Glocal Theological Education

Glocal Theological Education

Teaching and Learning Theology in the Light of Crisis

edited by BÅRD NORHEIM &
SHANTELLE WEBER

foreword by Bert Roebben

◆PICKWICK *Publications* · Eugene, Oregon

GLOCAL THEOLOGICAL EDUCATION
Teaching and Learning Theology in the Light of Crisis

Copyright © 2024 Wipf & Stock Publishers. All rights reserved. Except for brief quotations in critical publications or reviews, no part of this book may be reproduced in any manner without prior written permission from the publisher. Write: Permissions, Wipf and Stock Publishers, 199 W. 8th Ave., Suite 3, Eugene, OR 97401.

Pickwick Publications
An Imprint of Wipf and Stock Publishers
199 W. 8th Ave., Suite 3
Eugene, OR 97401

www.wipfandstock.com

PAPERBACK ISBN: 978-1-6667-6256-3
HARDCOVER ISBN: 978-1-6667-6257-0
EBOOK ISBN: 978-1-6667-6258-7

Cataloguing-in-Publication data:

Names: Norheim, Bård, editor. | Weber, Shantelle, editor. | Roebben, Bert, foreword.

Title: Glocal theological education : teaching and learning theology in the light of crisis / edited by Bård Norheim and Shantelle Weber ; foreword by Bert Roebben.

Description: Eugene, OR : Pickwick Publications, 2024 | Includes bibliographical references and index.

Identifiers: ISBN 978-1-6667-6256-3 (paperback) | ISBN 978-1-6667-6257-0 (hardcover) | ISBN 978-1-6667-6258-7 (ebook)

Subjects: LCSH: Religion—Study and teaching. | Theology—Study and teaching.

Classification: BV4020 .G65 2024 (paperback) | BV4020 .G65 (ebook)

09/24/24

Scripture quotations marked NIV are taken from the Holy Bible, New International Version®, NIV®. Copyright © 1973, 1978, 1984, 2011 by Biblica, Inc.® Used by permission of Zondervan. All rights reserved worldwide.

The publication of the book is supported by a grant from the UTFORSK funding programme by DIKU – Norwegian Agency for International Cooperation and Quality Enhancement in Higher Education.

Contents

Contributors | *ix*

Foreword by Bert Roebben | *xi*

Preface | *xiii*

Abbreviations | *xv*

CHAPTER 1
Introduction—Why Learn from Crisis? | 1
         Bård Norheim & Shantelle Weber

PART 1 | *WHERE* **CAN WE LEARN FROM CRISIS?**
    NAMING REALITY

CHAPTER 2
The Crisis of the Church and a Plea for Playful Theological Education | 17
              Bård Norheim

CHAPTER 3
Listening to the Voices of Students in Theological Education | 30
       Shantelle Weber & Gretchen Schoon Tanis

CHAPTER 4
Perspectives on the Climate Crisis, Sin, and Theological Education | 44
             Gunnar Innerdal

CHAPTER 5
The Social Crisis of Infertility in Sub-Saharan Africa: Repositioning Theological Education | 61
              Terese Bue Kessel

CHAPTER 6
Experiencing God as One's Opponent | 78
                                        Knut Alfsvåg

**PART 2 | *HOW* CAN WE LEARN FROM CRISIS?
EXPLORATIONS IN LEARNING THEOLOGY,
DIGITALLY, GLOBALLY, AND LOCALLY**

CHAPTER 7
Technology-Mediated Learning (TML) during a Time of Crisis: Reflecting on Experiences of Students and Lecturers during COVID-19 | 93
                                        Anita Cloete

CHAPTER 8
Teaching and Learning Theology in Crisis: Reflecting on the Benefits of Collaborative Online International Learning (COIL) | 111
                                        Ian Nell

CHAPTER 9
Student Creativity and Collaboration during Digital Learning: Glocal Theoretical Perspectives | 128
   Svitlana Holovchuk, Linnéa K. Jermstad, & Gunnvi Sæle Jokstad

CHAPTER 10
An Appreciative Inquiry of the Role of a Program Leader within Program Renewal Process at the Faculty of Theology, Stellenbosch University | 142
                                        Shantelle Weber

CHAPTER 11
Academic Support as a Success Factor for Augmented Teaching and Learning at the Faculty of Theology, Stellenbosch University | 156
                                        Dawid Mouton

CHAPTER 12
Colleague Observation in Interdisciplinary Academic Collaboration: Quality and Innovation in Education | 171
   Linnéa K. Jermstad, Svitlana Holovchuk, & Gunnvi Sæle Jokstad

PART 3 | *WHAT* CAN WE LEARN FROM CRISIS?

CHAPTER 13
Can You Be Trained in Courage—or Taught It? A Rhetorical and Theological Assessment of How to Carry Out Training in Courage as Part of Theological Education | 189

BÅRD NORHEIM & JOAR HAGA

CHAPTER 14
Reclaiming Joy and Tenacity through Online Learning: Teaching and Learning in Crisis | 206

NATHAN HUSSAINI CHIROMA

CHAPTER 15
The Transformative Power of Cultural Immersion Practices in a Master of Theology Module? Reflections on Opportunities and Challenges with Regards to Engaging Students on Poverty and Inequality in South Africa Today | 221

NADINE BOWERS DU TOIT & RALPH AFGHAN

CHAPTER 16
(Im)possibilities of Malawian Postgraduates Studying at Stellenbosch University during the COVID-19 Crisis | 234

CHRISPINE NTHEZEMU KAMANGA

CHAPTER 17
Learning and Teaching from the Margins: An Autoethnographic Reflection upon Theological Formation That Is Committed to the Cause of Justice | 253

DION A. FORSTER

CHAPTER 18
Epilogue: Learning Theology in Crisis by Reading the Times: A Question of Leadership | 274

BÅRD NORHEIM & SHANTELLE WEBER

Index | 289

Contributors

Ralph Afghan is a Minister of the Methodist Church of Southern Africa and Part-Time Lecturer at Stellenbosch University.

Knut Alfsvåg is Professor of Systematic Theology at VID Specialized University.

Nadine Bowers Du Toit is Professor of Practical Theology (Community Development) at Stellenbosch University and Director of the Unit for Religion and Development Research.

Nathan Hussaini Chiroma is Associate Professor of Practical Theology at Africa College of Theology in Kigali, Rwanda, and Research Associate at Stellenbosch University.

Anita Cloete is Professor of Practical Theology and Youth Work at Stellenbosch University.

Dion A. Forster is Professor of Public Theology at the Vrije Universiteit Amsterdam and a Research Associate in the Faculty of Theology, Stellenbosch University.

Joar Haga is Professor of Church History at VID Specialized University.

Svitlana Holovchuk is Associate Professor of Educational Studies at NLA University College.

Gunnar Innerdal is Associate Professor of Systematic Theology and Head of the Department for Theology, Religion and Philosophy at NLA University College.

Linnéa K. Jermstad is Associate Professor of Educational Studies at NLA University College.

Gunnvi Sæle Jokstad is Teaching Professor of Educational Studies at NLA University College.

Chrispine Nthezemu Kamanga is a PRACTEMUS Research Associate at the Theological Faculty of Stellenbosch University.

Terese Bue Kessel is Associate Professor of Practical Theology at VID Specialized University.

Dawid Mouton is Lecturer in Practical Theology and Missiology at Stellenbosch University.

Ian Nell is Professor of Practical Theology at Stellenbosch University.

Bård Norheim (Editor) is Professor of Theology at NLA University College and Project Coordinator of the TLC project—Teaching and Learning Theology in Crisis.

Bert Roebben is Professor of Religious Education at the Faculty of Catholic Theology of the University of Bonn and extraordinary professor at the Faculty of Theology of Stellenbosch University.

Gretchen Schoon Tanis is Associate Professor of Practical Theology at NLA University College.

Shantelle Weber (Editor) is Associate Professor of Practical Theology and Youth Work at Stellenbosch University and Project Coordinator of the TLC project—Teaching and Learning Theology in Crisis.

Foreword

SPOILER ALERT: this is not an easy book. You have to sit down with it and grant yourself time to read and reflect on it, and preferably in a group. The book originated in an inter-contextual learning process between academics from Northern Europe and sub-Saharan Africa, and that is how it should be read: as an ongoing inter-contextual learning process in times of crisis. For three reasons, it is an "unsettling" book. First, the text itself is a panopticon with many entries. Theoretical, empirical, and action-oriented perspectives follow one another. The reader and/or readership must make the book their own by reconstructing it. Second, the initial situation of "polycrisis" (global pandemic, climate crisis, injustice in the world) leaves the readership with an uncanny feeling. One must get out of one's comfort zone, move "on shifting ground" (as argued by Russel Botman, public theologian and the first rector of color at Stellenbosch University) and persevere in reality, that is, actually share reality with fellows in the same storm, an image often used in coronavirus times. And finally, the book does not provide ready-made recipes for theological education and pastoral ministry, but rather encourages critical thinking. The old schemes no longer fit, the curricula and patterns of action learned in academic centers are often no longer applicable to specific local developments. Why, where, what, how, and when act "in the night when all cows are black"?[1] The book's answer is in its conclusion: we need to act now and learn inter-contextually from the action!

In this respect, this book is particularly hopeful. It does not flee from reality but opens the space for a creative handling of crisis and a transformative attitude toward periods of transition. The Teaching and Learning Theology in Crisis project and the book that emerged from it offer, in my judgment, five interpretive keys to this "glocal" learning enterprise. Together they form the backbone of this book and take shape in the methodological polyphony of the contributions, which are quantitative and qualitative-empirical, descriptive and normative, autoethnographic and literature based:

1. G. W. F. Hegel, *Phenomenology of Spirit*, translated by A. V. Miller, with text analysis by J. N. Findlay, rev. ed. (Oxford: Oxford University Press, 1977), 9.

in short, unusually rich in substance for both systematic and practical theology. The five keys are interrelated:

- Performative discernment—The signs of the times should be read on the basis of action options concretely tried out in the field. Knowledge is gathered through action and interaction in the midst of everyday life.

- Theological resistance—The theological interpretation of these signs is an act of resistance, of consciously staying with the facts, detecting causes of structural evil and daring to relate theological interpretation also to oneself as a researcher, explicitly or implicitly autoethnographically. In this respect, even empirical-theological groundwork becomes an act of resistance.

- Responsible imagination—Improvisation and play are central attitudes in the development path for good leadership. Part 3 of this book unfolds virtues that have emerged in times of crisis and are significant in the lives of moral and spiritual leaders of the future.

- Collaborative inquiry—Part 2 presents innovative models of primarily online inquiry and learning that proved fruitful in times of pandemic and have since inspired and organized powerful learning environments, including in theological institutions. "Living, learning, and researching in the presence of the other" (even in a digital context) is the key phrase here, with all its opportunities and limits.

- Inter-contextual learning—This project and book were born from the collaboration of two youth leaders, Shantelle and Bård, current and former presidents of the International Association for the Study of Youth Ministry. They were and are close to the reality of future generations and know their sighs and questions, their existential needs and transcendent hopes. From their global theological focus on youth work and youth ministry, they proved to be the ideal interlocutors for this process of inter-contextual learning. Sometimes one just needs youthful enthusiasm to start anew!

Next to philosophy, theology is the oldest but often most stubborn discipline in the academic world. Change (in theory and practice) is wasted on it. In this book, however, theologians, religious scientists, and educational scholars take the lead in the academic enterprise: they call for realism and future perspective! Their eschatology is "presentic," their theologizing radically existentialist, their call to action urgent. So: urgently read and discuss this "unsettling" book!

Bert Roebben, University of Bonn

Preface

GOD'S FIRST QUESTION TO humans, in Gen 3:9, is both basic and simple: "Where are you?" Arguably the most fundamental theological question—*where is God?*—is a response to God's call to Adam and Eve on that day among the trees in the garden. Somehow the question of place, the question of *where*, seems to be primary to human existence: Where are you?

Whenever we ask "Where are you?," or in a more reflective manner, "Where am I?," we are reminded that we live in this world together with all of creation. And we do so both in times of peace and in times of crisis. Even doing theology is therefore in a certain sense a worldly practice.

Where do we then find ourselves as we try to teach and learn theology? Where do teaching and learning theology really start? In the church or at universities, in the streets or at home, in the calm peace of nature or in the burning heat of an exhilarating climate crisis? This book is an attempt to explore the meaning of *glocal* theological education. It looks at what it means to teach and learn together in a globalized, yet local, world.

For the last couple of years, NLA University College in Norway and Stellenbosch University in South Africa have come together in a project to examine what it means to teach and learn theology in times of crisis (Teaching and Learning Theology in Crisis). The aim of the TLC project is to develop new ways of teaching and learning theology in crisis by addressing the climate crisis, the challenge of youth citizenship, and the church's changed status in society. The aim is to train theological *judicium*, the ability to exercise sound judgment and practice discernment as the church and her leaders try to be church in the face of different crises the world face today.

In the book we present a vision for *glocal theological education*, an invitation to rethink and reshape theological training in times of crisis. We present what we have learned from developing shared, global learning within the framework of local learning communities in Norway and South Africa—and beyond. We discuss key practices, such as the combination of co-teaching online and learning in local contexts, and best-practice research on other educational activities and on student and teacher mobility. We also reflect more theoretically on *where*, *how*, and *what* we can learn from crisis, and how these theoretical insights can help us shape theological leaders for the future who can read the times.

Hopefully, the book will inspire and provoke anyone who cares about the future of theological education, or even education as a whole. However, we want to issue a warning: if the question of *where* is primary, we present this exploration of glocal, theological education consciously aware that our visionary framework is situational and perhaps even fragmentary. Doing theology and developing theological education is never a "copy-and-paste" exercise. Rather, it requires discerning the local complexities of any place or situation, to continuously rediscover the meaning of the gospel of Jesus Christ with those engaging theological education. So, wherever you are—*tolle lege!*—take it up and read, and then take a deep breath to remember where you are.

Bård Norheim and Shantelle Weber, editors
Bergen and Stellenbosch, February 2024

Abbreviations

AcT	Acta Theologica
BibInt	Biblical Interpretation
HvTSt	Hervormde teologiese studies
IJHE	International Journal of Higher Education
IRRODL	The International Review of Research in Open and Distributed Learning
JBL	Journal of Biblical Literature
JRT	Journal of Religious Thought
RelEd	Religious Education
SAJHE	South African Journal of Higher Education

Chapter 1

Introduction—Why Learn from Crisis?

BÅRD NORHEIM AND SHANTELLE WEBER

START WITH WHY

An important challenge for theological education today is to educate and form leaders of faith communities who are prepared to lead in a global and transnational world.[1] This creates an urgent need to rethink and restructure theological education around the globe. Lamentations on the shrinking status of theology have been prevailing over the last four decades at least, particularly in the Western world.[2] Where theology as a discipline was once the queen of sciences at the university, it has become an endangered species—often banished to seminars at best. Most teachers of theology still seem to hold to traditional teaching methods mainly because of the assumption that theology has been taught to the same communities that have historically had access to education, and less often to those who represent the complex world realities of the Christian church.[3] It is no exaggeration to claim that theology and theological education face both a global crisis and many local crises.

What do you when you are faced with a crisis? First, it is important to note that a *crisis* implies the arrival of one or more threats that challenge the way we think, act, and structure our lives, and calls for sound judgment and transformed ways of learning and acting together. The problem, however, is that in a crisis it is often tempting to simply fast forward to the *how* question:

---

1. Pui-lan et al., *Teaching Global Theologies*, 1.
2. See, e.g., Thiemann, "Making Theology Central."
3. Pui-lan et al., *Teaching Global Theologies*, 1.

How should this crisis be addressed in the most efficient and relevant manner? However, seeking simple how-to solutions, may turn out to be a sort of escapism that jumps the gun before the crisis has been carefully evaluated. When the going gets tough and people experience that their world is in a crisis, the reality of the crisis must be named somehow by someone giving a convincing answer to the most urgent question: *What* is really going on?[4]

Even more fundamentally, it could be argued, that when we face a crisis, we need to *start with why*.[5] However, the why question moves beyond mere cause and effect reasoning. It concerns the very nature of what a crisis is, not just tracing its possible origins. The why question in times of crisis even asks why a crisis moves us in the ways it does. It poses the fundamental questions: What is at stake in a crisis, and how should the different options be evaluated?

The word *crisis* originally stems from the Greek word *krisis*, which points to the division of two opposites. In antiquity a *krisis* demanded clear alternatives. A crisis involved differentiating right and wrong or determining which action that would lead to salvation and which would lead to condemnation. Therefore, Aristotle underlined that speaking in times of crisis required sound judgment or discernment—what the Romans later called *judicium*.[6] The one who is able to describe the reality of the crisis by offering calibrated discernment, often earns the right to set the "diagnosis" of the crisis, as well.

It is also important to remember that the word *crisis* points to the future. A crisis forces us to consider alternatives for the future: Are we on our way to a future utopia, that inspires a fight for change? Or should we rather anticipate the imminent emergence of a dystopia? The point is that any vision of the future serves as a prism through which the call to action is calibrated.

At the same time, from a theological perspective, a crisis calls for compassion for the other. In theology such compassion beckons what Walter Brueggemann calls *prophetic imagination*. In other words, theology is an academic, yet imaginative, discipline and therefore has a particular potential to speak into crisis. The task of prophetic ministry is to nurture, nourish, and evoke a consciousness and perception alternative to the consciousness and perception of the dominant culture around us.[7]

---

4. Norheim and Haga, *Four Speeches*, 29–35; Norheim and Haga, *Three Fears*, 6–8.
5. Sinek, *Start with Why*, 37–45.
6. Aristotle, *Rhetoric*, 20–23, 30–50.
7. Brueggeman, *Prophetic Imagination*.

Introduction—Why Learn from Crisis?

Universities are global institutions embedded in local contexts that are not homogeneous and unitary, yet they are impacted by disciplinary influences, ideological positions, and regimes of teaching and learning.[8] Faced with the fading influence of theology, one may of course ask *why* theological education is needed in the first place. A simple answer may be, that the God question is still integral to how humanity makes sense of life or perhaps quite simply that the church as an influential space, needs educated leaders. The bold claim in this book, however, is that we need theology, because theology, like no other academic discipline, offers a holistic and fundamental, yet practical, take on how to interpret and act in the face of crisis. This is not to say that theology is a sort of crisis management. Rather, theology offers a nuanced historical and hermeneutical framework to interpret the human condition in its most fundamental relations. Theology therefore trains the imaginative art of discernment, drawing on the dialectical learning that happens when encyclopedic and empirical sources of knowledge are juxtaposed in the midst of human life, even in the midst of crisis.

The *why* question regarding theological education is therefore not so much a question of the relevance of theological education per se, but it concerns ways in which theology can speak into crisis, offering reflection and leadership. For a theological education in crisis—and in times of crisis—a fundamental question is therefore: What does it mean, or what does it take to become an engaged theologian? Reformer Martin Luther argued that a theologian is born by exploring three modes of action—*oratio*, *meditatio*, and *tentatio*—prayer, contemplation (on the Bible and other sources), and the struggle and tribulations (*Anfechtung* in German) that humans face in their relation to God and the world.[9] Theological training should equip current and prospective leaders with competencies to empower Christians (believers) to participate in the mission of the church wherever they are active.[10]

Theological education concerns reflecting on and developing the social imaginary of those who study theology. Teaching and learning theology, particularly in crisis, has to do with the images, narratives, symbols, and myths that allows people to imagine and sense the reality of today, but also the preferred vision of tomorrow. Consequently, theological training is even an aesthetic enterprise, where one needs to develop educational practices for engaging with creation's beauty, drawing on aesthetic means like stories,

---

8. Trowler, *Cultures and Change*.
9. See Hütter, *Suffering Divine Things*, 72.
10. Nell, "Competency-Based Theological Education," 4.

images, music, liturgies, parables, symbols, etc.[11] Therefore, one goal of theological education, often expressed in an African context, is to bring out the beauty of each person, which then makes social justice education within theological education an imperative.[12]

In this book we are particularly interested in the hermeneutical struggle that grows out of being confronted with crisis. We make the plea that becoming an engaged theologian—in addition to prayer and formation (*oratio*), contemplation and interpretation of key sources (*contemplatio*)—involves developing sound judgment (or discernment) and a critical awareness of social justice by learning from crisis. It means getting involved in the struggle and disputes (*tentatio*) that any leader faces when a crisis strikes. South African faith leaders, such as Desmond Tutu, Frank Chikane, Allan Boesak, Beyers Naudé, and many others, played a significant role in advocating for justice for the poor. This was true of many Christian movements too. Their efforts were shaped by their theology, which in turn was formed by their interpretation of the core messages of Scripture. Although these pastors and teachers differed in many respects, their common insight was that the biblical interpretation was often influenced by a social perspective and an economic location. These leaders set an example of integrating their calling as Christians with their passion and engagement in politics and activism.[13]

The worldwide exchange or fusion of culture usually happens locally but the global and local are not opposing forces: they are interdependent and mutually influence each other.[14] To become an engaged theologian, therefore, involves developing a vision of the world. However, this vision of the world is always something contested. The danger is to become a theologian of glory, someone who claims to have a direct approach to God.[15] American theologian Robert W. Jenson suggests that theological hermeneutics should be understood as a *struggle*, drawing on Luther's notion of *tentatio* or *Anfechtung* (see above). Jenson argues that doing theology means getting involved in the practices and language of a discerning community.[16] Therefore the hermeneutics of theology is not placed solemnly in the academic classroom, but in the life of the church and the world, always

---

11. White, *Tending the Fire*, 17–42, 60–71.
12. Naidoo, "Ministerial Formation."
13. Weber, "Necessity of Intergenerational Dialogue."
14. Pui-lan et al., *Teaching Global Theologies*, 12.
15. See Norheim, "Cultivating a Vision"; De Kock and Norheim, "Youth Ministry Research."
16. Jenson, *Triune God*, 18.

shaped by *tentatio*, doing theology, and reading Scripture in particular, as a *struggle*, "because lives and behavior are at stake and folk are not going to let us off with evasions." Therefore "the struggle itself is the hermeneutical principle."[17]

In this book we explore ways to train theological students towards engagement in that hermeneutical struggle. More precisely, the book investigates how students of theology may become more capable of offering an innovative and theological response to three crises that stand out in our time: the *climate crisis* and the challenge of *youth involvement*, particularly with regards to active and participatory citizenship that challenges existing socioeconomic differences, and *the church's* need to renavigate its *role in society*. A core focus is on theological training relevant to the contextual realities people (and Christian leaders) face. Quite practically, this means that those affected by these crises must be engaged as stakeholders in theological education. As an example, it involves including the voices of young people in our classrooms.

As we have already pointed out, the emergence of a crisis requires exercise of discernment and sound judgment. This is where theology becomes important. Theology is a practice which deals with crisis, either by interpreting and giving meaning to various historical "crises" through biblical studies and church history and by assessing more contemporary "crises" with the help of systematic theology and practical theology. Training theologians means training scholars who can exercise sound judgment in the face of crisis so that they grow toward being engaged citizens wherever they may find themselves. Here we are reminded of Nussbaum's call for a liberative education which cultivates the humanity of our learners.[18] One of the ways we nurture such learning is through creating in our students the capacity for global citizenship. Here the student sees themselves not merely as locally engaged but also as a human being bound to other human beings by ties of recognition and concern. Mosha concurs that the goal of education is the making of good, responsible citizens motivated and sustained by a life of virtue grounded in community.[19]

---

17. Jenson, "Hermeneutics and the Life," 94–95.
18. Hinga, "Teaching to Transform," 127–30.
19. Mosha, *Heartbeat of Indigenous Africa*, 14–146.

TLC—TEACHING AND LEARNING THEOLOGY IN CRISIS

The book has evolved as part of the TLC project—Teaching and Learning Theology in Crisis. This is collaborative research focusing on theological education in times of crisis. It is a joint project with NLA University College in Norway and Stellenbosch University in South Africa, involving partners from other institutions in Europe and Africa, such as PAC University in Kenya and VID Specialized University in Norway. The project explores new ways of teaching and learning theology in crisis, and every year teachers and students meet to assess the new and old ways of teaching and learning theology.

The aim of the project is to address theology's response to the three above-mentioned crises in particular—the climate crisis, the challenge of youth citizenship, and the church's changed status in society. It may be helpful to distinguish two different kinds of crises. Some crises will never be repeated, such as a possible annihilation of the planet and humankind through a nuclear war. However, other crises represent repeatable phenomena, a pandemic, for example. How we relate to the different kinds of crises differs. The crucial challenge for theology is how to respond to the threats that any crisis represents with educated leaders that can examine both past sources and the contemporary contexts relevant in naming the reality of the current crisis.

The key activities of the project include co-teaching online and learning in local contexts, developing new modes of teaching; best-practice research on the development of joint, educational activities; student and teacher mobility and publication of peer-reviewed books based on the research. An important part of the project is the learning that takes place when teachers co-teach and meet at annual face-to-face conferences. Similarly, all the student exchanges so far have involved an element of internship, which the students find to be an indispensable way of the learning process. We train theological discernment, not simply by teaching and learning in more traditional ways, but by being together, sharing meals, practices, and language.

To many people, theology is a parochial discourse addressing only people in the church, with no significant import for the larger issues facing humanity and the planet. What is seen as global theology is contingent on one's social location, history, and background that is indeed also shaped by denominational histories, theological traditions, and institutional structures. What we fail to name is that theology developed in one part of the world has implications for other parts.[20] This project is an attempt at creating glocal communities of engaged theologians who also champion teaching and learning in our varying contexts.

Additionally, the COVID-19 pandemic has forced universities and colleges around the world to rethink the impact and meaning of education, beyond developing mere technical solutions to online teaching. Theological training of ministry leaders must adapt to the needs highlighted by the pandemic by developing a more comprehensive theological response to youth involvement and the churches' role in addressing climate change with training focused on ministry to those in crisis. The TLC project seeks to address these needs by developing new modes of co-teaching both online and locally, revising curriculum, and encouraging student and staff mobility.

THE IMPORTANCE OF CONTEXT: GLOCAL THEOLOGIES

The TLC project aims to explore what it means to teach and learn together in a globalized, yet local world. The focus is on *glocal learning*, which in this instance means developing shared, global learning within the framework of local learning communities in Norway and South Africa—and beyond. By developing co-teaching *online* and learning in *local* contexts, new modes of teaching, and hopefully a joint new course along with best-practice research, the overall aim of our research project is to strengthen theological education relevant to community practice that promotes a sustainable future. The term *glocal* resembles the slogan "think globally, act locally." The slogan may be read as an incitement for action in the light of crisis, like the evolving climate crisis.[21] In the TLC project, the student exchanges with internships and more traditional learning mix serve as an example of such glocal learning. The same accounts for the structure of the co-teaching, where teachers from NLA University College and Stellenbosch University teach together simultaneously online and then engage locally with the different student groups. Similarly, the face-to-face meetings at the annual project symposiums offer glocal learning loops as we alternate between meeting in South Africa and in Norway.

So, what does the notion of glocal theological education and glocal theologies imply? First, it is important to note that the question of "who is my neighbor" is becoming more complex and difficult to answer in a world

20. Pui-lan et al., *Teaching Global Theologies*, 23.
21. The idea behind the slogan supposedly dates to Scottish town planner and social activist Patrick Geddes; see Geddes, *Cities in Evolution*.

where geographical barriers are increasingly being broken down. It is only through seeing one's local context through the global that we truly honor the local and vice versa. An excellent theological education must expose teachers and students to the various worlds in which people dwell.[22] In this book we therefore present a new agenda for theological education, drawing on experiences of co-teaching online and "face-to-face," with the commitment that theological learning always needs to be fundamentally *global* and rooted in *local* contexts simultaneously.

Drawing on the TLC project, we present cutting-edge best-practice research on new modes of teaching and learning theology and theoretical explorations of what it means to do theology in the light of crisis. We believe that rediscovering the power of *glocal* co-teaching and co-learning will train theologians to exercise sound judgment in the face of crisis.

What are the possible implications of a theology that is both global and local in scope and content? This question really comes down to how we theologically interpret the presence of Christ in our world. Here it may be helpful to revisit a treatise from 1528, *Confession Concerning Christ's Supper*, written by Martin Luther. The Reformer argued that Jesus Christ is free to be present in any way God may want, but that there are three modes of Christ's presence that are known to humans through the promise of the biblical witness. The first mode is the *local* or circumscriptive mode of presence. This applies to the time when Jesus walked bodily on earth and occupied and yielded space according to his size from his birth to the death on the cross. The second mode, labeled the *diffinitive* or uncircumscribed mode, is a mode applied to the time from Christ's resurrection to ascension, where Christ passed through everything created as he wills. Luther finds this mode of the risen Christ to be a salvific mode of presence, even ascribed to the distribution of the sacraments, according to the promise of Christ. Finally, the third mode of presence, the *repletive* mode, is the mode ascribed to the exalted Christ, whom nothing can measure or circumscribe, but to whom all things are present so that he measures and circumscribes them.

The point for Luther, although he does not use that phrasing, is that the presence of Christ *migrates* as Christ is not confined to one place. The migrating presence of Christ is on one hand *centripetal*—drawing humans to explore places where the salvific presence of Christ is to be encountered according to the diffinitive mode of Christ's presence. On the other hand, the presence of Christ is *centrifugal* and missional, sending humans into

---

22. Fernandez, "Geopolitical and Glocal," 169–72.

Introduction—Why Learn from Crisis?

every corner of the world to encounter Christ according to his repletive presence.[23]

What does this conceptual understanding of the presence of Christ have to do with teaching theology? Well, it may shape the way theologians attempt to name reality in the face of crisis. In Gen 2:18–20, naming reality, giving names to the immediate surroundings, is human beings' first participatory act in God's creation. After the fall, humans are still called to participate in the act of naming reality, but the reality that is waiting to be named is a fallen world, a reality which is shaped by crisis. Naming this reality of crisis in a credible way is a dialectic enterprise of truthfully naming the reality of a fallen world and faithfully naming the promise of Christ's migrating presence. The promise of the gospel is that the presence of Christ migrates to the encounter with the other—and the Other. This may make theological education both prophetic and political at the same time.[24] Truthfully naming the dialectic of reality may be taken as a way of reinterpreting the slogan "think globally, act locally," by reminding us that the present Christ is a global body, with Whom theologians are encountered locally. Reflecting on the role of prophetic liturgy in the transformation of unjust socioeconomic systems from a Latin American liberation theology perspective, Junker notes that one of the core challenges the postmodern church faces is that of having prophetic awareness of socioeconomic injustice, while at the same time having to preserve that community's historical-cultural identity, its religious values and its spirituality.[25] This is because, as a prophetic voice the church is a countercultural voice that speaks God's word to the weak, the oppressed, the marginalized, and the helpless while also trying to mediate God's desire for goodness, life, and beauty. Allan Boesak (1946–) and Beyers Naudé (1915–2004) are African theologians well known for their prophetic stance against empire. This stance has had an impact on current Christian and ecumenical leaders around the world. They are known for their uncompromising stance against all kinds of oppression.

---

23. See Norheim, "Naming Glocal Fear." For an even lengthier elaboration on this subject, see Norheim, *Practicing Baptism*, 71–81.

24. It is here important to take into account Kathryn Tanner's plea to root political theology in Christology: "Christology (specifically, a discussion of the character of Jesus' relationships with other people) is the better avenue for making such judgments: it is less misleading, far simpler and much more direct" (Tanner, *Christ the Key*, 208).

25. Junker, *Prophetic Liturgy*. See also Pui-lan et al., *Teaching Global Theologies*, 12.

WHERE, HOW, AND WHAT—LEARNING THEOLOGY IN CRISIS

The book is structured in three parts, each part circling around one of the following three questions—*where* can we learn from crisis, *how* can we learn from crisis, and *what* can we learn from crisis? The idea is to start by naming reality faithfully, then move on to explore how it is possible to learn from crisis both digitally, globally, and locally. The third and final part studies the virtues and skills that may emerge as we try to learn from the experience of crisis in different forms and contexts. The three parts of the book with three questions—where, how and what—are framed by two other fundamental questions in the pursuit of developing discernment, *why* and *when*: the introduction chapter (ch. 1) and the epilogue (ch. 18) remind us of these two fundamental questions as we seek to develop theological discernment in the face of crisis. This introduction starts with the why, insisting why it is essential to learn in a glocal fashion as we try to develop theological discernment in the face of crisis. The epilogue emphasizes that exercising theological discernment in crisis is a question of leadership, and performing such leadership faithfully and truthfully by reading the times—asking *when* in a sense—is a key practice.

In more detail then, the first part of the book starts by naming reality and asks *where* we can learn from crisis. In chapter 2, Bård Norheim starts by assessing the contemporary crisis of the church with its numerical decline and loss of relevance in parts of the world, and how this relates to the crisis of theology and theological education. Next, Shantelle Weber and Gretchen Schoon Tanis take on the crisis of youth involvement and how theological education needs to question its understanding of youth and its involvement with youth. In the following chapter, Gunnar Innerdal examines how the climate crisis and theological conceptions of sin should inform how we conceptualize theological education. In chapter 5, Terese Bue Kessel asks how the crisis of infertility in many African countries challenges theological discourses and frameworks for learning. The final chapter of the first part, offers a fundamental, and systematic theological engagement with the theme of teaching and learning theology in and from crisis, where Knut Alfsvåg explores what it means to learn theology with God as your opponent.

The second part of the book explores *how* we may learn from crisis in developing theological studies. This part offers explorations of how theology may be learned digitally and glocally. The first chapter, by Anita Cloete, discusses the contours of technology-mediated learning in theology, reflecting on the experiences of students and lecturers during COVID-19.

In chapter 8, Ian Nell presents and examines the strengths of collaborative online learning in the glocal. In the next chapter, Svitlana Holochuk, Linnéa Jermstad, and Gunnvi Sæle Jokstad propose twenty-first-century skills for digital, glocal learning; chapter 10, by Shantelle Weber, evaluates the role of the program leader in developing theological education; while the next chapter, by Dawid Mouton, discusses what is implied in developing academic literacy in theological education. The final chapter of part 2 examines what it means for theological teachers to be learners through colleague observation. Here Linnéa Jermstad, Svitlana Holochuk, and Gunnvi Sæle Jokstad engage pedagogical theory reflecting on the experiences of the TLC project so far.

The third part of the book examines *what* we may learn from crisis, by discussing the virtues and skills of a glocal, theological learning community. In the first chapter of the third part, chapter 13, Bård Norheim and Joar Haga ask if and how courage can be taught and trained. In chapter 14, Nathan Hussaini Chiroma examines how it may be possible to develop joy and tenacity through glocal theological training. In the next chapter, Nadine Bowers Du Toit and Ralph Afghan discuss glocal, theological training as a sort of community development. And in the two last chapters of part 3, Chrispine Nthezemu Kamanga first explores what it means to practice and share hospitality away from home, through a study of Malawian postgraduates at Stellenbosch University during the COVID-19 pandemic. In the following and final chapter of part 3, Dion A. Forster proposes ways to train theologians to fight for justice glocally, through an autoethnographic reflection.

In the final chapter of the book, chapter 18—the epilogue—Bård Norheim and Shantelle Weber then examine what it implies to ask the *when* question. Or more specifically, how should theologians respond to the question "what time is it." The chapter argues that learning theology in crisis is a question of training theological leaders who can read the times and offer sound judgment.

TOWARDS GLOCAL THEOLOGICAL EDUCATION

Glocal theological education must be interdisciplinary and integrative. Theological education that does not stimulate critical thinking or empower students to engage with their context (as it connects to other contexts) could be termed irrelevant, as theological education plays a pivotal role in the liberation of these students from their local experiences of crisis. A crisis calls for leadership, and the leader—here the theologian—needs to give an adequate and persuasive account of reality. In a crisis, the use of words is of great importance, and theology has a thing with words. We hope that this book will help theologians in many different contexts to rediscover how theological studies may be formative in shaping leaders who are able to interpret faithfully and credibly what's going on when a crisis strikes and even propose a way forward to cope with that crisis. As such, the book strives to be an introduction to the fine art of theological discernment.[26]

BIBLIOGRAPHY

Apollis, Quinton, and Shantelle Weber. "Young Adults and Social Justice: Empowering Young Adults as Social Change Agents through Theological Education." In *Faith, Race and Inequality amongst Young Adults in South Africa: Contested and Contesting Discourses for a Better Future*, edited by Nadine Bowers Du Toit, 165–78. Beyers Naudé Centre Series on Public Theology 14. Cape Town: African Sun Media, 2022.

Aristotle. *Rhetoric*. Edited by Jenny Bak. Translated by W. Rhys Roberts. Mineola, New York: Dover, 2004.

Brueggemann, Walter. *The Prophetic Imagination*. 2nd ed. Minneapolis: Fortress, 2001.

De Kock, Jos, and Bård Eirik Hallesby Norheim. "Youth Ministry Research and the Empirical." *International Journal of Practical Theology* 22 (2018) 69–83.

Geddes, Patrick. *Cities in Evolution*. London: Williams, 1915.

Fernandez, Eleazar S. "The Geopolitical and the Glocal: Situating Global Theological Voices in Theological Education." In *Teaching Global Theologies: Power & Praxis*, edited by Kwok Pui-lan et al., 163–76. Waco: Baylor University Press, 2015.

Hinga, Teresia. "Teaching to Transform: Theological Education, Global Consciousness, and the Making of Global Citizens." In *Teaching Global Theologies: Power & Praxis*, edited by Kwok Pui-lan et al., 125–42. Waco: Baylor University Press, 2015.

Hütter, Reinhard. *Suffering Divine Things: Theology as Church Practice*. Grand Rapids: Eerdmans, 2000.

Jenson, Robert W. "Hermeneutics and the Life of the Church." In *Reclaiming the Bible for the Church*, edited by Carl E. Braaten and Robert W. Jenson, 89–106. Grand Rapids: Eerdmans, 1995.

———. *The Triune God*. Vol. 1 of *Systematic Theology*. Oxford: Oxford University Press, 1997.

Junker, Tércio Bretanha. *Prophetic Liturgy: Toward a Transforming Christian Praxis*. Eugene, OR: Pickwick, 2014.

Mosha, R. Sambuli. *The Heartbeat of Indigenous Africa: A Study of the Chagga Educational System*. Indigenous Knowledge and Schooling. London: Routledge, 2002.

Naidoo, Marilyn. "Ministerial Formation of Theological Students through Distance Education." *HvTSt* 68 (2012) art. 1225. https://doi.org/10.4102/hts.v68i2.1225.

---

26. See, for instance, White, *Practicing Discernment*.

Nell, Ian A. "Competency-Based Theological Education in a Postcolonial Context: Towards a Transformed Competency Framework." *Transformation in Higher Education* 5 (2020) 1–9.

Norheim, Bård, and Joar Haga. *The Four Speeches Every Leader Has to Know*. London: Palgrave Macmillan, 2020.

———. *The Three Fears Every Leader Has to Know: Words to Use in a Crisis*. London: Palgrave Macmillan, 2022.

Norheim, Bård Eirik Hallesby. *Practicing Baptism: Christian Practices and the Presence of Christ*. Eugene, OR: Pickwick, 2014.

———. "Cultivating a Vision of the Unseen: The Apophatic Mode in Ecclesiological Research." *Ecclesial Practices* 2 (2015) 40–56.

———. "Naming Glocal Fear in Local Youth Ministry—and the Migrating Presence of Christ." *European Journal of Theology* 26 (2017) 162–72.

Pui-lan, Kwok, et al., eds. *Teaching Global Theologies: Power & Praxis*. Waco: Baylor University Press, 2015.

Sinek, Simon. *Start with Why: How Great Leaders Inspire Everyone to Take Action*. New York: Portfolio, 2009.

Tanner, Kathryn. *Christ the Key*. New York: Cambridge University Press, 2010.

Thiemann, Ronald F. "Making Theology Central in Theological Education." Religion Online, 1987. From *Christian Century* (Feb. 4–11, 1987) 106–8 https://www.religion-online.org/article/making-theology-central-in-theological-education/.

Trowler, Paul. *Cultures and Change in Higher Education: Theories and Practice*. Universities into the 21st Century. Basingstoke, UK: Palgrave MacMillan, 2008.

Weber, Shantelle. "The Necessity of Intergenerational Dialogue on Social Justice within the South African Church." In *Powers, Inequalities and Vulnerabilities: Impact of Globalisation on Children, Youth and Families and on the Mission of the Church*, edited by Johannes L. Knoetze and Valentin Kozhuharov, 267–92. Reformed Theology in Africa 4. Cape Town: AOSIS, 2020. https://doi.org/10.4102/aosis.2020.BK229.13.

White, David F. *Practicing Discernment with Youth: A Transformative Youth Ministry Approach*. Cleveland: Pilgrim, 2005.

———. *Tending the Fire That Burns at the Center of the World: Beauty and the Art of Christian Formation*. Eugene, OR: Wipf and Stock, 2022.

PART 1

Where Can We Learn from Crisis?
Naming Reality

Chapter 2

The Crisis of the Church and a Plea for Playful Theological Education

BÅRD NORHEIM

CRISIS OR TRIUMPH?

In 2022, American theologian Andrew Root published the book *Churches and the Crisis of Decline*. Here, Root argued that "the church and its local congregations appear to be in a crisis," and that we tend to interpret the crisis as "the loss of people and resources, but it's really the radical transformation of belief itself."[1] Eleven years earlier, in 2011, American sociologist of religion Rodney Stark published *The Triumph of Christianity*. Here he concluded that "despite the low levels of religious participation prevalent in Europe . . . , more than 40 percent of the people on earth today are Christians and their number is growing more rapidly than that of any other major faith."[2]

So, which one is it? Are we facing the triumph of Christianity or a crisis for the church? Or could it perhaps be that we are facing both things at the same time? Either way, the role of the church in society is a very complex issue, both from a historical point of view and from a contemporary perspective. The story of Christianity is a multifaceted history with many surprising crises, changes, and turns. Historian Philip Jenkins has pointed out how radically the societal role of Christianity has changed over the centuries. In the year 500, "Christianity was the religion of empire and domination." Five

---

1. Root, *Churches and the Crisis*, x.
2. Stark, *Triumph of Christianity*, 418.

hundred years later, in the year 1000, "it was the stubborn faith of exploited subject peoples or of barbarians on the irrelevant fringes of great civilizations." In 1900, once again, "Christian powers ruled the world." However, as Jenkins sarcastically puts it, "knowing what the situation will be in 2100 or in 2500 would take a truly inspired prophet."[3] So, what shall we make of the current state of the church in the world? And how should the assessment of the status of Christianity influence how we conceptualize the future of theological education? Is the church in crisis due to a loss of hegemony over the public sphere or should we still anticipate the church's triumph due to the continuous influence of a Christian mindset?[4]

The purpose of this chapter is not to answer any of these questions in full. And for sure, the aim is not to present detailed statistics on the state of the church. Rather, the chapter wants to offer reflection on how theology and theological training should respond to the church's loss of hegemony, influence, and relevance in *some* parts of the world. This book addresses what it means to do glocal, theological education in times of crisis. This chapter explores the fundamental challenges that marks the crisis of the *church*, particularly in the Western world. It further asks where theology and theological training should look for inspiration to find ways of tackling the feeling of loss and decline, arguing for rediscovering play as a formative force in shaping glocal, theological learning communities around the world. The research question that this chapter seeks to answer is therefore: *What challenges does the experience of lost hegemony present to the church and to theological education, and how may a theology of play and the practice of play help reshape theological education in times of crisis?*

ECCLESIAL AGORAPHOBIA?

Before we move to the more constructive part of the chapter, we need to explore what sort of challenges the perceived crisis of the church represents for theology and theological education. The selective focus of this chapter is to examine the crisis that numerical decline and loss of status represent, particularly for the church in the West. However, the assessment of this crisis and the discussion on how the church may respond could be relevant to many a crisis that the church may face. After all, any crisis that puts the church's status and reputation at stake will probably involve challenges similar to the ones discussed below.

---

3. Jenkins, *Next Christendom*, 276.
4. Tom Holland argues that Christianity is "the most influential framework for making sense of human existence that has ever existed" (Holland, *Dominion*, 535).

A crisis implies that we face one or more threats that challenge the way we think, act, and structure our lives. It tests our perception of reality. The first step in any crisis is therefore to name reality faithfully.[5] So, let us start by doing exactly that, naming the reality of the church's loss of hegemony and influence with the purpose of determining what sort of challenges it represents for theology and theological training. When I started studying theology at the beginning of the 1990s, one of the lecturers in the introductory class of philosophy at the university proclaimed enthusiastically that secularization had been so successful that Christian faith would be extinct or irrelevant within the next generation or so. I was not sure whether to be offended, intrigued, or encouraged. Later, I learned that such rapid conclusions should be confronted with more careful examinations of the history of Christianity, a story characterized by rather swift and surprising changes. The point is that Christianity has always changed.[6] Perhaps even the reason behind the global success of Christianity, comes down to its "remarkable cultural flexibility": in other words, the story of Christianity is a story of how Christian faith adapts to local culture everywhere.[7]

Still, it seems quite evident that in the Western and Northern hemisphere, the church's position and role in society is changing. Perhaps, the most constructive way to interpret and address these changes is to look at the changing dynamics at the marketplace, at how religion is perceived in the public sphere. What is called the public—or the common, open space—has radically changed in recent times: First, the borders between the public and the private are not as fixed as they used to be. Second, the public sphere is also being radically democratized. It is no longer the playground of the educated public.[8]

These changes also influence the church's role and position in the public sphere. Previously, one could say the church fixed and determined time for most people. The church bells chimed when the day of work started, and when the day ended. The bells told you when to mourn and when to celebrate. Nowadays, the church does not configure life in the public sphere, nor our understanding of time, in the same way.[9] Similarly, Charles Taylor has argued that the church has lost its hegemonic influence over the public sphere, particularly in the Northern and Western hemispheres.[10] Where the

---

5. Norheim and Haga, *Three Fears*, 21.
6. Jenkins, *Next Christendom*, 6–7, 12.
7. Stark, *Triumph of Christianity*, 412.
8. Taylor, *Secular Age*, 181, 188, 210.
9. See, for instance, Davie, *Religion in Britain*, 197–218.
10. Taylor, *Secular Age*, 392.

role of church in society used to be a *given*, the church is now, along with most other institutions, something to be *chosen*. Religion has moved from an act of obligation to an act of consumption.[11] You define yourself through choices, and that is how you appear real and authentic.[12] Succinctly put, membership of a church, typically through infant baptism, is no longer a prerequisite for being a citizen. The local church is no longer the unquestioned plausible structure[13] that defines societal belonging through rites of passage like baptism, confirmation, weddings, and funerals.

My claim is that this loss of hegemony and influence presents the church with the challenge of *ecclesial agoraphobia*.[14] For human beings, loss aversion is a major driver of fear,[15] and for the church it seems to be no different. The term *ecclesial agoraphobia* is a metaphorical term that tries to capture the church's potential fear of open spaces, or the public sphere.[16] We learn from psychology that human beings are destined to respond to fear by means of aggression or withdrawal, what we usually refer to as "fight-or-flight-freeze-mode."[17] One may even say that fear is a basic and fundamental human experience,[18] and in a society formed by risks and threats, shaping our obsession with security, fear seems to determine the attitude towards life.[19]

When the church responds to the loss of influence and status by fleeing the public sphere or fighting back against any controversy in an increasingly aggressive manner, these reactions may be interpreted as symptoms of what is here labeled *ecclesial agoraphobia*. In other words, a church seeking refuge in a "safe spot" far from the heat of the public sphere, or a church presenting itself with intensified aggression in the public debate, may both be seen as symptoms of the church's struggle to cope with the loss of authority,

---

11. Davie, *Religion in Britain*, 133–74.
12. Taylor, *Ethics of Authenticity*.
13. Cf. Berger, *Sacred Canopy*, 45, 192; Berger and Luckmann, *Social Construction of Reality*. Plausibility structures define the sociocultural systems of meaning and the contexts in which these meanings appear meaningful.
14. See Norheim and Haga, "Four Speeches."
15. See Kahnemann, *Thinking Fast and Slow*, 300–309.
16. *Agora* means "marketplace" or "public" in Greek. See also Norheim and Haga, "Four Speeches"; Norheim, "Den norske kyrkjas retoriske sjølvforståing."
17. See, for instance, Donahue, "Fight-Flight-Freeze System."
18. Hankiss, *Fears and Symbols*, 6–7.
19. Beck, *World at Risk*, 8.

privilege, and power. Interestingly, ecclesial agoraphobia is both a global and local phenomenon. It represents a sort of *glocal fear*. The phenomenon of glocal fear is a reminder that theology and theological education are inscribed in the realities of a global(ized) world, where globalization of both information and popular culture inevitably globalizes the individual.[20]

PLAY AS A RESPONSE TO ECCLESIAL AGORAPHOBIA

How should the church respond to this loss of influence and hegemony—and the potential fear of engaging actively in the public sphere as a result? Generally, the answer is found to be the following—by becoming (even) more relevant.[21] The problem with the argument for relevance, is that it seems to presuppose that people are simply waiting for an excuse to go to church. But what if this not the case? What if another biker church, drive-in wedding, or drop-in baptism may not be the only solution to the church's experience of loss of hegemony? What if the church needs to rehearse living with the experience of putting being ignored, or even rejected, at the top of its list of priorities?

The fundamental question here is how to live with the fear of being rejected or not chosen. Or more proactively put: How should the church rehearse offering herself and her gospel message as an attractive alternative on the marketplace in an era of heightened autonomy and with intensified codes of authenticity? The claim in this chapter is that the church and her servants need to rehearse living with the fear of being ignored or even rejected without developing *ecclesial agoraphobia*. What strategy should the church, and theology develop then, when it may be captivated by the fear of losing hegemony, position, power, and influence?

In the following sections of the chapter, I will look at how play, as a fundamental mode of learning, may be a key factor in helping theological education address the challenges presented by potential ecclesial agoraphobia. The plea for more play in theological training is a plea to see play as the sort of basic training in theological education.[22] What do I mean by this? Basic training prepares you to endure more training, enables you to develop and explore new opportunities. It charges the learner with the potential to deal with change and challenges, as play helps to adapt to "different and

---

20. See Norheim, "Naming Glocal Fear."
21. Reiland, "Relevant Church."
22. Play may even boost academic performance, studies find; see Sahlberg and Doyle, *Let the Children Play*, 55.

changing contexts."[23] Play is therefore not a simple trick to help church leaders deal with decline and disappointments.[24] Rather, it offers a new way to explore a failure-friendly church, a church that prepares herself for a future of more experimentation and willingness to try out new things.[25]

The problem with play, however, is that we often tend to think of it as something different from the regular world. In play, other rules than the ordinary may apply. The impossible may become possible. Adults may become like children. The frightful may be bold, and the last may be the first. An important premise in play is that those playing accept that when playing they enter a special place and time, with its own rules for the sake of the game or the play only. Play is marked by open-ended, and often unstructured and imaginative, exploration and spontaneity.[26] The practice of play opens the door to a reality where risk-taking and being adventurous is the default setting. Simultaneously, as play explores the borders of human existence it connects the one who plays with a whole range of fundamental human experiences, like being found (hide-and-seek), failing, searching, learning new rules, breaking rules, and fundamentally how to relate to other people. Importantly, play even triggers curiosity.[27]

Play also challenges the tendency to tackle crisis merely by becoming gravely serious. Play offers an opportunity to develop a needed portion of self-irony, which may come in handy for any leader faced with a crisis. This is particularly true for theological leaders who need to deal with the experience of loss and decline. The importance of developing skills of improvisation through play is essential for a leader in a missional context.[28] Another key feature in play is that play stands in a certain opposition to planning and control. Play honors the unexpected, the incalculable, even the improbable.[29] This implies that play is not an instrument to achieve another end. It is not merely about jumping up and down while you learn to multiply ten times five or memorize the capitols of Europe by heart. Play is play for its own sake. Fundamentally, therefore, play embodies a bodily, creative, and explorative mode of learning.

---

23. Nell, *Together in God's Theatre*, 29.

24. These sections draw partly on reflections developed in Norheim, "Leik som retorisk basistrening."

25. Pohl-Patalong, *Kirche Gestalten*, 252–55.

26. Sahlberg and Doyle, *Let the Children Play*, 47, 49.

27. Sahlberg and Doyle, *Let the Children Play*, 309.

28. Nell, *Together in God's Theatre*, 115.

29. Taleb, *Black Swan*.

Play has been both valued and discredited throughout history. Plato, for instance, did not promote a very positive view on play, categorizing it in line with the mimetic arts, like poetry and painting. Later, as human life was compared to a great play in the baroque era, many thinkers expressed a more positive view on play. In his seminal book on play, *Homo Ludens*, Dutch historian and culture theorist Johan Huizinga focused on how the development of human culture is expressed through play and games. In German idealism, with Schiller and Goethe, a new view on play emerged with the concept that a sort of aesthetic humanity lies dormant in human beings and is being expressed as humans start to play. Human beings become their authentic selves when they play. We therefore tend to be intrigued by characters who play various roles and take on various identities, interpreting this sort of role play as a "delightful experience of freedom."[30] For Schiller, play—even in bringing up children—is the pathway to Beauty and the Good, ultimately to human freedom. Huizinga argues that play is a cultural phenomenon, although it exits pre-culture. Simultaneously, play connects humans to other creatures who also play and reminds us that not everything can be rationalized. Huizinga identifies five characteristics of play:

1. Play is voluntary.
2. Play is not real or ordinary.
3. Play can be distinguished from ordinary life in play's concept of time and place.
4. Play still creates order.
5. Play displays no material interest, and you cannot profit from play.

Drawing on these elaborations, Huizinga finds that it is possible to argue that our civilization is built on play in a certain manner, as law, knowledge, poetry, art, war, and many other practices draw on play.[31] Similarly, the former general secretary to the UN, the Swede Dag Hammarskjöld, has claimed in his famous reflective diary, *Markings*, that in play human beings learn their pattern for action, and the joy of playing may even show the importance of sacrifice and suffering.[32]

If we look at theological engagements with the practice of play, German theologian Jürgen Moltmann's *The Theology of Play* from 1972 stands out. Moltmann, much like Huizinga, is critical of the kind of play that is simply taken part in as a sort of spare-time activity or labor. Rather, Moltmann is

---

30. Hankiss, *Toothpaste of Immortality*, 72.
31. Huizinga, *Homo Ludens*.
32. Hammarskjöld, *Veimerker*, 108.

concerned with play's capacity to promote reform and change. He wants to explore how play may break the bonds, in contexts where the status quo keeps people down, particularly those living on the margins of society. Moltmann even argues that Christ suffered "that we may laugh again."[33]

In a certain sense, Moltmann advocates a more revolutionary view on play and the role of play. Theologically, he focuses on a God that plays—in creation, in the Christ event, and particularly in the emerging future, in the eschatological inbreaking of God's reign. Moltmann seems to think that we should play because God's transforming future rule may break through in play. Critically, one may argue that Moltmann promotes a quite optimistic view of play. Play is a like a worship song that never ends, an eternal dance in communion with the triune God. The optimistic take on play in many ways represent Moltmann's blind spot. The future-oriented and transformative moment is emphasized to such an extent that the role of play, and with it the nature of human beings, risk being idealized.

Another way to interpret the role of play theologically would be to argue that play offers a pathway for humans to find a way back to their origin. Through play, humans may rediscover that they belong to a Creator, the first one who invited anyone to play. In Proverbs, Wisdom is portrayed as rejoicing and playing in the presence of God:

> Then I was constantly at his side.
> I was filled with delight day after day,
> rejoicing always in his presence,
> rejoicing in his whole world
> and delighting in mankind. (Prov 8:30–21 NIV)

The first Christians interpreted this description of Wisdom's playful presence before God as an image of the Son, Jesus Christ. As Christ was rejoicing before God every day, playfully, playing may be an exercise in discipleship, following Christ. When the church strives to follow Christ, even in times of crisis, she returns to the presence of God, her Creator. Play may hence be an initiation into the presence of the triune God.

THE POWER OF PLAYFUL THEOLOGICAL EDUCATION IN TIMES OF CRISIS

How may these reflections on play help in reshaping theological education in times of crisis? In the age of authenticity, it seems obvious that the church and her theological training is challenged to develop a new kind

---

33. Moltmann, *Theology of Play*, 32–33.

of self-understanding which looks beyond mere *ecclesial agoraphobia*—the fear of the open space. The argument against play would be that the result of play cannot be measured straightforwardly. The uneasiness that the outcome of play cannot be measured that easily is a topic of discussion even in contemporary educational studies and pedagogics. Research shows that play-based learning is under pressure in schools and kindergartens due to the constraints of more instrumental and operational learning goals. The problem, many researchers would argue, is that there seems to be an implicit claim that there is a contradictory relationship between play and learning, suggesting that play cannot be learning, and learning cannot be play. However, if learning implies the creation of new ideas that enables us to see the world anew, play and learning are not that different after all. What the school—and perhaps even theological training—needs is a more exploratory approach to learning and life.[34]

These dilemmas need to be considered as we rethink theological education in times of crisis. Fundamentally, it would imply building a glocal, theological learning community committed to *deeper play*, which involves a focus on self-directed learners, intrinsic motivation, the use of imagination, process orientation and appealing to positive emotions.[35] Learning through play also means honoring the importance of *repetition*, as playing a game repeatedly is essential in developing fundamental habits and skills.[36] Playful theological learning would also be a noncompetitive mode of learning, which is critical in developing a resonant connection with the world.[37] Playing theology in this manner really comes down to rehearsing a "credible performance of the gospel drama," as play is the place where transformation takes place and opens the learner to future possibilities, which is fundamental in crisis.[38] A crisis may also force those affected by the crisis to wait for a better future. Andrew Root even finds that "a congregation that waits is a community of friends in play."[39] Practically, learning through play means setting up an education shaped by a mix of guided and free play and with abundant time for recess.[40]

---

34. See Barblett et al., "Pushes and Pulls"; Edwards, "Play-Based Learning."
35. Sahlberg and Doyle, *Let the Children Play*, 307.
36. Wells, *Improvisation*, 85.
37. Rosa, *Resonance*, 417: "Competition and resonance are thus two incompatible attitudes towards the world." See also Root, *Churches and the Crisis*, 273.
38. Nell, *Together in God's Theatre*, 7, 29.
39. Root, *Churches and the Crisis*, 188.
40. Sahlberg and Doyle, *Let the Children Play*.

Included in this vision for a more playful theological education is the conviction that the core practices of the church may be interpreted as forms of play: If we see both prayer and worship as forms of play,[41] it should influence the way we teach and learn, explore and assess, these spiritual disciplines in the framework of theological education. In a very concrete sense, it should imply that we emphasize developing skills of improvisation, rehearsing an openness to the unexpected, the incalculable, and even the improbable—that forms of play like prayer and worship may present to us.

It is also important to remember that the crisis of the church is often connected to numerical decline and loss of influence. However, putting play at the heart of theological education and church practice, may help the church and her leaders to frame the experience of decline in a different manner, by playfully and actively engaging with newcomers. Fundamentally, play is a practice that always welcomes newcomers. And more importantly, the arrival of a newcomer also changes the dynamic of the game. Therefore, theological education needs to offer abundant opportunities to engage with both outsiders and newcomers to church, as "a newcomer's presence within a congregation reminds the congregation that there are people who do not yet belong."[42] Theological training is not a therapeutic exercise to cope with the experience of decline, but an imaginative and welcoming practice of engaging playfully with the experience and questions of the newcomer and the outsider.

All in all, this playful approach to theological training implies that the process of theological teaching and learning would be conducted intentionally in a more explorative manner, following the pattern of innovation and creativity described in the process of preparing an act of communication in classical rhetoric.[43] According to this "training scheme," all learning starts with a stage of *inventio*, of searching for new themes and opportunities. This phase is impossible to imagine without play and exploration, and you need learn how to make mistakes and learn from them. Following the *inventio* stage, you enter the *dispositio* stage. This concerns collecting the different parts and creating a whole by seeing how the elements from the *inventio* stage may playfully interact. The third stage implies looking for the most fitting expression (*elocutio*). The fourth stage involves the playful memorizing of the speech by heart (*memoria*). The fifth stage marks the execution of the innovation process, presenting, or *action*, and this includes the playful

---

41. Edgar, *God Who Plays*, 13.

42. Ducksworth, *Wide Welcome*, 4.

43. For a longer elaboration on the connection between play, innovation, and change, see Wagner, *Creating Innovators*.

element any actor who appears on stage needs to handle, what role should I take on as I perform this.[44] In pursuing theological wisdom in this manner, we are building on our capacity to play,[45] and the theological curriculum and the practice of theological education have to be fundamentally challenged and changed as a result of this insight.

CONCLUSION

This chapter has looked at a phenomenon which emerges as the church is losing her given position in the public sphere: *ecclesial agoraphobia* describes the fear of sharing the Christian faith in the open space, at the marketplace (*agora* in Greek), responding to this fear by fighting back or fleeing the scene and withdrawing to the Christian catacomb or ghetto. However, neither aggression nor withdrawal are relevant responses to the challenge of lost privileges and hegemony. Rather, theological education needs to train leaders who rediscover and reinvent what it means to appear credible and speak with authority in the public sphere, even from a position of lost hegemony. I have argued that reshaping theological education through play is a key factor in this explorative endeavor.

Play may encourage theologians and church leaders to pursue the poetic and creative art of convincingly describing what the world looks like and envisioning a reality that requires a certain response in times of crisis.[46] By rehearsing how to live with the feeling of being ignored or rejected, the church and her theologians may be better equipped to rediscover the narrative art of responding to the three fundamental questions for all people: Where do we come from, where are we, and where are we going?

In times of crisis, and with the feeling of loss and decline, the church should explore play, but not as an instrument to achieve a particular strategic goal or as an attempt to ease the unpleasant feeling of influence lost. Rather, this kind of play may be capable of building another type of civilization, not based on destructive fear,[47] but teaching humans what it means to take risks and chances—in the light of being chosen in the mercy of God. This rests in the conviction that Christ once played in the presence of God Almighty (Prov 8:22–31). By relearning to play like children, the church may rediscover and experience what it means to be created over again, by

---

44. See Andersen, *I retorikkens hage*, 43–44; or Lausberg, *Handbook of Literary Rhetoric*.

45. Nash, "Being a Reflective Practitioner," 18.

46. Norheim and Haga, *Four Speeches*, 29–35; Norheim and Haga, *Three Fears*, 125.

47. Hankiss, *Fear and Symbols*.

an external force. It is the meaning of the *missio Dei*, of being sent by the triune God to the world. Fundamentally, play teaches humans a pattern for action, a return to the holy play in the presence of the Creator. It is a sort of *back to the future* move, where the church and her theological training may look forward to the promise of a time, when "the city streets will be filled with boys and girls playing here." (Zech 8:5 NIV)

BIBLIOGRAPHY

Andersen, Øyvind. *I retorikkens hage.* Oslo: Universitetsforlaget, 1995.
Barblett, Lennie, et al. "The Pushes and Pulls of Pedagogy in the Early Years: Competing Knowledges and the Erosion of Play-Based Learning." *Australasian Journal of Early Childhood* 41 (2016) 36–43.
Beck, Ulrich. *World at Risk.* Cambridge: Polity, 2009.
Berger, Peter. *The Sacred Canopy: Elements of a Sociological Theory of Religion.* New York: Anchor, 1967.
Berger, Peter, and Thomas Luckmann. *The Social Construction of Reality: A Treatise in the Sociology of Knowledge.* New York: Doubleday, 1966.
Davie, Grace. *Religion in Britain: A Persistent Paradox.* Oxford: Wiley-Blackwell, 2015.
Donahue, John J. "Fight-Flight-Freeze System." In *Encyclopedia of Personal and Individual Differences,* edited by Virgil Zeigler-Hill and Todd K. Schakelford, 1590–95. New York: Springer, 2020.
Ducksworth, Jessicah Krey. *Wide Welcome: How the Unsettling Presence of Newcomers Can Save the Church.* Minneapolis: Fortress, 2013.
Edgar, Brian. *The God Who Plays: A Playful Approach to Theology and Spirituality.* Eugene, OR: Cascade, 2017.
Edwards, Susan. "Play-Based Learning and Intentional Teaching: Forever Different?" *Australasian Journal of Early Childhood* 42 (2017) 4–11.
Hammarskjöld, Dag. *Veimerker.* Oslo: Lunde, 2003.
Hankiss, Elemèr. *Fears and Symbols: An Introduction to the Study of Western Civilization.* Budapest: CEU Press, 2001.
———. *The Toothpaste of Immortality: Self-Construction in the Consumer Age.* Baltimore: Johns Hopkins University Press, 2006.
Holland, Tom. *Dominion: How the Christian Revolution Remade the World.* New York: Basic, 2019.
Huizinga, Johan. *Homo Ludens: A Study of the Play Element in Culture.* Boston: Beacon, 1955.
Jenkins, Philip. *The Next Christendom: The Coming of Global Christianity.* 3rd ed. Oxford: Oxford University Press, 2011.
Kahnemann, Daniel. *Thinking Fast and Slow.* New York: Farrar, Straus and Giroux, 2011.
Lausberg, Heinrich. *Handbook of Literary Rhetoric: A Foundation of Literary Study.* Edited by David E. Orton and Dean Anderson. Leiden, Neth.: Brill Academic, 2002.
Moltmann, Jürgen. *Theology of Play.* New York, Harper & Row, 1972.

Nash, Sally. "Being a Reflective Practitioner and Lifelong Learner: Pursuing Wisdom and Fruitfulness." In *Christian Youth Work in Theory and Practice*, edited by Sally Nash and Jo Whitehead, 16–33. London: SCM, 2014.

Nell, Ian. *"Together in God's Theatre": Practical Theology in an African Context*. Wellington: CLF, 2020.

Norheim, Bård, and Joar Haga. *The Four Speeches Every Leader Has to Know*. London: Palgrave Macmillan, 2020.

———. "The Four Speeches Every Youth Leader Has to Know: The Preaching of Jesus as Model for a Public Rhetoric for Youth Ministry." *Journal of Youth and Theology* 18 (2019) 164–84.

———. *The Three Fears Every Leader Has to Know: Words to Use in a Crisis*. London: Palgrave Macmillan, 2022.

Norheim, Bård Eirik Hallesby. "Leik som retorisk basistrening for kyrkja i valfridomens tidsalder." *Luthersk Kirketidende* 153 (2018) 508–11.

———. "Naming Glocal Fear in Local Youth Ministry—and the Migrating Presence of Christ." *European Journal of Theology* 26 (2017) 162–72.

———. "Den norske kyrkjas retoriske sjølvforståing i valfridomens tidsalder: Å leva med frykta for å bli avvist." *Luthersk Kirketidende* 153 (2018) 408–11.

Pohl-Patalong, Uta. *Kirche Gestalten: Wie die Zukunft gelingen kann*. Gütersloh: Gütersloh, 2021.

Reiland, Dan. "The Relevant Church." Dan Reiland, n.d. https://danreiland.com/the-relevant-church/.

Root, Andrew. *Churches and the Crisis of Decline: A Hopeful, Practical Ecclesiology for a Secular Age*. Ministry in a Secular Age. Grand Rapids: Baker Academic, 2022.

Rosa, Hartmut. *Resonance: A Sociology of Our Relationship to the World*. Translated by James Wagner. Cambridge: Polity, 2019.

Sahlberg, Pasi, and William Doyle. *Let the Children Play: How More Play will Save our Schools and Help Children Thrive*. Oxford: Oxford University Press, 2019.

Stark, Rodney. *The Triumph of Christianity: How the Jesus Movement Became the World's Largest Religion*. New York: Harper One, 2011.

Taleb, Nassim Nicholas. *The Black Swan: The Impact of the Highly Improbable*. New York: Random House, 2010.

Taylor, Charles. *A Secular Age*. Cambridge, MA: Belknap, 2007.

———. *The Ethics of Authenticity*. Cambridge, MA: Harvard University Press, 1991.

Wagner, Tony. *Creating Innovators: The Making of Young People Who Will Change the World*. New York: Scribner, 2012.

Wells, Samuel. *Improvisation: The Drama of Christian Ethics*. Grand Rapids: Brazos, 2004.

Chapter 3

Listening to the Voices of Students in Theological Education

SHANTELLE WEBER AND GRETCHEN SCHOON TANIS

INTRODUCTION

"Theology's concern with spirituality is not only liturgical acts of worship but also to pass social, economic and political issues through the prism and microscope of the God-word, with the ultimate good of redeeming everything to and for God . . . Theology is not only to know the truth, it is also to do the truth, too."[1] Recognizing the need for academic flexibility in a dynamic post-pandemic world, theological education institutions are seeking new and improved ways to provide quality education. Advances in technology, the demands of an increasingly mobile and diverse population, economic realities, the emphasis on the democratization of education, and dissatisfaction with traditional models are some of the issues that continue to spark interest in theological education across the globe.[2]

This chapter reflects on the importance of listening to student voices, particularly from the Norwegian and South African contexts. Katherine Gough argues that space is central in the social construction of childhood and to a large extent in the social construction of students as well.[3] A research study comparing young people in South Africa, Finland, and Norway calls for a better understanding of the agency of youth, not only to understand

---

1. Pobee, "Foreword," vii.
2. Cannell, "Review of Literature," 6.
3. Gough, "Nordic Geographies," 220.

how youth survive but also how they live with dignity under difficult circumstances.[4] This study highlights the many differences between South Africa and Norway in terms of youth population sizes, socioeconomic status, and access to social welfare services, as well as experiences of violence and death. It shows how the large majority of young people in Norway are in education, employment, and training—or some combination of these activities—while a large proportion of young South Africans are not.[5] The difference between the South African and Nordic higher education enrolment rates (higher in Norway) are based on varying factors including access to free education, familial background in education, and familial gender role expectations.[6] Student movements (in South Africa) have in recent years called for access to free higher education because of the unequal access to such education. This chapter argues that students (mainly young adults in both contexts) in higher education have significant life experience that they bring to the classroom and ministry contexts. These include experiences of brokenness, chronic illness, inequality, privilege, marginalization, and climate change. Amid these varying contextual realities, decolonization of educational curriculum was prioritized. Theology students particularly called for access to indigenous theologies that are relevant and adaptable to their contextual realities. Faith communities are, therefore, critical in supporting and equipping their young adults to engage in society. Conversely, students calling for relevant theologies argue that the teachings they receive from their faith communities are often inadequate to assist youth in making sense of their lived realities, as the theologies which are popularly taught in their largely evangelical congregational contexts do not grapple with contextual issues they face.[7] Norwegian ministry contexts also call for contextual theology relevant to the contextual realities they face. One of the tenets of the Teaching and Learning Theology in Crisis project has been that we address the crisis of Christian leaders not being trained to engage the contexts they find themselves in. Theological education is called to a new way of being by the very text of our globally construed life.[8] Students call us to ask, who in this text is in power? Who is powerless, and whose side does God take?

Education is not merely the accumulation of a prescribed set of academic credits but includes the holistic formation of all aspects of the

---

4. Holte and Rabe, "Statistical Snapshots," 49.
5. Holte and Rabe, "Statistical Snapshots," 58.
6. Holte and Rabe, "Statistical Snapshots," 60.
7. Apollis, "Developing a Short Course," 40.
8. Gonzalez-Andrieu, "Good of Education," 59.

individual.[9] Theological education has in its very subject matter already taken a marginal position in the prevalent power structures of our contemporary society.[10] Theological training that embraces the experiences and voices of its students takes the formation processes during such training seriously. Ministerial formation then becomes a multifaceted activity involving critical thinking, the acquisition of knowledge, skills development, religious identity formation, and the development of ministerial and spiritual maturity expected of church ministers and Christian leaders.[11] Theological education should intentionally listen to the voices of the students it serves, paying particular attention to their contexts and taking formation during training seriously. In this instance, ecclesial practices and religious aspects of culture and society, as well as the spiritual dimension of individual life, are considered. This chapter reflects on our combined experience as practical theologians who specialize in the field of youth ministry. It is based on our experience in teaching and learning in higher education in South Africa and Norway which includes our journey alongside the students (young people) we serve. The research question explored asks: How do we engage with the voices of the theology students we are training to become contextually relevant theologians and Christian leaders amid the many complexities they face while studying at a university? Against this background, we reflect on two crises: 1) the voices of theological students are not being taken seriously within their theological education, and 2) the academic courses do not adequately train students for their vocational contexts.

CRISIS 1: THEOLOGICAL EDUCATION DOES NOT CONSIDER THE VOICES OF THE STUDENTS WE ARE TRAINING

Christians are becoming increasingly convinced that traditional approaches to theology do not really make sense within their own contexts. In order to create global conversation that unites a vision of life and a way of life, theological education must carefully inquire who is missing from the dialogue.[12] Research conducted with youth on the margins in South Africa and Norway reveals "that place of residence (or lack thereof), citizenship status, race, gender, class (although difficult to define across vastly different

---

9. Naidoo, "Ministerial Formation," 1.
10. Gonzalez-Andrieu, "Good of Education," 59.
11. Naidoo, "Ministerial Formation," 1.
12. Gonzalez-Andrieu, "Good of Education," 62.

societies) and religion" are important intersectional factors to consider for studies focused on these contexts.[13] The same study revealed that many, but not all, religious people are affiliated to Christian churches in South Africa and the Nordic countries with young people expressing mixed appreciation for the rituals and practices churches expect them to get involved in.[14] For this reason, Naidoo argues that one should consider that the type of students in our classrooms are also influenced by the theological tradition from which they come.[15] Denominational schools of theology, seminaries, and Bible colleges are one cluster, while theological faculties at universities are another. Some students (in the former cluster) come having been encouraged through their local faith communities while many (in the latter) do not. All the factors mentioned affect the competencies, curriculum, academic integrity, and professional identity of the theological student. In addition to this, theological education is expected to address tensions students face along their journey. How are their social and contextual realities addressed through theological application or praxis? How should the need for accredited theological training alongside the need for ministerial formation be navigated? What does a decolonized theological education include? How are gender and diversity taken seriously when training students who come from contexts where these issues are not taken seriously in relation to ministry? What does faith and moral formation in theological education include? Finally, what is the relationship between church and the academic institution when the goal is to serve ecumenical churches or organizations? These are all complex considerations when reflecting on the students being theologically trained. For many years, theological institutions, particularly vocational ones, have acknowledged the need to keep an eye on what end product is required, asking what sort of person churches need and designing programs of study accordingly.[16] At the same time, the goals of the traditional intellectual approach to the academic study of theology found in universities often omit personal formation elements, despite evidence that students in these courses often enrol for formational reasons.[17]

It was in light of these shifting patterns between theological academic programs and the ministerial location of the students that NLA University College proposed and began the master of theology and ministry program in 2016. It was perceived there was a population in Norway and across Europe

---

13. Rabe et al., 225.
14. Rabe et al., 229.
15. Naidoo, *Contested Issues*.
16. Naidoo, "Ministerial Formation," 2.
17. Graham, "Theological Education," 230.

working in nontraditional Christian ministries—be that nondenominational or charismatic churches, Christian organizations like mission and youth organizations, or Christian folk high schools. The implicit understanding of the NLA faculty was that, because of the unique ministry settings of this population, a program was needed that would allow for theological training to be done in a flexible and unique way. Because of this, a program with practical theology as its focus and with a hybrid schedule was started. Because the program is offered in English, NLA has received students from international settings from a plethora of Christian backgrounds. However, because of these unique backgrounds and experiences of the students, it is vital that faculty and staff pay attention to the ways in which the contexts both of upbringing and ministerial location are understood; it is vital that the voices of these students are heard. In doing so, we take an important step towards preparing theology students to maintain their heart and passion for ministry while recognizing the complex backgrounds they come from.

Rabe et al. highlight that space and race continue to be a critical intersection that contributes to the way that the lived experiences of young people in South Africa may be understood and analyzed.[18] Many young people in this context grew up in a space where there were almost no economic opportunities and their chances of finding or creating such opportunities were slim. The same research study revealed that people from various countries also cross borders to Nordic countries in search of better opportunities.[19] They not only shift their locations, but also their legal status, at least until they obtain a new citizenship, which can take a long time, resulting in many being immigrants or the children of immigrants. Young people from immigrant families were subject to certain forms of labeling. Physical location is important in determining young people's opportunities for education, training and employment in South Africa and Norway.[20] Against this background, one could perhaps say that students studying theology also experience a crisis of adjustment while studying. Conversations with many students over time allude to them dealing with the tensions between having a call to Christian ministry and the desire to obtain a theology degree, including familial and denominational expectations and preconceptions about what theology is before studying and then adjusting one's theological lenses from these preconceived notions of theology to understanding and grappling with the theology being taught to them. This is more complex for a first-generation student (whose family has no background in higher

---

18. Rabe et al., 237–38.
19. Rabe et al., 239.
20. Rabe et al., 240.

education), having an added pressure placed on them to succeed which results in a type of spiritual trauma experienced.

In 2018–2019 the Faculty of Theology, Stellenbosch University, embarked on a journey towards renewing its bachelor of theology degree program. Some of the motivating factors were the need to revise programs for funding or subsidy purposes, decolonization of curricula after the #FeesMustFall movements, and updating faculty offerings for the market of students arriving at the institution. A brief survey with alumni and students was also conducted.[21] A first survey was sent to both alumni and current BTh students (general and youth work, years 1 to 3) of the 2012 to 2016 cohort. This survey revealed that students studying theology came from over twenty different denominations, most from black communities and from families who did not previously have access to higher education. As part of the data gathering process, several workshops were conducted in which students, academic staff, and partners of the faculty participated. Data from these workshops revealed a need to take the role of social location of the students and the faculty into careful consideration. This impacts the jobs and skills required while studying. Some of these contextual issues were noted earlier in this chapter. This data also revealed that some of the challenges students faced along the way were related to finances, the social location of faculty, short time frame (three years) in which to adapt and succeed, and the varying contexts (familial, ecclesial, educational, dreams, fears, and personalities) that affected how they studied. Students in these workshops reported church, family, and friends as their main forms of support while studying.

In a similar fashion as Stellenbosch University, NLA University College also went through the process of examination and recertification with external examiners in 2021. Through the process of examination, it was discovered that the voice of their master in theology students needed to adapt to the changing landscape of ministry and mission in Norway and beyond. An important area for improvement, as discovered through the process of recertification, was to adapt the program to have more internationalization. It was articulated that there was need for "a radical willingness to listen to the empirical reality as it is and a radical willingness to search for theological significance and response as a mark of the Master in Theology and Ministry."[22] It was articulated that this would be essential when students encounter multicultural and ecumenical ministry environments. As students transitioned from their degree program to formal ministry

---

21. Weber, "Faculty of Theology," 6.
22. Weber et al., *Report*, 2.

positions it would be important to have a master's program focused on international ministerial experience and engagement. External examiners noted that there was a need for field research around, and in, the mission field of secularized Europe. Who are the ones the church is trying to reach who are not currently churchgoers? Is there resistance to the gospel in the various age groups? If so, why? What does the relevant church-planting literature recommend if one is to start up afresh in new areas or to go into unreached cultures in areas where churches already exist? What about the international, first- or second-generation immigrants? Many of them are believers, but what bridges can be made in new church plants that would help a smoother integration for many, and enrich everyone involved across the continent of Europe?[23]

Examiners prophetically pointed out specific areas of challenge in terms of the specific modules offered to theology students. They rightly challenged by asking, "It seems there is a lack of societal/developmental (diakonia) engagement and globalized/contextual theology. Were these modules chosen on the basis of the Norwegian partner's needs or on the desire to engage international students?"[24] More specifically, examiners challenged NLA's landscape of teaching and learning to make certain they included more Pentecostal churches/backgrounds, as well as international missions and ministries—including the background of their mission partners. It was suggested to include church planting/planters and understanding of varying denominational backgrounds. They emphasized there should be an inclusion of Free Churches and mission societies in the program. With the benefit of different perspectives on the changing landscape of Norway, as well as across Europe, external examiners assisted by pushing NLA to think of the contexts and experiences of students in order to adjust the theological courses on offer in order to prepare them for future vocational contexts.

Through the process of the examination of curricula and student experience at both NLA University College and Stellenbosch University, faculties at both institutions recognized the missing voices of students' backgrounds and experiences. Access to higher education that has the capacity to undermine the history of power and exclusion built into educational systems is thus inextricably joined to the very task of doing theology responsibly.[25] In both contexts, listening to the voices of students allowed a revision of the way in which we teach them and critical reflection on what we teach them. Listening to their contextual realities and the relevance of what we teach has

---

23. Weber et al., *Report*, 6.
24. Weber et al., *Report*, 9.
25. Gonzalez-Andrieu, "Good of Education," 63.

been integral toward renewed curriculum. It is against this backdrop that we now reflect on a second crisis: that what we teach should be contextually relevant to the student.

CRISIS 2: THEOLOGICAL CURRICULUM IS NOT RELEVANT TO THE CONTEXT STUDENTS SERVE

According to Villa-Vicencio, it is essential to educate people and advocate for democratic participation in the struggle for social renewal and shaping new mental constructs, ready to envision and build a new society.[26] Theological seminaries, moreover, play a pertinent role in the training of current and future clergy, as well as community practitioners, that serve both church and society. If we believe that churches should play a leading role in modeling this, they should take the lead in the journey of engaged citizenship for which this kind of training is imperative. As noted in the introduction to this chapter, young students in both Norway and South Africa still find religion important in their lives. Churches have a significant impact on the value systems of individuals and therefore have great influence in the work of reconstructing ideologies, belief systems, and behavioral patterns. For many students in South Africa, studying at an institution of higher education is a first in their family. Students studying theology are decreasing across Europe. For this reason, theological education that seeks to equip the church towards an intergenerational and intercultural passing on of their faith and heart for justice needs to take these marginalized voices seriously and seek to equip them with the skills and competencies to navigate society.[27] Botman notes that "education should play a role in changing the world for the better by stimulating critical thinking and empowering people so that they might free themselves from oppression, poverty, injustice and the difficult task of living peacefully with former oppressors after political liberation."[28] Theological education that does not stimulate critical thinking or empower students to engage with their context could be termed irrelevant, as theological education plays a pivotal role in the liberation of students from their marginalized situations. Students tend to operate at two extremes in the political arena. On the one hand, they are critiqued for being overly disengaged from conventional political participation, while on the other hand they are critiqued for being engaged in protest and political

---

26. Villa-Vicencio, *Theology of Reconstruction*, 279.
27. Apollis and Weber, "Young Adults," 172.
28. Russel Botman, in Leibowitz, *Higher Education*, xiii.

violence.[29] These varied perspectives of young people classify them as either apathetic, alienated from the political process, or as having internalized values that radically reject the new, democratic societies.[30] Young people are an integral part of any society in terms of the economy and workforce as well as an indicator of a sustainable future for both the present generation and generations to come. Delgado states that countries need to view their youth as social capital as opposed to a capital drain.[31]

Christian youth are taught, both formally and informally, that what they do within Christian spaces is separated from how they live in society. Their reading, interpretation, and application of the Bible is limited to church tradition and not their daily lived experiences.[32] Theological education faces the same challenges with growing diversity as the rest of higher education: new student constituencies reflect a wide spectrum of cultural backgrounds, personal histories, and theological commitments, representing diversity in race, ethnicity, culture, class, gender, age, and sexual orientation.[33] Theology students need to challenge such notions of dualism in their churches, communities, and society. Diversity within theology is both a blessing and a challenge since hearing and experiencing the other entails questioning one's theological convictions as part of one's intrinsic being. It calls for an unpacking of familial and theological tradition that for many theology students was never contested, or even taught, prior to engaging with the other at university level. The dichotomy between spirituality and politics in present-day South Africa and Norway reflects a failure of the promises of a political liberation without the transformational voice of faith in public life.

The earlier survey mentioned from Stellenbosch noted that 62 percent of the alumni indicated that their churches had referred them or supported them to study theology, while 55 percent from the current student cohort indicated that their church body supported their studies at Stellenbosch.[34] Many private theological seminaries in South Africa are also being closed for lack of adherence to government accreditation criteria. This is a challenge for the kind of theology offered and taught in local churches where a majority of ministers have not been formally trained. It was interesting that many alumni reported relevance of the practical theology offering to

29. Apollis and Weber, "Young Adults," 165.
30. Mattes and Richmond, "South Africa's Youth," 4.
31. Delgado, *New Frontiers*, 26–27.
32. Apollis and Weber, "Young Adults," 167.
33. Naidoo, *Contested Issues*, 71.
34. Weber, "Faculty of Theology," 6.

their ministerial situations. The practicing theologian is one who seeks to bridge action and reflection—or is challenged to put into practice *reflection* on said praxis. This has serious implications for theological training which takes the voice of its students seriously. Theological curriculum is not merely attaching Bible verses to what students are experiencing, rather it is about examining how divine action connects to human beings. Theology then is not the process of unveiling God to the world but rather the process of articulating how God has unveiled Godself in the world. It is about faithful discipleship,[35] which challenges notions of superficial theology. Faithful discipleship is so God-directed that it invites the Holy Spirit to consistently encroach into any assumptions, attitudes, and/or habits held dearly that may keep either a community or an individual believer from living out the call of the gospel. It is about equipping students towards outwardly driven ministries and exploring what God is doing in the communities they live or are going to. It is about taking the guidance of the Holy Spirit seriously. This approach to theological training also takes context seriously. The engaged theologian acknowledges that the lecturers' own experience, background, and training can affect how one views a given context. It is also realized that theological training is a communal process of reflection and discernment in which lecturers listen carefully to how students see and experience their world. Theological training should make students aware of the processes of social and systemic transformation of contexts in which these performances take place. Students become aware of their own and other cultural prejudices and the importance of approaching social analyses from different perspectives. It is a continual process (praxis-theory-praxis). Theological education should orientate students towards the world, further the telos of life, learning from engaged praxis, and be intentionally interdisciplinary by helping students to understand the world in all its complexities, as they need to understand all the other subjects in the curriculum.[36] The activist scholar and liberation theologian in this regard is crucial. They have to ask critical questions of society and of the university in relation to society; they are the ones to name the shackles and manipulations of power, but also to accompany processes dedicated to finding radically inclusive alternatives. But, finally, they are also the ones who have to start embodying the viable responses to their own questions.[37] Theological training should include solidarity with the local, solidarity with the poor, and solidarity with emerging and existing movements working for social justice.

35. Clark, *Youth Ministry*.
36. Nell, "Teaching Leadership and Administration," 10–13.
37. De Beer, "University, City, Clown," 4.

As noted above, diversity within theology entails unpacking the familial and theological traditions students embody while studying at university. We have argued that students bring significant life experience and Christian perspective when studying theology. With this in mind, it was important to approach joint learning between Stellenbosch University and NLA University College as a means in which students and professors could share their unique experiences and perspectives with one another. With this communal process of reflection and discernment, in August of 2021 and 2022 co-teaching (and thus co-learning) between Stellenbosch University of South Africa and NLA University College of Norway was started. In the August intensive weeks of 2021 and 2022 for the youth ministry course of the MATM program, the topic of youth participation in protest movements was discussed. Participation in student movements happens differently in both locations. While young adults in Norway were not as quick to join protests or movements in the streets (unless around the issue of climate change), young adults in South Africa have participated in mass protests around a number of issues over the course of the previous five to seven years.[38] In team teaching and collaboration, the theories and ideas discussed in the classroom in Norway were presented with grassroot examples of how youth movements look in South Africa. That included the movements of Fees Must Fall and Rhodes Must Fall protests. Weber showcased photographs from the protests themselves as well as discussions between Christian students and faculty around the issues of protest participation. In collaborating between institutions and locations, students from Norway were introduced to the issues and movements in South Africa, especially the issues that impact similar theology students in international and ecumenical situations. The hope and desire in pursuing these co-teaching opportunities was that students would be introduced to multicultural and international ministerial issues. One of the lessons we learn from global student communities is that such communities force us to reflect on what we assume are contextually bound realties and create opportunities to be rooted in the indigenous theological roots we come from. Without a sufficiently diverse group in the conversation, we are just reinforcing what we already know, and thus, the efficacy of education itself is lost.[39] We are then reminded that what we teach in glocal contexts is crucial. Such international collaboration relies on contextually rooted theologies that can be shared with the global community. Theology

---

38. We will discuss the movements such as #FeesMustFall and #RhodesMustFall below.

39. Gonzalez-Andrieu, "Good of Education," 62.

graduates need to be rooted in their local contexts yet globally aware of what is happening in situations and contexts that differ from their own.

CONCLUSION

This chapter reflects a response to the research question: How do we engage with the voices of the theology students we are training toward becoming contextually relevant theologians and Christian leaders amid the many complexities they face while studying at a university? Theological education that does not take the voices and subsequent lived experiences of the students we teach seriously is devoid of relevance to the student and the context in which they are called to work. Socioeconomic and ecclesial factors need to be considered in how we teach. Theological education needs to interrogate historical legacies that have led to the theological curriculum we currently teach. Our students are key in this regard. Through reflecting on two academic offerings in Norway and South Africa, we are reminded that glocal theological education is enhanced when students understand their own indigenous theologies and local contexts better. Listening to the voices of students in how and what we offer is crucial in higher education today.

In summary, as practical theologians engaged in both community and academy, the authors shared their experiences, emphasizing that the exploration of ways of international collaborative teaching will enhance both the local and global contexts.

BIBLIOGRAPHY

Apollis, Quinton. "Developing a Short Course: Engaging Youth, Church and Social Justice." MTh thesis, Stellenbosch University, 2020.

Apollis, Quinton, and Shantelle Weber. "Young Adults and Social Justice: Empowering Young Adults as Social Change Agents through Theological Education." In *Faith, Race and Inequality amongst Young Adults in South Africa: Contested and Contesting Discourses for a Better Future*, edited by Nadine Bowers Du Toit, 165–78. Beyers Naudé Centre Series on Public Theology 14. Cape Town: African Sun Media, 2022.

Cannell, L. "A Review of Literature on Distance Education." *Theological Education* 36 (1999) 1–72.

Chatterton, P., et al. "Beyond Scholar Activism: Making Strategic Interventions inside and outside the Neoliberal University." *ACME: An International e-Journal for Critical Geographies* 9 (2010) 245–75.

Clark, Chap, ed. *Youth Ministry in the 21st Century: Five Views*. Youth, Family, and Culture. Grand Rapids: Baker Academic, 2015.

De Beer, Stephan. "The University, the City and the Clown: A Theological Essay on Solidarity, Mutuality and Prophecy." *HvTSt* 71 (2015) art. 3100. http://dx.doi.org/10.4102/hts.v71i3.3100.

Delgado, Melvin. *New Frontiers for Youth Development in the Twenty-First Century: Revitalizing and Broadening Youth Development.* New York: Columbia University Press, 2013.

Dibeela, Prince, et al. *Prophet from the South: Essays in Honour of Allan Aubrey Boesak.* Stellenbosch, S. Afr.: Sun, 2014.

Du Pree, Ronel, et al. "Report on the 25th International Conference on the First Year Experience Held in Vancouver, British Columbia, Canada, July 16–19, 2012." Unpublished manuscript. Microsoft Word file.

First Generation Commission. "Report." University of Stellenbosch, May 2001. Unpublished manuscript. Microsoft Word file.

Foster, Charles R., et al. *Educating Clergy: Teaching Practices and Pastoral Imagination.* JB-Carnegie Foundation for the Advancement of Teaching. San Francisco: Jossey-Bass, 2006.

Frank, T. E. "Leadership and Administration: An Emerging Field in Practical Theology; Research Report." *International Journal of Practical Theology* 10 (2006) 113–52.

Garcia, Valerie. "First-Generation College Students: How Co-Curricular Involvement Can Assist with Success." *Vermont Connection* 31 (2010) art. 6.

Gonzalez-Andrieu, Cecilia. "The Good of Education: Accessibility, Economy, Class and Power." In *Teaching Global Theologies: Power & Praxis*, edited by Kwok Pui-lan et al., 57–74. Waco: Baylor University Press, 2015.

Gough, Katherine V. "Nordic Geographies of Children and Youth." *Geografiska Annaler*, ser. B, *Human Geography* 90 (2008) 217–26.

Graham, Susan Lochrie. "Theological Education on the Web: A Case Study in Formation for Ministry." *Teaching Theology and Religion* 5 (2002) 227–35. http://dx.doi.org/10.1111/1467-9647.00142.

Hansen, L. D., ed. *The Legacy of Beyers Naudé.* Beyers Naudé Centre Series on Public Theology 1. Stellenbosch, S. Afr.: Sun, 2005.

Herman, Judith. *Trauma and Recovery: The Aftermath of Violence—from Domestic Abuse to Political Terror.* New York: Hachette, 2015.

Holte, Bjørn Hallstein, and Marlize Rabe. "Statistical Snapshots: Contextualising the Lives of Youths in South Africa and the Nordic Countries." In *Stuck in the Margins? Young People and Faith-Based Organisations in South African and Nordic Localities*, edited by Ignatius Swart et al., 49–64. Research in Contemporary Religion 31. Göttingen: Vandenhoeck & Ruprecht, 2022.

Leibowitz, Brenda, ed. *Higher Education for the Public Good: Views from the South.* Stellenbosch, S. Afr.: African Sun Media, 2012.

Leibowitz, Brenda, et al. "Institutional Context Matters: The Professional Development of Academics as Teachers in South African Higher Education." *Higher Education* 69 (2015) 315–30. https://doi.org/10.1007/s10734-014-9777-2.

Mattes, Robert, and Samantha Richmond. "South Africa's Youth and Political Participation, 1994–2014." OpenUCT, July 2014. CSSR Working Paper 338. https://open.uct.ac.za/handle/11427/7905.

Naidoo, Marilyn, ed. *Contested Issues in Training Ministers in South Africa.* Stellenbosch, S. Afr.: Sun, 2015.

———. "Ministerial Formation of Theological Students through Distance Education." *HvTSt* 68 (2012) art. 1225. http://dx.doi.org./10.4102/hts.v68i2.1225.

Nell, Ian Alphonso. "Teaching Leadership and Administration at a Faculty of Theology: Practical-Theological reflections." *Scriptura: Journal for Contextual Hermeneutics in Southern Africa* 113 (2014) 1–18.

Pobee, John S. "Foreword." In *Contested Issues in Training Ministers in South Africa*, edited by Marilyn Naidoo, vii–x. Stellenbosch, S. Afr.: Sun, 2015.

Ramphele, Mamphela. *Laying Ghosts to Rest: Dilemmas of the Transformation in South Africa.* Cape Town: Tafelberg, 2009.

Villa-Vicencio, Charles. *A Theology of Reconstruction: Nation-Building and Human Rights.* Cambridge Studies in Ideology and Religion 1. Cambridge: Cambridge University Press, 1992. https://doi.org/10.1017/CBO9780511607592.

Weber, Shantelle, et al. *Report from External Evaluation Panel: Periodic Evaluation of Master in Theology and Ministry.* NLA, 2021. https://www.nla.no/globalassets/kvalitetsportalen/rapporter-fra-periodisk-evaluering-av-studietilbud/2021-external-matam-master-in-theology-and-ministry-evaluation-report.pdf.

Weber, S. M. "Faculty of Theology Program Renewal Progress Report." Unpublished manuscript, last modified May 22, 2018. Microsoft Word file.

Chapter 4

Perspectives on the Climate Crisis, Sin, and Theological Education

Gunnar Innerdal

INTRODUCTION

Many scientists, political leaders, and religious leaders agree that the crisis of environmental destruction, where the most urgent problem is human-induced climate change from excessive carbon emission, is the biggest and most complex crisis we face as global humanity. In recent years there have been many incidents with severe consequences for human beings that have been interpreted by scientists, and communicated to the public through the media, as very likely to have been caused or made much more likely by climate change. Global warming leads to what can be called global weirding—multiple extreme and unusual weather incidents.[1] In our April 2022 Stellenbosch symposium of the TLC project, I cited the huge 2020 Australian forest fires and the floods of Ahr Valley in Germany after extreme rain in 2021 as examples of this. Now we could add, from the summer of 2022, exceptional heat waves around the globe (in the UK/Europe, China, and other places) and the horrible floods in Pakistan from June to October, leading to the deaths of thousands of people. The countries involved in our project have also been affected, South Africa most severely through heavy rain, flooding, and landslides, the worst in April 2022. In Norway there have been few extreme incidents, but November 2022 saw a bunch of temperature records all over the country that fit well into the emerging pattern of

---

1. See the use of the term in Hayhoe, "Heat."

slow temperature growth. In the winter, parts of central Europe saw green hills where people would normally go for skiing holidays. Against this background, it should be easier than ever to make people take UN General Secretary Antonio Guterres's "Code red!" warning seriously.[2]

Is there any way out of the collective decision paralysis we are experiencing in facing this situation? It would be naïve to give a short and simple answer to such a question, given the overwhelming scientific/technological, economic, political/societal, cultural, and ethical complexity of the issue.[3] Climate change can certainly be called a "wicked problem" that eludes simplistic explanations and treatments.[4] In this chapter, I will nevertheless try to make a small contribution from the perspective of theology and theological education. Theologians have been addressing issues in environmental ethics and ecological hermeneutics for decades, covering a wide range of themes and perspectives.[5] My contribution here will be to address and discuss some aspects of the Christian doctrine of sin, as an important concept in the theological interpretation of climate change as a problem. The discussion will also serve as a resource for understanding and engaging with the decision paralysis of churches, Christians, and broader society individually and collectively. Departing from this discussion I will contribute to the broader discussion of how to integrate ecological perspectives in theological education. If the problem of climate change is rightly interpreted theologically as relating to sin, future theologians and pastors need to address it as part of their ministry of giving prophetic insights, correction, and hope.

Thus, we arrive at the following research questions for this chapter: *How can the concept of sin from Christian dogmatics contribute to the understanding and handling of the problem of climate change? How can future theologians and pastors be equipped through their theological education to engage with this issue?* The questions are related and have some connection with each other, but their selection and combination arises as much from the context of the Teaching and Learning Theology in Crisis (TLC) project as from a systematic discussion. By answering those two questions, I will

---

2. Guterres used the expression repeatedly after the issue of a new report from the Intergovernmental Panel on Climate Change in 2021 and continued to do so in 2022. See Guterres, "Deputy Secretary-General's Remarks"; Guterres, "Secretary-General's Statement."

3. My selective version of this list is based primarily on Conradie, "Emergence of Human Sin," 384. Thunberg, *Climate Book*, and different publications from the IPCC can fill out the picture.

4. Conradie, *Redeeming Sin*, xvi, with references.

5. A comprehensive overview focusing on the Norwegian context is found in Tomren, *Kyrkje, miljø og berekraft* [Church, environment, and sustainability].

contribute doubly to the project in the sense of reflecting on both the *what* and the *how* of the ecological aspect of theology and theological education preparing for ecclesial ministry.

The doctrine of sin and how to meet the climate crisis are both contextual questions. How to define and make sin concrete depends on cultural and social dynamics, as both contextualizing missionaries[6] and sociologists of religion[7] can attest. Likewise, climate crisis responsibility and urgency look very different in a Pacific Island threatened with being overcome by rising ocean levels, or in a high-emission industrialized economy, or to indigenous peoples living close to and caring for nature. In this chapter, the context is primarily North Atlantic[8] societies, churches, and higher education institutions. This is a shared context between Norway and South Africa to some extent, although Norway is a clearer oil-based economy, and South Africa is less industrialized and more socially and ethnically complex. The wisdom of indigenous people and the broader contextual aspects of sin, climate crisis, and theological education deserve more attention and discussion on other occasions. My priority here will be to address questions from a North Atlantic perspective both theologically and societally. In addition to being the context where I and the TLC project belong, this is also the place where most of the climate crisis responsibility and guilt (by sin) are located.

The contextuality of the questions discussed in this chapter can be seen with a short look at the notions of *prevention* and *adaptation* connected to climate crisis politics. While, for example, the agenda in the 90s that resulted in the Kyoto Protocol, emphasized *prevention* by means of carbon emission reduction as the most important action mode, more recent political discussions have given more attention to *adaptation* to the new climate. This includes the heavy and subtle moral question of who is to pay for necessary adaptations, especially for those changes that affect the people that suffer greatly from, but have contributed little to, global warming.[9] Which moves are to be taken in making and balancing prevention and adaptation will depend on both the kind of society and the type of economy that is your context. Wealth acquired through unsustainable use of natural resources should be shared. And prevention should be discussed with reference to general consumption patterns and public welfare in each context.

6. See, e.g., Dye, "Toward a Cross-Cultural Definition"; Strand, "Explaining Sin."

7. See, e.g., Sumerau et al., "Can't Put My Finger."

8. The term *North Atlantic* is used by Conradie to refer to all societies with roots in preindustrial Europe, including Australia and South Africa, among others (Conradie, "Emergence of Human Sin," 387).

9. Jan-Olav Henriksen reflects on the need for solidarity responsibility and action in this context in his recent small piece "Klimakrisens utfordringer."

SIN AS THEOLOGICAL INTERPRETATIVE LENS ON CLIMATE CHANGE

In recent years, the South African theologian Ernst M. Conradie has attempted through several publications to retrieve Christian sin-talk as a positive contribution to the public discourse over ecological destruction, especially climate change issues. In *Redeeming Sin* (2017) he argues that "the deepest roots of ecological destruction may be found in a three-letter word: sin."[10] Much of the argument concerns obstacles to a retrieval of Christian sin-talk in the context of ecological problems, and one of the major questions handled is the question about what is wrong with the world and how and when it became so.

In his 2020 work *Secular Discourse on Sin in the Anthropocene*, Conradie goes deeper into the analysis of what is wrong in the world, starting from an acute crisis understanding of the present ecological situation. He relates to the ongoing interdisciplinary discussion about whether the world has entered a new geological age, the *Anthropocene*, because human beings through practices such as the use of nuclear power, carbon emission, and removal of biodiversity are leaving a significant and lasting impression on the geological layers of the earth. Conradie suggests that perhaps the Anthropocene should rather be called the *Hamartiocene* (the age of sin, from Greek *hamartia*), "the age in which the global impact of human sin has become evident."[11] He thus joins other important Christian leaders such as Pope Francis and the ecumenical patriarch Bartholomew in addressing the current ecological crisis as not only a scientific, technological, and political problem, but also a profoundly *spiritual* problem.[12]

In his contribution to the *T&T Clark Handbook of Christian Theology and Climate Change* on "he emergence of human sin," Conradie is more careful in his conclusions regarding sin as the cause of the climate crisis, suggesting that "many Christians would be inclined to take a shortcut . . . to capture the root cause of climate change with three letters: sin."[13] The reason that reduction to Christian sin-talk may be a shortcut is that climate change is a profound sense a global problem, including people from different

---

10. Conradie, *Redeeming Sin*, xi.

11. Conradie, *Secular Discourse on Sin*, 14. Cf. Henriksen citing Hans Jonas: "It was once religion which told us that we are all sinners, because of original sin. It is now the ecology of our planet which pronounces us all to be sinners because of the excessive exploits of human inventiveness" (Henriksen, *Climate Change*, 179).

12. See Francis, *Laudato Si'*, esp. §§8, 9, 119; Conradie, *Secular Discourse on Sin*, 69–70; Conradie, *Redeeming Sin*, xvii, with references.

13. Conradie, "Emergence of Human Sin," 385.

religions and geographical contexts. And we have already pointed to the level of complexity of the issue, that makes single-faceted answers impossible.[14] Regardless of that, Christian sin-talk may make an important contribution to understanding the causes of the climate crisis and what is needed to address it properly.

Theological discussions on ecology have often focused on what has been called the stewardship model.[15] Starting from the doctrine of creation, this approach emphasizes human beings as responsible stewards within creation seen as the garden of God. In recent years many theologians have suggested that there is need for an adjustment of this focus to include more genuinely *Christian* perspectives, through an engagement with Christology. Notions such as deep incarnation[16] and the ecological Christ[17] serves to situate ecological issues at the heart of Christian theology. I suggest that the doctrine of sin can take cues from both models and contributes to their connection and mutual illumination. Sin as an ethical perspective arises from unfaithful stewardship, while sin as a spiritual/theological perspective relates what is wrong to the central part of the Christian story: the incarnate cosmic Christ as redeemer of humans and all creation.

A new and troubling insight becoming clear to theologians through climate change research is that the traditional distinction between moral and natural evils as the cause of human suffering and other forms of destruction of God's creation is fading. It becomes evident that the human entanglement in creation means that the sum of small-scale human action may add up to making natural catastrophes much more likely. Thus, "the cumulative impact of moral evil has become a (geological) force of nature" that results in human suffering.[18] The situation today is that "although much of the evil in the natural world cannot be said to have been caused by human sin, some undoubtedly is."[19] The falling apart of this distinction adds to the

---

14. Henriksen says similarly that "a reduction to either a mere scientific or a mere spiritual/theological interpretation of the situation will not suffice" (Henriksen, *Climate Change*, 71).

15. See Tomren, "How Green was Martin," 105–7; Haugen, "Hope, Fear, Anger, Courage," 42, 49. Baumgartner, "Transformations of Stewardship"; Henriksen, *Climate Change*, 142–46, give more comprehensive accounts of debates about the stewardship model.

16. See Deane-Drummond, "Who on Earth"; Gregersen, "Extended Body of Christ."

17. Tomren, *Kyrkje, miljø og berekraft*, 305–8. See also Jakobsen, "Kristus og naturen" [Christ and nature], where he forwards Christology as a central motivation for environmental engagement from evangelical theology.

18. Conradie, *Secular Discourse on Sin*, 14. A broader perspective on the moral aspects of climate change is found in Gardiner, *Perfect Moral Storm*.

19. Messer, "Sin and Salvation," 131.

urgency of the climate crisis from a theological perspective. As often, the most vulnerable ones are those who suffer the most from the actions of the privileged.[20]

There are some important close at hand pitfalls to avoid when introducing sin-talk to the field of ecology and eco-theology. The first is a passivism that can arise from the conviction that if sin is the cause, there is nothing we can do about it—God must intervene! Even though this may be true in a certain meaning in an Augustinian-Lutheran sense concerning our spiritual forces in combating sin generally, it should never be an argument against concrete confession and fighting of sin. On the contrary, the Christian doctrine of sin can be interpreted as a claim that it is possible to do something about problems. And because we can do something about climate change, we must. The second pitfall is the two problems already mentioned, namely, the reductionism involved in saying that sin is the (only?) cause of the climate crisis, and the challenges involved in making Christian notions such as sin and Christology relevant to the broader public debate and political landscape. Sin may be a fruitful interpretative category but cannot explain it all to everyone without nuanced communication. A third possible pitfall is that reference to the doctrine of sin may lead to avoidance of concreteness. Here it is important to remember that sin, both as wrongdoings and in its more structural dimension, is an aspect of concrete human lives, and can and must be addressed as such.[21] The prophetic task of church and theology is especially relevant here. Fourth, we have the pitfall of reductionism in the understanding of sin itself. Sin in context of the climate crisis cannot be reduced either to wrongdoing, what is left undone, broken relationships between human beings or the situation *coram deo*, guilt, power, or a specific claim about the historical origin of sin.

If these pitfalls are avoided, Christian sin-talk can contribute to the understanding of ecological problems in the following ways, among others. First, sin and connected theological notions can be used to understand and name the nuances of what is wrong. A central notion in Lutheran understandings of sin is the picture of human beings as curved in on themselves (Lat. *incurvatus in se*).[22] This is the problem behind anthropocentrism in its anti-ecological forms; the perspective becomes reduced to human inward-looking that can end up destroying nature. The concept clarifies how many of our problems arise from overfocusing on the ego, thus failing to letting

20. Cf. Henriksen, *Climate Change*, 45, 117, with references.

21. As Henriksen says, "If we ignore the empirical, that is, the structural and psychological dimensions of sin, we will not counter its consequences" (Henriksen, *Climate Change*, 191).

22. See Jenson, *Gravity of Sin*, ch. 2; Moe-Lobeda, *Resisting Structural Evil*, 58.

God be God and being open to his love. We need to lift our eyes beyond our own situation to our local and global neighbor if we are to understand and solve our problems. The Christian tradition of reflection on virtues and vices also contains much wisdom that can be mined in this respect. Some examples mentioned in different ways by Ernst Conradie and Neil Messer include:[23]

- *Greed* as the driving force behind environmentally destructive consumerism
- *Sloth* as the cause of action paralysis
- *Domination* as failed responsibility
- *Alienation* from nature as the cause of disengagement
- The *folly* or *falsehood* involved in climate change denial
- *Pride* as lack of consciousness of our entanglement in the world
- *Idolatry* as unhealthy attachment to worldly things resulting in a broken relationship with God

A second resource from Christian sin-talk is its claim that another and better world could and ought to exist, and that there is human responsibility involved in the situation as it is.[24] Christian faith makes it possible to make a moral judgment of the situation, say something about where we ought to be going, and expresses faith in the possibility of change. Through the notion of possibility of change, sin is thus a pathway to *hope*.[25] The Christian eschatological orientation envisioning a new creation without sin and suffering opposes a tragic fate for human beings and all creation.

Third, Christian sin-talk can help people understand the complexities of individual and corporate responsibility, and structural and personal elements, connected to the notion of original sin. Such an interpretation presupposes, as Conradie and others have shown, that this doctrine is not reduced to an account of the historical origin of sin and its transmission but is viewed as much as a predicament in our current situation. As Henriksen points out, sin "entails a structural element and cannot be reduced

---

23. See Conradie, "Emergence of Human Sin," 386–87; Messer, "Sin and Salvation."

24. Conradie notes that "the Christian confession of sin expresses a conviction that is widely held, namely, that things are not what they are supposed to be, *what they could have been* and should have been" (Conradie, *Secular Discourse on Sin*, xi [emphasis added]).

25. For a discussion of hope in relation to Christian action in response to the climate crisis, see Haugen, "Hope, Fear, Anger, Courage," esp. 52–53 and 57.

to individual failures."[26] Sin is our wrongdoings and the guilt connected to them, but also a power that threatens the good in our life and the world. Messer suggests that the notion of structural sin—that is, institutions, practices, customs, regulations, etc. that make it hard to do what is right or even encourage what is wrong—should be viewed as a part of original sin and not as an alternative to it.[27] We are always already entangled in a sinful world, where the global ramifications of human life in one sense make many of us sinners by our mere existence. Citizens of the North Atlantic world contribute to the economically and environmentally unjust world order even before their birth.[28] On this background, Christian hope and action in response to the climate crisis must happen both in individual and corporate contexts. Another aspect of sin closely connected to this is the difficulty of knowing oneself, our own good, and the consequences of our life. While ignorance is sometimes best addressed as personal sloth, at other times our lack of knowledge may be due to structures around us that sustain false ideas or suspend important information, willfully or not. To help people look out from their own inwardness also includes helping them to see themselves and the world in truth. Greta Thunberg points to the Swedish term *folkbildning* (meaning *Bildung* or formation of people, the whole public) as a central part of what is needed to address the climate crisis.[29] Human sinfulness is an important reason that this is necessary.

THEOLOGICAL EDUCATION AMID ECOLOGICAL DESTRUCTION AND CHANGE

The most central aim of theological education in a professional context is to prepare students for scholarly reflection and ministry in tomorrow's churches and societies. Good reasons can be given as to why questions concerning ecology and climate change should be given attention in theological education, reasons stemming from a theological perspective as well as from philosophical and ethical perspectives. Human-induced climate change seen as a heightened expression of global structural sin, as discussed above, is one of them. However, there are also signs that societies and churches are starting to undergo processes of radical change and innovation, both in the way pressing ecological problems are perceived and how they are met in

26. Henriksen, *Climate Change*, 191.
27. Messer, "Sin and Salvation," 129.
28. Moe-Lobeda, *Resisting Structural Evil*, esp. chs. 2 and 3, gives a thorough analysis of this complex ethical problem.
29. Thunberg, *Climate Book*, ch. 5.1.

practice and in decisions on different levels—individually, collectively, politically.[30] Thus, ecological awareness and knowledge of ecological matters becomes a necessity for future theologians not only for theological reasons, but also because of the importance these issues will have in the world they will be theologizing and ministering within. A church and theology not adapting to an eco-friendlier lifestyle, not showing awareness of ecological questions, will soon be an outdated church.

Churches and theologians can make contributions to the problems raised by climate change in many ways. I suggest gathering them under four labels. First, theological reflection on ecological matters can foster *motivation* for action in different contexts. Christian ethics and the practice of Christian living in community can be a powerful source of transformation. However, theologians as well as politicians should be careful about thinking about religious commitment in terms of having only an instrumental value in solving these problems. Effective and sustainable adherence needs to be voluntary. Second, church and theology can be a source of relevant scientific, ethical, and cultural *knowledge* needed to establish sustainable ecological habits—positively by drawing attention to relevant questions and connections that are possibly overlooked in other media and contexts, and negatively through resisting the sloth and folly expressed through ignorance or denial of ecologically relevant facts. A third possible contribution is churches and theologians raising a *prophetic voice*, addressing ordinary people, politicians, and leaders of corporations, reminding them of their responsibility for nature and fellow and future human beings.[31] Fourth, theological knowledge and reflection can encourage leaders and Christians into *modeling communities*, giving embodied examples of sustainable living.[32]

To make such contributions happen in the future, it is important that theological students are equipped with the knowledge and methods to tackle ecological questions.[33] The tendency has perhaps been that eco-theology

---

30. Put with a pun from Greta Thunberg in her address to the UN assembly: "Change is coming, whether you like it or not." Quoted in Philip et al., *Religion, Sustainability and Education*, 9.

31. See Marlow, *Biblical Prophets*. Walter Brueggemann has also written extensively on the relevance of biblical prophecy today, including for the climate crisis.

32. There are many examples of international (e.g., A Rocha; Plant with Purpose) or local initiatives (e.g., the *grønn menighet* [green congregation] label in the Church of Norway; Web of Creation) in this regard.

33. How to include eco-theology and ecological hermeneutics in theological education is a field with relatively few scholarly contributions. Some works in the growing literature on sustainability education in general are also relevant to the question. See, e.g., Tomren, "From Environmental Activism"; Tomren, "Climate Strikes and Curricula" (with further references); Rimmer, "Ecology and Christian Education."

first entered theological education as an extracurricular theme and activity, was given attention in ad hoc seminars, interdisciplinary happenings, and so on, but not discussed as an integral part of the theological problems and material addressed in the day-to-day activity in the theological disciplines. My own institution, NLA University College, where I studied and now work, is an example of this. I remember from my study days about twenty years ago, during an interdisciplinary student seminar, a visit from a radical activist pastor and missionary claiming provocatively that it is a sin to travel by plane. Discussions went (really) high, but I doubt that there was a serious scholarly work done about this within the disciplines either before or after. Today, we have taken further steps to integrate these perspectives in our ordinary courses, lectures, and reading lists, but there is still need for more. In the following, I will give an overview of some suggested ways and examples of how to deal with questions of eco-theology and ecological hermeneutics within different theological disciplines.[34]

Biblical studies is a basic element in all types of theological studies.[35] Different groups of scholars have through the years given multifaceted approaches on how to include a critical ecological hermeneutic in theological work on the Christian Scriptures. Prominent examples include the Earth Bible project, led by Norman C. Habel;[36] the Green Bible;[37] and *Ecological Hermeneutics*.[38] With different perspectives and approaches, scholars in these camps interpret biblical texts with their potential ecological relevance in mind. Some interpreters also stress that biblical texts should be interpreted ecologically, not only as criticism of ourselves or others, but also with a critical lens towards the texts themselves. To naïvely interpret the Scriptures as bringing only positive contributions to the forwarding of ecological ideas and action may be counterproductive. A critical perspective on the Bible's situatedness in a context of lower ecological consciousness and scientific knowledge is needed, as well as a critical approach to the application of the Bible's theological normativity today.

34. I want to thank Tom Sverre Tomren for input through private conversation on literature and questions concerning ecological aspects of theological education.

35. My presentation is dependent on Nilsen and Solevåg, "Expanding Ecological Hermeneutics"; and Hamon, "Teaching Environmental Activism."

36. See the project home page, including an extensive bibliography: https://www.webofcreation.org/Earthbible/earthbible.html.

37. The Green Bible is a version of the New Revised Standard Version translation that has an environmentalist ideology annotation framework.

38. A central publication is Horrell et al., *Ecological Hermeneutics*. Nilsen and Solevåg connect this to the Exeter project conducted from 2006 to 2009 (Nilsen and Solevåg, "Expanding Ecological Hermeneutics," 668–69). See also Horrell, *Bible and the Environment*.

Robin B. Hamon is among the few scholars who have given concrete didactic suggestions on how to teach ecological hermeneutics as part of biblical studies courses. Hamon notes that the standard approach of including ecological hermeneutics as one of the critical interpretative methods presented as part of a lecture series is good for teaching students what ecological hermeneutics is and how it has been and can be applied to biblical texts.[39] However, he also thinks that this approach can tend to disengage students from the physical world and their personal engagement within it, even if the interpretative approach itself arose from an activist intention. It puts, so to speak, urgent matters at arm's length and academic distance. Instead, he advocates a teaching style that encourages students to "think about ecological hermeneutics in the context of the wider environmental crisis and to reflect on the practical and tangible steps that they can take towards protecting our planet."[40] His main didactic move to achieve this is to require more preparatory reading from the students, thus giving space for more discussion in lectures and/or seminars.[41] Hamon is open about selectively choosing the issues of (over-)population and extinction of species as possible contemporary issues that can be addressed on basis of an ecological reading of concrete biblical texts.[42] Both issues could easily be related to and/or replaced by themes more directly impacting or impacted by the climate crisis. Hamon then suggest proceeding to an activism-oriented discussion of what we can do in response to the situation just described. His suggestions include options for political and societal involvement as well as personal choices regarding food, travel, and other aspects of consumer behavior.[43]

Hamon's suggestions are interesting. His intention of avoiding disengagement from serious and urgent matters is important; the tension between knowing and living the truth should be brought forward in theological studies. However, there are also fundamental pedagogical questions to reflect on in this context. Is the teacher's role in higher education to prescribe solutions for the students' personal and political life, to declare when and what the students need to take a stand on, or is the main goal to prepare

---

39. Hamon, "Teaching Environmental Activism," 68.

40. Hamon, "Teaching Environmental Activism," 76.

41. Hamon, "Teaching Environmental Activism," 69.

42. Hamon, "Teaching Environmental Activism," 71–73. The biblical texts he suggests are exclusively from the Old Testament. I suggest that this relates to his discipline training and should not be interpreted as a suggestion of excluding New Testament perspectives on these or any other given issue possibly arising from the ecological engagement with biblical texts.

43. Hamon, "Teaching Environmental Activism," 73–76.

the students to find good solutions based on their own knowledge and critical judgment? Hamon swings the pendulum quite far over from the normal approach in biblical studies here, perhaps as far as to raise questions about the self-understanding of biblical studies as a discipline and the academic freedom of the student. Furthermore, from my didactic experience I am not sure whether the emphasis on preparatory reading will work very well in practice. The choice of using "flipped classroom" elements in a course is more a question of teaching and learning cultures and didactics than a necessity arising from the need to act. The unintended result if preparatory reading is not done according to the plan may be that students are given the impression that the course presents pure activism without a firm scholarly basis.

Ecological hermeneutics can also be applied to other historical texts than the Bible. Tom Sverre Tomren offers an example of how this can be done through an ecocritical analysis of the arguably most important theologian in his own Evangelical Lutheran tradition, Martin Luther, asking "how green" he was. Through his reading of selected central Luther texts (the catechisms and the Genesis commentary), Tomren shows that there are possible resources for eco-theology in Luther's doctrine of creation, including humans as created beings among other created beings, a certain realism in the view of human ability to be good rulers of nature, and the notion of vegetarianism as having paradisiac origin as a possible source of opposition to excessive meat consumption. Luther's thinking is an important driving force behind the central position of the so-called stewardship model through which Protestant churches and theology relate to environmental questions. In recent years there has been much debate about the appropriateness of this model and whether it has been overemphasized, thus leaving other important perspectives overlooked. In any case, for better or for worse, Luther has been influencing the eco-theology of churches for the last fifty years, even if he was by no means an eco-theologian in a modern sense; he simply lived in another age when ecology or the environmental crisis was not understood in the same way as today.[44] Because of this centrality of Luther as a theological authority in many quarters, and his influence through the stewardship model, a comprehensive ecocritical theological education ought to include ecological approaches to his texts.

That ecological perspectives can be included in systematic theology courses is obvious on basis of my earlier discussions of themes as sin, creation, and stewardship, and Christology. These are all central themes of Christian dogmatics that must be treated as such, and that must be related

---

44. Tomren, "How Green Was Martin?," 108.

to the current ecological crisis to ensure their contemporary relevance.[45] Courses in systematic theology, including theological ethics, can be central spaces for training students to identify and critique structural sins related to environmental destruction. To my knowledge, there are very few discussions available on how to do this in practice as part of a course in theological education. While there is not room to present a complete toolbox for such analysis here, it should be noted that such an analysis must include both local, contextual aspects and common global aspects. There are many reading resources available for such an undertaking.[46]

According to Pamela R. McCarroll in a 2020 article, practical theology is currently predisposed to "ignore and fall silent before the enormity of the environmental crisis currently upon us."[47] In 2022 she coedited a special issue of the journal *Religions* that tries to break this silence.[48] Here Leah D. Schade reflects on the use of a "Who Is My Neighbor" mapping exercise as part of practical theological education and ecclesial practice.[49] One of Schade's main concerns is to expand "neighborness" to include even nonhuman nature, departing from the idea that a neighbor is someone you choose to care about. The exercise is a set of place-based questions, observations, and activities that encourage students to see the ecological relevance of concretely situated church life. According to her findings, completing the exercise "was a source of spiritual formation for many students."[50] The student presentation examples given in the article show that the approach is good for making students realize the ecological relevance of what is near and concrete.[51] However, the method may need to be supplemented by

---

45. See, e.g., the course plan of TEOL 304, Basic Questions in Systematic Theology and Dogmatics [*Systematisk-teologiske grunnlagsspørsmål og dogmatikk*], at NLA University College: "General competence. The student—can give an account of the character, validity and truth responding to challenges from contemporary culture, pluralism, and ecological problems [*Generell kompetanse: studenten—kan gjøre rede for den kristne tros egenart, gyldighet og sannhet i møte med utfordringen fra samtidskulturen, pluralisme og økologiske problemstillinger*]."

46. See, e.g., Conradie and Koster, *T&T Clark Handbook*; Northcott and Scott, *Systematic Theology*; Northcott, *Moral Climate*.

47. McCarroll, "Listening to the Cries," 45.

48. Published as McCarroll and Kim-Cragg, *Practical Theology*.

49. Schade, "Who Is My Neighbor." The article builds on material from her book *Creation-Crisis Preaching*.

50. Schade, "Who Is My Neighbor," §11.

51. Another example of contextual perspectives on ecological perspectives as part of theological education is the suggested model for coconut theological education in Kiribati made by Timon et al., "Re-Envisioning Tangitenbu Theological College."

other approaches that are good for identifying structures of larger societal and global character.

This overview of suggestions on how to integrate ecological perspectives in theological education shows that there are many available options. It is possible to integrate ecological elements in theological education through historical, systematic, and practical theological disciplines, to help prepare theological students for future ministry in a changing world. My reflection on these suggestions has pointed to two particular areas of tension in need of attention.

The first is the importance of integrating perspectives made relevant by the climate crisis in the ordinary curriculum in different courses and degrees, thus avoiding the issue being reserved for special occasions. However, when situated in day-to-day academic work it is also important to preserve the tensions involved in working with material that, so to speak, screams for action. The second area requiring attention is how to balance the need for action and activist approaches with the academic freedom of the teacher/researcher and student in an academic setting. It might be tempting to dismiss theological reflection and freedom in response to the need for action, and prescribe both the questions and the answers for students.[52] Here, it is important to underscore the necessity of informed, voluntary adherence as the way of disseminating truth and bringing about change through theological education. With these matters in mind, teachers involved in theological education should be encouraged to continue to bring forward ecological questions. The resources and possibilities are many, but for things to happen, there is need for change and innovation.

CONCLUSION

The climate crisis calls for reflection, critical judgment, and action on the part of theology and theological education. My contribution has been to show how the Christian doctrine of sin can be a relevant interpretative concept for the understanding of ecological questions, and to reflect on suggested ways in which ecological perspectives can be included in theological education. Christian sin-talk can be helpful in ecological matters by contributing to the naming of different aspects of the problem and their causes, giving grounded hope, and clarifying the relation between the individual and the collective in ethical matters. The global ramifications of sin in the context of the climate crisis are part of the reason that ecological questions should

---

52. Cf. Tomren, "Climate Strikes and Curricula," 111; citing Öhman and Östman, "Different Teaching Traditions," 78.

be well integrated in the curriculum of all disciplines of theological education. Historical texts can be read with contemporary questions in mind, and systematic and practical theology needs to respond to challenges from the wider society and other disciplines. A central part of theological education is to encourage students to take a stand on urgent matters, but it must also respect the academic and individual freedom of students, making room for action to happen on basis of informed, voluntary adherence. Although the engagement with sin might be a reason for despair, both individually and in theological education, I have also shown that one of the implications of this doctrine is that change is possible in God's future. Thus, I can end this contribution on a note of hope.[53]

BIBLIOGRAPHY

Baumgartner, Christoph. "Transformations of Stewardship in the Anthropocene." In *Religion in the Anthropocene*, edited by Celia Deane-Drummond et al., 53–66. Eugene: Cascade, 2017.

Conradie, Ernst M. "The Emergence of Human Sin." In *T&T Clark Handbook on Christian Theology and Climate Change*, edited by Ernst M. Conradie and Hilda P. Koster, 384–94. T&T Clark Handbooks. London: T&T Clark, 2019.

———. *Redeeming Sin: Social Diagnostics amid Ecological Destruction*. Lanham, MD: Lexington, 2017.

———. *Secular Discourse on Sin in the Anthropocene: What's Wrong with the World?* Lanham, MD: Lexington, 2020.

Conradie, Ernst M., and Hilda P. Koster, eds. *T&T Clark Handbook on Christian Theology and Climate Change*. T&T Clark Handbooks. London: T&T Clark, 2019.

Deane-Drummond, Celia. "Who on Earth Is Jesus Christ? Plumbing the Depths of Deep Incarnation." In *Christian Faith and the Earth: Current Paths and Emerging Horizons in Ecotheology*, edited by Ernst M. Conradie et al., 31–50. T&T Clark Theology. London: Bloomsbury T&T Clark, 2014.

Dye, T. Wayne. "Toward a Cross-Cultural Definition of Sin." *Missiology: An International Review* 4 (1976) 27–41.

Francis, Pope. "*Laudato Si'*: On Care for Our Common Home." Vatican, May 24, 2015. https://www.vatican.va/content/francesco/en/encyclicals/documents/papa-francesco_20150524_enciclica-laudato-si.html.

Gardiner, Stephen M. *A Perfect Moral Storm: The Ethical Tragedy of Climate Change*. Oxford: Oxford University Press, 2011.

Gregersen, Niels Henrik. "The Extended Body of Christ: Three Dimensions of Deep Incarnation." In *Incarnation: On the Scope and Depth of Christology*, edited by Niels Henrik Gregersen, 225–51. Minneapolis: Fortress, 2015.

---

53. I would like to thank colleagues involved in the TLC project and in the research groups Research in Theology and Ministry and *Tekststudier i teologi, religion og filosofi* at NLA University College and beyond for their feedback on different occasions in the process of writing this chapter. I would also like to thank my anonymous peer reviewer for valuable advice and literature suggestions.

Guterres, Antonio. "Deputy Secretary-General's Remarks at the Opening of the High-Level Segment of the Resumed Fifth Session of the United Nations Environment Assembly." UN, Mar. 2, 2022. https://www.un.org/sg/en/content/dsg/statement/2022-03-02/deputy-secretary-generals-remarks-the-opening-of-the-high-level-segment-of-the-resumed-fifth-session-of-the-united-nations-environment-assembly-delivered.

———. "Secretary-General's Statement on the IPCC Working Group 1 Report on the Physical Science Basis of the Sixth Assessment." UN, Aug. 9, 2021. https://www.un.org/sg/en/content/secretary-generals-statement-the-ipcc-working-group-1-report-the-physical-science-basis-of-the-sixth-assessment.

Hamon, R. B. "Teaching Environmental Activism and Ecological Hermeneutics." *Journal for Interdisciplinary Biblical Studies* 2 (2020) 66–80.

Haugen, Hans Morten. "Hope, Fear, Anger, Courage and Love in Times of Climate Crisis: Are Resources from Christian Faith and Tradition Useful?" In *Religion, Sustainability and Education: Pedagogy, Perspectives, and Praxis towards Ecological Sustainability*, edited by Mary Philip et al., 42–59. Steinkjer, Norw.: Embla, 2021.

Hayhoe, Katharyne. "Heat." In *The Climate Book*, edited by Greta Thunberg, §2.2. London: Lane, 2022.

Henriksen, Jan-Olav. *Climate Change and the Symbolic Deficit in the Christian Tradition: Expanding Gendered Sources*. Explorations in Theology, Gender and Ecology. London: T&T Clark, 2022.

———. "Klimakrisens utfordringer til solidarisk handling" [The climate crisis challenges to solidarity action]. *Luthersk kirketidende* 2 (2023) 50–51.

Horrell, David G. *The Bible and the Environment: Towards a Critical Ecological Biblical Theology*. Biblical Challenges in the Contemporary World. London: Routledge, 2014.

Horrell, David G., et al., eds. *Ecological Hermeneutics: Biblical, Historical and Theological Perspectives*. London: T&T Clark, 2010.

Jakobsen, Martin. "Kristus og naturen: Hvordan motivere til miljøengasjement i kirke og menighet?" [Christ and nature: How to motivate for environmental engagement in church and congregation]. *Scandinavian Journal of Leadership and Theology* 9 (2022) 26–44.

Jenson, Matt. *The Gravity of Sin: Augustine, Luther and Barth on 'homo incurvatus in se.'* London: Bloomsbury T&T Clark, 2007.

Marlow, Hilary. *Biblical Prophets and Contemporary Environmental Ethics: Re-Reading Hosea, Amos and First Isaiah*. Oxford: Oxford University Press, 2009.

McCarroll, Pamela R. "Listening to the Cries of the Earth." *International Journal of Practical Theology* 1 (2020) 29–46.

McCarroll, Pamela R., and HyeRan Kim-Cragg, eds. *Practical Theology amid Environmental Crises*. Reprint, Basel: MDPI, 2023. https://doi.org/10.3390/books978-3-0365-5794-6.

Messer, Neil. "Sin and Salvation." In *Systematic Theology and Climate Change: Ecumenical Perspectives*, edited by Michael S. Northcott and Peter M. Scott, 124–40. London: Routledge, 2014.

Moe-Lobeda, Cynthia D. *Resisting Structural Evil: Love as Ecological-Economic Vocation*. Minneapolis: Fortress, 2013.

Nilsen, Tina Dykesteen, and Anna Rebecca Solevåg. "Expanding Ecological Hermeneutics: The Case for Ecolonialsm." *JBL* 135 (2016) 665–83.

Northcott, Michael S. *A Moral Climate: The Ethics of Global Warming*. Maryknoll, NY: Orbis, 2007.

Northcott, Michael S., and Peter M. Scott, eds. *Systematic Theology and Climate Change: Ecumenical Perspectives*. London: Routledge, 2014.

Öhman, Johan, and Leif Östman. "Different Teaching Traditions in Environmental and Sustainability Education." In *Sustainable Development Teaching: Ethical and Political Challenges*, edited by Katrien Van Poeck et al., 70–82. Routledge Studies in Sustainability. London: Routledge, 2019.

Philip, Mary, et al., eds. *Religion, Sustainability and Education: Pedagogy, Perspectives, and Praxis towards Ecological Sustainability*. Steinkjer, Norw.: Embla, 2021.

Rimmer, Chad. "Ecology and Christian Education: How Sustainability Discourse and Theological Anthropology Inform Teaching Methods." In *Religion, Sustainability and Education: Pedagogy, Perspectives, and Praxis towards Ecological Sustainability*, edited by Mary Philip et al., 20–41. Steinkjer, Norw.: Embla, 2021.

Schade, Leah D. *Creation-Crisis Preaching: Ecology, Theology, and the Pulpit*. St. Louis: Chalice, 2015.

———. "Who Is My Neighbor? Developing a Pedagogical Tool for Teaching Environmental Preaching and Ethics in Online and Hybrid Courses." *Religions* 13 (2022) 322. https://doi.org/10.3390/rel13040322.

Strand, Mark. "Explaining Sin in a Chinese Context." *Missiology: An International Review* 28 (2000) 427–41.

Sumerau, J. E., et al. "'Can't Put My Finger on It': A Research Report on the Non-Existence and Meaninglessness of Sin." *Qualitative Report* 21 (2016) 1132–44.

Thunberg, Greta, ed. *The Climate Book*. London: Lane, 2022.

Timon, Tioti, et al. "Re-Envisioning Tangitenbu Theological College in the Context of Climate Change: An Emerging Model of Coconut Theological Education and Ministerial Formation." *HvTSt* 75 (2019). http://dx.doi.org/10.4102/hts.v75i1.5169.

Tomren, Tom Sverre. "Climate Strikes and Curricula: Insights from Norway." *Journal of Teacher Education for Sustainability* 24 (2022) 105–15.

———. "From Environmental Activism to Environmental Education: A Historical Overview, Evaluations and a Suggestion for a Path Forward for the Religious Institutions as Partners for a Global Green Shift." *Consensus* 41 (2020) art. 12.

———. "How Green Was Martin? An Ecocritical Analysis of Selected Luther Texts in Search for an Ecotheology Syllabus for a Theological Environmental Education." In *Religion, Sustainability and Education: Pedagogy, Perspectives, and Praxis towards Ecological Sustainability*, edited by Mary Philip et al., 82–113. Steinkjer, Norw.: Embla, 2021.

———. *Kyrkje, miljø og berekraft: Ein studie av miljøfråsegnene i dei store kyrkjesamfunna i perioden 1969–2019 og ein detaljanalyse av korleis Den norske kyrkja har arbeidd med det grøne skiftet gjennom 50 år* [Church, environment and sustainability: a study of environmental statements of large churches 1969–2019 and a detailed study of how the Church of Norway has worked on the green shift through 50 years]. Steinkjer, Norw.: Embla, 2019.

Chapter 5

The Social Crisis of Infertility in Sub-Saharan Africa

Repositioning Theological Education

Terese Bue Kessel

INTRODUCTION

Childlessness in Africa is a huge problem. Experts point at a magnitude of infertility across sub-Saharan Africa and Central Africa, from Tanzania in the east to Ghana in the west, identified as the "infertility belt." The social crisis that follows on a personal and communal level, challenges theological education and the training of future pastors. The focus of this chapter is on rethinking *diakonia* and pastoral counseling in the corresponding relationship to the stigmas of infertility.

Theological education and learning in Africa is an area of concern on the continent that hosts the fastest growing Christian churches in the world and is now the center of gravity for the Christian faith.[1] There is an urgent challenge to train sufficient leaders, pastors, women, and men, with "theological education that matches the actual needs of the churches, their members and communities."[2] The words of Bishop Dr. Jean Baïguelé in the Evangelical Lutheran Church in Cameroon (EELC), of the Lutheran

---

1. Bevans, "What Has Contextual Theology," 9.
2. LWF, "Cameroon," under question "What are your perspectives on theological education on the continent generally?"

Communion in Africa,[3] are in concert with similar concerns expressed by church leaders and scholars on the continent.[4]

Bediako Kwame contributed to Africa being included in contemporary worldwide Christian discourse and he was central in the development of an African Christian theology.[5] For African theology to be relevant, it must be rooted in local contexts, be developed within its cultural frame, and relate to people's lived experiences—in contrast to an imported Western theology that is often distant from people's lives. Scholars claim that African theology must be decolonized to be appropriate.[6] Contextual theology involves interaction and dialogue between faith and culture.[7] It considers "the experience of the past" presented in Scripture and the church's tradition and "the experience of the present" in persons and communities in current contexts.[8] When people of faith share their experiences, in whatever space is available to them, in women's and men's groups, and in youth groups, they are theologizing.[9] Some of these stories are neglected and overlooked in theological education; such as the social crisis of infertility. *Crises* here refers to the arrival of one or more threats that challenge the way people think, act, and structure their lives, and which calls for sound judgement and transformed ways of learning and acting together.[10]

The stigma that follows barrenness falls within the space of gender-based violence and domestic abuse and is relevant to the United Nations Sustainable Development Goal (SDG) 5: "Achieve gender equality and empower all women and girls." The SDG perspective reflects an invitation to theological education to engage with the topic of this chapter. I will, in the following, first describe the social crisis and stigma that follow infertility in sub-Saharan Africa. Then I will point to two significant contributions to the discourse of fertility, the rise of assisted reproductive technology (ART) in fertility clinics in urban areas of Africa, and various local fertility strategies. Last, I reflect on models of theological education and discuss how the crisis of infertility works with any of these models in reshaping theological learning in Africa.

---

3. The EELC is a member church in the Lutheran World Federation (LWF).
4. LeMarquand and Galgalo, *Theological Education*; Knoetze and Brunsdon, *Critical Engagement*; Mashabela, "Africanisation"; Pobee, "Foreword."
5. Bediako, *Christianity in Africa*; Bediako, *Jesus in Africa*.
6. Hadebe, "Commodification, Decolonisation."
7. M. Vähäkangas, "World Christianity," 227.
8. Bevans, "Contextual Theology," 9.
9. Galgalo, "Teaching of Theology," 5
10. See Norheim and Weber in the introductory chapter of this book.

BARRENNESS IN SUB-SAHARAN AFRICA

Infertility across sub-Saharan Africa is massive. The infertility belt stretches from Tanzania in the east to Ghana in the west. A study from 2020 reveals that if, on average, 15 percent of couples worldwide struggle to conceive, this figure climbs to 42 percent in West Africa, 30 percent in East Africa, and 40 percent in South Africa.[11] This context is believed to have the world's highest level of sterility. Cameroon is included here with some ethnic groups having over 40 percent combined infertility.[12]

Childlessness exists in all cultures. Available data from the World Health Organization (WHO) indicates that "infertility affects millions of people—and has an impact on their families and communities. Estimates suggest that approximately one in every six people of reproductive age worldwide experience infertility in their lifetime."[13] Infertility is either primary or secondary and prevails in developing countries for lack of general well-developed health systems.[14] The main cause for sterility is ascribed to infections and sexually transmitted diseases, such as HIV-related infertility.

A crucial study on the global impact of infertility released in 2002 by several internationally acknowledged social scientists is *Infertility around the Globe: New Thinking on Childlessness, Gender, and Reproductive Technologies*.[15] The original research examines how infertility is understood and experienced in several countries, including sub-Saharan Africa and Cameroon. It is the first book to examine reproductive technologies in non-Western countries. The study addresses a wide range of social issues and the gendered nature of infertility that blames women. Extensive research material from the African continent confirms that infertility in several contexts is generally viewed as intolerable. Children constitute marriage, therefore a marriage without children is living on borrowed time. According to Baloyi, infertility is viewed as a "disgrace and abnormal state."[16] In many traditional contexts, the culture claims that it is a child of your own seed that constitutes marriage, thus failure to conceive can cause adultery, polygamy, divorce,

---

11. Abebe et al., "Primary and Secondary Infertility."
12. A combination of male/female infertility.
13. World Health Organization, "Infertility."
14. WHO's International Classification of Diseases understands infertility as "a disease of the male or female reproductive system defined by the failure to achieve a pregnancy after 12 months or more of regular unprotected sexual intercourse" (see https://www.who.int/health-topics/infertility#tab=tab_1). Secondary infertility means failing to become pregnant after successfully having given birth in the past.
15. Inhorn and Van Balen, *Infertility around the Globe*.
16. M. Baloyi, "Gendered Character of Barrenness," 2.

and domestic violence.[17] In patriarchal communities, men are not believed to be infertile. While women are objects in marriage, men are agents, and womanhood relates to the ability to give birth. Such understanding puts pressure on women who will make any effort to combat infertility, to the extent of seeking pregnancy outside marriage. In traditional African society, the woman's duty is to procreate and secure the continuation of the family. Motherhood provides status and value.[18]

I referred above to the words of Bishop Baïguelé, current leader of the Evangelical Lutheran Church in Cameroon, which has about 700,000 members. The church holds a powerful women's movement, Women for Christ. The movement, present in all the congregations in rural as well as in urban contexts, has three central approaches. First is the focus on maintaining the Christian identity of the movement. Second is the focus on teaching and training women in social and biblical issues. Third is the diaconal work carried out by the women, expressed through prayer, pastoral care, and compassion for one another.[19] In my encounter with this grassroots movement, I came across the social burden of infertility.[20] The story of one informant can function as an example here. The informant introduced herself as the mother of ten children. It later came clear that she had not given birth to any of them. They were orphans of her husband's extended family of whom many had succumbed to the HIV/AIDS pandemic. She was scolded and despised because of her failure to conceive:

> My problem in my home has to do with my husband. When you do not have children, it is really a big problem, . . . we have been married for fifteen years. . . . I have done everything. I am tired. They have already operated on me once, and when I go to the hospital, they tell me they don't know what to do, they don't know what to tell me, they don't know what is going on. Since my thing [fallopian tube] is open, they don't know how to help me.[21]

Facing childlessness, she sought resolution through traditional strategies such as adoption within the lineage; however, the stigma remained. The couple had sought modern medical health care without success. Her

---

17. G. Baloyi, "African Woman's Dilemma"; Gerrits, "Infertility and Matrilineality," 242.

18. Gerrits, "Infertility and Matrilineality," 234.

19. Bue Kessel, "Between God's Sharing Power."

20. Bue Kessel, "Infertilitet."

21. Cameroon informant, conversation with author, Feb. 5, 2010. Author's translation from French to English, after 2010.

barrenness had put her in a state of crisis and contempt. In an effort to find a way of coping with the condition, God was declared to be responsible: "It is God who gives children." By making God accountable, she tried to rid herself of cultural stigma and shame. According to the leader of Women for Christ in 2019, "People get married to have children, but when that does not happen, they are made fun of and thrown out by in-laws."[22] Culturally acceptable means are largely utilized to resolve barrenness in Africa, such as adoption within the extended family. But fostering a relative's children does not always decrease women's mental suffering from barrenness.[23]

MODERN AND TRADITIONAL ACCESS TO INFERTILITY HEALTH CARE

Moving from a general description of barrenness in the traditional African context, I will now engage with the modern Africa and the diverse possibilities of technological resources that are available for barren couples in their quest to have children of their own. Assisted reproduction is providing new hope for both poor and rich families but is also challenging. It requires reshaping existing understanding of cultural and societal notions about kinship and the status of genetic ties.

WHO has identified infertility as a global health problem, hence universal access to reproductive health care is included in the United Nation's Millennium Developmental Goals for 2015.[24] Over the last four decades, the use of ART has increased significantly in both developed and developing countries.[25] Treating barrenness is a remarkable medical accomplishment throughout the world.[26] Assisted reproduction, such as in vitro fertilization (IVF) is a transnational undertaking, including Africa.[27] The first IVF procedure to succeed in Africa was in Ghana in 1995. There has since been seen the rise of the private fertility clinic, mainly in the capital, Accra.[28] However, in spite of the increase in access to reproductive technology in African cities, a recent study from Gambia concludes that the availability of infertility services is scarce, echoing a similar situation in other sub-Saharan African

---

22. Leader of Women for Christ, conversation with author, Nov. 11, 2019.
23. Gerrits, "Infertility and Matrilineality," 241.
24. Asemota and Klatsky, "Access to Infertility Care," 17.
25. Hiadzi et al., "God Helps."
26. Sharma et al., "Infertility & Assisted Reproduction," 14.
27. Gerrits, "Assisted Reproductive Technologies," 32.
28. Hiadzi et al., "God Helps."

countries.[29] Such development of infertility treatment and reproductive technology is mostly found in the private health sector, but insufficiencies on several levels cause lack of equal access for infertile couples in need of health care. There is shortage of equipment, lack of specialists, and lack of national guidance on infertility management, with costly treatment and geographical restrictions preventing treatment. Infertility services in resource-poor contexts is challenging, and infertility care is normally reachable first and foremost in well-off low-income countries in sub-Saharan Africa.[30] Infertility treatment creates hope, but often people are unable to pay the bill.

Reproductive technologies, skills, and knowledge are on the rise in Africa, but are inadequate to meet the needs. Public money is not used within this undertaking, but the services are subsidized by international health organizations. For instance, in Ghana, at present, "more affordable" IVF is being introduced in collaboration with the Belgium-based nonprofit organization the Walking Egg (tWE).[31] This reflects an innovative transnational networking. Couples in need of help to produce their own babies cross borders on the continent and return to Ghana from the diaspora. The new reproduction practices on the continent, such as surrogacy and the use of donor material, challenge existing cultural and societal understandings concerning bloodline and kinship and in the years to come will require further investigation.

Another way of seeking help is, that since biomedical health services are limited, the care of traditional healers and visits to sacred places are important alternatives.[32] From the perspective of "rural Africa" there is the growing popularity of traditional fertility shrines. One of the most important pilgrimage centers in the Horn of Africa is the shrine of Aw-Barkhadle, where sacred places and sacred wooden sculpture are significant mediums within fertility rituals.[33] Similar fertility shrines are documented in other parts of Africa.[34]

A case study from Mozambique depicts how traditional healers deal with rituals of fertility and pregnancy, seen also in other parts of the continent.[35] Various initiation rites for young men and young women separately, and pregnancy ceremonies for adults, serve to teach the secrets of fertility.

29. Afferri et al., "Availability of Services."
30. Asemota and Klatsky, "Access to Infertility Care," 17.
31. Gerrits, "Assisted Reproductive Technologies," 32.
32. Gerrits, "Infertility and Matrilineality," 250.
33. Mire, "Wagar, Fertility."
34. Werthmann, "Local Religion."
35. Gerrits, "Infertility and Matrilineality," 234–38.

Ritual practices related to medical plants serve the same goal, fertility. The rituals for women who cannot conceive often combine modern medical care with different traditional healers, such as herbal, spiritual, and Islamic healers. Husbands may accompany their wives to a traditional healer, but most often this is left to mothers or other female relatives.[36] The reason for infertility is more often explained using the words of the traditional healers than of the hospital, such as being caused by spirit possession, witchcraft, "incompatibility of blood," and poor-quality sperm. The last two explanations are interesting in respect of the Macua culture in Mozambique, where men are given the blame for infertility. This etiological explanation underlines the importance of continuity of the matrilineage in the Macua culture. Hence, traditional healers observe and judge critically a man's contribution to infertility since it is a "foreign element" to the matrilineage. If it is believed that the couple's blood is incompatible, pragmatic solutions are chosen. The wife may be encouraged to commit adultery and try to get pregnant with another man, or it could be an act of revenge if the husband has taken a second wife. If pregnancy is obtained by another man, it is most likely kept hidden, not because of fear of the husband and a possible divorce, but because the main goal is to have a child. In consequence, such fertility-seeking strategies involving unprotected sex with numerous partners are likely to cause sterility caused by infections and sexually transmitted diseases (STDs). The socially acceptable ways of handling barrenness challenge theological education in Africa to provide a critique.

THEOLOGICAL EDUCATION, DIAKONIA, AND PASTORAL COUNSELING

The editors of *Theological Education in Contemporary Africa* point to the phenomenon of HIV/AIDS as a crisis that has ravaged the African continent to the extent it requires urgent theological reflection and action that is relevant to peoples' everyday life, church, and society.[37] The infertility belt of sub-Saharan Africa is another such crisis in need of consideration.

Wahl identifies several models of theological learning, such as the classical, the vocational, the dialectical, the neo-traditional, the missional, and the ecumenical-diversified model.[38] Each model concentrates on a specific dimension of theological education. While the classical model's principal focus is an intellectual approach to Christian faith and tradition to develop

---

36. Gerrits, "Infertility and Matrilineality," 239.
37. Galgalo, "Teaching of Theology," 13.
38. Wahl, "Towards Relevant Theological Education," 273.

cognitive knowledge and wisdom,[39] the ecumenical-diversified model concentrates on contemporary matters. The aim is to offer contextualized and varied theological education to train pastors and church leaders to develop capacities that will address immediate and long-term needs in the local community. Theological formation of students includes all these models and is, according to Naido, "a multi-faceted activity involving critical thinking, the acquisition of knowledge, skills development, religious identity formation and the development of ministerial and spiritual maturity expected of church minister."[40] The ability to respond to social contexts is an urgent and needed skill in today's ministers and pastors. How, then, does the crisis of infertility fit or work with any of these models of theological education?

Practical theology is a central discipline in theological training with subdisciplines such as homiletics, liturgics, pastoral theology, *diakonia*, and pastoral counseling. Theories of *diakonia* and pastoral counseling, with perspectives from disability theories, could serve to reposition and renew theological education to equip future ministers to respond to an urgent crisis in the context, on a broader communal level (diaconal approach) and on an individual level (pastoral counseling).

Diakonia is among the younger disciplines in practical theology.[41] The ecumenical fellowship represented by the World Council of Churches (WCC) and the Lutheran World Federation (LWF) seeks to present a common understanding of diaconal reflection and action for the ecumenical community.[42] The use of the biblical concept of diakonia instead of "Christian social work," ensures a theological understanding of *diakonia*. Ecumenical *diakonia* seeks to integrate the DNA of mission and church. Diaconal reflection and action have three main motifs, the biblical motif of humankind as created in the image of God, the calling to act with compassion and justice on behalf of, and together with, those who are neglected and marginalized, and the calling for service and stewardship of the creation. *Diakonia* articulates a strong connection between what the churches are and what the churches do. Ecumenical *diakonia* refers to the worldwide communion of churches and Christians, to the commitment of unity, sharing, and participating in processes of empowerment, transformation, and reconciliation.

The terms *pastoral care* and *pastoral counseling* are often used interchangeably. While pastoral care refers to the broader caring activities by the

39. Wahl, "Towards Relevant Theological Education," 273, 284.

40. Naidoo, "Introduction," 3.

41. Nordstokke et al., *Serving the Whole Person*; Myers, *Walking with the Poor*; Haugen et al., *Just and Inclusive Communities*.

42. For the WCC, see World Council of Churches and ACT Alliance, *Called to Transformation*; for the LWF, see Nordstokke, *Diakonia in Context*.

Christian community, pastoral counseling refers to the dialogue between the counselor and the counseled.[43] The aim is to initiate processes of change of mind, attitude, and behavior.[44] Various models of pastoral counseling emphasize different dimensions in the encounter between the counselee and the counselor.[45] For the kerygmatic model, the aim was to preach the gospel and assist the counselee to come to terms with their own sin and be reconciled with God. In the 1920s, the kerygmatic model was assessed to be deficient because it put too much emphasis on Scripture, and little focus on people's life stories. The therapeutic model gave more attention to peoples' lived experiences, to the "living human document."[46] This model later came under criticism because it failed to take seriously the theological dimensions in pastoral counseling. This led to a quest to combine qualities from both models. Eide discusses the new perspectives in pastoral counseling, a fusion of the kerygmatic model and the therapeutic model, the theological perspectives in addition to the person-centered perspectives.[47] This merged model provides the possibility of a more holistic encounter and conversation with the wounded. After attentive listening to the counselee, if trust is created in a safe space of confidentiality, the counselor may apply appropriate biblical motifs to the counselee's account to assist in creating a new story of hope and meaning.

In Wahl's models of theological learning, the ecumenical–diversified model focuses on current issues.[48] This is relevant for diaconal reflection and action. According to the *Dictionary of the Ecumenical Movement*, *diakonia* refers to "responsible service of the Gospel by deeds and by words performed by Christians in response to the needs of people rooted in and modeled on Christ's service and teaching."[49] The intention is to develop sensitive attention to contemporary matters and respond to the identified needs. However, current challenges can also go unnoticed, be forgotten, or be experienced as too complicated to address, and therefore be neglected and go under the radar. This seems to be the case with the huge social challenge of barrenness in sub-Saharan Africa, where so many people are affiliated to Christianity and literature on this relationship is scarce.[50]

43. Magezi, "Reflection on Pastoral Care."
44. Kiriswa, *Pastoral Counselling in Africa*, 1–6.
45. Clinebell, *Pastoral Care & Counseling*.
46. Gerkin, *Living Human Document*.
47. Eide, *Forståelse og Fordypning*.
48. Wahl, "Towards Relevant Theological Education," 273, 284.
49. Lossky et al., *Dictionary of Ecumenical Movement*, 305.
50. Auli Vähäkangas has examined living with infertility among Christian couples

INFERTILITY IN VIEW OF DISABILITY THEORY, CULTURE, AND GENDER PERSPECTIVES

In an earlier article, I argue by way of disability theories, that marginalizing mechanisms follow the experience of infertility and create cultural disability.[51] Tøssebro has discussed different definitions of disability. The medical model analyzes the body from a mechanical perspective with a view to repairing the imperfect to adapt to what society perceives as normal. In the 1970s, organizations for disabled people promoted the social model of disability because the medical model put a mark of deviation on their bodies. They required societal acceptance for physical and mental differences. In analyzing mechanisms of exclusion, the social model of disability identified society as disabled.[52] From the social model of disability, it is possible to understand infertility in new ways. When local traditions and local healers push women who fail to conceive into vulnerable situations by way of infertility strategies, such as promiscuity and polygamy, the culture is disabled, not the barren woman.

To understand the mechanisms that cause this marginalization of barren women, tradition must be scrutinized from gender and cultural perspectives. The Circle of Concerned African Women Theologians (the Circle) has published widely on how culture and religion influence women's lives and has contributed to a theology of third world and indigenous women.[53] The Circle defines gender relations as power relations because male superiority is embedded in African cultures, as well as in religions.[54] Consequently, traditional religious beliefs and cultural practices influence everyday life, including the lives of Christian believers.[55] The Circle argues that the construction of gender relations is a root cause of the injustice that influences all of society on the continent, on a communal and individual level.

---

in two contexts in Tanzania (A. Vähäkangas,"Christian Couples").
51. Bue Kessel, "Infertilitet."
52. Tøssebro, *Funksjonshemming*, 15–27.
53. Kanyoro, *Introducing Feminist Cultural Hermeneutics*.
54. Ackermann et al., *Women Hold Up Half*.
55. Nwachuku, "Widow in African Culture," 72.

RETHINKING *DIAKONIA* AND PASTORAL COUNSELING

The following is a reflection on the models of theological education, *diakonia*, and pastoral counseling and how the crisis of infertility fits or works with any of these models.

Some years ago, I asked a church leader in Cameroon if the church at some point had publicly addressed the stigma of barrenness. From years of pastoral ministry, he could not recall any deliberate questioning of local traditions that stigmatize childless women. He did encounter personal stories of infertility in the ministry of counseling, but not as a prophetic diaconal approach from the church. He claimed that barrenness is taboo and concluded that "women are left to themselves with the pain."[56]

Further, in informal settings and conversations, I have asked a handful of teachers involved in theological education, primarily in Protestant contexts in Africa, if the social stigma of infertility is thematized in theological training. I have not yet come across any substantial information about this being the case in the discipline of practical theology. This could be an indication that theological training does not address local fertility strategies that enforce childless women's vulnerable condition. Practical theology in the seminaries concentrates mainly on equipping for service at the altar, through homiletics and liturgics, and is less concerned with the congregants' needs.

Pastoral counseling in Africa has a brief and little-documented history. Magezi and others claim that it has not been possible to critically engage with existing African challenges.[57] This has caused pastoral care and counseling to turn to public theology and engage with the larger society and address criticism of cultural disorder, injustice, and oppression. Pastoral counseling thus includes not only practices in faith communities but encompasses a wider commitment and interest in society, beyond the local community. While pastoral counseling addresses the individual's needs, *diakonia* has the capacity to address urgent issues on a broader systemic level.

The intention and purpose of prophetic *diakonia* is to address and critique the systematic oppression of groups of peoples and individuals and to unmask the unjust on behalf of those who have no capacity to resist and raise their own voice.[58] *Diakonia* is the church's practical response to the needs of the community and integrates the ministry of pastoral counseling

---

56. Pastor in the EELC, Nov. 12, 2019. See also Bue Kessel, "Infertilitet."
57. Magezi, "Reflection on Pastoral Care," 6.
58. Dietrich, "Prophetic Diakonia."

with caring presence and attentive listening to the one who is stigmatized and set aside.

African theologians have challenged the Western therapeutic or clinical model of pastoral counseling and argue that pastoral counseling in Africa must include the dimension of fellowship and community, contrary to looking at a person's problems only from an individualistic perspective. It must engage with people's culture and way of organizing life and include a more communal perspective.[59] This perspective fuses the *diaconal* approach and pastoral counseling in African contexts. In my research on women in Cameroon, informants identify domestic and gender-based violence as a significant individual and communal problem and state that women cannot solve the challenge on their own. They call upon the church to address the issue on a collective and communal level, with men on board in gender inclusion efforts.[60] Baloyi argues that in its pastoral ministry the church must contribute to increase knowledge among people in general about the gendered character of infertility, that infertility is also caused by men, and asks how the church can contribute to restoring the dignity of childless women.[61]

The advocacy of the church moves beyond the crisis of infertility as a subset in the subject of theological education in the quest to equip students for ministry. However, for theological education to be relevant, there is need for rethinking and reorganizing the programs and curriculum and direct it towards the burning issues of the congregants and their communities. The discourse on modern and traditional infertility treatment is an important cultural prism to bring to the classroom to contribute to shaping theological education and African Christian theology.

Theological education needs to engage with cultural propaganda on the efficacies of traditional fertility medicine. Understanding the impact of the fear of infertility,[62] the traditional and cultural acceptable means that are largely employed to resolve infertility, and the limitations of modern infertility treatment will engage the students' ethical and critical reflection. Levirate marriage and traditional surrogate motherhood,[63] adoption within extended family, polygamy, and other cultural acceptable means of handling infertility by African couples are essential topics for theological reflection. So is knowledge about infertility shrines, local healers' roles, and ART, which on the whole challenge religion. To some, the ART procedure is

---

59. Kimilike, "Integrating the African Perspective," 30.
60. Bue Kessel, "Between God's Sharing Power," 155.
61. M. Baloyi, "Gendered Character of Barrenness," 5.
62. Boivin et al., "Fear of Infertility."
63. Okwuosa, "Traditional Surrogacy."

experienced as religiously and ethically disturbing; while to others, religion provides a framework for navigation, with the hope of making responsible decisions in the treatment processes. The new treatment processes may be judged by religious institutions who underline sole trust in God to give children, rather than depending on human wisdom and technology.[64]

Surrogate motherhood is known from biblical stories such as that of Sarah's maid who slept with Abraham to give birth for the childless couple (Gen 16:1–4). Also, Leah and Rachel gave their maids to their husband Jacob to bear children for them (Gen 30:1–10). An interesting question about surrogate motherhood and modern surrogacy is how it influences cultural understanding of motherhood. The need to hold together various models of theological education, the classical and the practical approach, can be illustrated by the following example. According to Baloyi, misreading of Gen 1 ("be fruitful and multiply") in many contexts as a conditional clause for marriage adds to the burden of sterility.[65] Therefore, solid training in exegesis of Scripture is also much needed in theological education.

A theology that addresses the situation of infertile women in sub-Saharan Africa needs to be further explored. There are obvious challenges in the biblical material. Most infertile women in the Bible (such as Hannah, Rachel, Sarah, and Elizabeth) did give birth after some time. For African women who trust in God as their shield and protector, what kind of models, stories, and perspectives in Scripture can give them tools to cope with their situation and change the negative narrative of their lives? This question is an important challenge to address in *diaconal* theology, biblical studies, and systematic theology, in interaction with real life experiences. If the church is going to be a counterculture to the traditions of exclusion that follows infertility, both women and men need to be targeted in theological education.

An area of further research is a systematic empirical study of how some selected Protestant theological seminaries in Africa deal with burning issues in the congregants' lives, such as the topic of this chapter. A theology that speaks to the context involves a conversation between faith and culture,[66] between "the experience of the past" reflected in Scripture and "the experience of the present" in current contexts.[67] According to Bevans, "a theology that honors the experience of context will be one that is not tied

---

64. Hiadzi et al., "God Helps."
65. M. Baloyi, "Gendered Character of Barrenness," 5.
66. M. Vähäkangas, "World Christianity," 227.
67. Bevans, "What Has Contextual Theology," 9. See also Acolatse, *For Freedom or Bondage?*, 32–35.

to Western ways, themes, and methods of theology."[68] It should be carried out bottom-up, from local knowledge. Consequently, theological training must keep an eye on the ground.

CONCLUDING COMMENTS

This chapter has described the social stigma of infertility and its corresponding relationship to theological education in Africa with specific focus on *diakonia* and pastoral counseling. Ministerial formation needs contextual and intentional focus to influence the learning outcome of appropriate models of theological education in order to equip future pastors to address time and place. The stigmas that follow childlessness in Africa are pervasive, hence there is need to reposition theological education to engage, subvert, and shape the different negative perspectives of people towards infertility. In the view of disability studies, infertility renders couples culturally disabled and prevents their ability to live dignified lives within their various communities.

First, this chapter advocates encouraging knowledge of and reflection on the social crisis of infertility in Africa with a view to impacting theological education and African Christian theology. Second, with an eye on Cameroon, the chapter has presented various stigmas, fears, and cultural assumptions that generally characterize couples with infertility. Third, the chapter has engaged with the crisis of infertility using the cultural prism of socially acceptable ways of handling infertility to encourage a repositioning of theological education in Africa to address, critique, and challenge these socially acceptable ways.

BIBLIOGRAPHY

Abebe, Melese Shenkut, et al. "Primary and Secondary Infertility in Africa: Systematic Review with Meta-Analysis." *Fertility Research and Practice* 6 (2020) 1–20.
Ackermann, Denise, et al., eds. *Women Hold Up Half the Sky: Women in the Church of Southern Africa*. Pietermaritzburg: Cluster, 1991.
Acolatse, Esther E. *For Freedom or Bondage? A Critique of African Pastoral Practices*. Grand Rapids: Eerdmans, 2014.
Afferri, Anna, et al. "Availability of Services for the Diagnosis and Treatment of Infertility in The Gambia's Public and Private Health Facilities: A Cross-Sectional Survey." *BMC Health Services Research* 22 (2022) 1127.

---

68. Bevans, "What Has Contextual Theology," 11.

Asemota, Obehi A., and Peter Klatsky. "Access to Infertility Care in the Developing World: The Family Promotion Gap." *Seminars in Reproductive Medicine* 33(2015) 17–22.

Baloyi, Gift T. "An African Woman's Dilemma in *The Secret Lives of Baba Segi's Wives*: A Bosadi Perspective on the Challenges and Pains of Infertility." *Verbum et Ecclesia* 40 (2019) 1–8.

Baloyi, Magezi E. "Gendered Character of Barrenness in an African Context: An African Pastoral Study." *In die Skriflig/In Luce Verbi* 51 (2017) 1–7.

Bediako, Kwame. *Christianity in Africa: The Renewal of a Non-Western Religion*. Studies in World Christianity. Edinburgh: Edinburgh University Press, 1995.

———. *Jesus in Africa: The Christian Gospel in African History and Experience*. Theological Reflections from the South. Yaoundé: Clé, 2000.

Bevans, Stephen B. "What Has Contextual Theology to Offer the Church of the Twenty-First Century?" In *Contextual Theology for the Twenty-First Century*, edited by Stephen B. Bevans and Katalina Tahaafe-Williams, 3–17. Missional Church, Public Theology, World Christianity 1. Cambridge: Clarke, 2012.

Bevans, Stephen B., and Katalina Tahaafe-Williams, eds. *Contextual Theology for the Twenty-First Century*. Missional Church, Public Theology, World Christianity 1. Cambridge: Clarke, 2012.

Boivin, Jacky, et al. "A Rapid Scoping Review of Fear of Infertility in Africa." *Reproductive Health* 17 (2020) 142.

Bue Kessel, Terese. "Between God's Sharing Power and Men's Controlling Power: A Quest for Diaconal Empowerment and Transformation in Femmes Pour Christ in Cameroon." PhD diss., University of Stavanger, 2014.

———. "Infertilitet som sosial og kulturell funksjonshemming: Et perspektiv fra Kamerun." In *Religiøst medborgerskap. Funksjonshemming, likeverd og menneskesyn*, edited by Inger Marie Lid and Anna Rebecca Solevåg, 193–211. Oslo: Cappelen Damm Akademisk, 2020.

Clinebell, Howard. *Basic Types of Pastoral Care & Counseling: Resources for the Ministry of Healing and Growth*. Rev. and enlarged ed. Nashville: Abingdon, 1984.

Devor, Nancy Gieseler. "Pastoral Care for Infertile Couples." *Journal of Pastoral Care* 48 (1994) 355–60.

Dietrich, Stephanie. "'For Thus Says the Lord': Prophetic Diakonia as Advocacy and Fight for Justice." *Evangelism and Diakonia in Context* 32 (2016) 153–65.

Eide, Øyvind M. *Forståelse og Fordypning: Perspektiv på den sjelesørgeriske samtalen*. Oslo: Luther, 2014.

Galgalo, Joseph D. "The Teaching of Theology in Africa." In *Theological Education in Contemporary Africa* 5, edited by Grant LeMarquand and Joseph D. Galgalo, 5–27. Oxford: Zapf Chancery Africa, 2004.

Gerkin, Charles V. *The Living Human Document: Re-Visioning Pastoral Counseling in a Hermeneutical Mode*. Nashville: Abingdon, 1984.

Gerrits, Trudie. "Assisted Reproductive Technologies in Ghana: Transnational Undertakings, Local Practices and 'More Affordable' IVF." *Reproductive Biomedicine & Society Online* 2 (2016) 32–38.

———. "Infertility and Matrilineality: The Exceptional Case of the Macua of Mozambique." In *Infertility around the Globe: New Thinking on Childlessness, Gender, and Reproductive Technologies*, edited by Marcia C. Inhorn and Frank van Balen, 233–46. Berkeley: University of California Press, 2002.

Hadebe, Nontando M. "Commodification, Decolonisation and Theological Education in Africa: Renewed Challenges for African Theologians." *HvTSt* 73 (2017) 1–10.

Haugen, Hans Morten, et al. *Developing Just and Inclusive Communities: Challenges for Diakonia/Christian Social Practice and Social Work*. Regnum Studies in Mission. Oxford: Regnum International, 2022.

Hiadzi, Rosemond Akpene, et al. "'God Helps Those Who Help Themselves'... Religion and Assisted Reproductive Technology Usage amongst Urban Ghanaians." *PloS One* 16 (2021).

Inhorn, Marcia C., and Frank van Balen, eds. *Infertility around the Globe: New Thinking on Childlessness, Gender, and Reproductive Technologies*. Berkeley: University of California Press, 2002.

Kanyoro, R. A. Musimbi. *Introducing Feminist Cultural Hermeneutics: An African Perspective*. Cleveland: Pilgrim, 2002.

Kimilike, Peter Lechion. "Integrating the African Perspective." In *Restoring Life in Christ: Dialogues of Care in Christian Communities; An African Perspective*, edited by Øyvind M. Eide et al., 28–37. Makumira 19. Neuendettelsau, Germ.: Erlanger Verlag für Mission und Ökumene, 2008.

Kiriswa, Benjamin. *Pastoral Counselling in Africa: An Integrated Model*. Eldoret: AMECEA, 2002.

Knoetze, Johannes J., and Alfred R. Brunsdon, eds. *A Critical Engagement with Theological Education in Africa*. Reformed Theology in Africa. Durbanville, S. Afr.: AOSIS, 2021.

LeMarquand, Grant, and Joseph D. Galgalo, eds. *Theological Education in Contemporary Africa* 5. Oxford: Zapf Chancery Africa, 2004.

Lossky, Nicholas, et al. *Dictionary of the Ecumenical Movement*. Geneva: WCC, 2002.

LWF. "Cameroon: Addressing Gaps in Theological Education and Leadership." LWF, Sept. 23, 2022. https://www.lutheranworld.org/news/cameroon-addressing-gaps-theological-education-and-leadership.

Magezi, Vhumani. "Reflection on Pastoral Care in Africa: Towards Discerning Emerging Pragmatic Pastoral Ministerial Responses." *In die Skriflig/In Luce Verbi* 50 (2016) 1–7.

Mashabela, James K. "Africanisation as an Agent of Theological Education in Africa." *HvTSt* 73 (2017) 1–9.

Mire, Sada. "Wagar, Fertility and Phallic Stelae: Cushitic Sky-God Belief and the Site of Saint Aw-Barkhadle, Somaliland." *African Archaeological Review* 32 (2015) 93–109.

Myers, Bryant L. *Walking with the Poor: Principles and Practices of Transformational Development*. Maryknoll, NY: Orbis, 2011.

Naidoo, Marilyn. "Introduction." In *Contested Issues in Training Ministers in South Africa*, edited by Marilyn Naidoo, 1–10. Stellenbosch, S. Afr.: Sun, 2015.

Nordstokke, Kjell, ed. *Diakonia in Context: Transformation, Reconciliation, Empowerment; An LWF Contribution to the Understanding and Practice of Diakonia*. Geneva: Lutheran World Federation, 2009. https://www.lutheranworld.org/sites/default/files/DMD-Diakonia-EN-low.pdf.

Nordstokke, Kjell, et al. *Serving the Whole Person: The Practice and Understanding of Diakonia within the Lutheran Communion*. LWF Documentation 54. Minneapolis: Lutheran University Press, 2009.

Nwachuku, Daisy N. "Widow in African Culture." In *The Will to Arise: Women, Tradition, and the Church in Africa*, edited by Mercy Amba Oduyoye and Musimbi R. A. Kanyoro, 54–73. Maryknoll, NY: Orbis, 1992.

Okwuosa, Ikechukwu Kenneth. "An Ethical Evaluation of Traditional Surrogacy in Igbo Culture, South-East Nigeria." *Sapientia Global Journal of Arts, Humanities and Development Studies* 3 (2020) 13–24.

Pobee, John S. "Foreword." In *Contested Issues in Training Ministers in South Africa*, edited by Marilyn Naidoo, vii–x. Stellenbosch, S. Afr.: Sun, 2015.

Sharma, Radhey Shyam, et al. "Infertility & Assisted Reproduction: A Historical & Modern Scientific Perspective." *Indian Journal of Medical Research* 148 (2018) 1–14.

Tøssebro, Jan. *Hva er funksjonshemming*. Oslo: Universitetsforlaget, 2010.

Vähäkangas, Auli. *Christian Couples Coping with Childlessness: Narratives from Machame, Kilimanjaro*. American Society of Missiology Monograph. Eugene, OR: Pickwick, 2009.

Vähäkangas, Mika. "World Christianity as Post-Colonialising of Theology." In *Contextual Theology: Skills and Practices of Liberating Faith*, edited by Sigurd Bergmann and Mika Vähäkangas, 221–37. Routledge New Critical Thinking in Religion, Theology and Biblical Studies. New York: Routledge, 2021.

Wahl, W. P. "Towards Relevant Theological Education in Africa: Comparing the International Discourse with Contextual Challenges." *AcT* 33 (2013) 266–93.

Werthmann, Katja. "Local Religion or Cult-Shopping? A Sacrificial Site in Burkina Faso." *Anthropos* 109 (2014) 399–409.

World Council of Churches, and ACT Alliance. *Called to Transformation: Ecumenical Diakonia*. Geneva: WCC, 2022. https://www.oikoumene.org/resources/publications/ecumenical-diakonia.

World Health Organization. "Infertility." World Health Organization, Apr. 3, 2023. https://www.who.int/news-room/fact-sheets/detail/infertility.

Chapter 6

Experiencing God as One's Opponent

Knut Alfsvåg

THE UBIQUITY OF LAMENT

The Bible presents God as a loving Father (Ps 103:13; Matt 7:11). Still, suffering and misfortune are quite common experiences among his children, and there are more than a few passages in the Bible where the writer or speaker complains to God about this, often with the implication that God is somehow to blame. The most well known of these complainers is Jesus, who from the cross complained that God had forsaken him (Matt 27:46), but he is certainly not alone. His lament was a quotation from Ps 22:2, and similar complaints abound both in the book of Psalms and in other biblical writings (Pss 13:2–3; 44:25; 88:15; Lam 3:8; Job 19:7; 30:20). The persons writing and quoting these texts experience their trials and tribulations as divine absence and/or divine opposition, and for that reason find it adequate to complain to God about what God does or does not do. Why do they behave in this way, what is the alternative to expressing life's trials as a criticism of God, and how do we teach ourselves and our students to make sense of and express our crises and negative experiences in an adequate way? These are the questions I want to explore in this chapter.

GOD AS TRANSCENDENT SOURCE

According to the Bible, God is the origin of all there is (Gen 1:1). Irrespective of which other characteristics apply, all phenomena in the world therefore

Experiencing God as One's Opponent

have a God-relationship.[1] There are passages in the Bible that express this dependence of everything on God without reserve, both as a present reality (θεὸς ὁ ἐνεργῶν τὰ πάντα ἐν πᾶσιν [God who works all in all] [1 Cor 12:6]) and an eschatological one (1 Cor 15:28), and there are other passages that emphasize that neither death nor nonexistence make any difference in this respect. Death does not remove us from the God-relationship (Ps 139:8; Matt 22:32), and God even calls on the nonexistent as existing (ἐπίστευσεν θεοῦ τοῦ . . . καλοῦντος τὰ μὴ ὄντα ὡς ὄντα [Rom 4:17]). There are no thinkable limits before the infinite One.

The divine origin accounts for both the existence and the structure of the world as we experience it. Genesis 1 tells us how the world is called forth by the word of God from nonexistence into the structured *kósmos* that can only be described as good. There is thus a close correspondence between existence, structure, meaning, and goodness. The world in its created goodness makes sense to us and we are able to make use of it in a good way. Among created beings, as far as these are known to us today, humans are by far the ones who are best able to make sense of, meditate on, and communicate the structured goodness of the created world. It therefore makes sense to single out humans as the ones who are created in the image of God and subjected to his fatherly love in a particular way. We communicate with God's addressing us through the created world in a unique way.[2]

There is a problem, though. While we have no problem understanding what is meant by the description of the goodness of the completed creation in Gen 1:31, neither the Bible nor our experience find the present reality of the world to be unambiguously good. On the contrary, it contains large amounts of evil, some of which is related to humans behaving in ways that are at variance with divinely determined goodness, and some of which is related to the created world behaving in ways that, from our point of view, can only be called disastrous. This calls for an explanation of a phenomenon, usually called the problem of (moral and natural) evil, that from the presuppositions of the biblical worldview cannot be explained—the biblical authors do not even try. If structure and meaning equal goodness, evil as lack of goodness defies explanation. It is not a definable entity in the way goodness, meaning and structure are. This is suggested already by the lack of transition from Gen 1 and 2, where all is "very good," to the snake and its treacherous question in chapter 3.

By refraining from an explanation, the Bible maintains the reality of evil without any concession either to a dualist worldview according to

---

1. Schwöbel, "Creatureliness."
2. For interesting reflections on this topic, see Bayer, *Schöpfung als Anrede*.

which God has an equally powerful, but evil, opponent[3] or to an understanding of God as a powerless deity whose main contribution is to show solidarity with suffering humans.[4] These attempts at a solution integrate evil in a meaningful structure and are for that reason unacceptable.[5] The Bible never loses sight of either the asymmetry between the substantiality of goodness as structure and meaning and evil as its destruction, or of the corresponding conviction of God's ultimate victory where the goodness of and unambiguous divine presence in everything will be restored. The unconditional promise of this restoration is arguably the very point of the biblical narrative and the center of the Christian message.[6]

The contradiction caused by the experience of evil and the conviction of divine goodness is what produces lament. What is expressed through the lament is that God is somehow behaving improperly; he is the origin of justice and goodness but will not let the one who complains take part in it. On the contrary, the one who laments experiences life exposed to the ploys of enemies to the extent that the days are filled by sorrow.[7] Somehow this sad situation is felt to be God's responsibility; God does not fulfill his divine obligation to show fatherly care and love. Still, the lament is addressed to him with a hope of deliverance. As deliverance is regularly postponed, the lament is often expressed as the cry of "How long?" Lamentations can be expressed either as individual (e.g., Ps 13) or as collective (e.g., Ps 74), but usually with the same basic elements.

None of the complaints contains anything in the direction of a theoretical solution of the problem that is addressed through the lament. A fair number of them, though, still end with an expression of trusting faith, the reason for which we are not informed about (Ps 13:6). It is as if the ability to complain without any kind of restraint in itself is felt as satisfactory. The most important exception to this rule is Ps 88, which contains only lament, though even this psalm addresses God as "the God of my salvation" (יְשׁוּעָתִי אֱלֹהֵי יְהוָה; Κύριε ὁ θεὸς τῆς σωτηρίας μου).

The structured world of goodness of which God is the ultimate origin is thus never unambiguously present. The idea that this should suggest something in the direction of the nonexistence of God or the irrelevance of meditating on the God-relationship is, if not entirely beyond the horizon

---

3. Torchia, "Manichaeism."

4. Moltmann, *Gekreuzigte Gott*.

5. For a further discussion of this topic, see a number of the contributions in Keating and White, *Divine Impassibility*.

6. The first Christian thinker to give a philosophically ambitious account of evil along these lines was Augustine; see Maker, "Augustine on Evil."

7. Natural disasters are not in the same way included in the lament; see, e.g., Ps 46:3.

of the biblical writers, felt as the characteristic of the fool and something that immediately results in bad and irresponsible behavior (Ps 14:1).[8] The injustice of bad people being blessed far beyond the pious and just is felt to be something that might induce a lack of trust in God, but this is a temptation that it should be possible to resist (Ps 73).

We may therefore conclude that within the biblical context, it is felt to be much less of a problem to find God to be unjust and accuse him of being so than to use his alleged injustice and lack of love as a pretext for withdrawing from the God-relationship. Lament is still a form of belief and thus adequate far beyond disengagement and neglect.

DIVINE INJUSTICE AND THE NEED FOR A RATIONAL JUSTIFICATION

Within the context of a secularized modernity, this situation no longer obtains, and the experience of trials and tribulations is felt to be a relevant argument in the debate on whether there is a God, and in the corresponding debate whether the idea of a God-relationship is a relevant notion or not.[9] If God does not satisfy his job description of being the source of love and goodness, do we have any use for him anymore? This is now felt to be the adequate question. What is the reason for this change in attitude, and how should we evaluate it?

For the biblical and premodern way of thinking, the world's making sense for us is something that is granted by its transcendent source. This is true both for Plato and Aristotle, the Bible, and the synthesis between Greek and biblical thought established by the church fathers and maintained through most of the intellectual history of medieval Europe. As the precondition for making sense of our experiences, belief in God may be challenged by, but is eventually not seriously affected by, the experience of evil, which is felt to be adequately handled through prayers of lamentation.

However, during the fourteenth century it was suggested that the idea of God as the precondition for the appreciation of the truth of the world should be replaced by the idea of truth as founded on unambiguous conceptual representation, thus allegedly making it possible to reach a higher degree of precise knowledge.[10] According to this way of thinking, the phe-

---

8. As quoted by Paul in Rom 3:10; however, the situation described in this psalm is considered universally valid. Godlessness may thus be more prevalent than it appears to be.

9. This is, e.g., the position of a number of authors in Rowe, *God and the Problem*.

10. For a more detailed discussion of this shift and its implications, see Alfsvåg, "Unknowability and Incarnation."

nomena we experience are given a conceptual representation in the human mind, and truth is what occurs when these representations are sorted in a way that is logically satisfying. This reorientation was controversial and resisted by, among others, the main Reformers,[11] but it made sense as a way of interpreting the modern scientific breakthrough as occurring in the work of Kepler, Galileo, and Newton,[12] and was ultimately accepted as the common frame of reference for European intellectuals during the time of the Enlightenment.

If truth is what can be given an unambiguous conceptual representation, the conditions for thinking through the relation between God and the world, and between God and evil, change. In the latter case, it introduces the problem of what was now called *theodicy* (the word was introduced by Leibniz in 1710), which investigates whether the idea of divine justice is defensible given the existence of evil—Leibniz thinks it is.[13] In the former case, the question of the relation between God and the world, it introduces the problem of proving the existence of a Creator, a problem unknown to Christian theology before the fourteenth century.[14] The question whether God exists or not was regularly answered positively; there were no serious atheists in Europe until the eighteenth century.[15] It is still significant, though, that the question that in the Bible is referred to the margin of thought, to the extent that it is thought to be the prerogative of the fool, is now considered a question worthy of serious thought.[16]

What is significant concerning these attempts at giving a rational justification of God's existence is not how the questions were answered. The interesting thing is what these attempts reveal about the presuppositions commonly taken for granted.[17] If unambiguous conceptual representation is the key to the understanding of the truth of the world, then truth is defined with reference to the human, and in this way becomes the judge of what

11. Alfsvåg, "Contra Philosophos."
12. Funkenstein, *Theology and Scientific Imagination*.
13. Malcolm, "Theodicy," 500.
14. According to Mühling-Schlapkohl, natural theology "developed as an intensive discipline" with Thomas Aquinas (Mühling-Schlapkohl, "Existence of God," 751). But Thomas's five ways are not proofs in a technical sense.
15. According to Hyman, *Short History of Atheism*, 6–7, Denis Diderot (1713–84) "is widely recognized as being the first explicitly ... atheist philosopher." In Britain, this was not a socially acceptable position until the end of the nineteenth century (Hyman, *Short History of Atheism*, 13).
16. For a critique of the attempts of proving God's existence as inherently inconsistent, see Schwöbel, "Systematic Theology."
17. This is what Charles Taylor calls "social imaginaries" (Taylor, *Secular Age*, 171).

may be considered consistently unambiguous and for that reason rationally justifiable. Hidden in the agenda of Enlightenment, modernity is thus the deification of the human.[18] This does not in itself exclude the possibility of humans finding God useful and for that reason continuing to believe in his existence, but it seriously affects the points of orientation for the relationship between God and the human. This relationship is no longer understood as the reverent thankfulness of the created towards its Creator but is seen as a relationship between equal partners in negotiation. This also affects the understanding of the world, which can no longer be seen as structured goodness called forth by the word of God and communicating itself to humans for the sake of a participatory, but inexhaustible, exploration. It is rather seen as an, in itself, possibly unstructured[19] compilation of facts without inherent value and governed by mutual causal relationships, the structure of which is forcibly imposed by humans. For this reason, they are knowable by humans and something we are free to manipulate to our benefit.[20]

On these presuppositions, there are two possible solutions to the problem of evil. We can reject the idea of the world's ultimate goodness, or we can understand evil as an intentional part of the original creation. In the former case, a good God does not exist;[21] in the latter case, a good God (or at least a God with positive intentions) may still exist, but the world is given a kind of independent existence at variance with the biblical idea of divine omnipresence and the unconditional trustworthiness of salvation by grace. At least the moral evils are then due to humans making the wrong choices, the problem being why God gave humans this freedom in the first place. Did he intend it as a possible area for growth?[22] Was he surprised by humans acting as they did? However, even if this solution is accepted, the problem of the natural evil is still unaccounted for; it is hardly plausible to see all natural evils as caused by humans making the wrong decisions, even if some of them may be.

---

18. For an interesting discussion of how this reorientation plays out in the thought of Descartes, see Hyman, *Short History of Atheism*, 19–26.

19. The question of whether the world has an inherent structure independent of our structuring of it can on this presupposition neither be asked nor answered, as the beginning of our investigation of the world is our conceptualizing it (nominalism). Scientists often do not quite understand this and continue to work from a realist perspective that presupposes a theology of creation they usually are not willing to grant.

20. This is now often referred to as the philosophical and theological origin of the ecological crisis; see, e.g., Tyson, *Theology and Climate Change*.

21. Mackie, "Evil and Omnipotence."

22. Hick, "Soul-Making Theodicy."

The implication of these attempts at explaining the problem of evil, unsatisfactory as they may seem, is that they make it impossible to let the lamentations keep the significance they have in the Bible, where the pure fact of humans crying to God about the injustice they experience is as close to a solution of the problem of evil as we get. As the Bible presents God, God accepts any number of accusations irrespective of whether they are fair or not, the question of the fairness of the accusations being one that is never asked. What humans feel is real, irrespective of its philosophical justifiability. The only attitude toward the problem of evil the Bible never accepts is the one preferred by modernity, i.e., the attempt at solving it.

Today, modernity's one-sided emphasis on conceptual rationality does not enjoy quite the prestige it once enjoyed. While still being seen as basic for what is considered commonly accepted truths both in science and society, it has been challenged as being dependent on a narrative of progress for which there is no justification,[23] and which has landed us in the trouble we experience as pollution and climate change.[24] Where does that leave us as Christians and theologians struggling with the problem of evil and informed by the biblical inclination to consider the infinitely good God the source of our sufferings and misfortunes?

CHRISTIAN PROCLAMATION AND CONTEXTUAL COMPATIBILITY

When the message of Christ's victory over sin and death was first proclaimed, this happened in a Jewish context where the basic points of orientation for a Christian worldview were taken for granted, the main issue being whether Jesus was the proclaimed Messiah or not. This changed dramatically as the apostles moved into the Hellenistic context. The attitude chosen by the apostles and the church fathers was to maintain and proclaim what they considered the truth of the world (monotheism, incarnation, atonement) in a way that was critical of differing, but commonly accepted, positions in the prevailing culture, while still looking for points of contact and possible dialogue. To some extent they found that in the monotheism of Neoplatonism.[25]

Protestant post-Enlightenment theology is a variation of this approach, with the added complication that the surrounding culture is now informed by nearly two thousand years of Christian proclamation, thus raising the

---

23. Smith, "Postmodernism."
24. Tyson, *Theology and Climate Change*.
25. See Alfsvåg, *What No Mind*, 33–50, for a summary of this development.

question whether a sharply critical attitude toward contemporary culture is now the appropriate one. Even the added awareness of the dignity of the individual that structures modernity's emphasis on nominalist rationality is arguably the outcome of a Christian emphasis on the liberty of the individual.[26] The question of how to relate to the surrounding culture is then not a clear-cut question of message and context, but a question of how to relate different aspects of the biblical revelation seemingly at odds with each other. Should we go for the emphasis on divine unknowability implicated by the worldview of the lamentations, or should we favor the need for explanations implicated by the new emphasis on anthropocentric rationality?

The outcome has been a compromise where the intellectually more ambitious forms of Christian theology favored at the universities and in the revival movements have prioritized rationality and explicability, whereas the liturgical traditions with their closeness to the biblical texts maintained the significance of lament without necessarily adding an explanation.[27] The most obvious examples of the former attitude are the moralism of classical nineteenth-century liberal theology[28] and the Arminianism prevalent in many of the revival movements.[29] Even within the Bultmann school, "evil is a by-product of man's misuse of his freedom."[30] The price to pay for this emphasis on the piety of the individual is a (probably unintended) openness for a theology of merit that short-circuits the biblical possibility of unrestrained lament. If the success of one's God-relationship, at least to some extent, is dependent on one's own contribution, then one will have to blame the apparent lack of success on oneself.[31]

We do not solve the problems related to this compromise either with an appeal to the formal authority of the Bible or with an appeal to the significance of contextual awareness, for the traditions I have here referred to (liberal theology, revivalism, and Bultmannian kerygma theology) are paying attention to both sets of criteria. They want to be both scripturally

26. This is repeatedly emphasized in, e.g., Hart, *Atheist Delusions*.

27. The liturgy of the Church of Norway refers to human sinfulness and to the body and blood of Christ given for the atonement for our sins—*har nå gitt oss sin kropp og sitt blod som han gav til soning for alle våre synder* (Norske Kirke, "Ordning for hovedgudstjenesten," 14)—without attempting anything in the direction of an explanation for why we are sinners.

28. On the reinterpretation of soteriology in ethical and moral categories in the work of Albrecht Ritschl, see Hägglund, *History of Theology*, 375–76.

29. Bosch, *Transforming Mission*, 343.

30. Lee, "Bultmann's Existentialist Interpretation," 72.

31. Barth has a different approach; see Krötke, "Evil and Nothingness." One could argue, however, that the openness toward universalism allegedly implicated by his understanding of election ultimately lands Barth on the side of rational intelligibility.

sound and culturally relevant, and, at least to some extent, they succeed on both accounts. The problem is rather the way they relate the two sets of criteria, which they do from the presupposition of a basic compatibility, the implication of which is that the attempt to be culturally relevant in the context of modernity is ultimately based on accepting the basic dogma of modernity, i.e., the world's being essentially reducible to rational intelligibility. There is no doubt that even this criterion, prevalent as it is in the post-Enlightenment Western world, is ultimately informed by central elements of biblical anthropology, and for that reason easily accepted as a candidate for contextually relevant reformulations of the Christian message. The problem is, however, that there clearly are central biblical passages, the ubiquitous lamentations and their insistence on the inexplicability of the God-relationship being the most obvious example, which are incompatible with this way of contextualizing Christian theology.

There are two sets of problems that the prevailing schools of Protestant theology under modernity have never been able to solve. One is the problem of what to do with experiences that are most adequately expressed as accusations of divine injustice, thus not easily lending themselves to rational explanations. The other is the problem of what to do with one's models of contextualization when the cultural context changes and the models appear obsolete. The question of how to do theology after the Holocaust highlights both problems. As the carefully thought-out models of theodicy suddenly appear hollow and useless, culture shifts and raises the question of the goodness of the world, which is the quest for the Creator, in a way that lets the theoretical proofs of God's existence and God's goodness appear outdated.[32] The only possible answer may be to revert to the theology of unrestrained lament and accusation.[33] But if this is a possibility theology left behind generations ago, where does that leave us?

TO LIVE WITH THE INEXPLICABLE

There are obvious reasons to believe in a good Creator. The world is a well-structured whole, which from the point of view of human rationality is intelligible to an amazing degree.

There are equally obvious reasons not to believe in a good Creator. Moral and natural evils abound, and while humans are to blame for some

---

32. It is a common emphasis of the authors discussed in Pinnock, *Beyond Theodicy*, that theoretical theodicy in the footsteps of Leibniz (and Hegel) does not work; one needs practical and existentialist approaches.

33. Mandolfo, "Psalm 88 and Holocaust."

of them, they are not to blame for all, and hardly for the existence of evil as a metaphysical reality.

There are different ways of solving this dilemma. One may or may not insist on its rational solvability, and if one does insist on its solvability, prefer to go with either belief or disbelief as the preferred option. Both rationally argued belief and disbelief come with obvious drawbacks, though. A one-sided belief in God's goodness ultimately leaves the human experience of evil speechless, and the one-sided rejection of the existence of a good Creator is logically inconsistent, as the rationality that informs the argument then becomes a mere fact without an explanation. If there is no God, the idea of a universal rationality is difficult to maintain, and the goodness and the intelligibility of the world must be accepted as brute facts without any hint of an explanation.

Teaching theology in a time of crisis, our first challenge is to invite our students and ourselves to reflect on which of these solutions we are able to live with. How to make sense of a world that combines ineffable beauty and natural mysteries that are both unsolvable and intelligible to an amazing degree with the astounding cruelty of both the natural world and the human mind? In my view, neither the insistence on rationally defended belief nor its rejection, which after all is but a variation of the understanding of reality as ultimately intelligible on human terms, are consistent and convincing solutions. The way of the lamentations, insisting on the apparent contradiction between divine goodness and divine injustice as the ultimate reality of the world as experienced by us, is remarkably resilient, and is thus certainly a candidate worthy of serious consideration.

If the way of the lamentations is accepted as a candidate worthy of serious consideration, the next step should be to find the experiences that invites us to cry out against divine injustice. Referring to our collective memory, these experiences are not hard to find after a century that has seen more than its fair share of human suffering through war, by persecution and brought about by famine caused by the cruelty and incompetence of dictators. And as we listen to the daily news, we are repeatedly reminded that this is not only a thing of the past. Simply from solidarity with our fellow human beings, we can today use the biblical lamentations with reference to experiences of evil and cruelty far beyond what was experienced and imagined by their original authors.

The real test, however, is whether the lamentations speak to and meaningfully interpret the experiences of our own lives. We differ in the way we experience evil, and some are familiar with it to an extent others do not understand. But we all have our experiences, and we may all feel entitled to complain about divine injustice. Let us do so and let us invite our students to do the same. We may all make the experience of God having left us. It may not be the final word, but it is as long as the experience lasts. Let us then try to emulate the courage of the biblical authors and leave it there. In some situations, that may be the only responsible thing to do.

BIBLIOGRAPHY

Alfsvåg, Knut. "Contra Philosophos: The Lutheran Reformation as Critique of the Rationality of Modernity." In *Justification in a Post-Christian Society*, edited by Carl-Henrik Grenholm and Göran Gunner, 192–206. Church of Sweden Research 8. Eugene, OR: Pickwick, 2014.

———. "Unknowability and Incarnation: Creation and Christology as Philosophy of Science in the Work of Nicholas Cusanus." *International Journal of Systematic Theology* 21 (2019) 141–56.

———. *What No Mind Has Conceived: On the Significance of Christological Apophaticism*. Studies in Philosophical Theology 45. Paris: Peeters, 2010.

Bayer, Oswald. *Schöpfung als Anrede: Zu einer Hermeneutik der Schöpfung*. Tübingen: Mohr Siebeck, 1986.

Bosch, David J. *Transforming Mission: Paradigm Shifts in Theology of Mission*. Maryknoll, NY: Orbis, 1991.

Funkenstein, Amos. *Theology and the Scientific Imagination from the Middle Ages to the 17th Century*. Princeton, NJ: Princeton University Press, 1986.

Hägglund, Bengt. *History of Theology*. Translated by Gene J. Lund. 4th rev. ed. St. Louis: Concordia, 2007.

Hart, David Bentley. *Atheist Delusions: The Christian Revolution and Its Fashionable Enemies*. New Haven, CT: Yale University Press, 2009.

Hick, John. "Soul-Making Theodicy." In *God and the Problem of Evil*, edited by William L. Rowe, 265–81. Blackwell Readings in Philosophy. Malden, MA: Blackwell, 2001.

Hyman, Gavin. *A Short History of Atheism*. London: Tauris, 2010.

Keating, James F., and Thomas Joseph White, eds. *Divine Impassibility and the Mystery of Human Suffering*. Grand Rapids: Eerdmans, 2009.

Krötke, Wolf. "Barth on Evil and Nothingness." In *Wiley Blackwell Companion to Karl Barth*, edited by George Hunsinger and Keith L. Johnson, 1:207–16. Hoboken, NJ, 2020.

Lee, Jung Young. "Bultmann's Existentialist Interpretation and the Problem of Evil." *JRT* 26 (1969) 65–80.

Mackie, J. L. "Evil and Omnipotence." In *God and the Problem of Evil*, edited by William L. Rowe, 77–90. Blackwell Readings in Philosophy. Malden, MA: Blackwell, 2001.

Maker, William. "Augustine on Evil: The Dilemma of the Philosophers." *International Journal for Philosophy of Religion* 15 (1984) 149–60.

Malcolm, Lois. "Theodicy." In *The Cambridge Dictionary of Christian Theology*, edited by Ian A. McFarland et al., 499–501. Cambridge: Cambridge University Press, 2011.

Mandolfo, Carleen. "Psalm 88 and the Holocaust: Lament in Search of a Divine Response." *BibInt* 15 (2007) 151–70.

Moltmann, Jürgen. *Der gekreuzigte Gott: Das Kreuz Christi als Grund und Kritik Christlicher Theologie*. Munich: Kaiser, 1972.

Mühling-Schlapkohl, Markus. "Existence of God, Proofs of the." In *Religion Past & Present*, edited by David E. Orton, 4:751–55. Leiden, Neth.: Brill, 2008.

Norske Kirke, Den. "Ordning for hovedgudstjenesten." Den Norske Kirke, 2011. https://www.kirken.no/globalassets/kirken.no/om-troen/gudstjeneste---liturgi/gudst2011_2012_ordning_hovedgudstj_bokm.pdf.

Pinnock, Sarah K. *Beyond Theodicy: Jewish and Christian Continental Thinkers Respond to the Holocaust*. Albany, NY: SUNY Press, 2002.

Rowe, William L., ed. *God and the Problem of Evil*. Blackwell Readings in Philosophy. Malden, MA: Blackwell, 2001.

Schwöbel, Christoph. "Creatureliness." In *Religion Past & Present*, edited by Hans Dieter Betz et al., 3:561–62. Boston: Brill, 2007.

———. "Systematic Theology." In *Religion Past & Present*, edited by Hans Dieter Betz et al., 5:471–75. Boston: Brill, 2009.

Smith, James K. A. "Postmodernism." In *The Cambridge Dictionary of Christian Theology*, 399. Cambridge: Cambridge University Press, 2011.

Taylor, Charles. *A Secular Age*. Cambridge, MA: Harvard University Press, 2007.

Torchia, Joseph. "Manichaeism." In *The Cambridge Dictionary of Christian Theology*, edited by Ian A. McFarland et al., 295–96. Cambridge: Cambridge University Press, 2011.

Tyson, Paul. *Theology and Climate Change*. Routledge Focus on Religion. London: Routledge, 2021.

PART 2

How Can We Learn from Crisis?
Explorations in Learning Theology, Digitally, Globally, and Locally

Chapter 7

Technology-Mediated Learning (TML) during a Time of Crisis

Reflecting on Experiences of Students and Lecturers during COVID-19

Anita Cloete

INTRODUCTION

Technology-mediated learning is not new, not even in developing countries like South Africa. Although that may be the case, the impact of technology-mediated learning on the educational process is far from linear and therefore needs continuous theoretical reflection coupled with empirical research. TML can enhance the educational process, yet it can also cause distraction and disruption, resulting in some educators and learners embracing it and others trying to avoid it and even rejecting it. For this chapter it is important to establish how the sudden change to fully online teaching during the lockdown period shaped the behavior and attitudes of both lecturers and students, specifically towards TML. The chapter, therefore, focuses on TML during the crisis caused by COVID-19, which forced many institutions to pivot their teaching and learning activities to mainly online. First, the chapter will summarize four empirical studies focusing on different aspects of the learning process during TML, which will provide the theoretical framing for this study. The findings of these empirical studies also inform the aspects that will be covered as part of the empirical investigation. The second aim of the chapter is to dissect and compare, where possible, the experiences of lecturers and students regarding TML and how they envision the future relationship between TML and education. Third, the data gained will be used to provide guidance and suggestions regarding TML that could assist with identifying best practices regarding the use of technology, especially at a residential university.

TECHNOLOGY-MEDIATED LEARNING (TML) AND THE LEARNING PROCESS

TML has become popular in higher education. Therefore, evaluating the effect thereof on teaching and learning has become an important research focus. A very insightful article on technology-mediated learning and the learning process states that mediated learning refers to a context where teaching and contact with learning materials, peers, and instructors (lecturers) are mediated through information technologies.[1] TML includes both asynchronous and synchronous teaching and learning.

Wang et al. identified the following important factors about the effect of TML on the learning process that need continuous attention to make teaching and learning effective.

1. Currently not enough attention is paid to the learning process, which includes how information is dealt with. In other words, the learner's psychological process whereby information is absorbed during the learning process is an important aspect that is often neglected in research on TML.
2. The learner's behavioral, emotional, and cognitive engagement are other important factors that are often ignored.
3. The application of a task-technology fit (TTF) model is necessary. This means that TLM is effective only when technology matches the task requirement and the individual abilities.[2]

Moreover, they identified several aspects that make up the learning process and should be considered if we wish to determine the impact and efficacy of technology-mediated learning. First, it is important to gain the learners' attention; we cannot assume that we have their attention simply because they are online or even physically present in a face-to-face class. Wang et al. caution that learners' attention is restricted. It is a scarce resource in

---

1. Wang et al., "Development and Measurement Validity," 131.
2. Wang et al., "Development and Measurement Validity," 132–33.

the educational process because it is selective and limited. Second, it is important that students understand the information effectively.[3] The process of understanding depends on two aspects: First, the information must move from the sensory memory to the short-term memory (STM) and eventually to the long-term memory (LTM). Second, the new information needs to be connected to previous knowledge. Third, the existing knowledge needs to be modified. And finally, the knowledge needs to be applied mainly through students' performance.[4] This discussion serves as a reminder of the comprehensive and complex process of teaching and learning, which is dependent on and influenced by many factors inside and outside the classroom as well as the attitudes and views of both teachers and learners towards TLM.

BACKGROUND AND MOTIVATION FOR THE STUDY

Although the empirical aspect of this study wishes to focus on TML during the lockdown period in South Africa brought about by COVID-19, it is important to remember that most universities participated in a form of TML before then, although the use of technology was limited. But during COVID-19 it became the default mode of teaching and learning under different circumstances that I wish to refer to as a time of crisis. The sudden and therefore drastic move to fully online teaching caused a lot of uncertainty for both learners and lecturers and the whole learning process was put under immense pressure due to the number of changes that were introduced almost overnight. This was especially the case for residential universities where in-person teaching was previously the norm. Secondary data from four empirical studies, focusing exclusively on TML, will form the theoretical backdrop of this study and inform the aspects to be covered in the empirical investigation. Two of the studies were conducted in South Africa and the other two abroad. Two studies were done before the lockdown and the other two during or after lockdown. The timeline of the studies is important because it confirms the understanding that technology was used, albeit to a limited extent, before COVID-19, but TML during COVID-19 was experienced differently and has the potential to change significantly the expectations regarding the future direction of the learning process of both learners and teachers. Each of the four studies focused either on students or lecturers, but this exercise will gather data from all the studies and where possible compare the views and experiences of both students and lecturers regarding TML.

    3. Wang et al., "Development and Measurement Validity," 134–35.
    4. Wang et al., "Development and Measurement Validity," 134.

SECONDARY DATA

In this section I will introduce the above-mentioned studies and briefly describe their aims, methodologies, and key findings. The studies performed before lockdown will be presented first, followed by those during lockdown.

The first study was carried out among school children in South Africa and aimed to establish the effect on learners' attention when using technology compared to when not using technology. Attention is understood as being focused on something specific and, therefore, closely linked to concentration, which is described as "focusing single-mindedly on one object without interruption."[5] Without attention, which includes concentration, optimal learning cannot take place. According to Bester and Brand, the integration of technology in education could stimulate learners and gain and hold their attention.[6] This is especially true of the use of visual content. Due to learners' exposure to visual content outside the classroom, it has become part of how learners learn. Therefore, the use of visual content in teaching is encouraged as part of TML. The research design was an experiential inquiry that included two phases. The learners first completed a questionnaire about concentration and motivation. In the second phase, one group was exposed to lessons where technology was used but with the second group technology was not used. The unit of analysis was school learners between twelve and thirteen years of age, and subjects used for the investigation were geography, English, and mathematics. One of the three hypotheses tested was that there would be a significant difference between the average achievement and attention of the two groups. It was also assumed that there is a significant relationship between the motivation and concentration of learners. The findings confirm that the average achievement and attention in all three subjects was higher when technology was used. Therefore, the researchers concluded that the use of technology in teaching should be promoted since a significant relationship between motivation and concentration was confirmed.[7]

The second study investigated the negative possibilities introduced with the use of technology by focusing on an interesting concept, namely, cyber-slacking. Cyber-slacking diverts students' attention away from course material and what is going on the classroom. Therefore, it points to the negative or adverse impact technology could have on the learning process.[8] Al-

---

5. Bester and Brand, "Effect of Technology," 3.
6. Bester and Brand, "Effect of Technology," 4.
7. Bester and Brand, "Effect of Technology," 14.
8. Taneja et al., "Cyber-Slacking in the Classroom," 144.

though, as the previous study demonstrated, technology can gain and keep students' attention to enhance learning, the opposite is also possible due to the interactive nature of technology. The second study wished to establish how students' intentions and planned behavior are related to cyber-slacking in the classroom. The unit of analysis was undergraduate students between twenty-one and twenty-three years of age at a college in the United States of America (USA) who completed a survey on the reasons for cyber-slacking during class time.

The study identified several factors that could lead to cyber-slacking. One is consumerism, according to which students regard their studies as something that does not require any effort from them; they expect to receive the degree simply because they are paying for it. Escapism can also lead to cyber-slacking—when students' attention starts wandering and they try to escape the current situation, especially when they are not interested in the topic or subject. Lack of attention and cyber-slacking anxiety were other factors mentioned. If students know that there will be consequences for cyber-slacking, they will most probably refrain from it, and vice versa.[9] The main drivers that impact students' behavior towards cyber-slacking were found to be escapism and lack of attention.

The third study included 624 educators across the world, but the majority were in Australia, New Zealand, Singapore, and the USA, where the researchers were based. A narrative approach was used since part of qualitative methodology is conducting interviews, and the researchers wished to establish the lived experiences of teachers during COVID-19.[10] Areas of concern to teachers were the fact that many students did not engage during synchronous and asynchronous contact. Another serious concern was that students with disabilities and those that are disadvantaged could suffer exclusion through online teaching. Lecturers also reported that they missed their students and especially the reciprocity of embodied teaching and learning/meaning making. Using online teaching in support of face-to-face teaching is felt to be very different from teaching fully online. Another interesting and important finding is that they experienced the hybrid mode of teaching, where some students are present in class and others attend online, to be complicated, and therefore less effective. Online teaching is also conceived to be more time consuming because lecturers must redesign their programs and adjust or change the form of assessments.[11]

---

9. Taneja et al., "Cyber-Slacking in the Classroom," 144.
10. Davis and Phillips, "Teaching during COVID 19," 68.
11. Davis and Phillips, "Teaching during COVID 19," 75–78.

The fourth and final study was carried out with theology students at the University of Pretoria and the University of the Free State during the COVID-19 pandemic between 2019 and 2020. The aim was to establish students' experiences of the different modes of teaching and learning such as face-to-face, online, and hybrid. This chapter provides a helpful background to the unique contextual challenges and opportunities of higher education in South Africa, with specific reference to theological education.[12] The main finding, given the aim of the study, is that students prefer a hybrid or blended learning mode of teaching rather than fully online or only face-to-face teaching. Although it seems that they understand the value of face-to-face teaching, they do not view that as the norm anymore, especially after their experiences of fully online teaching during COVID-19. Those who prefer face-to-face teaching are motivated by the embodied experience of teaching, for example, the value of socializing, including physical contact and discussions with both students and lecturers. Interestingly, some relate online teaching and learning more to content, and face-to-face learning more to understanding and meaning making. The importance of socioeconomic context and factors is highlighted by the fact that those who prefer online teaching referred to factors like saving time, having the opportunity to structure their study time better—especially if they are working—cost of traveling, etc. Finally, there was an indication that some subjects, in this case practical theology, should rather be taught face-to-face.[13]

These studies demonstrate that students have insight about their own learning behavior and possess value knowledge about what they regard as the most effective teaching and learning process.

RESEARCH DESIGN AND PARTICIPANTS

The research question is: What are the views and experiences of both students and lecturers of TML during the lockdown period and how could that inform the effective integration of TML in teaching and learning at the faculty in the future? On March 15, 2020, the president of South Africa, Cyril Ramaphosa, declared a national state of disaster and followed this with the announcement on March 23 of a national lockdown that was effective from March 27, 2020. On April 4, 2022, the national state of disaster was terminated.[14] Therefore, the period between March 2020 and April 2022 is the focus of the empirical investigation. The unit of analysis was

12. Knoetze, "Online Theological Education," 3–7.
13. Knoetze, "Online Theological Education," 6.
14. See "COVID-19 Pandemic."

lecturers and students at the Faculty of Theology, Stellenbosch University. The data-gathering method was basic online individual interviews with open-ended questions. MS Teams was used by the university as the online platform for teaching and learning during the lockdown; therefore it was utilized for this study, because students and lecturers were familiar with the online platform. Interviews were recorded using voice, not video call, to provide a comfortable and effective distance between the researcher and participants. Ethical clearance was obtained from the Ethics Committee of Stellenbosch University (Project THE-2022–26382).

Purposive sampling was used[15] as students and lecturers were in the best position to answer the research question and provide guidance on the meaningful integration of TLM at the faculty. I taught students in both the year groups used in the study during the lockdown and relied on the relationship that we built during a difficult time of teaching and learning for a positive response rate. Currently approximately seventy students in each of the selected year groups are enrolled for a compulsory module, meaning students of all programs offered should take the module. I had a better response rate from third-year students (seven) than second-year students (five) and four out of twenty-eight lecturers at the faculty. In total I conducted sixteen interviews, which is an efficient representation of the chosen units of analysis.

FINDINGS

The next section will report on the findings using identified themes with supporting quotes from the empirical investigation, followed by a short discussion. Content or thematic analysis is used to interpret the data,[16] where recurring words or themes are identified and used to systematically present the data. L identifies a lecturer, SY a second-year student, and TY a third-year student. During the interviews I used the phrase "fully online teaching," because that was the term used at Stellenbosch University and was therefore familiar to participants.

---

15. Babbie and Mouton, *Practice of Social Research*, 289.
16. Babbie and Mouton, *Practice of Social Research*, 249.

DEVICES USED DURING ONLINE TEACHING AND LEARNING (FOTL)

Most students used both their smart phones and laptops to access online teaching and learning (FOTL). Initially, many had only a phone while waiting for a laptop provided by the university. Phones were used to listen to classes and submit assignments because it was easier to download applications on phones than on laptops. Although students were familiar with using their phones for communication and entertainment, it seems it was difficult to use the same device for teaching and learning.

TY: "I used both my phone and laptop, sometimes I struggled with laptop then I used the phone because the phone has all applications."

TY: "I used my phone for online classes and the laptop to do assignments. My laptop could not download SunLearn, but my phone is not suitable for studies as the screen is too small and the sound is not good."

SY: "I used both, but the layout is different on the devices. Laptop is better for your eyes. The situation with the devices can get complicated."

Students who did not have smart phones or a laptop experienced serious problems in proceeding with their studies during online teaching.

TY: "It was a bad experience because I did not have a cell phone that was working or a laptop. I was staying in private accommodation and had to walk far to campus to borrow other students' devices. I waited five weeks for a laptop, and I am not good with technology I am still struggling with it."

Most lecturers acknowledged that they did not think much about which devices students used but realized later that it could have had an impact on their experience of OTL during the pandemic.

L: "I did not check that, but I guess they have used both phones especially in the beginning as all did not have laptops."

L: "We were much focused on ourselves in other words self-absorbed and to find a suitable space to present lectures online. I recorded and presented my lecturers from my car as I could not find a quiet enough spot in the house during the hard lockdown."

L: "A cellphone is extension of them [the students], not a laptop."

CHALLENGES EXPERIENCED WITH FULLY FOTL

Lack of computer skills, time constraints, and emotional stress/strain

Most described their overall challenge as feeling overwhelmed and unprepared for the sudden move from face-to-face classes to fully online classes. What contributed to this experience was the fact that many had limited knowledge and skills to use a laptop. A few second-year students explained that they started the year late during their first year and therefore they never managed to use the university's academic platform, SunLearn, effectively.

SY: "I missed the orientation week and was sometimes using the wrong link to submit assignments and tests—I did not understand the difference between the links."

SY: "I had very basic knowledge about how to use a laptop and the people at home could not assist because they don't have laptops. I watched YouTube videos for guidance on how to use a laptop. Study time become limited because you must learn all these other things. Nobody assisted me but I had the burden of assisting many others."

TY: "The quality of your experience depends on your computer skills."

TY: "Online is more tiring, in person communication energises me. Online is not the same, I still feel tired because online drains you emotionally and physically."

TY: "I felt stuck, stressed out, in a corner."

A lecturer made a striking comment regarding how online teaching impacted especially the third-year students:

L: "They have been in COVID longer and were not exposed to lecturers and other students. There is an intellectual ethos formed, in an informal way through contact with senior students. They have not been exposed to this process and, therefore, missed out on the formation of critical faculties outside class."

For others there were too many transitions in a short period of time, and they could not manage all the demands made by fully online classes in particular.

SY: "It was a stressful transition from school to university and the fully online was very difficult as I was not used to online services."

TY: "We did not have time to release the stress; things just keep on changing."

L: "Effective communication because there could easily be miscommunication when you work online. Effective OTL depends a lot on the skills of lecturers."

L: "The modality change was huge and immediate, and I was anxious about it."

Workload: Overassessing?

Many students felt the workload was more than what they experienced during face-to-face teaching. This should be viewed in conjunction with the time they needed to train themselves to use their laptops, applications, and other software effectively.

TY: "Workload was the biggest challenge for me—there were more assessments all these tasks and the reading was too much."

SY: "The workload was too much, even the online resources were overwhelming."

SY: "There were too many small assignments."

TY: "We just submit for the sake of submitting and not because we are learning."

L: "COVID caught us by surprise without training for both students and lecturers."

L: "I used some assessments as preparation for class."

L: "We should think carefully about our assessment strategy."

Disembodied teaching and learning

Many students and lecturers referred to the loss of contact and feeling of disconnectedness. One lecturer made an interesting point in this regard:

L: "Students were mostly muted behind these devices."

L: "I felt disconnected because I could not read the students' facial expressions. I felt mechanistic."

L: "We were robbed from feedback from students, their facial expressions, and body language—the devices create a nonresponsive environment."

L: "It felt like speaking into this void and that was frustrating. It felt more like [a] package I deliver."

SY: "An impersonal situation was enforced on us."

TY: "I felt lonely—I study better with others."

SY: "I had a lot of assistance in my first year, now I was on my own."

TY: "We cannot see each other, and we are afraid to answer questions online."

TY: "Students forget their identity as students when they are online—because you are at home and not at the university."

TY: "You cannot connect online—you can do more in person for instance you can see when people struggle and help them."

Cyber-slacking and how it impacts on attention

Most students agreed that they participated in behavior that could be described as cyber-slacking. Students gave examples of things they are interested in like football and TikTok, which led to cyber-slacking during FOTL.

SY: "It does occur with many students."

SY: "I developed that, when something pops up, I lose concentration. Like I am interested in the war in Ukraine so I will read any news about that."

SY: "It is a big disturbance. Students log in but don't listen to the lecture."

TY: "Honestly it is a big challenge."

TY: "My Facebook was open all the time during class. I minimize teams during class time. I never had TikTok but downloaded it during online classes. My attention was diverted most of the time."

    Some students recommended that lecturers ask students not to use devices during classes in order to help the whole class to focus, although others thought some students may not respond positively to such a request. Others indicated they prefer not to take out their devices during class—although this seems to refer only to in-person classes where lecturers have more control over what happens in the classroom.

For most lecturers, cyber-slacking does not seem to be a challenge when teaching, which is understandable because they must keep the class going albeit in person or online. They did, however, admit that when they are only listening during a lecture or a meeting, they lose concentration and do other online work like answering emails. One lecturer made an interesting observation about the role of the internet even before COVID-19:

L: "Our minds are always distracted, and this became a radical crisis during COVID-19. We were already isolated due to the use of the internet and COVID just legitimized this isolation."

L: "Social media waste our time."

L: "I don't use a lot of applications on my phone and put my phone face down during online classes."

LESSONS LEARNED AND SKILLS DEVELOPED

Apart from learning how to use a laptop and online platforms more effectively, many students pointed to growth points developed that could be described as autonomous learning. Alizadeh and Ebrahimi define *autonomous learning* as when there is a transition of control of the learning process from the teacher to the students.[17] Autonomous learning includes learning outside and inside the classroom or education system as well as willingness, motivation, and confidence in students.

Autonomous learning, learning styles, and spiritual growth

SY: "I was very determined because I waited four years to come to an Institution of Higher Education and I was not going to give up and was determined to make this work also for my family. I taught myself to master the laptop."

SY: "I learned to manage my time better and feel I matured quicker because you have to set your own schedule. I think these are skills that are growing more."

TY: "I learned to be more disciplined, better time management and took control of my own schedule. We did not have connections and had to learn to balance everything and persevere."

17. Alizadeh and Ebrahimi, "Investigating Medical Students' Readiness," 3290.

TY: "I learned how to adapt as the situation was constantly changing and to be flexible."

TY: "I learn more when I read than listen and prefer to wrestle with material; that is my learning style. I also remember better when I read."

TY: "Online study taught me to appreciate my studies—forced me to self-discipline and to read more than what is prescribed, to do research. I discovered new websites and applications on my laptop."

TY: "Online learning taught me to be more disciplined, to be on time, which was important at the beginning. I made summaries before class, something I did not do before and keep on doing now."

Lecturers, however, are not convinced that students became more autonomous during fully online teaching.

L: "I received many emails. I think students became more dependent on lecturers, maybe because we did not see each other, and they want to make sure we are still there for them."

L: "Not sure about that one—some ways yes, some ways no. They could not see you after class, so they sent many emails. Many dropped out and did not attend class."

Lecturers also reported that they learned and practiced new skills that were not as evident when they were teaching in person classes.

L: "Yes it takes extra work to get students into online classes. I have experience of online teaching and had 80 percent class attendance because I did not only send a link for the class but also sent an extra reminder to students with a personal message on the importance of the class and their responsibility to attend."

L: "I learned to think critically not only about what I will present but also how I will present myself."

L: "We as human beings are resilient, and we can adapt. Sometimes we can become very dependent on tried exercises and pedagogical tools and COVID disrupted this, and we had to rethink the pedagogical tools we use."

Others referred to spiritual growth experienced during this difficult time that also impacted positively on their learning process.

TY: "My relationship with God grew and became stronger and we prayed for others."

TY: "Conversation with God and people is much better now although I am an introvert."

SY: "I was very unsure on this new journey and wondered where is God? Later I realized God was present through friends, because they helped to improve my computer skills."

TY: "I thought to worship God I must go to church, but I learned that I could worship God in my own space. COVID took me out of my comfort zone to know God better."

HYBRID/BLENDED TEACHING AND LEARNING

On a question about the hybrid options available during COVID-19, most students believe having these options (online or in person) was relevant during that time, but since we are at a different (safer) stage regarding the pandemic, these options should not be available anymore. Others prefer the option when it is indicated on the course outline that some classes will be only in person and others only online. Others complained about the impact on class attendance when there is an online option. Students who prefer the online options relate this to their circumstances, like having a family, having to travel, lack of funding, etc.

SY: "Online option should stay because it is best due to my circumstances. I am staying far away, and I will therefore choose online."

TY: "Students that are at risk [are] students [who] never go to class even though they are struggling."

One of the third-year students explained how the experience of being taught fully online for two years is affecting the group now:

TY: "We are struggling in person and there are different reasons like we have never been a group/unity/community. We became used to studies online. It is comfortable doing studies from home, now travelling becomes a challenge. Many have mental health challenges; do we recognize that? The expectation is we should just go back while we don't see the value of making that change again—it is too many adjustments."

L: "It is going to stay—basically because it is a bigger change in culture of universities and as business model it is believed to be more successful. The question if it is better is not necessarily the most important question. Therefore, residential priorities need to be enforced and hybrid options can't just be a duplication of residential classes and activities. A different model is needed to do hybrid and that places lots of pressure on staff. To prevent a faculty without bodies a definitive strategy is needed to have embodied interpersonal teaching that creates community."

L: "I have mixed feelings about hybrid and think there need to be very strong arguments for hybrid teaching. A lot of energy goes into managing a technological environment and teaching becomes a secondary aspect. I felt tired and discontented—felt like it was a waste of time."

L: "Many were online but not really there; it was if they were wearing masks in class. I felt stuck—a sage of the stage. I make use of case studies and group work during teaching and that did not work with hybrid teaching."

TEACHING THEOLOGY IN FUTURE: FACE-TO-FACE TEACHING

Responses to a question about what the best option (hybrid or in person) is for teaching and learning theology provided data about participants' understanding of theology and how they learn.

SY: "Like for instance practical theology, service learning, group work make sense to be in person."

SY: "To have theology in person is very good choice—learn from other students and lecturers."

SY: "It is better to study theology in community because you can hear different opinions and grow."

TY: "You need the learning community to grow as spiritual leader."

TY: "Theology is very personal, and we need to use the library."

TY: "I think it will be best that the subject of theology be taught in person because there are different aspects to theology, and it is good to hear more than one perspective, different voices. It is a broad field and geared toward practice. Embodied presence makes a difference in how info is communicated and how you learn. Body language helps you to understand information and what is important or where you need to do more research. In person you can see the body language of both students and lecturers."

L: "Hybrid is possible to some extent, but I don't know how many lectures are ready for that—lecturers should get more training. I will encourage hybrid mode for postgraduate programs."

L: "The focus must be residential learning and if any form of hybrid is offered it should be well managed. Embodied teaching and learning should not become optional."

L: "Theology is learned in a community—it is about relationships. In online it remains a simulation—students miss that connection."

DISCUSSION: COMPARING EXPERIENCE OF STUDENTS AND LECTURERS

It is evident from the data that the impact of the lockdown on teaching and learning as well as mental health was significant. The question is, how do we bring this into consideration in the teaching space going forward? It seems that the third-year students' experiences differed from those of the second years, mainly because they had to rely on FOTL for a greater proportion of their course. Lecturers also experienced challenges in terms of how they facilitated teaching and learning in a virtual space. Both students and lecturers could identify new skills gained. Lecturers differ from students in regard to whether students developed autonomous learning skills during FOTL. This however does not mean we can disregard what students learned. They also disagree about the impact of cyber-slacking on their attention. Lecturers do not have as many applications on their devices that could divert their attention and, therefore, cyber-slacking among lecturers is limited. Students, on the other hand, could explain, with appropriate examples, what causes them to cyber-slack. In general, lecturers and students agree on their choice of in-person teaching for a discipline like theology. Students could describe their preference for in-person teaching quite eloquently, in considering their understanding of theology. This is in line with how both groups articulated their negative experience of disembodied teaching and learning. For both groups, embodiment and the learning community are essential for teaching and learning theology. However, some students believe hybrid options should be available, especially considering the socioeconomic challenges students experience. It seems that for these students the quality of the learning experience is not their first concern, accessibility is their main concern. A few students also argued for any online or hybrid option because they found that they learn better that way and prefer to study at their own pace and time. An interesting finding is that, although the online platform used for online teaching provided options for interaction, both lecturers and students reported that interaction was extremely limited. Students' feedback regarding being overassessed to the point that it does not necessarily facilitate learning, deserves attention. Although these results cannot be generalized, the study does provide valuable information that could inform future teaching and learning strategies.

CONCLUSION

This chapter draws on secondary data on TML that also provides theoretical framing for the empirical work done. The question remains, how does the new data generated by this research correlate—or not—with the secondary data used? In considering this question, I would like to highlight a few findings that stood out concerning the medium used and its impact on the learning process. Although technological devices can enable interactive communication, it seems that was mostly not the case as became clear through both the responses of lectures and the study carried out by Davis and Phillips, who postulated that students were not engaging during online class discussions.[18] Another factor regarding the medium is that although it could connect students and lecturers, students indicated that they felt isolated and lonely despite being connected via online platforms. As mentioned at the beginning of this chapter, students' attention is necessary for learning to happen. Students' attention, however, is a limited and scarce resource and therefore cannot be assumed. It was clear that despite the fact that online platforms connect students and lecturers, the same medium can also provide a great deal of other information that can cause students to cyber slack during online teaching and learning.[19] Therefore, online classes are competing with other platforms that interfere with the student's attention. Many students indicated that they were not digitally literate and struggled to use a computer, a reflection of the digital divide. "Access to technology and technological literacy are a part of the challenges faced in a developing country like South Africa. These challenges are often described as the digital divide referring to those that have access to technology and technological skills and those that do not."[20] Most students believed they were overassessed during FOTL and that it took a lot of their time, while the assessments did not necessarily prepare them for summative assessments like tests or examinations. In a study on assessment during COVID-19, Almossa reached similar

18. Dawis and Phillips, "Teaching during COVID 19," 75–78.
19. Taneja et al., "Cyber-Slacking in the Classroom."
20. Cloete, "Technology and Education," 4.

conclusions and states: "Online teaching has become an online assessment crisis."[21] Moreover, lecturers tried to cover too much work in a short period, which led to information overload and overassessing students. These findings imply that being connected online does not automatically result in engagement, and therefore lecturers need to use activities and visual material as proposed by Bester and Brand to get students' attention.[22] Furthermore, assessment should not increase during online teaching, because it does not necessarily assist students to learn. Therefore, assessment strategies should be carefully planned and executed.

BIBLIOGRAPHY

Alizadeh, Iman, and Faridah Ebrahimi. "Investigating Medical Students' Readiness for Technology—Mediated Autonomous Learning Situations in ESP Programs." *Education and Information Technologies* 24 (2019) 3289–309.

Almossa, Samar Yakoob. "University Students' Perspectives towards Learning and Assessment during COVID-19." *Education and Information Technologies* 26 (2021) 7163–81. https://doi.org/10.1007/s10639-021-10554-8.

Babbie, Earl, and Johann Mouton. *The Practice of Social Research*. South African ed. Cape Town: Oxford University Press, 2012.

Bester, G., and L. Brand. "The Effect of Technology on Learner Attention and Achievement." *South African Journal of Education* 33 (2013) 1–15.

Cloete, Anita. "Technology and Education: Challenges and Opportunities." *HvTSt* 73 (2017) 1–7.

"COVID-19 Pandemic in South Africa." Wikipedia, last edited Jan. 5, 2024. https://en.wikipedia.org/wiki/COVID-19_pandemic_in_South_Africa.

Davis, Susan, and Louise Gwenneth Phillips. "Teaching during COVID 19 Times: The Experiences of Drama and Performing Arts Teachers and the Human Dimensions of Learning." *Drama Australia Journal* 44 (2020) 66–87.

Knoetze, Johannes J. "Online Theological Education within the South African Context." *HvTSt* 78 (2020) 1–7. https://doi.org/10.4102/hts.v78i1.7232.

Taneja, A., et al. "Cyber-Slacking in the Classroom: Potential for Digital Distraction in the New Age." *Computers & Education* 82 (2015) 141–51.

Wang, Sufen, et al. "Development and Measurement Validity of and Instrument for the Impact of Technology-Mediated Learning on Learning Process." *Computers & Education* 121 (2018) 131–42.

---

21. Almossa, "University Students' Perspectives," 7169.
22. Bester and Brand, "Effect of Technology," 14.

Chapter 8

Teaching and Learning Theology in Crisis

Reflecting on the Benefits of Collaborative Online International Learning (COIL)

Ian Nell

INTRODUCTION

South Africa, like many other countries, was caught off guard by COVID-19. Not only did urgent plans have to be made regarding the management and control of the pandemic, but its effects on education were devastating. We have seen how many educators and teachers have experienced this threat firsthand, and there are many who actually became very ill, and some who even died. There are numerous scholars who believe that the pandemic brought to the surface many of the underlying problems in education, specifically tertiary education. But it is not only in South Africa that we experienced the challenges of the pandemic; countries all over the world were hit hard.

As a faculty member, I became interested in how we could also share some of these experiences in international exchange by collaborating with faculty members in other countries. An opportunity for me came to the fore after Stellenbosch University started a joint research project with NLA University College in Bergen, Norway, during 2021. From the start I was interested to see what the benefits of using collaborative online international learning (COIL) could be. I was interested in looking at content, pedagogy, and methodology. From the literature I realized that COIL can be used as a method to encourage collaboration between students and lecturers on two campuses to enhance their academic skills. COIL presents a rich learning experience for students, particularly during a pandemic and distance learning. I was also convinced that COIL could be continued even when face-to-face instruction resumed. Many universities can adopt this model. In this contribution I want to explore these different themes.

COLLABORATIVE PRACTICAL THEOLOGY

Before we pay attention to some theoretical perspectives, it is important to remember that collaboration is not something that is totally new in the world of academia and more specifically within the field of practical theology. The recent publication by the Dutch practical theologian Henk de Roest uses the telling title: *Collaborative Practical Theology*. According to De Roest, we are all part of a common and global research community.[1] As practical theologians, we have all already experienced how this collaborative research takes place in a community of colleagues in seminars, journals, conferences, and both online and offline gatherings. Research that takes place in collaboration between practical theologians, practitioners, and everyday believers helps to make the process a truly communal enterprise. De Roest puts it this way: "I envisage a 'communal' or 'relational' turn in the process of collaborative research on Christian practices."[2]

According to Phillips et al., collaborative research can be understood as part of a "dialogic turn" across diverse fields of social practice:

> In the dialogic turn, communication is conceived as a dialogue among participants in which knowledge is co-produced collaboratively. . . . Common to all the fields of social practice in the dialogic turn is a retreat, at least rhetorically, from the idea of communication as one-way flow—that is, knowledge transmission, diffusion, dissemination, or transfer—from experts to less knowledgeable target groups. Instead, a conception of communication as processes of dialogue is embraced in which the different participants co-produce knowledge collaboratively on the basis of the different knowledge forms that they bring into play when they meet and collaborate.[3]

---

1. De Roest, *Collaborative Practical Theology*, 1.
2. De Roest, *Collaborative Practical Theology*, 2.
3. Phillips et al., "Tackling the Tensions," 1–2.

According to De Roest, the so-called dialogic turn is not only good news for practical theology in different contexts, but is also full of promise for both teaching and research in the communities it serves and where practitioners work.[4] When practitioners are spoken of, one thinks of pastoral workers, parish evangelists, pastors, pastoral counselors, teachers of theology, and ministers, among others. Research in practical theology often has to do with these practitioners' concerns, challenges, and experiences, although the rest of the community's activities are never out of sight. One of the challenges of practical theology is to reflect on these practitioners' practices and offer knowledge and sometimes even give instructions about the "know-how," "know-why," and "know-what."

What is important to understand here is that many of the questions that end up being researched emerge from shared experiences and challenges. This is also the case with our project. Our research arose from our shared experience of the crisis that the pandemic caused in our teaching and learning activities, not only at the local level, but also at the international level. Collectively, we have a need to find out how we can teach better and differently, conduct research, develop programs, and learn new competencies. That is why it is gratifying to see how many new methods of collaborative research in the field of practical theology have developed over the last decade in all the different subdisciplines. In this regard, it is especially action research that has received a renewed focus, and Elaine Graham was at the forefront of this development. Collaboration in action research methods enjoys particular attention and enables practical theologians to help people "in the well-springs of tradition from which practical wisdom flows."[5]

The pandemic forced us into COIL projects. It was also one of the objectives of the Teaching and Learning in Crisis project to explore the mutual processes of teaching and learning. Religious communication, which needs to be defined in more detail, can be traced online and offline in the context of social networks. Online practices form part of the connections found in everyday life, resulting in fluid transitions. In other words, the separation between online and offline practices seems less and less plausible. Research must react to this through a "conceptual shift" that focuses on the "in-between."[6] Marres explains as follows:

> The main attraction of digital sociology is precisely that it enables the development of experimental forms of inquiry that cut across the divides between the sciences and the humanities. It

---

4. De Roest, *Collaborative Practical Theology*, 26.
5. Graham, "Is Practical Theology," 178.
6. Przybylski, *Hybrid Ethnography*, 4.

may develop and inform richer approaches to 'data interpretation', more adventurous ways of introducing social theory into the space of digital research.[7]

Before going into the details of how COIL works, it is important to reflect on some creative models around the world deployed in online teaching/learning of theology.

CREATIVE MODELS AROUND THE WORLD

The South African scholar Jennifer Roberts explores the connections between online learning and distance education, specifically in the context of theology. The author argues that online learning can be viewed as a form of distance education, and as such, it can be understood through the theories and practices that have developed in the field of distance education. The author notes that distance education has evolved over time, with the shift towards online learning and the use of technology in education. Roberts draws on the work of several scholars in the field of distance education to explore the different models and theories of distance education. These include transactional distance theory, social constructivist theory, and the community of inquiry framework. The author then applies these theories to the context of online learning in theology, exploring how they can inform the design and delivery of online courses. Her article concludes by emphasizing the importance of understanding online learning as a form of distance education, and the need to apply theories and practices from the field of distance education to the design and delivery of online courses.[8]

Selçuk et al. examined the impact of the COVID-19 pandemic on the online learning experience of theology students in Turkey. The study involved seventy-five participants, who completed a survey and participated in focus group interviews. The findings suggest that while the transition to online learning was challenging for both students and instructors, it also presented new opportunities for theological education, such as increased access to resources and a more flexible learning environment. However, participants also expressed concerns about the lack of personal interaction and community building that typically occur in traditional classroom settings. The authors argue that the pandemic highlighted the need for a new disposition for religious education, one that embraces the potential of technology while also recognizing the importance of interpersonal relationships

---

7. Marres, *Digital Sociology*, 6.
8. Roberts, "Online Learning."

and community building. They suggest that this new disposition can be fostered by incorporating more collaborative and interactive learning activities into online theological education, as well as by emphasizing the importance of community building and personal relationships in both online and traditional classroom settings.[9]

Two American scholars, Lowe and Lowe, discuss the challenges and opportunities for spiritual formation in theological distance education from their context. The authors propose an "ecosystems model" that considers the interconnectedness of various factors that impact spiritual formation, including the student, the instructor, the institution, the curriculum, and the (online) community. The article explores each of these factors in detail and offers suggestions for how they can be integrated to create a holistic approach to spiritual formation in theological distance and online education. Ultimately, the authors argue that spiritual formation is essential in theological education and that online distance education can provide unique opportunities for students to grow spiritually, despite the challenges it presents.[10]

Melinda Thompson, another American scholar, explores the challenges and opportunities of providing theological education through online platforms for students from different cultural backgrounds. The author argues that online theological education offers greater accessibility to students from different parts of the world, but cultural differences and language barriers can pose significant challenges. Thompson emphasizes the importance of cultural sensitivity in designing and delivering online theological education programs. She suggests that instructors should take into consideration the cultural context of their students, their communication styles, learning preferences, and theological perspectives. The author also discusses the potential benefits of online theological education, such as the ability to connect with diverse theological perspectives and learn from experienced instructors from around the world. However, she also notes that online education can lack the personal interaction and community-building opportunities of traditional classroom education. Overall, Thompson's article highlights the need for online theological education to be culturally sensitive and responsive to the needs of diverse learners.[11]

With some presentation of past research around collaborative online teaching and learning from different contexts and continents, we can now move to the distinctiveness of COIL among these other different models of

9. Selçuk et al., "Online Learning Experience."
10. Lowe and Lowe, "Spiritual Formation."
11. Thompson, "To Ends of Earth."

online teaching/learning collaboration. For this purpose, I want to start by asking the following question:

WHY IS IT IMPORTANT TO "REFLECT" ON COLLABORATIVE TEACHING AND LEARNING?

According to Roebben, there are three important reasons why a process of good reflection is needed on what and how we teach and learn. The first is a "professional" reason. Anyone who wants to act professionally must know what he/she is doing. In order to plan, carry out, and evaluate a learning process well, one must have one's own identity. Therefore, one must be certain about the field in which one can provide guidance. One's words, thoughts, and actions must be recognizable to colleagues and students. In other words, it is about professional durability and credibility.[12]

The second reason to reflect on teaching and learning is a "pedagogical" reason. Here it is important to notice and value each student in his/her own development. However, the distinctiveness of a pedagogical profession also goes beyond simply noticing students and it is namely to challenge them intellectually to grow further and develop new insights and make these insights their own. Good pedagogy therefore also often has to do with resistance from students and demands that we must still try to keep "seeing" them in the midst of their resistance.[13]

Finally, there is a "spiritual" reason to reflect on learning and teaching. If one bears in mind that most of the students feel called to what they are doing, this is equally true of those who do the teaching. In fact, the awareness of one's calling to participate in the learning process is at the heart of what it means to act professionally, pedagogically, and didactically. Those who want to improve the world also experience a certain "holy restlessness," because they want to make a difference. Roebben refers in this regard to a poster he once saw in Boston that read: "Make a difference: become a teacher."[14] Vocation is connected to this motto; one feels called upon and responsible to make a difference. With a better idea of why we want to reflect on COIL, we can now dwell on the question: How does it work?,

---

12. Roebben, *Scholen voor het leven*, 10.
13. Roebben, *Scholen voor het leven*, 12.
14. Roebben, *Scholen voor het leven*, 13.

HOW DOES IT WORK?

Online international collaboration is basically about connecting two classrooms in different parts of the world with two lecturers in different continents teaching about some topics in the same or different disciplines.[15] In the case of the collaboration between Stellenbosch and NLA, it was master classes where we taught together in the fields of practical theology, rhetoric, and leadership. The teaching and learning can be done through projects, assignments, or an already-designed curriculum. COIL projects can be structured in terms of time over different periods, but usually include an icebreaker during which participants are introduced to one another and introductory remarks are made, collaborative teaching, a common assignment, and then time for reflection afterwards.

COIL is therefore an enabling enterprise with a view to involving everyone in the classroom in the subject under discussion, and there are different ways of organizing projects around these subjects. According to Chun, there are several benefits for both the lecturers and the students, which will be addressed in the next section.[16] However, we must bear in mind that there are also some constraints regarding the technology, which can often lead to great frustration and of which we also have firsthand experience.

THEORETICAL PERSPECTIVES

In this part I will try to build a theory around the benefits of COIL by making use of the work of Chun, Dweck, Gokcora, Simpson, Wenger, and Gokcora and Everson.[17] Taking my cue from their writings, the following six perspectives are discussed:

1. COIL projects provide academic freedom and pluralistic points of view

Wenger introduced us to communities of practice and the way in which learning, meaning, and identity take shape in these communities. According to Wenger, "Communities of practice are groups of people who share a concern or a passion for something they do and learn how to do it better

---

15. Guth, *COIL Institute*.
16. Chun, "Language and Culture Learning."
17. Chun, "Language and Culture Learning"; Dweck, "What Having a 'Growth Mindset' Means"; Gokcora, "Benefits"; Simpson, "Integrating Technology with Literacy"; Wenger, *Communities of Practice*; Gokcora and Everson, "Making Connections."

as they interact regularly."[18] In COIL courses, the aim is to build a community of practice with a community of students with a view to creating space for students to learn from one another in a successful way. Students from different backgrounds bring different perspectives to the classroom, talk about them, and therefore share knowledge with one another, which in turn enriches the curriculum. Lecturers, in turn, work together to bring topics to the program that would be difficult to integrate without collaboration. For example, in a lecture on leadership, we had input from Professor Bård Norheim from NLA, after which Norheim asked the students from Stellenbosch to explain their understanding of his theory from their context. In this way, we all came to a shared understanding or the cultural significance of the topic. This ensures that all the students are involved with one another and develop a mindset that helps them to grow and learn in diverse contexts.

2. Peer-to-peer learning motivates students to become engaged in projects

One of the most important things that happens when students learn together is that they become information providers for one another. In a collaborative learning environment, knowledge is transferred and shared while working on joint projects and paying attention to certain learning objectives. In this way, they also develop a shared understanding of the subject and at the same time develop a common problem-solving ability. We must remember that students are not passive agents of the learning process, but that they play an active role in the process of knowledge acquisition. The latter happens as they discuss the topics together, look for information together, and exchange it with one another. As peers, they therefore create knowledge together and there is no one specific student who is in possession of the course material or who may have received it from the lecturer. The students can of course also assess one another's work as peers.

3. Lecturers are less concerned about the violation of academic integrity

Without consulting any written sources, the students generate new ideas and original knowledge and, in the process, also give feedback on one another's work. By engaging in conversation with one another, the students gain new information from their fellow students and maintain their academic

18. Wenger, *Communities of Practice*, 3.

integrity. COIL projects therefore, in a way, prevent the acquisition of information from external sources, as the information is created through the interaction of the students in their group. Through the collaboration of the students, a primary source of information is therefore created.[19] Peer assessment of one another's projects provides an opportunity to build knowledge together and enables students to establish a certain degree of autonomy.

4. Students establish critical thinking and global awareness

Many students, especially in South Africa, do not have the financial support to participate in programs abroad. In this regard, COIL offers an excellent opportunity to gain something of a foreign experience. Lecturers with writing skills also create important learning opportunities and, in the process, bring new ideas to students' attention. According to Simpson, it can also help the students with the development of critical thinking skills, writing skills, and a global consciousness.[20] For example, in discussing the different challenges facing practical theology in South Africa, it was interesting to listen to the way the students related the challenges to their own contexts, and we could all learn from one another's perspectives. It also helps to understand that one social problem at one location (for example, poverty) can be a global issue.

5. Students can become engaged in interdisciplinary learning

A further advantage of COIL projects is related to the fact that it is possible to bring courses that do not have a direct connection with one another into conversation with one another. Two lecturers from different countries can therefore work together to develop certain outcomes and objectives for these courses. In our case, it was related to rhetoric, leadership, and homiletics (Norheim) on the one hand, and cultural hermeneutics and leadership competencies (Nell) on the other hand. This form of interdisciplinary exchange helps promote careers in both faculties in question. In this way, students establish better networks and career skills, and the lecturers in turn find opportunities for scholarly collaboration.

---

19. Gokcora and Everson, "Making Connections."
20. Simpson, "Integrating Technology with Literacy."

6. Students gain digital literacy by engaging in online tasks

One of the important advantages of COIL projects is that they can be presented in different modes. It is possible to offer them fully online or in hybrid or face-to-face classes. In the process, the students also get exposure to the use of online tools that they can practice using in their projects and assignments. Furthermore, it is a case that each lecturer makes use of his/her own learning management system. In our case, Norheim (Norway) used Zoom, while Nell (South Africa) used MS Teams. It is interesting to see that as students learn to use these platforms, they improve and develop cross-cultural communication. In the process there is also the refinement of academic writing skills and research skills, assessment, and peer review skills, as well as critical technical literacy skills.

The six perspectives discussed above are also consistent with many of the general learning objectives found in higher education all over the world. The attractiveness of a variety of technologies and instruments at our disposal does not mean that lecturers must make use of them all. COIL does motivate students to participate in joint projects and it is important for lecturers who are in partnership with one another to strategically place the students in groups. The latter is the case because the so-called matching also requires a psychological and emotional exchange. Furthermore, it is also essential that lecturers should remember to encourage intrinsic motivation in students, as this form of behavior produces the best results.

METHODOLOGY

Making use of the theoretical perspectives developed in the previous section, a qualitative study was conducted to explore and understand the factors that the students found the most interesting concerning COIL. I also tried to find out what their thoughts were about the pedagogy used in the class and where they lost interest and what they found less interesting. Three research questions were posed to eleven students who all formed part of the master of divinity course at Stellenbosch University. Responses were captured in paper format and then sealed in an envelope. Participants could choose to respond in depth or briefly, at their own choosing.

Interpretative phenomenological analysis has seen a growth curve during the last twenty years.[21] This type of analysis forms part of qualitative research methodologies and is used in a wide variety of research contexts.

---

21. Shaw et al., *Sage Research Methods Cases*; Smith, "Interpretative Phenomenological Analysis."

This methodology provides a helpful way to "study lived experience with particular interest in the meaning-making processes involved in understanding individual experiences within certain contexts."[22] The data from the answers to the questions were powerful and graphic, and prompted the need for some reflection.

The three questions that I asked were the following:

1. What were the most interesting things you learned from the lecture? And how will it shape your ministry?
2. What did you think about the teaching methods used (pedagogy) in the class?
3. What did you find less interesting? Where did you lose attention?

FINDINGS

Concerning the *most interesting things learned* from the data taking the theoretical perspectives into consideration, I found that most of the students did indeed enjoy the theoretical framework put forward by the lecturer, and from the data we can see that peer-to-peer learning did indeed occur (perspectives 1–3). The theoretical framework that was discussed is the theory that was developed by Norheim and Haga in their book *The Four Speeches Every Leader Has to Know*. After an introduction on a rhetoric of suffering, the authors discuss the opening speech (envisioning the future), the executioner speech (communicating tough decisions), the consolation speech (the leader as comforter), and the farewell speech (leaving a legacy worth suffering for).

Here are three examples from the data:

- "The four aspects of the speech really helped me to know that there are different approaches that can be used to form a sermon and more specifically how the two middle speeches, suffering 1 and suffering 2, are used in speeches to address an audience more specifically."
- "One of the most interesting things that I learned was the importance of trust in ministry. There is often the assumption that leaders always have influence over the people they lead. This is however not true. Learning how to build and maintain this trust through making use of the four speeches is definitely something that I will make use of in ministry, especially as we are starting in our own ministries very soon."

22. Holland, *Teaching in Higher Education*, 12.

- "The three main thoughts regarding influence, persuasion, and trust, as well as the four parts of a speech—introducing yourself, naming reality, forming/stating a communal 'we,' and naming the cause, are the most interesting things that I would take from the lecture. I really enjoyed the lecture and felt that this is a practical guide that I can use in any context—ministry or any speech in any context. These are core concepts that will shape my ministry, because this will influence the way I present myself and calibrate myself according to the context and reality. Thus, I will be able to give a speech or sermon and know what will be needed for people to listen attentively."

From the data one can see that the students found the different theoretical perspectives (perspective 1) very helpful and could even apply the insights to some ministry fields, for example, preaching (perspectives 2 and 5). It is obvious that trust was important for many of the students. The fact that one student saw the lecture as a practical guide that he could use in any context underlines the importance of perspectives 3 and 5.

Concerning the *teaching methods* (pedagogy) used in class and once again taking the theoretical perspectives into consideration, I found that most of the students did indeed find the pedagogy very stimulating and helpful and it did enhance their critical thinking and global awareness (perspectives 4–6).

Another three examples from the data:

- "I absolutely loved the teaching method. I think that it is a great privilege to be able to listen to a lecturer from Norway while still in South Africa. It provided a unique opportunity for the class to learn about leadership from a different context."

- "It was one of the best online lectures I have experienced. Prof. Norheim held my attention throughout, and I enjoyed the reflection and feedback components, this also 'forced' us to engage with the content and formulate an understanding and practical example of the specific components. This was very informative and as I stated, one of the best lectures."

- "I remained captivated throughout the lecture; however, I struggled with the process of naming oneself. Although it is true that we must win the approval of our audience for them to even consider the content of our message, I am unsure whether I agree that I should market myself to my audience. I believe that the content should speak for itself and that my audience should remember my message and not me—especially when I am sharing the gospel. However, the lecture was fascinating, and I am positive that I will employ many of the strategies in the future."

From the data one can see that the students really did find the teaching method (pedagogy) helpful and stimulating. "Listening to a lecturer from Norway while in South Africa," as one student wrote, directly speaks to perspective 4 on global awareness. Describing the lecture as one of the best online lectures the student had experienced and the enjoyment coming from the reflection and feedback components are a feather in the cap of the lecturer. I found the last response above very interesting in the sense that is paradoxical. One the one hand, the student found that he was captivated during the lecture; however, he struggled with the process to name himself and then he goes on to reflect on this struggle. This struggle in himself underlines the importance of perspective 4 on critical thinking.

Concerning *what they found less interesting and where they lost attention* and taking the theoretical perspectives into consideration, especially perspectives 4 and 6 (critical thinking and digital literacy), I found that some of the students were a bit frustrated by the pedagogy.

Here are four examples from the data:

- "While the class was one of the best online classes I have ever participated in, I do think that the physical distance can still be 'felt.' The question of how we should talk about a 'pedagogy of the body' within the context of increasing online engagement still remains a challenge (as it did before the worldwide pandemic)."

- "It was frustrating that there were some technical issues at the beginning of the class; I do feel that it could have been sorted out ahead of class time. I would also have loved it if we could have received reading work, especially from Prof. ***'s book, before the class time. I found the work so interesting, but would have enjoyed coming to class prepared, as I know I would have had a lot more questions that I would have loved to discuss with him."

- "The focus in the beginning on introducing the speaker went on a tad too long. I lost a bit of focus in the beginning, but the reflective sessions got me fired up again."

- "There wasn't really a low spot, but there was one moment where I lost attention. This was where Prof. Norheim described the speech of John F. Kennedy in Berlin. Kennedy said: 'Ich bin ein Berliner.' Of course, the audience understood what he had wanted to say. However, due to the idiosyncrasies of the German language, Kennedy had inadvertently stated that he was a donut, as a Berliner also refers to a specific type of donut. Therefore, my attention was lost more to the funniness of the statement rather than due to the lecture itself."

From the data it is interesting to hear that even though the online class was a good experience, there was still the feeling that the physical distance could be "felt." In this regard, the student's reflection on a "pedagogy of the body" is very interesting and warrants some further exploration. Like so many times when technology is involved, many things can go wrong, and it indeed did go wrong, as the second participant above pointed out. I found the last response also very interesting, showing how cross-cultural communication can indeed play a misleading role in the communication process (perspective 6).

DISCUSSION

This research suggests an intricate symbiosis between the different theoretical perspectives and the experience of the students in class. The findings, for example, the positive reactions of the students in terms of the most interesting things that they learned from the lecture and the ways in which it will shape their ministries, as well as their appreciation of the teaching methods used (pedagogy), what they found less interesting, and where they lost attention, agitate for an expansive understanding of the role of COIL.

The study was done in an African context, where access to tertiary education has expanded significantly in recent years and where demands on lecturers have increased exponentially. Findings from this idiographic study may therefore suggest a need for deeper reflections on the benefits of COIL, and some more research in this regard is very necessary. Thinking and reflecting on COIL is therefore not a luxury; it is a necessity. The study found that students regard this kind of collaborative teaching very helpful. It seems as though the students find understanding and meaning through participating in this pedagogy and value the fact that their exposure challenges how they see the world.

Parpala et al. refer to the fact that within the field of ministry and theology, the motivation of students is closely connected to their values, spiritual convictions, and positive learning experiences.[23] A similar study by Erwich showed that 80 percent of theology students showed strong motivation when entering their studies, encountering different perspectives, and engaging with fellow students from different backgrounds. This is even

---

23. Parpala et al., "Students' Approaches to Learning."

more the case when they enter postgraduate studies such as the master of divinity. This motivation is often based on all kinds of spiritual experiences, which in turn connect to their callings.[24] In this regard it is also interesting to take note of the research of Henrico, who links positive self-evaluations of competence, task-related goals, and interest in academic tasks to the enjoyment of studies.[25]

LIMITATIONS OF THE STUDY

The limitations of the study include the relatively low number of students (only eleven) from only one institution (Stellenbosch University) who participated in the research. However, this is counteracted by the fact that one needs only a relatively low number of participants in these kinds of qualitative research projects to reach data saturation. Furthermore, I limited myself to only three research questions. In hindsight, I could have asked more, and other, questions. Finer nuances of discussions on COIL may therefore not have been captured. The study did, however, set out to capture the main complexities and nuances of the benefits of COIL. I came to the conclusion that in a network culture within the global village, COIL provides many wonderful opportunities to engage with peers all around the world in interdisciplinary learning and to enhance one's global awareness. From my own experiences as a lecturer, it was a fruitful engagement with my colleague from Norway.

CONCLUSION

I started this contribution by reflecting on the importance of collaborative practical theology and the importance of the "communal" or "relational" turn in the process of collaborative research on Christian practices. Next, I looked at why it is important to reflect on collaborative teaching and learning and how it works. This was followed by some theoretical perspectives on COIL and then a discussion on some empirical research that has been done among master of divinity students participating in a COIL project. Some of the findings were the positive reactions of the students in terms of the most interesting things that they learned from the lecture and the ways in which it will shape their ministries, as well as their appreciation of the teaching methods used during the teaching (pedagogy).

24. Erwich, "Studying Theology."
25. Henrico, "Sustaining Student Wellness."

BIBLIOGRAPHY

Chun, Dorothy M. "Language and Culture Learning in Higher Education via Telecollaboration." *Pedagogies* 10 (2015) 5–21.
De Roest, Henk. *Collaborative Practical Theology: Engaging Practitioners in Research on Christian Practices.* Theology in Practice 8. Leiden, Neth.: Brill, 2019.
Dweck, Carol. "What Having a 'Growth Mindset' Actually Means." *Harvard Business Review*, Jan. 13, 2016. https://hbr.org/2016/01/what-having-a-growth-mindset-actually-means.
Erwich, René. "Studying Theology: Between Exploration and Commitment; Researching Spiritual Development of Higher Education Students of Theology." *International Journal of Christianity & Education* 22 (2018) 214–32.
Gokcora, Deniz. "Benefits of Collaborative Online International Learning Projects." *Academia Letters* (2021) art. 202. https://doi.org/10.20935/AL202.
Gokcora, Deniz, and Shaun Everson. "Making Connections: Social Justice Issues across the Globe through COIL." Digital presentation, L2DL Symposium, "Critical Transnational Dialogue and Virtual Exchange: A Hybrid Symposium on Research and Practice," online through Florida International University, Oct. 21, 2020.
Graham, Elaine. "Is Practical Theology a Form of 'Action Research'?" *International Journal of Practical Theology* 17 (2013) 148–78.
Guth, Sarah. *The COIL Institute for Globally Networked Learning in the Humanities: Final Report.* New York: SUNY COIL Center, 2013.
Henrico, Karien. "Sustaining Student Wellness in Higher Educational Institutions: Possible Design Principles and Implementations Strategies." *Journal for Transdisciplinary Research in Southern Africa* 18 (2022) 1–9.
Holland, Fiona. *Teaching in Higher Education: An Interpretive Phenomenological Analysis.* New York: SAGE, 2014.
Lowe, Stephen, and Mary Lowe. "Spiritual Formation in Theological Distance Education: An Ecosystems Model." *Christian Education Journal* 7 (2010) 85–102.
Marres, Noortje. *Digital Sociology: The Reinvention of Social Research.* Malden, MA: Polity, 2017.
Norheim, Bård, and Joar Haga. *The Four Speeches Every Leader Has to Know.* London: PalgraveMacmillan, 2020.
Parpala, Anna, et al. "Students' Approaches to Learning and Their Experiences of the Teaching-Learning Environment in Different Disciplines." *British Journal of Educational Psychology* 80 (2010) 269–82. https://doi.org/10.1348/000709909X476946.
Phillips, Louise, et al. "Tackling the Tensions of Dialogue and Participation: Reflexive Strategies for Collaborative Research." In *Knowledge and Power in Collaborative Research: A Reflexive Approach*, edited by Louise Phillips et al., 1–10. Routledge Advances in Research Methods. London: Routledge, 2012.
Przybylski, Liz. *Hybrid Ethnography: Online, Offline, and in Between.* London: Sage, 2021.
Roberts, Jennifer. "Online Learning as a Form of Distance Education: Linking Formation Learning in Theology to the Theories of Distance Education." *HvTSt* 75 (2019).
Roebben, Bert. *Scholen voor het leven: kleine didactiek van de hoop in zeven stappen.* Leuven: Acco, 2011.

Selçuk, Mualla, et al. "The Online Learning Experience of Theology Students in Turkey during the COVID-19 Pandemic: A New Disposition for RE?" *RelEd* 116 (2021) 1–17.

Shaw, Rachel, et al. *Sage Research Methods Cases Part 1: Interpretative Phenomenological Analysis in Applied Health Research*. London: Sage, 2014.

Simpson, Alyson. "Integrating Technology with Literacy: Using Teacher-Guided Collaborative Online Learning to Encourage Critical Thinking." *ALT-J, Research in Learning Technology* 18 (2010) 119–31.

Smith, Jonathan A. "Interpretative Phenomenological Analysis: A Reply to Amedeo Giorgi." *Existential Analysis* 21 (2010) 186–93.

Thompson, Melinda. "'To the Ends of the Earth': Cultural Considerations for Global Online Theological Education." *Theological Education* 49 (2015) 113–25.

Wenger, Ettiene. *Communities of Practice: Learning, Meaning, and Identity*. Learning in Doing: Social, Cognitive and Computational Perspectives. Cambridge: Cambridge University Press, 1998.

Chapter 9

Student Creativity and Collaboration during Digital Learning

Glocal Theoretical Perspectives

Svitlana Holovchuk, Linnéa K. Jermstad, and Gunnvi Sæle Jokstad

INTRODUCTION

The COVID-19 pandemic has had a significant impact on the global higher education sector,[1] prompting educators to refer to the situation as a crisis.[2] This crisis has presented new challenges, but has also created possibilities, such as increased "openness towards innovation and new learning opportunities that were not as evident before."[3] An article published on the World Economic Forum's website states that the pandemic has permanently changed education.[4] In the post-COVID era, there is a need for reforms in higher education practices in theology that prioritize teachers' all-around competencies and didactic approaches. The changes in education after the corona virus crisis require flexibility, interdisciplinary collaboration, co-creation, innovations, new approaches and perspectives, and strategies that can

---

1. Crawford et al., "COVID-19," 10.
2. Biesta, "Paying Attention," 221.
3. Rapanta et al., "Balancing Technology, Pedagogy," 716.
4. Li and Lalani, "COVID-19 Pandemic."

improve quality.⁵ To address the challenges during different crisis periods, it is necessary to create a flexible education program that can be used both in the classroom and in the digital learning space. Several higher education institutions have implemented a blended learning format, which combines traditional classroom learning with online learning, and have prioritized the development of twenty-first-century skills.⁶ These skills, also known as "soft skills" or "transferable skills," have been grouped into three categories according to P21's Frameworks for 21st Century Learning, which were developed with input from teachers and education experts⁷ *Learning skills*, such as critical thinking, creativity, collaboration, and communication; *literacy skills*, such as information, media, and technology; and *life skills*, such as flexibility, leadership, initiative, productivity, and social skills are valuable for teaching and learning theology in times of crisis.⁸

This study is part of a series of articles related to the project Teaching and Learning Theology in Crisis, conducted by NLA University College and Stellenbosch University. To gain more knowledge, the phenomenon of twenty-first-century skills was explored as a glocal theoretical perspective before empirical research is conducted in subsequent articles. Since twenty-first-century skills are varied, we focused on two skills that were deemed most important in this study: collaboration and creativity. The interdisciplinary approach and insights gained from this exploration can be used in further empirical research and teaching practices and are valuable and meaningful both to theology and pedagogy. The research question of the chapter is: *What are the success criteria for students' collaboration and creativity during digital learning, based on a rapid literature review of studies from 2020 to 2022?*

METHODOLOGY

The rapid review methodology was used in this study.⁹ This involves a rapid overview of studies to produce key conclusions with facts, theories, professional perspectives,¹⁰ and systematization of knowledge¹¹ related to creativity and collaboration during digital learning. In our search strategy,

5. Khamis et al., "COVID-19 Pandemic," 187.
6. Laar et al., "Determinants of 21st-Century Skills."
7. Battelle for Kids, *Framework for 21st Century Learning*.
8. Stauffer, "21st Century Skills."
9. Jesson et al., *Doing Your Literature Review*, 192.
10. Befring, *Sentrale forskningsmetoder*, 51.
11. Støren, *Bare søk*, 17.

we used various databases, such as Oria, Idunn, Google Scholar, EBSCO, ERIC, ProQuest, JSTOR, Nora, and Norart. Due to the extensive number of hits, we focused on the databases Oria and ERIC. The inclusion criteria were search keywords *21st-century skills, student collaboration, student creativity, digital learning, crisis,* and the relevant articles in English, published within the last two years (2020–2022). Twenty-one scientific articles were included in our study. Data materials were sorted, based on the topic, and analyzed.[12] As an analysis tool, we used a content analysis approach and focused on the following elements: *author, year, focus,* and *research method.*[13] The study has been carried out in line with guidelines for research ethics in the social sciences and the humanities scientific norms.[14] The ethical approach is based on our own interpretation and inclusion of the relevant literature related to the research.[15]

RESULTS AND DISCUSSION

To fulfill the aim of the chapter, the results and discussion section centers on two distinct aspects: the first being the phenomenon of student creativity and collaboration, and the second being the success criteria for student's collaboration and creativity during digital learning. These two approaches are presented in the following sections.

Author	Year	Focus	Research Method
Student creativity and collaboration as a phenomenon			
F. M. Ciğerci	2020	The study is focused on collaboration, communication, team- and individual work, and digital storytelling as a tool in this process.	Explanatory Sequential Design
E. Laar and others	2020	The article combines two definitions—twenty-first-century skills and digital skills—and describes students' competencies as creativity, communication, collaboration, critical thinking, and problem-solving skills.	Systematic Literature Review

12. Persson, *Hvordan skrive en litteraturgjennomgang*, 11–25.

13. Mosvold and Fauskanger, "Innholdsanalysens muligheter i utdanningsforskning."

14. National Committee for Research Ethics in the Social Sciences and the Humanities, "Guidelines for Research Ethics."

15. Suri, "Ethical Considerations," 41.

O. Agaoglu and others	2020	The study has presented the importance and use of twenty-first-century skills (collaboration and creativity as well) in the student's learning environment.	Survey and Reflection
A. Lazareva and others	2020	The project concerns which effect has "a collaborative digital storytelling project" on the student's active learning in the "higher education context."	Survey
H. Semilarski and others	2021	The project presents a comparative analysis of how to develop twenty-first-century skills (we are focused on collaboration and creativity) in the two student groups: experimental and nonexperimental.	Experiment
H. Aifan	2021	In this study, the author investigates collaborative learning and focuses on the students' perspectives.	Experience Based
W. Hazaymeh	2021	This project builds on the students; creativity, innovation, communication, and collaboration during online learning and their opinion and attitudes regarding this process.	Survey
N. Komang and others	2022	In the study, the researchers give an overview of theoretical perspectives and vectors related to twenty-first-century skills (collaboration and creativity as well).	Literature Review
Success criteria for students' collaboration and creativity during digital learning			
R. Alves and others	2020	The project presents and highlights the important factors related to the teacher's professional development during the coronavirus pandemic.	Online Questionnaire
U. Goth and others	2020	The studies focus on the students' experiences and their reflections related to online teaching via Zoom. The study describes also changing motivation and learning outcomes during digital learning.	Online Survey
J. Crawford and others	2020	The research describes COVID-19 challenges "for the global higher education community." The study presents the teacher's experience across twenty countries.	Desktop Analysis

T. Karalis and others	2020	The project is focused on the university experience during the first two months of the coronavirus time. They also discuss the effect that the crisis conditions had on university education.	Online Questionnaire
V. Ahmed and others	2021	The article describes students' and teachers' experiences during digital learning under COVID-19 and what challenges and possibilities they had.	Survey and Interview
S. Metscher and others	2021	The article presents the students' and teachers' adaptation to online teaching during COVID-19 and their experiences of using digital tools and programs.	Reflection, Observation Notes, and Systematic Discussion
C. L. Teo and others	2021	The study is focused on the teachers' collaboration and new ideas that can be used with the students during digital learning under crisis.	Case Study
M. Treve	2021	The article describes the teachers' challenges during digital learning (connection and interaction with the students, lack of digital competence, etc.).	Narrative Review of Literature
S. Nuere and others	2021	The study has an experience-based approach and is related to the teachers' and students' experiences during digital learning.	Experience Based
T. Towip and others	2022	The project describes students' challenges (transition from campus-based learning to digital, collaboration and social interaction, etc.).	Survey
A. Dewi Anggraeni and others	2022	In the article, the researchers explore how to use Canva as a digital platform during online learning and how this tool can promote student collaboration and interaction.	Observation and Survey
M. Händel and others	2022	The project investigates students' reflections on the coronavirus crisis and how the pandemic influenced their socio-emotional perceptions.	Online Survey
M. Li and others	2022	The researchers present the teacher's professional role and challenges during the COVID-19 pandemic and how they can combine "traditional face-to-face teaching methods" with digital skills and competencies.	Systematic Literature Review

STUDENT CREATIVITY AND COLLABORATION AS A PHENOMENON

The phenomenon of student creativity and collaboration has gained significant attention in higher education.[16] It is seen as an active learning process that facilitates interaction, knowledge sharing, and improvement among students. Collaboration is recognized as a cognitive and emotional process that enhances meaningful teaching and learning practices. Studies have highlighted the importance of collaboration in promoting competence development, learning outcomes, and social interaction through activities and common projects.[17] Creativity, on the other hand, is defined as an intellectual ability that is related to intelligence and an active learning environment. Modern theoretical understanding emphasizes the need for students to be active participants who give constructive feedback, take part in reflective interaction[18] and have "an open mind,"[19] motivation, and independence.[20]

The collaborative and creative processes require a common understanding, responsibility, and respect for each other. Challenges can arise from a lack of knowledge and information, inclusion, mutual support, openness within the group, and respect.[21] Studies have shown that teachers' and students' expectations play a crucial role in promoting collaboration and creativity in higher education. Abbas and several other researchers emphasize that "the teachers expect better learning outcomes from the students, while students expect expertise, support, and balance between creativity and criticism during their study period."[22] Kivunja in his research develops Abbas's meaning regarding student support and points out that this includes giving and receiving feedback from the teacher and other students to improve a common task, sharing and creating new ideas, acknowledging other student's skills, developing creativity, "stating personal opinions and areas of disagreement tactfully, listening patiently to others in conflict situations, defining the problems, supporting group decisions even if not in total agreement."[23] Collaborative processes involve reflection and

16. Nerantzi et al., "Human Relationships," 3.
17. Ağaoğlu and Demir, "Integration of 21st-Century Skills"; Van Laar et al., "Determinants of 21st-Century Skills."
18. Gibson, "Art of Creative Teaching," 610.
19. Kivunja, "Innovative Pedagogies," 45.
20. Goth et al., "Nærhet, eller distanse?," 201.
21. Hussein, "Addressing Collaboration Challenges."
22. Abbas et al., "Elements of Students' Expectation," 1.
23. Kivunja, "Innovative Pedagogies," 44.

knowledge consolidation for improving student outcomes and fostering interpersonal bonding among participants. Individualized approaches that promote creativity, improvisation, and open-mindedness are essential for student development in higher education.

In addition to enhancing student outcomes through reflection and knowledge consolidation, the collaboration also facilitates deeper levels of interpersonal bonding among participants.[24] As students' professional development relies on their knowledge, competencies, and skills, it is crucial in higher education to adopt an individual approach to each student, fostering their creative potential, improvisation skills, and open-mindedness. Ciğerci observes that collaboration involves providing feedback, sharing experiences, and being open and responsive to new and diverse perspectives, allowing students to work creatively with each other.[25] Semilarski et al. suggest that interdisciplinary approaches can significantly promote students' creativity and collaboration.[26]

SUCCESS CRITERIA FOR STUDENT COLLABORATION AND CREATIVITY DURING DIGITAL LEARNING

Based on the analyses of the studies from the two years presented above, we would like to highlight some success criteria for student creativity and collaboration in digital learning. As mentioned above, the post-COVID period required new reforms in higher education, focusing on didactic approaches and methods. Crises give us new paradigms and vectors for digital learning. In addition, the pandemic "forced" us to be more flexible, find new approaches, ideas, and some success criteria that increase teachers' knowledge of how to create collaborative learning processes and creativity.

One of the new approaches is to develop flexibility in the learning process and allow students to learn online regardless of where they are studying, "these educational provisions are successful in meeting the needs of working life and help ensure that education and skills are available where people live and with different life situations."[27] Moreover, a flexible educational approach gives students the opportunity to acquire knowledge and develop competencies not only in a classroom but also via digital learning.[28] The

---

24. Chenault, "Building Collaborative Pedagogy."
25. Ciğerci, "Primary School Teacher Candidates."
26. Semilarski, "Promoting Students' Perceived Self-Efficacy."
27. Ministry of Education and Research, "Students Are Happy," para. 1.
28. Ahmed and Opoku, "Technology Supported Learning," 366.

theoretical and empirical studies related to online education in COVID-19 focus on the various core elements of quality. Researchers are examining the success criteria, principles, and factors that can improve the quality of online education, promote flexible education, and benefit students and teachers.

Student collaboration and creativity normally takes place in the traditional classroom, but is this also possible with digital learning? Teachers face pedagogical dilemmas when it comes to building relationships with students in the digital classroom and engaging them in collaborative active learning and creativity.[29] The several studies that we have included in our chapter mention that the crisis gave space to new ideas on how to improve student's potential during digital learning through collaboration and creativity.[30] One of the success criteria in this process is student co-creation, reflection, and discussion. Student interaction and reflection consistently impact student learning outcomes and professional development, provide quality in education, and offer creative potential, which can be used in education as part of the blended learning format.[31] On the one hand, the digital classroom requires planning and structure for the learning process, but on the other hand, it also offers room for flexibility and improvisation.

To engage students in creativity and collaboration during digital learning, the teacher should have *professional digital competence* that "can facilitate social online-based interaction among the students and between teacher and student"[32] and make the learning process valuable and meaningful. The studies analyzed also indicate that the dominant role in the digital learning environment is the teacher's professional competence. Based on Mishra and Koehler's TPACK framework,[33] we can suggest that professional digital literacy during theology learning involves three types of knowledge: content knowledge (teachers' knowledge of the subject of theology), pedagogical knowledge (teachers' knowledge of instructional processes, the use of different didactic approaches that can foster students' creativity and collaboration in a digital learning environment), and technological knowledge (teachers' knowledge of how to use technology, tools, and resources that can be used in the context of the traditions of theological subjects). The studies by Stenberg and Maaranen and Nuere et al. also point out that teaching

29. Barnes et al., *How Has Covid-19 Affected*, 7.
30. See Nuere and Miguel, "Digital/Technological Connection"; Towip et al., "Students' Perceptions and Experiences"; Khamis et al., "COVID-19 Pandemic"; Crawford, "COVID-19."
31. Barnes, *How Has Covid-19 Affected*, 7.
32. Goth et al., "Nærhet, eller distanse?," 205.
33. Mishra and Koehler, "Technological Pedagogical Content Knowledge."

is "a complex profession with a multitude of dimensions," which requires knowledge and skills, open-mindedness, and flexibility to change pedagogical practice, new methods, and didactic approaches.[34]

In the process of student collaboration and co-creation, digital technologies and tools are tools that can foster a creative learning environment,[35] discovery, motivation, and curiosity and create a context that "imposes certain constraints, establishes preconditions for students' behaviors and opens up a range of learning opportunities."[36] Moreover, the use of digital technologies in the learning space promotes a diversity of possibilities and innovations.[37] Technology can be used as a support in the classroom and can promote learning outcomes and flexibility. Fayed and Cummings's study indicates that online learning can be challenging for both students and teachers due to a lack of digital literacy and skills, social and emotional interaction, contact with other students,[38] lack of commitment and concentration, and demotivation. Several articles point out that motivation can influence student creativity and collaboration and promote student learning outcomes. To motivate students, teachers should follow the new global trends in education and have expertise in using digital tools in learning. Händel emphasizes that active student learning should be part of the digital learning environment, and the teacher's role is to work both with students as a community and use an individual approach.[39] The learning environment is "the sense that it is consistently transformed according to contextual learning conditions, either being conducted face-to-face or delivered remotely or about students' needs and expected learning outcomes."[40] The quality of higher education depends on student learning outcomes that can be developed in interdisciplinary programs, and teachers' professional competence, qualifications, and skills are essential.

Based on the studies, we can highlight that other aspects make digital learning successful and can promote student creativity and collaboration. First, *teacher-student interaction* is based on new opportunities for sharing knowledge in online discussion among students and between a student and a teacher. Second, *feedback and reflection* can have a positive effect on the

34. Stenberg and Maaranen, "Promoting Practical Wisdom," 627. See also Nuere and Miguel, "Digital/Technological Connection," 933.
35. Selfa-Sastre et al., "Role of Digital Technologies," 8.
36. Selfa-Sastre et al., "Role of Digital Technologies," 4.
37. Rapanta et al., "Balancing Technology, Pedagogy," 734.
38. Fayed and Cummings, *Teaching*, 3.
39. Händel et al., "Digital Readiness," 276.
40. Rapanta et al., "Balancing Technology, Pedagogy," 734.

students' learning outcomes and support the students' learning process. And third, *innovative pedagogy approaches*—pedagogical innovations that promote the development of creativity and collaboration, new approaches to teaching and learning, and provide new concepts in online education—require "teachers to comprehend and decide the optimized way of delivering the course lectures to help students learn appropriately and e-learning requires altogether different pedagogy, especially in online assessment and individual and group interactions."[41]

SOME CONCLUSIONS AND FUTURE EMPIRICAL RESEARCH

In summary, student collaboration and creativity as twenty-first-century learning skills are the competencies students need to succeed today, especially in times of crisis and change. These skills can be developed in both traditional and digital environments. The analysis of the studies from the two years (2020–2022) included in our chapter can confirm that the core elements and success criteria for students' creativity and collaboration during digital learning are the teacher's professional digital literacy (knowledge of the subject and skills in how to use technology as helpful tools for creativity and collaboration), which can promote students' participation in active learning and engagement, involvement in the digital learning environment, social interaction, and motivation. The above core elements promote quality of higher education, flexibility, new approaches, and innovation. Teachers play a crucial role in higher education, and their professional development is one of the success criteria of modern education. Undoubtedly, the digital learning environment should be further developed, improved, and technically supported.

Theoretical research show that the use of digital technologies in education can generate new ideas for teachers and students. In addition, the effectiveness of digital learning as a form of education can provide flexibility and accessibility to students. However, the challenges in the digital learning environment are related to the lack of knowledge, digital literacy, and understanding of how to work with digital resources and platforms. The results of our study show that there are several articles that explore the phenomenon of twenty-first-century skills and highlight the phenomenon of "collaboration and creativity" as part of twenty-first-century skills and combine them with other skills. The studies related to digital learning during the pandemic provided a general overview of post-crisis challenges

---

41. Treve, "What COVID-19 Has Introduced," 214.

and opportunities, but we did not find any studies that provided detailed practical recommendations on how we, as teachers, can foster student creativity and collaboration in digital learning. In addition, the results show the need for more practical knowledge about how to use the digital space to promote collaborative learning and creativity. Therefore, in our further empirical studies, based on the empirical material, we will try to provide practical guidelines and recommendations on how teachers can develop creativity and collaboration in digital learning. Our chapter has highlighted the importance of the above-mentioned skills for teaching and learning in crisis, and interdisciplinary approaches can be a support in this process. By focusing on the success criteria for student creativity and collaboration during digital learning, we have gained valuable insights that can be applied to further empirical research and teaching practice in theology.

BIBLIOGRAPHY

Abbas, Asad, et al. "Elements of Students' Expectation towards Teacher-Student Research Collaboration in Higher Education." *IEEE Frontiers in Education Conference (FIE)* (2020) 1–5. https://doi.org/10.1109/fie44824.2020.9273902

Ağaoğlu, Onur, and Murat Demir. "The Integration of 21st-Century Skills into Education: An Evaluation Based on an Activity Example." *Journal of Gifted Education and Creativity* 7 (2020) 105–14.

Ahmed, Vian, and Alex Opoku. "Technology Supported Learning and Pedagogy in Times of Crisis: The Case of COVID-19 Pandemic." *Education and Information Technologies* 27 (2021), 365–405. https://doi.org/10.1007/s10639-021-10706-w.

Aifan, Hanan. "Implementing a Project-Based Collaborative Learning Approach Using PowerPoint to Improve Students' 21st-Century Skills." *E-Learning and Digital Media* 19 (2021) 258–73. https://doi.org/10.1177/20427530211030642.

Barnes, Jan, et al. *How Has Covid-19 Affected How Teacher Educators Engage Their Students in Learning? Project Report.* Education & Covid-19. London: BERA, 2021. https://www.bera.ac.uk/publication/how-has-covid-19-affected-how-teacher-educators-engage-their-students-in-learning.

Battelle for Kids. *Framework for 21st Century Learning.* Battelle for Kids, 2019. https://static.battelleforkids.org/documents/p21/P21_Framework_Brief.pdf.

Befring, Edvard. *Sentrale forskningsmetoder: med etikk og statistikk.* Oslo: Cappelen Damm Akademisk, 2020.

Biesta, Gert. "Have We Been Paying Attention? Educational Anesthetics in a Time of Crises." *Educational Philosophy and Theory* 54 (2022) 221–23. https://doi.org/10.1080/00131857.2020.1792612.

Chenault, Krystel H. "Building Collaborative Pedagogy: Lesson Study in Higher Education." *College Quarterly* 20 (2017) 1–23. https://files.eric.ed.gov/fulltext/EJ1131159.pdf.

Ciğerci, Fatih Mehmet. "Primary School Teacher Candidates and 21st Century Skills." *International Journal of Progressive Education* 16 (2020) 157–74. https://doi.org/10.29329/ijpe.2020.241.11.

Crawford, Joseph, et al. "COVID-19: 20 Countries' Higher Education Intra-Period Digital Pedagogy Responses." *Journal of Applied Learning & Teaching* 3 (2020) 1–20. https://doi.org/10.37074/jalt.2020.3.1.7.

Fayed, Ismail, and Jill Cummings, eds. *Teaching in the Post Covid-19 Era: World Education Dilemmas, Teaching Innovations and Solutions in the Age of Crisis*. Cham, Switz.: Springer, 2021.

Gibson, Robyn. "The 'Art' of Creative Teaching: Implications for Higher Education." *Teaching in Higher Education* 15 (2010) 607–13. https://doi.org/10.1080/13562517.2010.493349.

Glăveanu, Vlad P. "Educating Which Creativity?" *Thinking Skills and Creativity* 54 (2018) 25–32. https://doi.org/10.1016/j.tsc.2017.11.006.

Goth, Ursula S., et al. "Nærhet, eller distanse? Lærerstudenters erfaringer med Zoomundervisning under Covid-19." In *Fra barnehage til voksenliv: utdanning, didaktikk og verdi*, edited by Linnéa K. Jermstad and Ursula S. Goth, 193–212. Oslo: Novus, 2020.

Händel, Marion, et al. "Digital Readiness and Its Effects on Higher Education Students' Socio-Emotional Perceptions in the Context of the COVID-19 Pandemic." *Journal of Research on Technology in Education* 54 (2022) 267–80. https://doi.org/10.1080/15391523.2020.1846147.

Hazaymeh, Wafa' A. "Students' Perceptions of Online Distance Learning for Enhancing English Language Learning during COVID-19 Pandemic." *International Journal of Instruction* 14 (2021) 501–18.

Hussein, Bassam. "Addressing Collaboration Challenges in Project-Based Learning: The Student's Perspective." *Education Sciences* 11 (2021) 1–20. https://doi.org/10.3390/educsci11080434.

Jesson, Jill K., et al. *Doing Your Literature Review: Traditional and Systematic Techniques*. London: SAGE, 2011.

Khamis, Tashmin, et al. "The COVID-19 Pandemic: A Catalyst for Creativity and Collaboration for Online Learning and Work-Based Higher Education Systems and Processes." *Journal of Work-Applied Management* 13 (2021) 184–96. https://doi.org/10.1108/JWAM-01-2021-0010.

Kivunja, Charles. "Innovative Pedagogies in Higher Education to Become Effective Teachers of 21st Century Skills: Unpacking the Learning and Innovations Skills Domain of the New Learning Paradigm." *IJHE* (2014) 37–48.

Lazareva, Alexandra, and Gibran Cruz-Martinez. "Digital Storytelling Project as a Way to Engage Students in Twenty-First Century Skills Learning." *International Studies Perspectives* 22 (2020) 383–406. https://doi.org/10.1093/isp/ekaa017.

Li, Cathy, and Farah Lalani. "The COVID-19 Pandemic Has Changed Education Forever. This Is How." World Economic Forum, Apr. 29, 2020. https://www.weforum.org/agenda/2020/04/coronavirus-education-global-covid19-online-digital-learning/.

Li, Ming, and Zhonggen Yu. "Teachers' Satisfaction, Role, and Digital Literacy during the COVID-19 Pandemic." *Sustainability* 14 (2022) 1–19. https://doi.org/10.3390/su14031121.

Ministry of Education and Research. "Students Are Happy with Flexible Study Options." Government.no, Dec. 19, 2022. https://www.regjeringen.no/no/aktuelt/studenter-er-fornoyde-med-fleksible-studietilbud/id2952239/.

Mishra, Punya, and Matthew J. Koehler. "Technological Pedagogical Content Knowledge: A Framework for Teacher Knowledge." *Teachers College Record* 108 (2006) 1017–54.

Mosvold, Reidar, and Janne Fauskanger. "Innholdsanalysens muligheter i utdanningsforskning." *Norsk Pedagogisk Tidsskrift* 98 (2014) 127–39. https://doi.org/10.18261/ISSN1504-2987-2014-02-07.

National Committee for Research Ethics in the Social Sciences and the Humanities, The. "Guidelines for Research Ethics in the Social Sciences and the Humanities." National Research Ethics Committees, 2021 (Eng. translation 2022). https://www.forskningsetikk.no/en/guidelines/social-sciences-humanities-law-and-theology/guidelines-for-research-ethics-in-the-social-sciences-humanities-law-and-theology/.

Nerantzi, Chrissi, et al. "Human Relationships in Higher Education: The Power of Collaboration, Creativity and Openness." *Journal of Interactive Media in Education* (2021) 1–11. https://doi.org/10.5334/jime.668.

Nuere, S., and L. de Miguel. "The Digital/Technological Connection with COVID-19: An Unprecedented Challenge in University Teaching." *Technology, Knowledge and Learning* 26 (2021) 931–43. https://doi.org/10.1007/s10758-020-09454-6.

Persson, Mats. *Hvordan skrive en litteraturgjennomgang? En praktisk guide.* Oslo: Universitetsforlaget, 2021.

Rapanta, Chrysi, et al. "Balancing Technology, Pedagogy and the New Normal: Postpandemic Challenges for Higher Education." *Postdigital Science and Education* 3 (2021) 715–42. https://doi.org/10.1007/s42438-021-00249-1.

Selfa-Sastre, Moisés, et al. "The Role of Digital Technologies to Promote Collaborative Creativity in Language Education." *Frontiers in Psychology* 13 (2022) https://doi.org/10.3389/fpsyg.2022.828981.

Semilarski, Helen, et al. "Promoting Students' Perceived Self-Efficacy towards 21st Century Skills through Everyday Life-Related Scenarios." *Education Sciences* 11 (2021) 1–18. https://doi.org/10.3390/educsci11100570.

Stauffer, Bri. "What Are 21st Century Skills?" iCEV, Jan. 10, 2022. https://www.aeseducation.com/blog/what-are-21st-century-skills.

Stenberg, Katariina, and Katriina Maaranen. "Promoting Practical Wisdom in Teacher Education: A Qualitative Descriptive Study." *European Journal of Teacher Education* 45 (2020) 1–17.

Støren, Ingeborg. *Bare søk! Praktisk veiledning i å skrive litteraturstudie.* Oslo: Cappelen Damm Akademisk, 2013.

Suri, Harsh. "Ethical Considerations of Conducting Systematic Reviews in Educational Research." In *Systematic Reviews in Educational Research: Methodology, Perspectives and Application*, edited by Olaf Zawacki-Richter et al., 41–54. Research Methods in Education. Wiesbaden: Springer, 2020. https://doi.org/10.1007/978-3-658-27602-7_3.

Towip, Towip, et al. "Students' Perceptions and Experiences of Online Cooperative Problem-Based Learning: Developing 21st Century Skills. *International Journal of Pedagogy and Teacher Education* 6 (2022) 37–42. https://doi.org/10.20961/ijpte.v6i1.56744.

Treve, Mark. "What COVID-19 Has Introduced into Education: Challenges Facing Higher Education Institutions (HEIs)." *Higher Education Pedagogies* 6 (2021) 212–27. https://doi.org/10.1080/23752696.2021.1951616.

Van Laar, Ester, et al. "Determinants of 21st-Century Skills and 21st-Century Digital Skills for Workers: A Systematic Literature Review." *SAGE Open* 10 (2020) 1–14. https://doi.org/10.1177/2158244019900176.

Chapter 10

An Appreciative Inquiry of the Role of a Program Leader within Program Renewal Process at the Faculty of Theology, Stellenbosch University

SHANTELLE WEBER

INTRODUCTION: BACKGROUND, RATIONALE, AND PURPOSE OF STUDY

This chapter reflects on a study focused on the nature of educational leadership practices within the Faculty of Theology, Stellenbosch University. Program renewal was one of the core strategic priorities in the 2017–2021 "Strategy for Teaching and Learning" at Stellenbosch University, motivated by factors such as the need to revise programs for funding or subsidy purposes, decolonization of curricula after the #FeesMustFall movements, and updating faculty offerings for the market of students arriving at our institution.[1] It is this process that has highlighted the need to investigate what the role of program leaders within academic programs should be.

The rationale for the study focused on contributing to understanding of the role of a program leader in the process of program renewal. The aim in this chapter is to interrogate and reflect on the experience of the program leaders involved in the renewal of the bachelor of theology degree at Stellenbosch University (SU).

---

1. Director, "Strategy for Teaching."

THEORETICAL FRAMING AND LITERATURE REVIEW

The 2015/2016 student protests about access to higher education in South Africa were one of the key drivers of curriculum or program renewal. Research conducted by Leibowitz et al. reflects on some of the features that may constrain or enable professional development, quality teaching, and the work of teaching and learning in such an educational environment.[2] Founded on the work of critical realists Margaret Archer and Dave Elder-Vass,[3] Leibowitz et al.'s work opposes the way in which institutional contexts have hindered or enabled the implementation of national or international imperatives regarding quality teaching and professional development in South Africa. In terms of leadership, they argue that not all institutions have created high-level positions for teaching and learning leaders, and not all incumbents have the interest or inclination to support teaching initiatives—many of the teaching-intensive universities in the study had experienced considerable instability, disruptions, and changes in leadership, and concomitant changes in institutional direction. This has led to significant socioeconomic disparities between institutions that confirm the way in which historical inequalities continue to play themselves out in the current era. They argue that amid the diverse and unequal academic staff workloads, timetables, and teacher-to-student ratios across South African higher education institutions, reflexivity alone is not sufficient to characterize how individuals respond to their conditions. Policy directives need to consider not only varying socioeconomic conditions of higher education institutions, but how the varied features at each institution play themselves out in relation to each other.

Another theoretical framework important for this research study is curriculum leadership.[4] Here the complexities of specialist knowledge production amid struggles for recontextualizing these knowledge systems become apparent. One challenge that comes to mind is the role of student voices and engagement in our conceptualization of specialist knowledge. Another is the role of the program leader during curriculum development processes. Msila describes an African philosophy of education as one that addresses issues of equity and enables student appreciation of the curriculum as their own.[5] This type of education is not individualistic but is somewhat

2. Leibowitz and Bozalek, "Access to Higher Education."
3. Archer and Elder-Vass, "Cultural System."
4. Young, "What Is a Curriculum."
5. Msila and Gumbo, *Africanising the Curriculum*.

reflective of *ubuntu* within education.[6] An African philosophy of education deliberately engages with a holistic (aesthetic, cultural, political, and social) African experience. In reaction to Bantu and Calvinistic education, how Africans learn and construct knowledge is taken seriously. Transformation and learner-centered education is key! This makes it an emancipatory education is which all citizens are able to learn, resulting in research being conducted from Africa by Africans. Msila's research study takes this approach to education seriously.

RESEARCH PROBLEM AND QUESTION

The 2018 "Teaching and Learning Policy" of the university requires that the roles and responsibilities of various figures involved in the proposed continual program renewal be clarified.[7] One such clarification would be that of a program leader or program coordinator. The SU draft "Guidelines for Programme Committee Chairs and Programme Leaders" define a program leader as "an academic staff member, appointed by a Faculty Board ... to lead, manage and coordinate a particular academic program for a fixed, rotating term."[8] In a chapter entitled "Leading Course Delivery," Parkin describes the "program leader's role as both liberating through supporting and mentoring individuals and modeling through enabling learning, championing learning values and teaching pedagogy through modelling the type of teacher you expect people to exhibit in a given program."[9] This description calls for a program leader who will model the academic values and behaviors we want our students to experience while in the program, be responsible for creating appropriate learning environments in which both staff and students strive toward the shared mission of the program, and be involved in the actual content that the curriculum would entail. Workshops held during phase 1 of the program renewal process highlighted the overwhelming nature of such a role amid other pressures of being a full-time academic staff member within the context of higher education in South Africa. The program renewal process was both exhilarating and exhausting. It enabled enormous personal and faculty-wide growth yet consumed much time and intellectual engagement from all stakeholders involved.

---

6. The notion of *ubuntu* is properly used within the African (and global) context as embracing community in which the perspective of the other is taken seriously.
7. Senior Director, "Teaching and Learning Policy," esp. §8.
8. Senior Director, "Guidelines," 3.
9. Parkin, *Leading, Learning, and Teaching*, 170.

As noted above, higher education places varying expectations for program and educational policy renewal that enhance equitable teaching and learning praxis with the aim of transformation. I also argue that we take the communal learning process of students seriously, and by doing this we include students in our transformation endeavors. In most higher education institutions in South Africa, a full-time academic is usually given the responsibility of holding all of the above together in a role that is described as a program leader. It is against the above-mentioned background that this research study explores the question: What is the role of a program leader in the renewal processes for an undergraduate degree? I explored this within the context of theology.

RESEARCH DESIGN AND METHODOLOGY

The overarching research design employed in this chapter is action research by specifically focusing on appreciative inquiry as hermeneutical lens. I write from the perspective of being appointed as the program leader of the bachelor of theology program (which is the program that has undergone renewal). Beylefeld et al. note that action research enables me as a researcher to be critical of my own circumstances in a subjective, yet rigorous, manner.[10] Action research is flexible in its methodology, yet never either haphazard or routine.[11] McNiff adds a few more reasons why action research is important in studies such as the present one. (1) Action research aims to improve the learning and educational growth of those participating in the endeavor. It is driven by a central value, namely, respect for others. This is important when embarking on program renewal processes in which one wants to include all possible stakeholders (staff, students, partners, etc). (2) The aim of action research, however, is to assume responsibility for self-improvement. Through various cycles, the researcher develops as an educational leader while remaining accountable to the above-mentioned stakeholders. This is crucial to the faculty's renewal processes. (3) The action researcher writes in the first person with the aim of sharing newly gained insights with influential members and encourages collaboration between staff teaching subject content and skills development specialists. Influencing others is one of the forms of knowledge creation embodied in action research.[12] One of the expectations of being a program leader has been the ability to influence process and relationships on various levels within program renewal. (4) Action

---

10. Beylefeld et al., "Action Research," 147.
11. Beylefeld et al., "Action Research," 153.
12. McNiff, *Action Research*, 18–33.

research enables the presence of a strong conviction that things could be better and, second, a commitment to one's own values as well as the recognition that one may be mistaken and thus, openness to other people's points of view. This comes with a responsibility towards students and staff and the researcher's commitment to encouraging collaborative practices and creating cultures of inquiry is evident. My willingness to question my motives, to suspend personal judgments, and to remain open to other people's points of view have been foundational. Finally, I opt for (5) action research in the hope that I will moved toward a changed understanding of my own teaching and learning practice, and my understanding of how this change has come about.

Given describes appreciative inquiry (AI) as a deliberate search for the positive core of an individual or collective system.[13] It was developed by David Cooperrider, a professor of organizational behavior at Case Western Reserve University. It rests on a belief that there is something that works in every system. This goodness can be identified and drawn out. AI, then, is an inquiry into what is valued and good about the individual or collective system. It generally employs a four-phase process of discovery, dream, design, and destiny. The discovery phase is focused on identifying what already exists in the system that is good. Once that is identified, it is possible to imagine an even better system, which is the dream phase. Creating an infrastructure to support this ideal system is the work that takes place during the design phase. As the new system comes into being, it must be maintained and sustained in such a way that its affirmative capacity is continuously strengthened; this is the destiny phase. As a social construction philosophy, a working assumption of AI is that systems (even individual ones) are socially constructed. Regardless of its history, any system can be altered. Images of the future are grounded in the system's past positive history, which means it does not disregard history. Branson notes that people have more confidence in the journey to the future when they carry forward parts of the past. If we carry parts of the past into the future, they should be what are best about the past.[14] For these reasons the outcomes of the renewal process should be useful. This is specifically important in the context in which this research study is being conducted. The Faculty of Theology is more than 150 years old and has a rich history within the South African story. As such, we have many senior colleagues who have prided themselves in the past as connected to the historical roots of theology (and consequently the curriculum we now have) and connected to the political history of this

---

13. Given, *Qualitative Research Methods*, 2:21.
14. Branson, *Memories, Hopes, and Conversations*, 24–28.

country. Valuing the worth of institutional memory and affirming what has been accomplished before my term as program leader are crucial in moving the current curriculum renewal process forward. This hermeneutical lens has helped me reflect on the complex history of the bachelor of theology degree within the larger discussion on equitable transformation of higher education in our country.

AI is an action research method that encourages collecting data through conducting interviews, making it well suited to qualitative research methods that allow engagement from other colleagues in leadership in my context. Here an inquiry questionnaire is aimed at finding out what works in the organization. These questionnaires are offered as an invitation, using conversational language and encouraging storytelling. The intent is for the stories to be directed at the positive core and the strengths of the program or policy and how to build on them.[15] There are several program and departmental leaders active in academic environments like our faculty. Gathering data through the voices of these colleagues puts my role into perspective and expresses the importance of collaboration in such program renewal processes. During the interviews (addendum A), four primary types of questions were asked: deep story, value, core factors, and future or miracle. The deep story question was designed to draw out stories about best experiences and to begin to get people thinking appreciatively. People were encouraged to provide rich, thick description by talking about who was involved, what made it a peak experience, what they did to make it a peak experience, and what others contributed to make it a peak experience. The first question posed to participants was "Can you describe what your understanding of leadership within an academic environment is?"

The value question was crafted to discover what it is that people value about the individual or collective system under inquiry. This begins to personalize the factors mentioned in the deep story response. Here I asked, "Can you give me examples of how you have experienced leadership in this faculty?"

The third type of question, core factors, was meant to identify what people believe are the core factors that give life to the system under discussion. This question elicits the specifics about what gives life to the individual or collective and seeks to understand why it gives life. SU prides itself in its systemic processes. Here I reflected on the recent policy document on program leaders and asked two questions: "What were your first impressions of this document and how would you describe the role of a program leader within our faculty? What could be expected from such a leader? Finally, the

---

15. Branson, *Memories, Hopes, and Conversations*, 23.

future or miracle question is an invitation to dream and imagine the ideal future."[16] Here I asked: "Reflecting on our current program renewal process, how would you describe the role of a program leader during this process?" I should note that the role of program leader as policy was a new designation for all participants despite it being operational in our program committee structure before this. Participants had experiential knowledge that could be shared and reflected on.

The data sources used for this empirical study were staff and students in leadership positions at the Faculty of Theology. Departmental leaders, student leaders, and program leaders were purposefully sampled based on their being leaders at the faculty during the program renewal process. Seven leaders were selected and individually interviewed. These interviews were recorded and transcribed after consent for this was obtained from participants. Institutional clearance was granted to conduct the study. The unit of analysis was the bachelor of theology program. A limitation of this study is that the data gathered is contextually and discipline bound, and its value is therefore not in its generalizability but rather in its transferability. This is the reason that I have endeavored to use all available institutional documentation to guide this research process.

DATA ANALYSIS

Qualitative researchers make claims about their ability to reveal the local practices through which the end products are assembled.[17] Qualitatively, thematic analysis is the method of data analysis used in this study. Thematic analysis is a method for identifying and reporting patterns (themes) within data to interpret various aspects of the research question.[18] This form of analysis is used for reporting the experiences, meanings, and realities of participants and for acknowledging the ways in which meaning is made within participants' social contexts.[19] It is considered most valuable in contexts where new theories and interpretations are required.[20] It is not restricted to one specific theoretical framework, which makes it attractive in a study of this nature. In alignment with appreciative inquiry as my lens, I find thematic analysis flexible enough to gain a rich description of the entire data set or give a more detailed account of one theme or group of

16. Branson, *Memories, Hopes, and Conversations*, 22.
17. Silverman, *Interpreting Qualitative Data*, 12.
18. Braun and Clarke, "Using Thematic Analysis," 79.
19. Braun and Clarke, "Using Thematic Analysis," 81.
20. Ezzy, *Qualitative Analysis*, 85.

themes.[21] Using the above-mentioned five research questions (addendum A) as thematic guide, Braun and Clark's six phases of thematic data analysis was employed for the study. The themes presented in the following section were derived through a manual process of tabulating the responses to each question and thereafter clustering responses into categories that became codes and later drawn into thematic mind maps.

FINDINGS OF THE STUDY

The core research findings can be divided into four responses and subsequent thematic foci to the research question: What is the role of a program leader in the renewal processes for an undergraduate degree? Participants reflected on their understanding of leadership (theme/code 1); their experience of leadership (theme/code 2) within the Faculty of Theology; their perceptions of the draft policy document on program chairs and leaders at the University of Stellenbosch (theme/code 3); and how they understood leadership through the lens of program leadership during curriculum renewal processes (theme/code 4). The following was discovered:

Participants understood leadership as *influence*, *collaboration*, and *position*. They also outlined specific characteristics of leaders. These correlate to how they perceive the role of the program leader within the faculty.[22]

Leadership is influential

Leaders who influence are the lecturing and administrative staff. Lecturing staff "know what they are teaching, they know how to teach, they know who their students are." Administrative staff help these people and understand their roles. Through these influential voices, leaders "impact what is considered to be normal or abnormal, or the way things always have been."

Leadership is collaborative

Leaders reflect a collaborative approach through "creating space for people, enabling and inspiring" people. In this approach, "relationships are important, [people are given] a voice when there is confusion and everyone has a voice." It is "not about forcing people but rather motivating, moving or

21. Silverman, *Interpreting Qualitative Data*, 83.

22. All quotations in "Findings of the Study" are verbatim from participants' responses.

inspiring people towards direction" and "pulling a team together and saying this is where we are going."

Leadership is positional

This study confirmed that leadership "takes places within a specific context" and "depends very much in terms of the different environments." Most participants reflected on the authority that either comes through a position or is placed onto one in leadership. Most also contested this as the norm of leadership, stating that leadership is "not supposed to be from the front, if that makes sense. Leadership to me is almost from the back where you are guiding people or walking amongst them." Some reported that "as soon as the position came authority also came with it" or that "authority is placed on you despite you trying to shift."

Participants highlighted that leadership is not management but later listed various management functions as part of the role of the program leader. Positional leaders should not be the norm in the faculty. It was emphatically acknowledged that leadership "lies on different levels" from ground staff to student leaders. One participant highlighted that "some of our students they are actually senior leaders, they are coming from faith-based communities where they have been leaders for twenty-five, twenty years [yet are] not acknowledged." These students "have been professional leaders."

An interesting contrast arose during this discussion. Most participants compared their experience of church leadership and that of academic leadership. Leadership in the academic context comes with "a lot more committees; more pressure to perform and bureaucracy."

Leadership characteristics

Most characteristics listed revolved around the *leader's personal leadership style* because leaders must "be true oneself and one's own leadership style" and enjoy "your own personal leadership journey." Leadership lies "deep within a person's value system, notions like calling and compassion, character those things matter to me." One's "experience of having gone through hardships and having self-have struggles and challenges would be a help for students." It is a "certain type of person that is drawn to academia" compared to being a church academic leader. Academic leaders have "a lot more responsibility, a lot more pressure, a lot more eyes on you, you have to do extra learning as well and extra reading just to be, to behave well in certain spaces and be the voice of the students to know what is good for them." Leadership is not restricted to any gender, race, or class, according to the participants of this study.

Participants experience leaders in the Faculty of Theology through various role players, they had both positive and negative experiences, and they see *leaders working collaboratively.*

The various leadership roles experienced in the faculty have been the Dean, faculty committee chairs, student (TSC and first-year representatives) leaders, tutors, and spiritual leaders. Most participants shared personal stories of the impact these leaders have had on their journey to becoming leaders today. These were reflected as positive, delivered through opportunities "to take a leadership role, show respect for each other's contributions, and through modeling, being able to create social collusion, with everyone from the janitor up to the Dean participating and joining in, being enabled to take a stand if there is a sort of injustice (and having the freedom) to articulate and able to express what they think." One voiced that they "have never felt like there was a dictatorship or authority." Conversely, some noted their negative experiences as when we experienced a "leadership vacuum for eighteen months. Processes are pretty much prescribed in how we identify leaders, [it is] pragmatic, managerial and still to a large extent top-down" and "[they have] really not distributed leadership intentionally." Complaints that we esteem "positional leadership—by default" and "sometimes do not know how the leaders are elected." "My experience is always this powerful system" was highlighted by a colleague who has been around for a while.

Participants described what they understood as the *role and expectations of the program leader* and also challenges they foresee for someone in this role. They also highlighted possible areas where this program leader would need to undergo leadership development, and suggested a few benefits to the faculty of this role.

It was interesting to note that participants related the role of program leaders directly to how they read the policy document yet also reflecting on our faculty processes. Besides the planning, networking, and quality assurance expected of this leader, the idea of a prescribed way of leading popped up again in this section. A program leader "does not prescribe where a program should go but rather links it to the university's vision." This was also highlighted through the actual process of program renewal. Colleagues were cautious about any possible ulterior motives of the program leader. Once they noticed that it was about a shared mission of the BTh, greater cohesion took place. This was evidenced through an expectation that the program leader is relational and able to collaborate with all stakeholders. Two benefits of having a program leader highlighted by disciplinary chairs was that having this role in place "would make the chair's work much easier" and "assessment would be 100 percent because you are a leader connected to all the others."

Finally, in direct response to the research question, the role of a program leader within the Faculty of Theology was highlighted both generally and during program renewal processes.

Relating the above-mentioned responses to the specific needs of the Faculty of Theology during program renewal, one notices that participants realize the *enormity of this role*. Aligned with the description of leadership as personal style, above, one participant emphasized that because this role required much of the person filling it, the "heartbeat of the one wanting to be a program leader" would also need to be taken seriously. This relates to earlier comments that "not everyone would be good at filling this role." Among the long list of responsibilities assigned to this person were scholarship within the discipline and an understanding and knowledge base of teaching, learning, and higher education; the ability to work with and manage people throughout the process; having a shared mission or purpose in mind; and, lastly, prioritizing the voice, role, and experience of students throughout.

DISCUSSION

The top two themes noticed throughout the data analysis process were first, that the *program leader needs to be relational and collaborative* in their approach to curriculum renewal. The second seems quite contradictory: most participants still ascribed greater authority and respect to positional leadership. Despite all the characteristics given to this program leadership role, examples given were still examples of those who held positions of authority within the faculty.

In terms of theological training, some of the themes that developed from our broader curriculum renewal process were:

- Exploring what the identity of a theologian is. This applies to the student studying and to the academic teaching theology.
- There are varying tensions between an inherited theological education and the proposed Africanized theological education, which also speaks to the distinction of global and local epistemology of knowledge.
- The role that the social location of the student and the faculty building plays in doing theology is crucial. There is a "need for theological discernment in view of South African context."

- As a faculty, we agreed that "we want students to understand what it means to be a Biblical scholar and the authenticity of its history, but you're also wanting the students to be able to apply this in their own context. As faculty, we also need to ask how the students are not getting this richness that we say is in the text."
- We would need to focus on continuous capacity building for program renewal as new staff are appointed and new students enroll.

The findings of this research study cannot be understood without awareness of the broader process that the Faculty of Theology has journeyed through for the past few years. In terms of theological training, an academic leadership competency framework is proposed. This includes:

- Integration that acknowledges professional learning within varying contexts as imperative!
- An intercultural approach for globalized impact
- Ethical leadership practices within classroom, faculty, and broader institution
- An intersection of communities of practice inclusive of all stakeholders[23]

CONCLUDING REMARKS

Program renewal is a continual process within higher education. For many faculties of theology, these processes require input from the same teaching and support staff and collaboration. The role of program leaders is to assist in streamlining demands placed on faculty and staff yet also calls for much from such a leader. This chapter highlighted what we need to consider when appointing people as program leaders, taking into consideration all the other workload they may have. The role of program leaders is indispensable and integral to program renewal processes in any faculty at a university.

BIBLIOGRAPHY

Archer, Margaret S., and Dave Elder-Vass. "Cultural System or Norm Circles? An Exchange." *European Journal of Social Theory* 15 (2012) 93–115.
Barnett, Ronald. "University Knowledge in an Age of Supercomplexity." *Higher Education* 40 (2000) 409–22.

23. Leibowitz and Bozalek, "Access to Higher Education."

Beylefeld, Adriana, et al. "Action Research: A Wonderfully Uncomfortable Mode of Creating Knowledge." *Acta academica* 39 (2007) 146–75.

Branson, Mark Lau. *Memories, Hopes, and Conversations: Appreciative Inquiry and Congregational Change*. Plymouth, UK: Rowman & Littlefield, 2004.

Braun, Virginia, and Victoria Clarke. "Using Thematic Analysis in Psychology." *Qualitative Research in Psychology* 3 (2006) 77–101.

Director of Centre for Teaching and Learning. "Strategy for Teaching and Learning 2017–2021." Stellenbosch University, 2017. https://www.sun.ac.za/english/learning-teaching/ctl/Documents/SU%20TL%20Strategy.pdf.

Ezzy, Douglas. *Qualitative Analysis: Practice and Innovation*. London: Taylor & Francis, 2002.

Given, Lisa M., ed. *The SAGE Encyclopedia of Qualitative Research Methods*. 2 vols. Los Angeles: SAGE, 2008.

Grønhaug, Kjell, and Olov Olson. "Action Research and Knowledge Creation: Merits and Challenges." *Qualitative Market Research* 2 (1999) 6–14.

Leibowitz, Brenda, and Vivienne Bozalek. "Access to Higher Education in South Africa." *Widening Participation and Lifelong Learning* 16 (2014) 91–109.

McNiff, Jean. *Action Research: Principles and Practice*. 3rd ed. London: Routledge, 2013.

Msila, Vuyisile, and Mishack T. Gumbo, eds. *Africanising the Curriculum: Indigenous Perspectives and Theories*. Cape Town: African Sun Media, 2016.

Parkin, Doug. *Leading, Learning, and Teaching in Higher Education: The Key Guide to Designing and Delivering Courses*. Key Guides for Effective Teaching in Higher Education. London: Routledge, 2016.

Perry, Chad, and Ortun Zuber-Skerritt. "Action Research in Graduate Management Research Programs." *Higher Education* 23 (1992) 195–208.

Senior Director of Learning and Teaching Enhancement. "Guidelines for Programme Committee Chairs and Programme Leaders." Stellenbosch University, 2018. http://www.sun.ac.za/english/learning-teaching/ctl/Documents/Guidelines%20for%20Programme%20Committee%20Chairs%20and%20Programme%20Leaders.pdf.

———. "Teaching and Learning Policy." Stellenbosch University, 2018. https://www.sun.ac.za/english/learning-teaching/ctl/Documents/TeachingLearning%20Policy%202018.pdf.

Silverman, David. *Interpreting Qualitative Data*. 5th ed. York: Sage, 2015.

Trowler, Paul, et al. *Change Thinking, Change Practices: A Guide to Change for Heads of Department, Programme Leaders and Other Change Agents in Higher Education*. York: Learning and Teaching Support Network, 2003.

Weber, S. M. *Faculty of Theology Program Renewal Progress Report*. University of Stellenbosch, 2018.

Young, Michael. "What Is a Curriculum and What Can It Do?" *Curriculum Journal* 25 (2014) 7–13.

ADDENDUM A

An appreciative inquiry into the role of a program leader within a program renewal process at the Faculty of Theology

Interview questionnaire:

Date: _____
Duration of interview: _____
Interview no.: _____

Questions:

1. You have been asked to partake in this interview because you serve as a leader within this faculty. Can you describe what your understanding of leadership within an academic environment is?
2. Can you give me examples of how you have experienced leadership in this faculty?
3. Have you read through the document sent on the role of program leaders? If so, what were your first impressions of this document?
4. How would you describe the role of a program leader within our faculty? What could be expected from such a leader?
5. Reflecting on our current program renewal process, how would you describe the role of a program leader during this process?

Chapter 11

Academic Support as a Success Factor for Augmented Teaching and Learning at the Faculty of Theology, Stellenbosch University

Dawid Mouton

INTRODUCTION

This reflective chapter is based on the author's subjective experience and perceptions in teaching the Academic Literacy Modules for Theology ALT 114 during the first semester of 2021. Even though no formal ethical clearance was required, care is taken to protect the identity of students.

The Faculty of Theology, Stellenbosch University (SU), offers an extended degree or curriculum program (EDP/ECP) option to students who may otherwise be excluded from higher education due to marginally missing admission criteria, especially when impeding socioeconomic conditions play a role.[1] This is in line with the strategic objective of the Department of Higher Education and Training (DHET), South Africa, as well as that of SU, to intentionally improve equitable access and academic success for such students.[2] In this article, the use of the term *extended curriculum program (ECP)* is preferred, in line with an increased preference among key role players in the higher education sector in South Africa.[3] The academic literacy modules offered as part of the ECP are intended to enhance the potential of these students and their success at university. In contrast to the structure

---

1. Council on Higher Education, "Extended Programs," 1.
2. Van Niekerk, "Verlengde program"; Stellenbosch University, "Guidelines."
3. Council on Higher Education, "Extended Programs," 1.

followed at other faculties at the university, the ECP at the Faculty of Theology simply spread the number of mainstream courses over two years and added two academic literacy modules as foundational courses. This changed in 2023 when the faculty implemented a fully accredited ECP in accordance with the guidelines from the DHET (SA) and included foundational courses up to the third year of studies. The implication of the ECP is that students take an additional year to complete their degree program.

During 2021, SU followed an augmented remote teaching approach. During the first semester of 2021, the faculty offered a one-week block teaching at the start of each term, followed by weekly online engagements for the rest of the term. This placed tremendous pressure on first-year students given the high-paced nature of the block-teaching model and the fact that students often have limited access to, and skills in, the use of information technology. Although this included both full-time and part-time cohorts, the discussion here pertains only to the engagement of the full-time cohort. This reflective chapter looks at the role the academic literacy module and associated interventions played during the first semester of 2021 in helping students to settle in at university and to acquire the necessary skills and attributes to enhance their success during the first year of studies.

The uncertainty and possible impacts on students and the academic program of the COVID-19 pandemic and the accompanying restrictions imposed by the government, as well as past experiences with the academic literacy modules, necessitated an inclusive and supportive approach. As the semester progressed, the approach also became more flexible in response to the particular challenges of students and with regard to the delivery of teaching and learning.

The chapter will give a brief background to the ECPs at South African universities, including SU, which links up with the following section, discussing some important considerations regarding ECPs and academic literacy. The chapter argues that an intentional and structured, yet flexible, approach to enhancing academic skills and attributes significantly enhances students' success, even amid the disruptions of a global pandemic that necessitated, among others, an augmented approach to teaching and learning.

BRIEF HISTORICAL BACKGROUND

The education system in South Africa prior to democracy in 1994 primarily catered for the minority white population, with access to higher education disproportionately limited for people of color.[4] Broadening access to

---

4. Badat, "Redressing the Colonial/Apartheid Legacy," 3–5; Bunting, "Higher Education Landscape," 36–38.

higher education was, and still is, seen as an important means to redress past inequalities and transform the higher education landscape in South Africa. One such pathway is the EDP, more recently referred to as the ECP. Leani van Niekerk describes the EDP (or ECP) as being "based on the same curriculum as the mainstream program, but students are granted an additional year of study along with supplementary learning opportunities and student support to complete the requirements for the qualification."[5] However, improved access does not guarantee success[6] and cannot be seen as the goal itself. Rather, it must culminate in improved success if it is to contribute to redressing past inequalities. Hence equity of access can only serve the redress "project" if the same emphasis is placed on the issue of equity of success. ECPs must therefore be designed, structured, and delivered in such a way that students are empowered to acquire the necessary social and academic skills to successfully complete their degree programs. This is particularly important given the past, and current, disparities in terms of quality basic education that still serve to marginalize students from poorer communities, which are predominantly also communities of color. ECPs at South African universities have been funded by the DHET since 2004.[7]

The Faculty of Theology at SU had been offering a "quasi-ECP" for ten years, so termed because the ECP merely split the first academic year in two and offered two basic academic literacy modules in the first year of study. This contrasted with the standard accredited programs aimed at improving student academic success that offered additional foundational modules to provide broader opportunities for academic and social skills development. This changed in 2023 when the faculty offered a fully accredited ECP to students in the three-year bachelor of theology (general and youth work) programs. The program under consideration here thus still offered only the two academic literacy modules to assist students in acquiring and building foundational academic skills. This will be followed by discussions on the academic literacy modules offered by the faculty and the approach followed in 2021. A brief discussion on student performance, followed by a reflective discussion on experiences and lessons learned, will precede the conclusion.

SOCIAL JUSTICE, LITERACY, AND ECP

In discussing academic support to ECP students, particularly academic literacy development in the context of the Faculty of Theology, it may be

5. Van Niekerk, "Verlengde program," 938–39.
6. Leibowitz and Bozalek, "Access to Higher Education," 97.
7. Liebowitz and Bozalek, "Foundation Provision," 9.

Academic Support as a Success Factor

worthwhile to consider a few key aspects and concepts. These include, but are not limited to, social justice imperatives and epistemic access, issue of academic literacy or literacies, the scope of academic support in undergraduate studies, and aspects pertaining to social practices, communities, and discourses.

Furlong and Cartmel assert that "social justice relates to the principle that every effort should be made to ensure that individuals and groups all enjoy fair access to rewards."[8] However, John Rawls argues that social justice in this sense would "require the equal distribution of 'all social primary goods—liberty and opportunity, income and wealth.'"[9] Alternatively, this would imply a type of access to "equal opportunity" only to "access unequal positions." Folashade Oloyede, reflecting on the value of a remedial English program for theology students in Nigeria, refers to the reality that many underprepared students come from challenging backgrounds that often include poor preparation for the higher education environment and its demands. To assume that these students, because of the equal opportunity for access to higher education and resources of higher education institutions, can compete on the same level as students from privileged environments and higher levels of preparedness, does not hold. Oloyede speaks of "involuntary academic injustice" as "a [naturally occurring] situation where the instructors treat all candidates as equal regardless of the disparities in their previous academic exposure thereby being unfair to the academically disadvantaged candidates."[10] In other words, without an intentional program to address, or at least reduce, the academic disparities with which students arrive at university, academic injustice is simply perpetuated, making it impossible to speak of social justice in the higher education context.

June Pym and Joseph I. Kioko are among many scholars who highlight the social justice imperatives of ECPs in South Africa, especially considering the persistent social, economic, and racial inequalities, historical and current, that impact students' ability to access and perform in higher education environments.[11] ECP students are often also first-generation, at-risk students who may struggle to perform optimally in a system designed to predominantly cater for the dominant culture in these environments.[12] Access to university is therefore only one part of the equation, as it means

---

8. Furlong and Cartmel, *Higher Education*, 3.
9. John Rawls, quoted in Furlong and Cartmel, *Higher Education*, 4.
10. Oloyede, "Remedial English Programme," 2.
11. Pym, "Voice, Identity, and Belonging," 186; Kioko, "Foundation Provision," 40.
12. De Klerk et al. "Small Victories over Time," 154.

relatively little if equity of success cannot be achieved.[13] Part of the process of achieving equity of success implies opening the space for reciprocal access to information, knowledge, and skill, broadly referred to here as epistemological access. For Crain Soudien, this requires from universities to be not only more inclusive, but also to be open to "engage with the whole spectrum of knowledges and understanding that live on the South African social and cultural landscape, those that are described as Western, African, modern, traditional, 'powerful,' 'useful,' and so on, and, fundamentally, the whole spectrum of people that are the living bearers of these knowledges."[14] In a way, this creates an opportunity for students to bring their own cultural and experiential knowledge and wisdom into the learning spaces to the benefit of all. However, this also comes with the responsibility for lecturers, academics, and institutions to find new ways to incorporate this and to make new knowledge and skills accessible to all students as part of the meaning-making process.

Another important aspect related to this is our understanding of what is meant by the concept of academic literacy. Lea and Street argue for a shift away from a deficit model when dealing with student literacy. They considered three overlapping approaches or models to teaching academic skills, namely, the study skills model, the academic socialization model, and the academic literacy model. Whereas the study skills model focuses primarily on individual cognitive and language skills, the academic socialization model deals with "acculturation into disciplinary and subject-based discourses and genres."[15] The academic literacy model on the other hand is concerned with "meaning-making, identity, power, authority" and institutional perspective on "knowledge."[16] These models are not mutually exclusive and share important overlaps. However, Lea and Street argue for a shift towards the academic literacy model as it "foregrounds the variety and specificity of institutional practices and students' struggles to make sense of these."[17] Jacobs warns against a restricted and limiting understanding of academic literacies and concurs with Lea and Street in the sense that a more nuanced view of academic literacies, which includes epistemological and ontological considerations, is required.[18] A view that moves away from

---

13. Pym et al., "Does Belonging Matter?," 37; Smith, "Creating Learning Communities."

14. Soudien, "Inclusion, Innovation and Excellence," 909.

15. Lea and Street, "'Academic Literacies' Model," 369.

16. Lea and Street, "'Academic Literacies' Model," 369.

17. Lea and Street, "'Academic Literacies' Model," 376.

18. Jacobs, "Academic Literacies," 134–36.

one-dimensional thinking of what I would call singular literacies, to a more comprehensive and holistic one that fosters meaning making in context. In the end, academic development is about more than just the acquisition of skills or language development. For Donovan and Erskine-Shaw, academic development and success relate to both study skills and socialization, whereby academic engagement should give meaning to knowledge and process.[19] This resonates with similar views by Jacobs and Van Dyk and Van de Poel, who argue for an understanding of literacy as a broader framework incorporating study skills, academic socialization, and academic literacies.[20] In the end, the chosen approach must serve the social justice imperative and provide equitable epistemological access.[21]

ACADEMIC LITERACY FOR THEOLOGY—STELLENBOSCH UNIVERSITY, 2021

During the first year of their studies, ECP students are required to complete two semester academic literacy modules, namely, Academic Literacy for Theology 114 (ALT 114) in the first semester, and Academic Literacy for Theology 144 (ALT 144) in the second semester. According to the module description, these modules have the following objectives and expected outcomes.

ALT 114 Objectives

In essence, the module aims to equip students with the basic skills required to successfully function and perform within the higher education environment, including a basic understanding of essential university environments, processes, and expectations, and the acquisition of a basic understanding, competencies, and skills to work on some online and offline technological platforms.

ALT 114 Expected Outcomes

Upon completion of the module, the successful student will be able to:

---

19. Donovan and Erskine-Shaw, "Maybe I Can," 326.
20. Jacobs, "On Being an Insider"; Van Dyk and Van de Poel, "Towards a Responsible Agenda," 48.
21. Boughey, "Contrasting Constructions," 308.

1. Demonstrate an understanding of the higher education academic environment, processes, and expectations by:

    a. Using critical thinking in cross-cultural academic contexts by engaging in discussions on the multicultural nature of the higher education context.

    b. Practicing and exercising, according to the course framework, scenarios that demonstrate their understanding of readings.

    c. Being able to take relevant notes during lectures and make annotations to indicate an understanding of lectures.

    d. Offering their own understanding, either orally or in annotations, by explaining expectations of academic tasks and assignments for assessments.

    e. Showing the detailed layout of their own academic planning.

2. Demonstrate an acquired understanding and competency to work on online and offline technological platforms by:

    a. Describing, comparing, and analyzing the difference between the functions of the laptop and computer.

    b. Knowing and performing the basic operations of computers

    c. Organizing and saving files.

    d. Understanding and navigating the Internet (Websites, Emails, URLs, Links, Networks, etc.).

    e. Confidently communicating with lecturers and peers using mobile technology.

    f. Identifying appropriate and effectively using and communicating how to use online help options.

ALT 144 Objectives

This module aims to promote and develop academic and digital literacy and the appropriate knowledge, skills, and attitudes to become a successful theology student and competent professional. This includes the development of reading and writing strategies, referencing techniques, time-management and learning skills, as well as basic ICT communication skills.

ALT 144 Expected Outcomes

Upon completion of the module, the successful student will be able to:

1. Apply effective reading strategies to read theological texts.
2. Apply effective writing, summarizing, paraphrasing, and referencing skills for theological essays.
3. Do a literature search through the proper use of a library system and research database.
4. Strategically and appropriately use the internet for academic purposes.
5. Compile electronic documents using MS Word that meet the requirements of academic work.
6. Create electronic presentations at a basic level of proficiency
7. Apply communication strategies and effectively present individual and group presentations.
8. Use time-management skills appropriately.
9. Understand and apply different learning strategies for personal learning and content-specific needs.

APPROACH, INTERVENTIONS, AND STUDENT PERFORMANCE

In deciding on a possible and potentially appropriate approach, the following were considered, in addition to the objectives of the modules and the broader teaching and learning framework of the university.

- Uncertainty related to the progression of the COVID-19 pandemic and the accompanying restrictions imposed by the government, including its impacts on the preparation of first-year students during their final year at school. It was expected that this would also add to the psychological challenges that many first-year students experience in general.
- Full-time and part-time students were combined for the block teaching and online sessions during the first semester. As a result, wide age and skills gaps existed for this cohort. For example, while some of the students had already mastered the basic ICT skills needed to access learning information and perform basic tasks, others had significant limitations in this regard. In addition, some students could only access

ICT resources while on campus as they had no access to these at home. The university, through its laptop loan scheme, eventually did well in minimizing the impact of this to some extent.

- In general, most students experienced a significant gap between their reading, writing and other academic skills, and that which is required to function effectively at university.

Course development at SU, including the development of objectives, expected outcomes and assessments, is usually done in accordance with SU's broader philosophy of constructive alignment, and Bloom's taxonomy plays a significant role in this.[22] The constructive alignment approach, according to John Biggs, incorporates "the idea that students construct meaning through relevant learning activities" and requires the lecturer/teacher to "set up a learning environment that supports the learning activities appropriate to achieving the desired learning outcomes."[23] In this, the "curriculum, and its intended outcomes, the teaching methods used, the assessment tasks— are aligned to each other" to optimize learning.[24] The general approach in these modules, in addition to the above, was very much influenced by my own understanding of Fink's taxonomy, particularly because of its high regard for socialization and the integration thereof in learning spaces.[25] My own philosophy is that the intentional facilitation of socialized engagement in learning spaces improves relationships, eases psychological pressure, enhances peer-to-peer learning, and has the potential to build confidence. This, among other things, may serve to improve students' perceptions about the challenges in the learning environment as well as their own potential, which may positively affect their academic outcomes.

During the block teaching sessions, the initial focus was on cultivating an awareness of the multicultural nature of the university environment and the academic demands of university studies, as well as the importance of self-awareness. In addition, students, through facilitated engagements, reflected on the importance of relationship building, networking, and socialization as important resources to help cope with both the academic and psycho-social demands of higher education environments. Accessing and optimizing digital resources and learning spaces, including the university library, and guidance on academic ethics were covered on an introductory level, with more guidance and exercises given during online engagements.

22. See https://wwwo.sun.ac.za/ctlresources/constructive-alignment/.
23. Biggs, "Aligning Teaching," 1.
24. Biggs, "Aligning Teaching," 3.
25. Fink, "What Is 'Significant Learning'?"

Online engagements served to reinforce content dealt with during the block session, as a scaffolding approach is also generally followed regarding teaching and learning. The development of academic reading and writing competencies, source integration, referencing standards, task analysis and completion, academic planning, and communication skills, were addressed during the online sessions. The varied skills and competency levels among students required extensive input. The availability of a learning assistant, who was readily accessible, fairly flexible, and responsive, allowed for continuous support. It was found that the initial input to build relationships and rapport with students, contributed to them reaching out for assistance when needed. Ad hoc online learning interventions, in addition to scheduled sessions, provided additional opportunities for students to develop the skills and competencies needed for their studies. It remains important that material, activities, tasks, and any other learning interventions relate to other mainstream modules the students are taking. For example, teaching and activities related to task analysis, essay planning, and writing, would normally make use of assignments given to students in other modules. Throughout the semester, opportunities for reflexive exercises were created, and at the end of the semester, students reflected, for instance, on their experience and the impact on the academic literacy module. They were then required to compile and submit a presentation on the exercises as a way to further enhance their ability to collate and structure information, and present that in a logical format, while at the same time getting practice in producing PowerPoint presentations. Unfortunately, they could not present these in person due to COVID-19-related restrictions.

When considering student performance in the respective modules, one is encouraged to note that most of them passed their respective modules. However, one must keep in mind that the residential student cohort was very mall, with eight students only, and not all took the same mainstream modules. The pass rates for modules taken during the first semester were as follows (theology modules considered only and not any of the modules taken at the Faculty of Arts and Social Sciences), with the overall pass rate for the combined cohort in brackets:

- Academic Literacy = 87.5 percent
- Old and New Testament = 62.5 percent (56 percent)
- Practical Theology = 100 percent (79 percent)
- Practical Theology and Missiology = 100 percent (97 percent)
- Systematic Theology and Ecclesiology = 100 percent (95 percent)

SOME REFLECTIVE NOTES

The experience with this module in 2021 underscored what has been referred to earlier in the chapter, namely, that academic literacy is about much more than just language, reading, and writing skills. Personal, social, and ICT competency development prove pivotal for academic success, as does students' ability to connect and build relationships in the learning environment. Facilitating the building of trust and cohesion among students enhances the learning atmosphere as well as peer-to-peer learning opportunities. Lecturer and facilitator accessibility and approachability, as embodied in a caring and encouraging approach, not only improved the relationship with students but also served to maintain a positive and hopeful atmosphere among students. Maintaining contact with students outside of scheduled sessions greatly contributed to allaying fears of falling behind as additional inputs into the learning process seemed to have improved the skills and competencies taught. Feedback from students indicated that the acknowledgment, right from the start, of the challenges as they transition into the academic environment, the uncertainties at the time, and the psycho-social dynamics anticipated, helped them to become aware of and sometimes respond timeously to challenges in these respects. The focused, yet flexible, approach to teaching at the time not only benefited the students. This also afforded a valuable learning opportunity for the learning assistant who had not been involved in this module before. The collaborative and reflexive approach taken at the time also led to personal growth, as well as general improvements in teaching and student engagement for the lecturer. It further strengthened the awareness of and focus on reflexive teaching praxis, not only as a means to improve teaching and learning but also with regard to embodiment and positioning in teaching and learning, and other spaces.

Unfortunately, it is not possible to always maintain the high levels of contact experienced during the first semester of 2021. Additional resources were made available to mitigate the potential negative impacts of the pandemic, but this cannot be sustained under so-called normal circumstances. It is, therefore, necessary to continue to find innovative ways to maintain such contact and to effectively assist students to develop the competencies needed to successfully navigate the demands of higher education. All students enrolled for the ECP spoke English only as a second language. Although Afrikaans-speaking students have the option of doing their first-year courses in Afrikaans, most ECP students did not go for that option. Teaching students a high level of command in English reading and writing remained a challenge, not least since neither the lecturer nor learning assistant were native English speakers. Having a consultant from the Language Centre of the university teaching language development, among others, addressed some of the challenges to an extent. A strong emphasis on "accurate English" introduced quite a bit of anxiety and insecurity for the students. Although the focus shifted to clarity in communication rather than the correctness of grammar, one cannot ignore the fact that a reasonable command of academic English is still required, also in preparation for future careers, even though some would argue that many of the students may go back to work in their own or similar communities. The disparities in terms of ICT access and competency also created challenges as it was not always possible to maintain the same tempo in terms of teaching and assessments. This was to some extent managed through the learning assistant, but also through a flexible and adaptable approach to assessments that allowed for individualized time frames and multiple opportunities for students to master the necessary skills and competencies.

The faculty will implement a more structured and expanded ECP in 2023. The following suggestions will serve the program and students well going forward:

- Consider the institutional and environmental context—enablers, restrictors, expectations, stressors—and how these can be incorporated in the planning and teaching of the academic literacy modules.

- Further develop and enhance the integration between the academic literary modules and mainstream offerings, including embedding academic literacy development in mainstream modules.

- Actively promote a culture of continuous learning for students and teaching personnel.

- Incorporate relevant research and best practices on ECPs, pedagogical and taxonomy frameworks, and teaching and learning in general, into the continuous planning and delivery of learning opportunities.

- Continued research on aspects of teaching academic literacy as well as on the implementation of the ECP, focusing, for instance, on reflective, organic development, course delivery, and learning opportunities. Such research should be collaborative, including students, lecturers, and educational experts.

- Critical reflection and engagements on prevalent ontological and epistemological frameworks at work within the faculty, the institution and the higher education space in South Africa and attempt to respond to these in a participatory and collective manner.

CONCLUSION

This chapter reflects only superficially on issues of teaching academic literacies at a South African university. It is also subjective and "teacher-centered" with the voices of students silent, which is a major limitation. This was mainly due to this contribution being developed from a retrospective perspective, but also due to the fact that, although student feedback is available, ethical clearance was not obtained for its use prior to the collection thereof. The reflection is further based on a very limited time frame, for a course with limited scope that involves a relatively small number of students, and should be read with these caveats in mind. However, from this limited reflection, it would appear that prioritizing academic literacies has the potential to improve the outcomes for ECP students, enhance the potential for a collaborative learning environment and process, and stimulate growth for students and lecturers. Through an inclusive, caring, and growth-enhancing approach, student mental health can be supported. It remains important to follow an inclusive approach to teaching in learning, actively including the diverse student body in the teaching and learning process, as it may further enhance the agenda of decolonization in the higher education space in South Africa. At the same time, one needs to remain cognizant of the downstream and contextualized impact of theological training, making the social justice imperative not only applicable to the teaching and learning of these students, but also in preparing them in a broader sense for the challenges and inequalities many communities face. The potential of ECPs and academic literacy programs as vehicles for improving access and success as a social justice response to past and current inequalities should be maximized as much as possible. In the end, particularly in the South African context, the implementation of the ECP at the Stellenbosch Faculty of Theology needs to nurture a social justice ethic, work towards the transformation of students, lecturers and the community, and remain rooted in a pedagogy of hope that resists narrow and marginalizing outlooks, expectations, and the pitfalls of a deficit approach to student academic development.

BIBLIOGRAPHY

Badat, Saleem. "Redressing the Colonial/Apartheid Legacy: Social Equity, Redress and Higher Education Admissions in Democratic South Africa." Paper presented at conference, "Affirmative Action in Higher Education in India, the United States and South Africa," New Delhi, Mar. 19–21, 2008.

Biggs, John. "Aligning Teaching for Constructing Learning." *Higher Education Academy* 1 (2003) 1–4.

Boughey, Christine Mary. "Contrasting Constructions of Students' Literacy-Related Experiences at a Historically Black South African University." PhD diss., University of Western Cape, 2002.

Bunting, Ian. "The Higher Education Landscape under Apartheid." *Transformation in Higher Education: Global Pressures and Local Realities* (2006) 35–52.

Council on Higher Education. "Extended Programs with an Integrated Foundation Phase: Theoretical Considerations for Curriculum Design." *Briefly Speaking* (2020) 1–16.

De Klerk, Edwin, et al. "Small Victories over Time: The Impact of an Academic Development Intervention at Stellenbosch University." *Education as Change* 10 (2006) 149–69.

Donovan, Christina, and Marianne Erskine-Shaw. "'Maybe I Can Do This. Maybe I Should Be Here': Evaluating an Academic Literacy, Resilience and Confidence Program." *Journal of Further and Higher Education* 44 (2020) 326–40.

Fink, L. Dee. "What Is 'Significant Learning'?" WCU, 2003. https://www.wcu.edu/webfiles/pdfs/facultycenter_significantlearning.pdf.

Furlong, Andy, and Fred Cartmel. *Higher Education and Social Justice*. Society for Research into Higher Education. N.p.: McGraw-Hill Education (UK), 2009.

Jacobs, Cecilia. "Academic Literacies and the Question of Knowledge." *Journal for Language Teaching = Ijenali Yekufundzisa Lulwimi = Tydskrif vir Taalonderrig* 47 (2013) 127–39.

———. "On Being an Insider on the Outside: New Spaces for Integrating Academic Literacies." *Teaching in Higher Education* 10 (2005) 475–87.

Kioko, Joseph I. "Foundation Provision in South African Higher Education: A Social Justice Perspective." In *Beyond the University Gates: Provision of Extended Curriculum Programmes in South Africa*, edited by Catherine Hutchings and James Garraway, 40–49. Cape Town: Cape Peninsula University of Technology Press, 2010. https://www.cput.ac.za/storage/services/fundani/beyond_the_university_gates.pdf.

Lea, Mary R., and Brian V. Street. "The 'Academic Literacies' Model: Theory and Applications." *Theory into Practice* 45 (2006) 368–77.

Leibowitz, Brenda, and Vivienne Bozalek. "Access to Higher Education in South Africa: A Social Realist Account." *Widening Participation and Lifelong Learning* 16 (2014) 91–109. https://doi.org/10.5456/WPLL.16.1.91.

———. "Foundation Provision: A Social Justice Perspective." *SAJHE* 29 (2015) 8–25.

Oloyede, T. Folashade. "Remedial English Programme as an Antidote to Involuntary Academic Injustice in Theological Education in Africa." Academia, 2018. From *West African Journal of Higher Education*. https://www.academia.edu/41623177/REMEDIAL_ENGLISH_PROGRAMME_AS_AN_ANTIDOTE_TO_INVOLUNTARY_ACADEMIC_INJUSTICE_IN_THEOLOGICAL_EDUCATION_IN_AFRICA.

Pym, June. "Voice, Identity, and Belonging: Making a Difference." In *Socially Just Pedagogies, Capabilities and Quality in Higher Education: Global Perspectives*, edited by Melanie Walker and Merridy Wilson-Strydom, 177–99. Palgrave Studies in Global Citizenship Education and Democracy. London, Palgrave Macmillan, 2017.

Pym, June, et al. "Does Belonging Matter? Exploring the Role of Social Connectedness as a Critical Factor in Students' Transition to Higher Education." *Psychology in Society* 42 (2011) 35–50.

Smith, Mitzi J. "A Case for Creating Learning Communities to Address the Challenges of At-Risk Students in Theological Education." Academia, 2016. https://www.academia.edu/21741351/A_Case_for_Creating_Learning_Communities_to_Address_the_Challenges_of_At_Risk_Students_in_Theological_Education.

Soudien, C. "Inclusion, Innovation and Excellence: Higher Education in South Africa and Its Role in Social Development; Part 2: HELTASA 2012 Special Section." *SAJHE* 28 (2014) 907–22.

Stellenbosch University. "Guidelines to the Extended Degree Programmes of Stellenbosch University." Stellenbosch University, 2010. https://www.sun.ac.za/english/learning-teaching/ctl/Documents/EDP%20guidelines.pdf.

Van Dyk, Tobie, and Kris Van de Poel. "Towards a Responsible Agenda for Academic Literacy Development: Considerations That Will Benefit Students and Society." *Journal for Language Teaching = Ijenali Yekufundzisa Lulwimi = Tydskrif vir Taalonderrig* 47 (2013) 43–69.

Van Niekerk, Leani. "Die verlengde program as'n instrument vir breër toegang tot Suid-Afrikaanse hoër onderwys—'n besinning oor die ervaring van die Fakulteit Regsgeleerdheid aan die Universiteit van die Vrystaat." *Litnet Akademies: 'n Joernaal vir die Geesteswetenskappe, Natuurwetenskappe, Regte en Godsdienswetenskappe* 14 (2017) 937–58.

Chapter 12

Colleague Observation in Interdisciplinary Academic Collaboration

Quality and Innovation in Education

LINNÉA K. JERMSTAD, SVITLANA HOLOVCHUK, AND GUNNVI SÆLE JOKSTAD

INTRODUCTION

Over the past decade, the educational system has faced significant challenges.[1] COVID-19, in particular, has been described as the "worst educational crisis on record," which "forced educational systems worldwide to come to a halt."[2] The crisis significantly impacted the quality of education, as educational systems had to reinvent overnight, with neither students nor teaching staff prepared for the sudden shift.[3] The COVID-19 pandemic, along with several other crises and unforeseen events in recent years, highlighted the need for innovation and collaborative practices in higher education. According to Chemi and Krogh, it is essential to conduct research and establish practices that facilitate the acquisition of knowledge among higher education individuals and groups, in particular the practices linked to co-creative experiences.[4]

---

1. Økland, "Perspectives on Globalization."
2. UNESCO et al., *Global Education Crisis*, 5.
3. Goth et al., "Nærhet, eller distanse?," 195.
4. Chemi and Krogh, "Setting the Stage."

A lesson from the pandemic is to create a more resilient system by preparing for disruption, promoting global collaboration on research and development in education, and strengthening the teacher workforce: "The crisis revealed that, in most countries, teachers were not ready to ensure continuity of learning. Teachers require high-quality initial teacher education and continuous professional development that prepares them to assess student learning."[5] This raises questions about what competencies are required to adjust and, perhaps even more importantly, how to adopt entrepreneurship in the way we teach and collaborate with colleagues.

The development of theoretical frameworks at the individual level that are concerned with the necessary knowledge structures (competence areas) for handling crises and unforeseen events is currently limited.[6] This DIKU project aims to develop an innovative educational system that fosters both established and novel approaches to teaching and learning in a glocal setting. The project constitutes a collaboration between the disciplines of pedagogy and theology, within the broader DIKU project Teaching and Learning Theology in Crisis, which involves NLA University College, Norway, and Stellenbosch University, South Africa. Such interdisciplinary glocal collaboration provides ample opportunity to investigate quality development in higher education. As members of the pedagogy department, our initial role was to observe theology lessons and enhance the quality of teaching and learning. However, our observations in this unfamiliar research field left us humbled and contemplative, prompting us to delve into the singular phenomenon of observation and the experience of being an outsider in another teacher's world. The aim of this inaugural chapter is to investigate the impact of interdisciplinary observation on the self-reflection of the observer. The research question that will guide this study is as follows: *How does interdisciplinary observation impact the self-reflection of the observer, and what are the underlying explanations for this phenomenon as elucidated by Bronfenbrenner's ecological systems theory and the parameter levels of observation categorized by semantic theory construction?* Using an autoethnographic approach, a comprehensive interview was conducted with a project member, and the resulting observations were thoroughly analyzed in the context of academia. The study drew upon research on collaboration and observation to inform its analysis.

Moreover, we meticulously analyze and deconstruct the phenomenon of observation through the lens of Kvernbekk's semantic theory construction, providing a model that offers a comprehensive depiction of observation. Our

---

5. UNESCO et al., *Global Education Crisis*, 39.
6. Torgersen, *Interaction*.

ultimate goal in this project is to assess the efficacy during times of crisis of colleague observation as a suitable approach for promoting innovation and professional development among pedagogy and theology educators.

HIGHER EDUCATION—OBSERVATION AS A COLLABORATIVE APPROACH TO INNOVATION

The role of educators in higher education is multifaceted and requires a complex set of competencies. Ulvik and Smith contend that collaboration with colleagues will be a crucial factor in promoting professional development in the future, as evidenced by colleague observation.[7] Collaborating with colleagues locally or globally can be viewed as a socially constructive process, emphasizing the social and cultural environmental demands as integral dimensions of the learning process. According to social constructivist theories, culture and the global dimension are regarded as constituent parts of the individual, embedded in everyday practices and mediated through language.[8] The aim of the researchers is to comprehend the world in which they work and to recognize that the practices they engage in are indispensable to the observer's interpretation.[9] By inviting colleagues to observe teaching, a dialogue between professionals may create an environment for further reflection for all involved.

The investigation of quality elements in higher education literature highlights observation as a crucial factor in enhancing dialogue and reflection, leading to improved teaching.[10] Traditionally, observation has been used as a method for monitoring, assessing, and supporting the quality of teaching and the development of teachers' pedagogic practices in education.[11] Classroom observation focuses on various dimensions of teaching, such as classroom management, involvement and motivation, assessment for learning, and learning strategies. As a formative tool, observation models didactic skills, and fosters sharing and developing of teachers' professional learning.

Research on colleague observation emphasizes feedback, aimed at providing a response to the observed teacher's teaching according to specific criteria. The feedback is primarily intended to benefit the observed teacher,

---

7. Ulvik and Smith, "Lærerutdanneres profesjonelle utvikling," 437.
8. Vélez-Agosto et al., "Bronfenbrenner's Bioecological Theory Revision."
9. Cresswell, *Qualitative Inquiry*, 34.
10. Bloch et al., "Does Quality Work Work?," 711.
11. O'Leary, "Rethinking Teachers' Professional Learning," 1.

serving as a starting point for reflection. However, in this specific academic context, where observation serves the purpose of reflection, it is necessary to define the concept of observation. Saussure posits that meaning is not fixed, but rather changes over time as language adapts to new social and cultural contexts.[12] To understand the significance of observation in a contemporary academic context, we can use the semantic theory construction to establish a model that captures the meaning of observation. In Kvernbekk's theory of semantic theory construction, models of phenomena have several parameters that together provide a picture of the concept's meaning. According to Kvernbekk, meaningful semantic structures are what define theories. Theories do not directly address phenomena but rather selective parameters that form abstract models of reality. A phenomenon is characterized by a small number of selected parameters that are abstracted from the phenomenon.[13] The main problem with our knowledge of the world, according to Kvernbekk, is how the abstract system and the phenomenon are connected, or how the knowledge we have represents the world. An abstract system is a radical simplification of the phenomenon and therefore does not represent the actual phenomenon but rather represents the phenomenon based on the selected parameters. Thus, there is an indirect relation between theory and phenomenon, and it possesses a certain state. As shown in our newly created "Higher Education Observation Model," the observation cycle is divided into four selected parameters intended to represent the phenomenon of observation as a self-reflective process in global collaborative academic colleague observation: assessment, interpretation, self-evaluation and judgment:

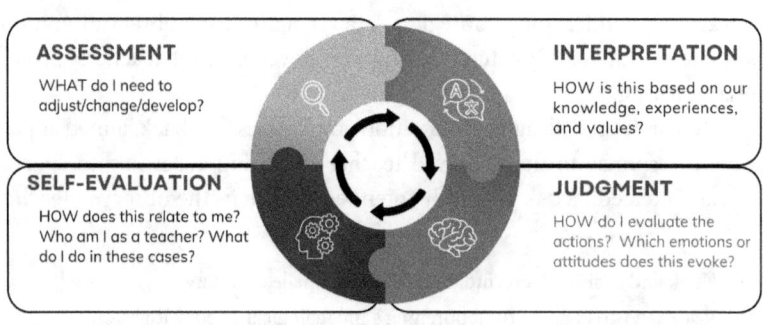

12. Saussure, "Nature of Language."
13. Kvernbekk, *Pedagogisk teoridannelse*, 65.

The four parameters indicate that reflective processes during observation yield several educational benefits for the observer. These include acquiring authentic experiences, heightened awareness of one's own practices, and exposure to novel didactic approaches.[14] As stated by Cosh: "The greatest influence on the way we teach is neither theories of education nor our training but is instead our notion of good teaching derived from our own experience of being taught."[15] Therefore, it can be argued that observation is a method that invites the observer into the "world" of another teacher, providing an opportunity for authentic experiences. In many ways, teachers who enter the world of another teacher, despite the uncertainty and discomfort it may bring, and reflect on their own actions, take an active and innovative position as lifelong learners.

THE INTERACTION OF WORDS—A GLOCAL SYSTEM THEORY APPROACH

Observation as an approach in glocal collaboration implies stepping out of our comfort zone as teachers, recognizing that "every local is connected in a global network of connectivity."[16] The term *glocal*, local *and* global, is here cited and described, according to the phenomenon of observation, as a dialectical space where new understandings emerge from polarities. The act of observing various teaching methodologies and teaching design can potentially stimulate innovation and entrepreneurial thinking,[17] while also offering fresh perspectives by breaking away from one's own disciplinary boundaries. Furthermore, observing teachers cross-nationally engaging in everyday contexts may seem highly localized, but the landscape and system of engagement is always already glocal: locally situated and globally influenced. The quality of higher education is both locally and globally influenced and is therefore a "complex phenomenon that can be affected by various social and historical practices such as academic habits, discourses, educational policies, and social values of the given community."[18] The local, glocal, global can be analyzed in themes of Bronfenbrenner's system theory as it sees the individual's environment in individual and composite systems, micro-, meso-, exo-, and macro-system. The micro-system relates to the

14. Bloch et al., "Does Quality Work Work?," 708.
15. Cosh, "Peer Observation," 173.
16. Varner et al., "Glocal Challenges," 9.
17. Iversen and Pedersen, "Co-Creating Knowledge."
18. Mulisa, "Bioecological Systems Theory," 107.

local and the closest relationships and activities in the individual's life, and the interactions that influence the individual on a day-to-day basis, such as the family, the teacher–student-relationship, or relationship and interaction between peers at the workplace, teaching methods, educational and supportive recourses.[19] The next level is the meso-system. A meso-system is the interconnections of two or more micro-systems, e.g., involvement in the activities.[20] The third system is called the exo-system and is defined as one or more settings in which the individual is not directly involved, but that can affect the individual, by affecting their experiences indirectly.[21] The macro-system describes trends in the culture and global phenomena that influence the other systems, i.e., the local education system. Macro-systems are social systems, economic frameworks, cultural values or national guidelines, or political systems, and thus the macro-systems will affect not only a single person but whole generations or social classes. The single individual teacher or researcher who is observed and observes is therefore influenced by global trends that manifest in the culture, by economic and political systems, colleagues, leadership in the workplace, and so on. In this view, teaching shouldn't be analyzed decontextualized from the social ecology of higher education.

The act of observing teachers in different educational systems will always implicitly carry each researcher's local engagement and presuppositions and can be a fruitful road to a broad understanding of knowledge in higher education. Varner et al., as cited earlier, show that educators lack the authentic experiences needed to connect across differences locally and globally. Building global collaboration, in higher education as a platform for engaging in a larger context and gaining authentic experience, enhances innovation and professional development as it allows the teacher to dive into a new world through observation.

METHOD

The data for this study was collected using a qualitative research design, specifically an autoethnographic methodology. The aim of the research project was to gain insight into the work life experiences of a teacher, while taking into consideration sociocultural aspects. "Autoethnography is a way of analyzing (graphy) the personal (auto) and how it relates to the wider

---

19. Bronfenbrenner, *Ecology of Human Development*.
20. Goth et al., "Tilrettelegging for trivsel."
21. Bronfenbrenner, *Ecology of the Family*.

socio-cultural (ethno) experience."[22] Autoethnography is a different way of studying experiences and gives academic life a new perspective. Autoethnography is valuable as a method of gaining access to social, political, and cultural aspects, and revealing emotions, hidden power structures, and norms.[23] Autoethnography is an experience-based path to knowledge: "It is also about challenging the alignment of what is understood as knowledge, and about making room for the 'small' and personal stories that are often swallowed up by the big, shared stories in more traditional research approaches."[24]

The overall purpose of this research is to contribute to knowledge in the area of colleague observation, and to explore how colleague observation in a glocal setting can yield valuable authentic experiences. These experiences and insights can be a resource for teachers' professional development and innovation using an autoethnographic approach.[25] The fieldwork notes were obtained during digital theology classes in higher education in Norway and South Africa. The interviewee works in higher education in Norway and views the observed teachers through her own eyes, situated in a Norwegian educational setting. The observed colleagues were from two different continents, Europe/Norway and Africa/South Africa, making that the study encompassed both local and global contexts.

This chapter focuses on the theme of observation itself and discusses the digital aspect only superficially. Although research has shown that using digital platforms raises questions about teaching and learning in higher education, the aim of this study was to explore the experience of gaining access to the world of another teacher and the experience described by the observer.

The study was conducted in accordance with "Guidelines for Research Ethics in the Social Sciences and Humanities,"[26] and the author acknowledges the critical reflections and pitfalls associated with autoethnography. Balancing the personal and professional, showing respect and sensitivity, and understanding the social-cultural system of the observed are crucial aspects of this research method.

---

22. Boncori, "Learning and Doing Autoethnography," 84.
23. Klevan et al., "Ensretting, standardisering og kunnskapsbasert," 108.
24. Klevan et al., "Ensretting, standardisering og kunnskapsbasert," 108.
25. Cresswell, *Qualitative Inquiry*, 70.
26. National Committee for Research Ethics in the Social Sciences and the Humanities, "Guidelines for Research Ethics."

RESULTS AND DISCUSSION

In our project the researchers involved agreed that college observation could benefit the observer as observation on a glocal level is a rare opportunity for authentic experience. However, there are some aspects to consider. Interaction between students and the lecturer, such as lectures and conversations, are created as a result of evaluation, assessment, judgment, and interpretation influenced by the context in which they live and work. The observer may not have an insight into all of these. Despite this, one can say that the observer's reflection is both useful for the individual professional teacher and enables collaboration and learning from peers.[27] Both the observer and the observed experience peer observation as valid and useful. Being able to place the experience and understandings in a larger context depends on the observer's reflective judgment.[28] The result of the study is analyzed and discussed according to Bronfenbrenner's system theory and the previously shared semantic theory–constructed model with parameters for observation: assessment, interpretation, self-evaluation, and judgment. According to Bronfenbrenner, we present our reflection from the observation in these categories: 1) micro-level, 2) meso-/exo-level and 3) macro-level.

1. MICRO-LEVEL

The initial stage of the analyses and discussion involves the observer's reflection on their observation as a form of judgment and self-evaluation. At this level, the individual researcher/teacher is examined, along with the proximal processes that exert an influence on them at the closest level. These processes may include colleagues, students with whom they interact over time, courses, teachers, mentors, and so on.[29] As individuals, we are closest to ourselves and our everyday situations when observing and analyzing data. Hence, we must acknowledge our biases and how they influence our interpretations. We possess personal knowledge-based ideas based on our field of theoretical expertise, our experiences, and values and these can affect our perception of observations made on colleagues from different cultural or professional backgrounds, as is the case in this interdisciplinary research. The encounter between colleagues can lead to unfair judgments and requires ethical reflection. When asked about this, the interviewee reflected: "Who am I to judge the interaction that takes place in this classroom? Why

---

27. Yurtseven and Altun, "Role of Self-Reflection," 209.
28. Jokstad, "Med kunst som veiviser," 185.
29. Bronfenbrenner, *Ecology of Human Development*.

am I trusted to be an observer in this classroom? Do I deserve such trust?" Moreover, the interviewee questioned said, "How would I feel if someone else observed me?" The interviewee's introspective reflection highlights the self-evaluation that arises from being invited into another teacher's world. She further continues:

> I recall from my own teaching some years back when several of the students in my higher-level course were colleagues and among them one student who stated that she had a higher degree in Pedagogy than myself. This made me uncomfortable, and I started to think that my teaching would be judged as weaker compared to hers. Not until after addressing this in a private conversation with her did I feel at ease.

These reflections draw upon the interviewee's personal history, demonstrating how vulnerability and uncertainty are integral components of a teacher's everyday work, where unforeseen circumstances may enter even the familiarity of the teacher's own classroom. When asked about the self-evaluative questions that arise from observation, the interviewee stated: "Would I have organized my lecture this way? Am I able to activate my students in conversation? And even: Do I offer my students lessons that fulfill the opportunities given me in class?" Such self-evaluation is a crucial starting point for new assessments of teaching. The observer's personal dialogue provides a unique opportunity for reflection, as it is useful for the individual professional teacher and enables collaboration and learning from colleagues, as noted by Yurtseven and Altun.[30] Both the observer and the observed may find colleague observation to be a valid and useful means of collaboration. According to Bakhtin, the word fulfills the listener, implying that individuals involved in a conversation may personally benefit from hearing the thoughts of others involved, resulting in their personal subjectification.[31]

These reflections on observation are predicated on the notion that observation can lead to active self-development, an intra-personal process that encourages awareness and sharing of good practice across academic disciplines. Self-directed learning through observation presupposes that individuals oversee their own learning,[32] as Schön introduced the term *reflective practitioner* to describe this type of learning that is necessary due to the new demands of professional practice. The reflective practitioner constructs personal meaning from knowledge and experience, including not only reflection in action but also reflection on action, as extended by

30. Yurtseven and Altun, "Role of Self-Reflection," 209.
31. Bakhtin, *Spørsmålet om talegenrane*.
32. Mueller and Schroeder, "From Seeing to Doing."

others. Self-reflection and self-evaluation strengthen teachers' professional development, raising awareness of their own strengths and weaknesses as well as those of others.[33] Throughout his work, Schön posits that technical rationality as a science-based position is replaced by approaches that emphasize artistic and intuitive methods, often employed by practitioners in circumstances involving uniqueness, fluctuation, and clashes in principles. Embracing a position of unfamiliarity helps us learn by thinking about what we do while we're doing it, and also later when we look back at our actions.

Brunstad and Oliverio discuss the term *reflective practitioner* as a catchword in educational discourse and introduce Biesta's term when asking, "How can we become an educational wise person?" They argue that professional skills "can be learned through study, training, and repetition, but the art of knowing which skills are most useful—and when and how best to use them—can only be gained through an active, sensitive interaction with our environment."[34] Therefore, reflective practice must be complemented by professional subjectification. The dialogue is a unique environment for this to occur and benefits all persons involved, as noted by Chemi and Krogh, and is essential for promoting co-creative processes in interdisciplinary collaboration.

2. MESO-/EXO-LEVEL

The subsequent level of our analysis and discussion entails an examination of departmental culture and structures, the college, general students, and other factors that indirectly influence the researcher/teacher, which are not necessarily a part of the everyday process. Regarding these levels, the interviewee reflects on how the interaction between students and lecturers may allow the exchange of some personal ideas as colleagues. The context and culture within our workplace or specific department have a substantial impact on our teaching. Since students are a product of society, they carry expectations associated with it. Reflecting on these realities, the interviewee states, "Lecturers might find themselves in a situation where several aspects must be considered, and where neither is as good as wished for. Teaching is a creation and cannot follow fixed rules." As mentioned above, Schön substitutes technical rationality with artistic, intuitive methods, relevant in uncertain, unstable, and value-conflicting situations.[35] These artistic, intuitive processes may be observed, but never fully understood by other than

---

33. Schön, *Reflective Practitioner*, 15.
34. Brunstad and Oliverio, "Practical Wisdom," 75.
35. Schön, *Reflective Practitioner*.

the lecturers themselves. In the observation we find ourselves in the trap of making judgments based on our own context. Seen from the perspective of Bronfenbrenner's theory, the meso-/exo-level and the context and disciplines we work within to some extent influence how we are as practitioners. The uniqueness is easily disregarded, but nevertheless of the utmost importance. When asked to interpret the experience of didactic approaches of some of the theology lectures, and assessing the lecture and her own didactic approaches, the interviewee said:

> To observe a lecture based on statements or facts presented in writing to the students took me back to my time as a student at the university. The lecturer delivered the speech and we, the listeners, took notes. In a way one can say that the knowledge of the lecturer was transported to the students. In my experience we rarely find monologues like this within the teacher education where I belong. I started to wonder: What benefit would the students have if we did? To give our students an overall view of the topic and then invite them for a discussion, would that be a better outcome for the students?

Observing theology lectures raised the observer's awareness of her own teaching in pedagogy and provided understanding of the complex aspects needing to be addressed while preparing for class. It also brings a new aspect into consideration, how to prepare for international students who are accustomed to different educational systems and how to initiate global co-creative collaborative processes with teachers who have different didactic approaches.

3. MACRO-LEVEL

At this level, we aim to discuss the broader role of teaching institutions and the teaching profession within their local and global contexts. National politics and policies can significantly impact programs and frames, potentially limiting a lecturer's professional autonomy. In discussing the macro-level, the interviewee noted, "As an observer of two different national institutions, it became clear how the student's environment might influence didactic planning." For instance, Norwegian students usually have access to necessary equipment for self-studies and may be accustomed to digital platforms for instructions and presentations, whereas other countries may not have such established practices. The interviewee found it fascinating to see the digital meeting place and how students interacted with it, interpreting it as a new way of classroom communication.

In this project, participants were both locally based and at the same time global citizens collaborating on a shared project with shared virtual lectures. As Hancock points out, "Global citizenships are empowered by a lack of physical and virtual boundaries, all members are individual identities and at the same time, members of the global community."[36] Virtual classrooms facilitate collaboration, observation, and co-creative practices. However, the interviewee reflected on the challenges of teaching on digital platforms during the COVID-19 pandemic, as it forced higher education systems to adapt their usual lesson-planning methods: "How did we handle those challenges and how did our students experience those lessons? If we judge the way of teaching online as better or weaker due to our own national influenced way of practice, am I being fair?" During the interview, the entertainment approach of the Norwegian system, as observed in some of the theology lectures, sparked a conversation that led the interviewee to question the prevailing ideas about teaching and learning. Over the decades, there has been a significant shift in how these concepts are perceived in Norway, where students were once expected to be attentive and listen to the teacher who held a position of power in society. As the status of the teacher's position has diminished, monologues have become less used as a didactic method, and more interactive techniques, such as student activities and colorful presentations, are now commonly used to engage students. She continued: "Am I influenced by the students' responses to my teaching, to my didactical performance? Do I accept that some students would rather have me lecturing on a topic in a monologue way, and even prefer to not be addressed in class?" This assessment prompts the interviewee to develop a deeper understanding of the teacher's autonomy to decide on teaching approaches that prioritize student and professional gains in the long run, rather than following societal expectations or feeling the need to entertain. At the macro-level, we assess the efficacy of these teaching methodologies and examine their impact on the holistic development of students. Exposure to diverse didactic approaches fosters innovative thinking in higher educational practices, which can be advantageous for interdisciplinary studies. This not only challenges conventional teaching and learning practices during times of crisis, but also prepares for unforeseen events in future in higher education.

---

36. Jermstad et al., "Dannelse til globalt medborgerskap," 35.

CONCLUSION

Ultimately, questions about pedagogy lie at the heart of the education dilemma—about what education should be and how to create an educational system that can adapt to crises such as global economic regression, diseases, and rapid change. Higher education systems face the challenge of addressing both local and global perspectives while fulfilling their role in educating and shaping the future generation in various professions in society.

Using an autoethnographic approach, this study has examined the phenomenon of observation and the impact on self-reflection from the perspective of the interviewee. It offers a valuable method for accessing social, political, and cultural aspects and for revealing emotions. Moreover, autoethnography challenges traditional research approaches by making room for personal stories that are often overlooked. The data in this study was analyzed using a four-parameter observation model, incorporating semantic theory construction to gain a comprehensive understanding. This approach offers both authors and readers an understanding of the phenomenon's meaning within the context of the study. Furthermore, the study has showcased Bronfenbrenner's system theory as an effective analytical tool in examining different facets of teaching and learning in a glocal setting during a crisis.

BIBLIOGRAPHY

Bakhtin, Mikhail. *Spørsmålet om talegenrane*. Translated by Rasmus Slaattelid. Bergen: Ariadne, 1998.

Bloch, Carter, et al. "Does Quality Work Work? A Systematic Review of Academic Literature on Quality Initiatives in Higher Education." *Assessment and Evaluation in Higher Education* 46 (2020) 701–18. https://doi.org/10.1080/02602938.2020.1813250.

Boncori, Ilaria. "Learning and Doing Autoethnography: Resonance, Vulnerability and Exposure." In *Organizational Ethnography: An Experiential and Practical Guide*, edited by Jenna Pandeli et al., 83–99. London: Routledge, 2022.

Bronfenbrenner, Urie. *The Ecology of Human Development: Experiments by Nature and Design*. Cambridge, MA: Harvard University Press, 1979.

———. "Ecology of the Family as a Context for Human Development: Research Perspectives." *Developmental Psychology* 22 (1986) 723–42.

Brunstad, P. O., and S. Oliverio. "Practical Wisdom and Spiritual Exercises in Teacher Education." In *Validity and Value of Teacher Education Research*, edited by Kari Smith, 59–78. Bergen: Fagbok, 2022.

Chemi, Tatiana, and Lone Krogh, eds. "Setting the Stage for Co-creation in Higher Education." In *Co-creation in Higher Education: Students and Educators Preparing Creatively and Collaboratively to the Challenge of the Future*, edited by Tatiana Chemi and Lone Krogh, vii–xvi. Creative Education 6. Rotterdam: Sense, 2017.

Cosh, Jill. "Peer Observation in Higher Education: A Reflective Approach." *Innovations in Education and Training International* 35 (1998) 171–76. https://doi.org/10.1080/1355800980350211.

Creswell, John W., et al. *Qualitative Inquiry and Research Design: Choosing among Five Approaches*. 3rd ed. Los Angeles: SAGE, 2016.

Goth, Ursula S., et al. "Nærhet, eller distanse? Lærerstudenters erfaringer med Zoomundervisning under Covid-19." In *Fra barnehage til voksenliv: utdanning, didaktikk og verdi*, edited by Linnéa K. Jermstad and Ursula S. Goth, 193–212. Oslo: Novus, 2020.

———. "Tilrettelegging for trivsel: mangfold i det norske klasserommet." In *Fra barnehage til voksenliv: utdanning, didaktikk og verdi*, edited by Linnéa K. Jermstad and Ursula S. Goth, 65–79. Oslo: Novus, 2020.

Iversen, Ann-Merete, and Anni Stavnskær Pedersen. "Co-Creating Knowledge: Students and Teachers Together in a Field of Emergence." In *Co-Creation in Higher Education: Students and Educators Preparing Creatively and Collaboratively to the Challenge of the Future*, edited by Tatiana Chemi and Lone Krogh, 15–30. Creative Education 6. Leiden, Neth.: Brill, 2017.

Jermstad, Linnéa K., et al. "Dannelse til globalt medborgerskap: solidaritetsarbeid i en barnehagekontekst." In *Fra barnehage til voksenliv: utdanning, didaktikk og verdi*, edited by Linnéa K. Jermstad and Ursula S. Goth, 33–47. Oslo: Novus, 2020.

Jokstad, Gunnvi Sæle. "Med kunst som veiviser til profesjonell utvikling." In *Fra barnehage til voksenliv: utdanning, didaktikk og verdi*, edited by Linnéa K. Jermstad and Ursula S. Goth, 177–192. Oslo: Novus, 2020.

Klevan, Trude G., et al. "Ensretting, standardisering og kunnskapsbasert praksis—autoetnografi som motstand?" *Forskning og forandring* 2 (2019) 105–23.

Kvernbekk, Tone. *Pedagogisk teoridannelse: Insidere, Teoriformer og Praksis*. Bergen: Fagbok, 2005.

Mueller, Robin, and Meadow Schroeder. "From Seeing to Doing: Examining the Impact of Non-Evaluative Classroom Observation on Teaching Development." *Innovative Higher Education* 43 (2018) 397–410. https://doi.org/https://doi.org/10.1007/s10755-018-9436-0.

Mulisa, Feyisa. "Application of Bioecological Systems Theory to Higher Education: Best Evidence Review." *Journal of Pedagogical Sociology and Psychology* 1 (2019) 104–15.

National Committee for Research Ethics in the Social Sciences and the Humanities, The. "Guidelines for Research Ethics in the Social Sciences and the Humanities." National Research Ethics Committees, 2021 (Eng. translation 2022). https://www.forskningsetikk.no/en/guidelines/social-sciences-humanities-law-and-theology/guidelines-for-research-ethics-in-the-social-sciences-humanities-law-and-theology/.

Økland, Øyvind. "Perspectives on Globalization and Culture in Intercultural Communication Textbooks." In *Møter og mangfold: Religion og kultur i historie, samtid og skole*, edited by H. V. Kleive et al., 9–36. Oslo: Cappelen Damm Akademisk, 2022.

O'Leary, Matt. "Rethinking Teachers' Professional Learning through Unseen Observation." *Professional Development in Education* (2022). https://doi.org/10.1080/19415257.2022.2125551.

Saussure, Ferdinand de. "On the Nature of Language." In *Structuralism: A Reader*, edited by Michael Lane, 43–56. London: Cape, 1970.
Schön, D. A. *The Reflective Practitioner: How Professionals Think in Action*. New York: Basic, 1983.
Torgersen, Glenn-Egil. *Interaction: "Samhandling" under Risk: A Step Ahead of the Unforeseen*. Oslo: Cappelen Damm Akademisk, 2018.
Ulvik, Marit, and Kari Smith. "Lærerutdanneres profesjonelle utvikling." *Uniped* 41 (2018) 425–40.
UNESCO, et al. *The State of the Global Education Crisis: A Path to Recovery*. World Bank, Dec. 3, 2021. https://www.worldbank.org/en/topic/education/publication/the-state-of-the-global-education-crisis-a-path-to-recovery.
Varner, Kenneth J. "Glocal Challenges to Teacher Education and a Glocally Sustaining Pedagogical Framework." *Global Education Review* 8 (2021) 8–20.
Vélez-Agosto, Nicole M., et al. "Bronfenbrenner's Bioecological Theory Revision: Moving Culture from the Macro into the Micro." *Perspectives on Psychological Science* 12 (2017) 900–910.
Yurtseven, Nihal, and Sertel Altun. "The Role of Self-Reflection and Peer Review in Curriculum-Focused Professional Development for Teachers." *Hacettepe Üniversitesi Eğitim Fakültesi Dergisi (H. U. Journal of Education)* 33 (2018) 207–28. https://doi.org/10.16986/HUJE.2017030461.

PART 3

What Can We Learn from Crisis?

Chapter 13

Can You Be Trained in Courage—or Taught It?

A Rhetorical and Theological Assessment of How to Carry Out Training in Courage as Part of Theological Education

Bård Norheim and Joar Haga

INTRODUCTION

When a crisis strikes, fear is imminent. This pertains to most crises, both personal and collective, such as the climate crisis. But how should we respond to fear? The short answer is of course, *it depends*. It depends on the situation, the magnitude of the threat, and how the challenges and fears are assessed practically and ethically.[1] Traditionally, however, the preferred virtue in the face of fear is *courage*. But *what is courage, and can courage be taught—and can someone be trained to be courageous—even in theological education?*

Courage—Greek ἀνδρεία, from "manly"—is one of the four classic cardinal virtues in the Western tradition, along with prudence, justice, and temperance. To Aristotle, real courage is on display during war. There, the greatest and noblest of fears is encountered, namely, fear of death in battle. Courage was considered the middle road between heedlessness and cowardice. Practicing courage required moderation. Exercising courage and taking on risks in a crisis should be proportional to the ends (telos) you

---

1. Norheim and Haga, *Three Fears*, 4–21, 125.

seek to fulfill. Aristotle also argued that a true virtue was worth training or cultivating. This implied that courage materializes at its most virtuous when it is connected to knowledge and practical wisdom, what the Greeks used to call *phronesis*.[2]

Aristotle believed that courage could be developed by training—by practicing the ability to endure situations that bring about fear. A person who is afraid of speaking in public should practice public speaking. A person who is afraid of the dark should walk in the dark. The aim of such an exercise was to develop a balance between fear and confidence. Aristotle therefore argued that developing courage is a rational endeavor on the bandwidth between extreme fear and unrestricted rashness. It is the ability to assess a situation rationally and calibrate one's response, balancing fear (*fobos*) and confidence (*tharros*). Training to become courageous therefore comes down to developing a virtue that has the ability of situational discernment.[3] In the *Nicomachean Ethics* Aristotle defines a courageous person in the following manner:

> The courageous man withstands and fears those things which it is necessary (to fear and withstand) and on account of the right of the right reason, and how and when it is necessary (to fear or withstand) them, and likewise in the case of being bold.[4]

Contemporary research on courage has revisited Aristotle's treatment of courage and extended the assessment of courage with insights from psychology, neuroscience, and leadership theory.

In this chapter we will offer a theoretical assessment of courage as a virtue with the aim of exploring how it may be possible for courage to be taught and made part of training in theological education—to prepare pastors and ministers to respond to the fears and challenges of a complex, *glocal* crisis. The theoretical foundations developed here are the basis for the follow-up action research study, which involves experiments with students and teachers as part of the TLC project to explore ways in which courage can be taught and form part of training in theological education. A first preliminary case study on the meaning of courage and how to train it has already been conducted. A group of students of homiletics at NLA University College were introduced to South African Archbishop Thabo Makgoba's sermon at midnight Mass in St George's Cathedral in Cape Town in 2014. Stellenbosch University professor Ian Nell offered a contextual introduction

---

2. Pangle, "Anatomy of Courage."
3. Vigani, "Aristotle's Account of Courage."
4. Aristotle, *Nicomachean Ethics*, 1116b17–19.

to the sermon and its message. In the sermon Makgoba preached on courage and proclaimed that Jesus is the one who "has already triumphed and broken all barriers."[5] The sermon was then discussed in groups of students, and the students were challenged to reflect on how it may be possible to train courage and what it means to display courage, given the situation at hand.

PART 1: COURAGE IN TIMES OF CRISIS—A THEORETICAL EVALUATION

Courage is narrowly defined as the capacity to face death in feud or war, but more broadly, courage is understood as fortitude. Traditionally, courage was necessary to defend oneself and family from external threats.[6] However, courage, like loyalty, is a grey virtue; it can be used to serve both good and bad purposes.[7] Courage is therefore some sort of psychological mystery, and, typically, both moral philosophers and soldiers are interested in theorizing courage.[8]

From the point of view of psychology and leadership studies, courage is a morally attractive, but still little-researched virtue that implies the ability to face personal risk in order to pursue worthy goals on a voluntary basis.[9] In other words, courage is a cherished quality that is necessary for social order. It involves an individual's ability to stand apart from the crowd, and at the same time the individual's ability to internalize the values and aims of the collective.[10] Interestingly, researchers of neuroscience have identified a particular cluster of neurons in mouse brains that seem to produce fear responses to perceived threats. Similarly, when an adjacent cluster of neurons is activated, courage and more bold patterns of behavior are exhibited.[11]

Courage may also be interpreted as an inherent and perhaps biological quality of human beings. It may also be taken as the outcome of a process of nurture and training. At the same time, as we have already seen, it is both an individual and collective feature. It is both personal and situational. In contemporary leadership studies and psychological research, courage is often portrayed as an individual virtue for self-fulfillment and self-realization.

5. Makgoba, "Welcome Season of Light," para. 19.
6. Miller, *Mystery of Courage*, 5.
7. Miller, *Mystery of Courage*, 8.
8. Miller, *Mystery of Courage*, 27, 29.
9. Pury, "Courage."
10. Worline, "Courage."
11. Goldman, "Researchers Find Fear."

Bottom line, if you fight your fears, you may develop courage. To the Stoics, however, being courageous is a rational operation; it has a distinguished intellectual character. After all, they underlined, we will all die in the end, and if we act cowardly in the face of fear, trembling over a threat that may possibly lead to death, it is taken to be a demonstration of irrational behavior. Seneca, for example, defined fortitude as the ability to distinguish between what is bad (*malum*) and what is not. The point was to develop a *vir fortis*, a stable and strong soul that is able to carry the burden of fate.

Whereas many of the church fathers continued to promote the virtue lists of antiquity, Augustine provided a significant framework for courage through his teachings on martyrdom. One of the incidents that prompted Augustine to write about the issue, was the sack of Rome in AD 410. Fearing rape, many virgins committed suicide. Understandable as it was, given the Roman tradition of an honorable death, Augustine based a rejection of suicide on the fifth commandment. He offered an interpretation of Cato's suicide as an example. His fear of being humiliated by Caesar caused it, but Augustine claimed that it was not courageous. True courage was, rather, suffering whatever God sends, he claimed.[12] In the same manner, Thomas Aquinas saw courage as the power to stand in the most dangerous situations, even to the point of death. This was labeled the virtue of martyrdom.[13] The point here is that the appeal to courage and the demonstration of courage may be seen as a response to fear. To be courageous is the ability to fine-tune an appropriate and rational calibration of fear, and craft an adequate response to the current fear.[14]

How we define courage, however, depends on the situation at hand. When a child falls into the ocean, it may be considered courageous to react swiftly and jump in to save the child. However, a soldier who runs ahead of his platoon may be taken as an expression of hubris and risky rashness. Similarly, a climate or free speech activist who rushes ahead of everything and everyone may risk losing both the audience and the cause. To the virtue ethics tradition, courage, rather, is unveiled in calibrated, collective, and concerted action.

If we seek to define courage, it is often emphasized that courage implies taking risks or making sacrifices for the benefit of protection of others in the face of danger. Courage is therefore the exemplary virtuous response to fear. A morally courageous person is often found to be brave and demonstrating perseverance and endurance, integrity, and honesty. What is courage then?

---

12. Straw, "Martyrdom," 540.
13. Qiaoying, "Aquinas's Transformation."
14. Norheim and Haga, *Three Fears*, 119–24.

It is, for sure, nothing given. To be courageous depends on the situation at hand. Fundamentally, courage is instrumental to the context in a certain sense.

PART 2: THE APPEAL TO COURAGE—A RHETORICAL CASE STUDY

"The secret of happiness is freedom, and the secret of freedom is courage." These are the words of the great fifth-century BC Greek orator Pericles, as accounted by the historian Thucydides.[15] Whether Pericles was right in his definition of happiness could be debated, but the history of speech demonstrates that courage and freedom, and the appeal to both, are intertwined. Appealing to courage seems to play a critical role in the defense of freedom, particularly freedom of speech.

We have so far examined the complex contextual nature of courage as a virtue, but how may a leader appeal to courage, particularly in times of crisis? Training theologians implies training leaders who can address a particular audience at a particular time and at a particular place. It obviously involves delivering a sermon from a pulpit, but the nature of a theologian's work goes beyond merely addressing a congregation during church service. The theologian is called to address the public at large. To develop the art of public speaking for theologians, rhetoric represents an important framework—both as a tool for theoretical analysis and as an instrument for practice and the developing of skills. Basically, rhetoric concerns the art of persuasion and helps the speaker to reflect on the available means to present a credible message (*logos*), a trustworthy character (*ethos*), and a convincing appeal to the audience and their feelings (*pathos*).[16]

Mastering the art of persuasion is particularly critical when a crisis strikes. In the following paragraphs we will examine two famous speeches given in times of crisis, to explore and identify the essential elements of an appeal to courage in times of change and upheaval. In the final, constructive section of the chapter, we will use these elaborations to discuss how to make theologians better equipped to appeal to courage and exercise courage in times of crisis. The two speeches are both given amid crisis and controversy. They are similar, but still different, in that their message was not uncontroversial at the time of delivery. Hopefully, engaging with these speeches will

---

15. Thucydides, "Pericles' Funeral Oration," 2.43; better translated as "esteeming courage to be freedom and freedom to be happiness."

16. Norheim and Haga, *Four Speeches*, 17–18, 115–22; see also Lausberg, *Handbook of Literary Rhetoric*.

help theological students in reflecting on the fundamentally complex and comprehensive enterprise of appealing to courage in times of crisis.

On June 12, 1987, former US president Ronald Reagan stood at a podium by the Brandenburg Gate to give a speech to the people of West Berlin. Behind him was the Berlin Wall, the most prominent symbol of the division between East and West following the Second World War. Reagan described Berlin as "a place of freedom," and commended the Berliners for their "courage and determination."[17] The main topic of the speech was freedom, and how freedom "leads to prosperity," and "replaces the ancient hatreds among the nations with comity and peace."[18] In the speech Reagan even argued that security and freedom belong together: "We in the West stand ready to cooperate with the East to promote true openness, to break down barriers that separate people, to create a safer, freer world."[19]

Quoting German president Richard von Weizsäcker, who had said that "the German question is open as long as the Brandenburg Gate is closed," Reagan went on to proclaim:

> Today I say: As long as this gate is closed, as long as this scar of a wall is permitted to stand, it is not the German question alone that remains open, but the question of freedom for all mankind.[20]

The US president then paraphrased West German and West Berlin post-WWII history. Using humor and making references to familiar Berlin symbols, he described how the city had prospered and developed:

> From devastation, from utter ruin, you Berliners have, in freedom, rebuilt a city that once again ranks as one of the greatest on Earth. The Soviets may have had other plans. But, my friends, there were a few things the Soviets didn't count on Berliner herz, Berliner humor, ja, und Berliner schnauze. [Laughter][21]

Reagan then turned to address Mikhail Gorbachev directly, the general secretary of the Soviet Union. The US president paused, lowered his voice, and slowly pronounced the words that later have become famous:

> General Secretary Gorbachev, if you seek peace, if you seek prosperity for the Soviet Union and Eastern Europe, if you seek

---

17. Reagan, "Remarks on East-West Relations," para. 2.
18. Reagan, "Remarks on East-West Relations," para. 10.
19. Reagan, "Remarks on East-West Relations," para. 17.
20. Reagan, "Remarks on East-West Relations," para. 5.
21. Reagan, "Remarks on East-West Relations," para. 9.

liberalization: Come here to this gate! Mr. Gorbachev, open this gate! Mr. Gorbachev, tear down this wall!²²

And the audience started to applaud enthusiastically. In the rest of the speech, Reagan used the story of Berlin as a city of freedom to promote how liberty and free markets should transform the globe.

Ronald Reagan appealed to courage in 1987, both the courage of the people of West Germany and Berlin, and even the courage of General Secretary Gorbachev. To Reagan, courage in this situation entailed changing the status quo, and not accepting the border between East and West Germany. It meant tearing down the Berlin Wall. The wall did indeed come down in the dramatic events of November 1989, but that was not necessarily the most likely future scenario when Reagan spoke in June 1987. To many, Reagan's appeal represented a bold and rather courageous attempt during an ongoing crisis.

What does it mean to be courageous, and what does it involve appealing to courage? To Reagan, exercising courage meant changing the status quo and not accepting the set borders between East Germany and West Germany. Let us fast forward to February 22, 2022. On the brink of Russia's invasion in Ukraine, Kenya's ambassador to the UN, Dr. Martin Kimani, delivered a statement to an emergency session of the UN Security Council on the situation in Ukraine. The statement was received by many as an example of courage and wisdom amid a very critical time for world peace and freedom. Kimani, with a PhD from King's College London on the role of Christian symbolism and racialism in the 1994 Rwandan genocide, appealed to Russia to accept the given borders of Ukraine, and that of any sovereign nation, and not try to change them by force. In a certain sense, Kimani seemed to argue that it is wise and courageous to accept the status quo to keep freedom and peace.

Kimani started his speech by naming the reality, describing how the borders of Kenya and almost every African country "were not of our own drawing." Rather, they were "drawn in distant colonial metropoles of London, Paris, and Lisbon, with no regard for the ancient nations that they cleaved apart."²³ The Kenyan US ambassador further emphasized that *if* the same nations "had chosen to pursue states on the basis of ethnic, racial, or religious homogeneity," there would still be "bloody wars" many decades later.²⁴ Kimani went on to argue the importance of settling "for the

22. Reagan, "Remarks on East-West Relations," para. 12; see also Reagan, "Mr. Gorbachev."

23. Kimani, "Statement to Emergency Session," para. 7.

24. Kimani, "Statement to Emergency Session," para. 8.

borders we inherited," still pursuing "continental political, economic, and legal integration."[25] As a nation you are faced with a choice of either looking "ever backwards into history with a dangerous nostalgia," or choosing "to look forward to a greatness none of our many nations and peoples had ever known," Kimani advocated.[26] He pointed out that Kenya chooses to follow the rules of the Organization of African Unity and the United Nations charter, "not because our borders satisfied us, but because we wanted something greater, forged in peace."[27] In his final appeal, Kimani made an implicit plea to Russian president Vladimir Putin and other world leaders to show courage by leaving empire ambitions behind:

> We believe that all states formed from empires that have collapsed or retreated have many peoples in them yearning for integration with peoples in neighboring states. This is normal and understandable. After all, who does not want to be joined to their brethren and to make common purpose with them? However, Kenya rejects such a yearning from being pursued by force. We must complete our recovery from the embers of dead empires in a way that does not plunge us back into new forms of domination and oppression.[28]

The meaning of courage, in the context of these two speeches, displays the situational nature of any appeal to courage. It also confirms courage as an ambivalent and grey virtue. From a rhetorical perspective, the meaning of courage therefore rests on the speaker's argumentative discourse on the meaning of rationality in the given context by naming reality and exercising sound judgment based on that assessment. For Reagan, and those applauding Reagan, courage implied working to change the status quo. For Kimani, and those commending Kimani, courage meant accepting the status quo, or at least refraining from using force to challenge it.[29] In other words, appearing courageous and appealing to courage requires careful training in what it means to name reality in a rational manner and exercise sound judgment based on that evaluation.

---

25. Kimani, "Statement to Emergency Session," para. 9.
26. Kimani, "Statement to Emergency Session," para. 9.
27. Kimani, "Statement to Emergency Session," para. 9.
28. Kimani, "Statement to Emergency Session," para. 10.
29. Kimani's speech was met by much praise, but also some criticism for embracing the colonial legacy of Africa; see Gathara, "Kenyan UN Ambassador's Ukraine Speech."

PART 3: TRAINING FOR COURAGE—A THEOLOGICAL ASSESSMENT

How do you then train in the ability to name reality and exercise sound judgment? How do you educate theologians and pastors who are able to read the signs of the times and exercise and appeal to courage based on that assessment? In other words, how may the ability to exercise an appropriate type of courage, given the situation at hand, be developed in training? More specifically: How may theological education offer teaching and training in the development of sound judgment in the face of fear, the virtue of performing calibrated and careful consideration of what the most courageous response may be?

Psychologist and leadership expert Manfred Kets de Vries has argued that a person acts courageously by a combination of "genetic predisposition, acquired psychological characteristics, social norms, and the context of the decision requiring courage."[30] He defines courageous behavior as taking a course of action where you accept a risk in order to protect or benefit others. Kets de Vries finds that this sort of behavior is possible to learn, particularly by developing greater openness to experience. Quite practically, Kets de Vries finds that training courage requires creating scenarios, practicing going out of your comfort zone, working with different body techniques, etc.[31]

Aristotle, on the other hand, believed that an individual develops courage by doing courageous acts. The simple axiom from virtue ethics is therefore that we become (more) courageous by acting courageously when the situation demands it. This may be taken as an argument in favor of case study training, like working with particular speeches that are taken to appeal to and demonstrate courage.

One study on training for social courage surveyed more than two hundred workers and found that grit and proactive personality were prominent features among those who demonstrated social courage.[32] Another study emphasized the importance of empowering leadership for a learning environment seeking to provide training in social courage. Empowering leadership was here defined as the ability to provide guidance and a calibrated combination of autonomy and collaboration among those who trained together. The findings suggested that leaders in less hierarchical organizations were more likely to "produce" courageous workers.[33] Bottom line, it is both

---

30. Kets de Vries, "How to Find," summary.
31. Kets de Vries, "How to Find," paras. 13–18.
32. Greenberg, "New Research," para. 5.
33. Greenberg, "New Research," para. 6.

possible and morally attractive to train in and try to increase the influence of a particular virtue. That a true virtue is worth cultivating is obvious to Aristotle and the virtue ethics tradition.

The key with all virtues, Aristotle argued, is to point to a mean, a midpoint of moderation between extremes. Both of the opposite extremes should be avoided, like acting too boldly or too calmly, being almost paralyzed with fear. As we have seen with the theoretical evaluation and the rhetorical case study, exercising courage therefore requires developing *judicium*, sound judgment. If you want to appeal to and display courage, you need to be able to read the signs and interpret the context. Training in courage, therefore, requires an element of self-reflection. How could theological training foster the sort of self-reflection that develops courage? In the following constructive part on how theological education may develop courage and train in the ability to appeal to courage, we will draw on German theologian Dietrich Bonhoeffer's work with courage and theological education.

Dietrich Bonhoeffer (1906–1945) was a German Lutheran pastor and theologian who became known for his staunch resistance to Hitler's Nazi dictatorship. In 1935 he established and led the illegal preacher's seminary of the Confessing Church in Finkenwalde, today Zdroje, a suburb of the Polish city of Sczezin, by the Baltic Sea. In Finkenwalde, Bonhoeffer trained future pastors by focusing on theological training shaped by a communitarian and ascetic way of life. Bonhoeffer's book *Life Together* describes the key elements of the rule of life at the seminary. The seminary in Finkenwalde was closed by the Gestapo in September 1937, and later twenty-seven pastors and former students were arrested. At this time Bonhoeffer published one of his best-known books, *The Cost of Discipleship*, which is a study of the Sermon on the Mount. Here Bonhoeffer criticizes "cheap grace" and promotes "costly grace." In 1943, after having joined the *Abwehr*, Bonhoeffer was accused of having been part of the so-called July 20 plot to assassinate Adolf Hitler. He was imprisoned and later taken to Flossenbürg Concentration Camp where he was hanged on April 9, 1945, just as the Nazi regime was about to collapse.

Bonhoeffer on Courage

History has praised Dietrich Bonhoeffer for his ability to display courage during the reign of Nazi-Germany. However, like courage, Bonhoeffer is a somewhat ambivalent figure—a martyr—in the sense that his heroic *Widerstand* is capitalized and idolized by groups with very different political and theological purposes. Similarly, Bonhoeffer's theology is both complex and part fragmentary. His Christocentric approach often attracts conservative Protestants. On the other hand, his focus on justice and his vision of a religionless Christianity is embraced by more liberally leaning Protestants. For the purposes of this chapter, we focus on Bonhoeffer's ability and call to practice *judicium* during a crisis. In Hitler and in the Nazi rule, Bonhoeffer found a dangerous connection between the will of the masses and what he labeled an idolatrous concentration of power that lacked accountability and responsibility to any higher authority. Bonhoeffer's fundamentally Christocentric take on reality is also reflected in his understanding of the world. He argued that the world has no reality of its own, "independently of the revelation of God in Christ."[34]

Reading Bonhoeffer's treatment of courage is also a complex endeavor. Fundamentally, Bonhoeffer claimed that civil courage can "grow only out of the free responsibility of free men."[35] Bonhoeffer also found that in a crisis, where accepted norms of ethics may not provide simple answers and perhaps even prevent responsible action, one must still try to act freely and courageously. The measure of courageous practice lies in the pattern of the incarnate, crucified, and risen Christ. To be conformed to the incarnation of Christ implies being involved fully and vicariously—hence the key word *Stellvertretung*—in the struggles of the world. To be conformed to the crucifixion of Christ means identifying with the suffering of victims and acting in solidarity with the oppressed. Further, to be conformed to his resurrection implies living and practicing hope for the sake of future generations.[36] Assessing Bonhoeffer's treatment of courage one is also compelled to ask whether courage is an inherent quality or not. Succinctly put, is a courageous person courageous because he is simply more wholesome or truthful? At one point, Bonhoeffer even claimed that "it is better for the truthful person to tell a lie than for the liar to tell the truth."[37]

---

34. Bonhoeffer, *Ethics*, 58.
35. Bonhoeffer, *Letters and Papers*, 5.
36. See De Gruchy, "Playing God."
37. Bonhoeffer, *Ethics*, 77.

Martyrdom and Courage

Bonhoeffer famously wrote that "when Jesus Christ calls a man, he calls him to come and die."[38] In a 1932 sermon, Bonhoeffer said on martyrdom:

> The blood of martyrs might once again be demanded, but this blood, if we really have the courage and loyalty to shed it, will not be innocent, shining like that of the first witnesses for the faith. On our blood lies heavy guilt, the guilt of the unprofitable servant who is cast into outer darkness.[39]

When discussing theological education and the training in courage, it is also worth consulting Bonhoeffer's contemporary, Erik Peterson. He wrote a much-ignored essay on the church and martyrdom, "Witness to the Truth" (1937). Facing the Nazi regime in Germany, Peterson underlined the *public* character of the Christian message. His point of departure was Jesus's address in the Gospel of Matthew, prior to their sending out into the world. A main element for Peterson was Christ's framing of the apostles as "sheep" among "wolves." They will be "hated by all," Peterson wrote, pointing to a rather dim reality without much expectation of applause. Still, the call was to give witness, publicly, at the places where political power was found. In the case of the apostles, that meant being accused at the courts where suffering awaited. For Peterson, it belonged to the concept of the martyr

> to be brought for reckoning before the public organs of the state—in councils, and synagogues, before governors and kings—to be subjected to a public judicial proceeding and the penalties of public law.[40]

Witnessing to Christ publicly breaks the idea of the worldly understanding of public, however, because Jesus would immediately proclaim it before God and the angels. Such a parallel reality was not meant to downplay the importance of the witness as a political act. Peterson was not interested in a "pie in the sky when you die." On the contrary, the publicity in heaven was meant to strengthen the importance of the witness on earth. Peterson illustrated the effect by referring to the analogy of Romans 6, where baptism was paralleled with the death of Jesus.

An important aspect of the martyr theology of Peterson was the role of the Revelation of John. The testimony of John enters the public sphere through the book, in analogy to Jesus "who is the faithful witness" (Rev

---

38. Bonhoeffer, *Cost of Discipleship*, 89.
39. Bethge, *Dietrich Bonhoeffer*, 155.
40. Peterson, "Witness to the Truth," 157.

1,5). Peterson points to Revelation's portrayal of the *glorious* appearance of Christ in the second coming as opposed to his *mysterious* first coming. This transformation was important for the receivers of the book, because they partook in the sufferings of their Lord. It meant that it was also a participation in Christ's power, his glory, his rule, and his status as revealed. The latter contrasted the hiddenness of their suffering. As the dying Stephen, the first martyr, they saw the majesty of the Son of Man.[41]

The Finkenwalde Learning Community

In training for courage, it is, among other things, important to assess the situation, contemplate dangers, and endure hardship.[42] The curriculum of the illegal seminary at Finkenwalde was founded in the discipleship of Christ as presented in Jesus's Sermon on the Mount, focusing on a Christ-centered daily life, contemplative prayer, service to others, and the healing power of confession. The learning environment in Finkenwalde was formed through games, discussion, and the mutual confession of sins.[43] In the context of what it implies about the formation of courage in theological training, we ask: Could the mutual confession of sins to each other be a way of training in courage? Dietrich Bonhoeffer writes that "confession in the presence of a brother is the profoundest kind of humiliation. It hurts, it cuts a man down, it is a dreadful blow to pride."[44] Bonhoeffer explained the importance of the confession of sins, by emphasizing that "Christ himself bears the sins of the individuals, which are laid upon the church-community."[45]

Fundamentally therefore, for Bonhoeffer, to train the ability to exercise courage implies rehearsing to live a selfless life. In this training, the mutual confession of sins among Christian brothers is essential. He argued that "only those who are selfless live responsibly, which means that only selfless people truly live."[46] Bonhoeffer also found that "the person who loves God must, by God's will, really love the neighbor."[47]

---

41. Peterson, "Zeuge der Wahrheit," 187–88.
42. Kidder, *Moral Courage*.
43. Root, *Bonhoeffer as Youth Worker*.
44. Bonhoeffer, *Life Together*, 114.
45. Bonhoeffer, *Sanctorum Communio*, 190.
46. Bonhoeffer, *Ethics*, 259.
47. Bonhoeffer, *Sanctorum Communio*, 169.

Theological and Pedagogical Implications: Confession and Deeper Play

If we emphasize the importance of confession in theological training, this conviction also comes with a set of theological and pedagogical implications. First, the confession of sins implies that fearing God is worthy. This theological axiom also presents us with two other fundamental convictions that are formative for a learning environment for theological training: First: failure is possible. To be better at showing courage, you need to be able to learn in a learning community where experimentation, innovation, and, as a result, failure, are accepted and perhaps even encouraged. Second: human beings are subjects to God's judgment.

Interestingly, courage, unlike the other cardinal virtues and theological virtues, seems to thrive "in certain restricted comedic veins." Trying to capture the mystery of courage William Miller has underlined that:

> In some cultural settings the heroic style demands insouciance or the grim mordancy of gallows humor, whether this functions as a way of stealing oneself against one's own fears or, as is often the case, as a way of instilling fears in others, when you joke in the face of their deaths: "Go ahead, make my day."[48]

Bonhoeffer may not have prescribed gallows humor in courage training, but rather the mutual confession of sins. At the same time, humor and play were also important ingredients at the Finkenwalde learning community. We know that play triggers curiosity, and that play is a key ingredient in children's emotional development.[49] What Bonhoeffer and the teachers and students practiced at Finkenwalde may perhaps be described as "deeper play." Deeper play has five main ingredients: self-direction, intrinsic motivation, use of imagination, process orientation, and positive emotions.[50] Both humor and confession require an acknowledgment of human vulnerability and a vulnerability of the self and may be key ingredients in necessary self-reflection and self-knowledge to foster courage and practice of sound judgment in times of crisis. Perhaps the use of play and humor along with the mutual confession of sins may be key practices in fostering self-reflection and the development of sound judgment in theological training in the face of crisis?

---

48. Miller, *Mystery of Courage*, 41.
49. Sahlberg and Doyle, *Let the Children Play*, 309, 312.
50. Sahlberg and Doyle, *Let the Children Play*, 307.

CONCLUSION

In this chapter we have explored courage as phenomenon and as a moral virtue, and we have investigated on what grounds and by what means it may be possible to teach and provide training in courage as part of theological education. The first part of the chapter gave a theoretical evaluation of courage as a virtue, drawing on classical rhetoric and philosophical, psychological, and theological assessments of courage, emphasizing courage as a "grey" and situationally embedded virtue. The second part presented a case study in rhetoric that analyzed two speeches, one by former US president Ronald Reagan, and the other by the Kenyan ambassador to the UN, Dr. Martin Kimani. These two speeches also display the situational nature of any appeal to courage, exemplifying how courage may be seen as an ambivalent and grey virtue. From a rhetorical perspective, the meaning of courage, therefore, builds on the speaker's ability to offer rational and persuasive arguments for the practice of courage in a given context, by credibly naming reality and exercising sound judgment based on that assessment. The final part of the chapter offered a theological and pedagogical assessment of the pursuit to teach and train courage as a collective practice, by drawing on Dietrich Bonhoeffer's theology and the experiences of the Finkenwalde Predigerseminar as learning community. We concluded that the teaching and training of courage may use deep play and humor along with the mutual confession of sins as key practices in developing the necessary self-reflection and *judicium* required to exercise courage in the face of crisis.

BIBLIOGRAPHY

Aristotle. *The Nicomachean Ethics*. New York: Penguin, 2004.
Bethge, Eberhard. *Dietrich Bonhoeffer: A Biography*. Edited by Victoria J. Barnett. Minneapolis: Fortress, 1999.
Bonhoeffer, Dietrich. *The Cost of Discipleship*. Translated by R. H. Fuller and Irmgard Booth. London: SCM, 1959.
———. *Ethics*. Translated by Charles C. West et al. Minneapolis: Fortress, 2005.
———. *Letters and Papers from Prison*. Edited by Eberhard Bethge. New York: Touchstone, 1997.
———. *Life Together*. Translated by John W. Doberstein. New York: Harper & Row, 1954.
———. *Sanctorum Communio: A Theological Study of the Sociology of the Church*. Edited by Clifford J. Green. Translated by Joachim von Soosten. Minneapolis: Fortress, 1998.
De Gruchy, John W. "Playing God during the Pandemic: Bonhoeffer on Civil Courage, Responsibility, and the Ethics of Necessity." *Ecumenical Review* 72 (2020) 660–72. DOI:10.1111/erev.12546.

Gathara, Patrick. "The Kenyan UN Ambassador's Ukraine Speech Does Not Deserve Praise." *Al Jazeera*, Feb. 23, 2022. https://www.aljazeera.com/opinions/2022/2/23/what-the-kenyan-un-ambassador-got-wrong-about-colonialism.

Goldman, Bruce. "Researchers Find Fear and Courage Switches in Brain." *Neuroscience News*, May 2, 2018. https://neurosciencenews.com/fear-courage-8942.

Greenberg, Melanie. "New Research Shows How to Facilitate Social Courage." *Psychology Today*, Jan. 30, 2018. https://www.psychologytoday.com/intl/blog/the-mindful-self-express/201801/new-research-shows-how-facilitate-social-courage.

Kets de Vries, Manfred F. R. "How to Find and Practice Courage." *Harvard Business Review*, May 12, 2020. https://hbr.org/2020/05/how-to-find-and-practice-courage.

Kidder, Rushworth M. *Moral Courage*. New York: Morrow, 2005.

Kimani, Martin. "Statement to an Emergency Session of the UN Security Council on the Situation in Ukraine." American Rhetoric, Feb. 22, 2022. https://www.americanrhetoric.com/speeches/martinkimaniunitednationsrussiaukraine.htm.

Lausberg, Heinrich. *Handbook of Literary Rhetoric: A Foundation of Literary Study*. Edited by David E. Orton and Dean Anderson. Leiden, Neth.: Brill Academic, 2002.

Makgoba, Thabo. Archbishop Thabo Makgoba, Dec. 25, 2014. "Welcome the Season of Light by Becoming a Society of Long Spoons." https://archbishop.anglicanchurchsa.org/2014/12/welcome-season-of-light-by-becoming.html.

Miller, William Ian. *The Mystery of Courage*. Cambridge, MA: Harvard University Press, 2002.

Norheim, Bård, and Joar Haga. *The Four Speeches Every Leader Has to Know*. London: Palgrave Macmillan, 2020.

———. *The Three Fears Every Leader Has to Know: Words to Use in a Crisis*. London: Palgrave Macmillan, 2022.

Pangle, Lorraine Smith. "The Anatomy of Courage in Aristotle's *Nichomachean Ethics*." *Review of Politics* 80 (2018) 569–90.

Peterson, Erik. "Witness to the Truth." In *Theological Tractates*, edited and translated by Michael J. Hollerich, 151–81. Cultural Memory in the Present. Stanford, CA: Stanford University Press, 2011.

———. "Zeuge der Wahrheit." In *Theologische Traktate*, 167–224. Munich: Wild, 1951.

Pury, C. L. S. "Courage." In *Oxford Handbook of Positive Psychology*, edited by Shane J. Lopez and C. R. Snyder, 375–82. Oxford Library of Psychology. Oxford: Oxford University Press, 2009.

Qiaoying, LU. "Aquinas's Transformation of the Virtue of Courage." *Frontiers of Philosophy in China* 8 (2013) 471–84.

Reagan, Ronald. "Mr. Gorbachev, Tear Down This Wall." YouTube, June 12, 1987. https://www.youtube.com/watch?v=GCO9BYCGNeY.

———. "Remarks on East-West Relations at the Brandenburg Gate in West Berlin." Reagan Foundation, June 12, 1987. https://www.reaganfoundation.org/media/128814/brandenburg.pdf.

Root, Andrew. *Bonhoeffer as Youth Worker: A Theological Vision for Discipleship and Life*. Grand Rapids: Baker Academic, 2014.

Sahlberg, Pasi, and William Doyle. *Let the Children Play: How More Play Will Save our Schools and Help Children Thrive*. Oxford: Oxford University Press, 2019.

Straw, Carole. "Martyrdom." In *Augustine through the Ages: An Encyclopedia*, edited by Allan D. Fitzgerald, OSA, 538–42. Grand Rapids: Eerdmans, 1999.

Thucydides. "Pericles' Funeral Oration." Human Rights Library, n.d. http://hrlibrary.umn.edu/education/thucydides.html.

Vigani, Denise. "Aristotle's Account of Courage." *History of Philosophy Quarterly* 34 (2017) 313–30.

Worline, M. C. "Courage." In *The Oxford Handbook of Positive Organizational Scholarship*, edited by Kim S. Cameron and Gretchen M. Spreitzer, 304–15. Oxford Library of Psychology. Oxford: Oxford University Press, 2012.

Chapter 14

Reclaiming Joy and Tenacity through Online Learning

Teaching and Learning in Crisis

NATHAN HUSSAINI CHIROMA

INTRODUCTION

Throughout the COVID-19 crisis, many wondered whether education would ever be the same again. The pandemic forced us to innovate rapidly, plan for the unexpected, and learn how to teach well in any modality. It is evident that online learning will be an integral part of education, hence, as theological educators, we must seek ways to reclaim joy and tenacity through online learning. Studies have indicated how many teachers and students were affected mentally and psychologically and how many lost joy and tenacity in their pedagogical engagements. Most notably, teaching and learning during crisis could limit joy and tenacity, key concepts that are deeply rooted in education—and even more so in theological education where students are exploring their interests, skills, and calling for career paths.

    Joy and tenacity are critical elements of teaching and learning. The teaching and learning process, especially in theological education, is supposed to bring joy and tenacity to both the teacher and the students. However, teaching and learning in crisis can pose a challenge to the attainment of joy and tenacity. Various studies have shown the negative aspects of online learning,[1] where learners' involvement is commonly described as "disrupted and leading to feelings of insecurity, anxiety, and hopelessness."[2] Research shows a pandemic is a disrupting occurrence triggering "stress that negatively affects students' learning performance and psychological well-being. For instance, studies show such harmful effects of lockdowns as increased levels of students' social avoidance, anxiety, and a decreased quality of general life."[3]

Responding to the current demand for investigation into the impact of teaching and learning in crisis, especially online learning,[4] this chapter will attempt to speak to the following research question: *Is there a possibility of reclaiming the sense of joy and tenacity in teaching learning during a crisis?*

This chapter argues that theological educators, students, parents, and caregivers are able to create a positive community of teaching and learning by creating a sense of joy and tenacity during crises and especially in online learning.

DEFINITION OF TERMS

In order to clarify some key concepts used in this chapter, some working definitions will be provided that will serve as a contextual framework for the chapter.

Tenacity

Narrowly defined, tenacity is the ability to stay persistent and determined, despite difficulty or difficult circumstances. The *Merriam-Webster Dictionary* defines tenacity as "mental or moral strength, to resist opposition, danger or hardship." The synonym for tenacity is perseverance. Similarly, Bakker and Demerauti define academic tenacity as the "cognitive ability to persevere and work hard in the face of challenging circumstances."[5] In this chapter, tenacity is defined as the ability and determination to forge ahead in teaching and learning during a crisis, despite the challenges.

---

1. Dubey and Tripathi, "Analysing the Sentiments."
2. Hajdúk et al., "Psychotic Experiences," 520.
3. Al-Rabiaah et al., "Middle East," 689.
4. Nicola et al., "Socio-Economic Implications."
5. Bakker and Demerauti, "Job Demands-Resources Model," 309.

Joy

Joy is a short word that means a lot of different things to different people. The *Merriam-Webster Dictionary* defines joy in this way: "The emotion of great delight or happiness caused by something exceptionally good or satisfying."

In this chapter, I will adopt the biblical definition of joy, which connotes that joy is a feeling of good pleasure and happiness that is dependent on our theological framework rather than on who we are or what is happening around us.

DYNAMICS OF ONLINE LEARNING

Online learning is not a new phenomenon. Several scholars have alluded to the fact that online learning dates back to the 1990s. According to Arenson, "Universities and colleges began trialing online courses in the early to mid-1990s with the development of the world wide web."[6] Online learning has not only changed the landscape of teaching and learning in theological education but has significantly influenced the teaching-learning process across the world.

The dynamics and the efficacy of online learning cannot be overemphasized. Several studies have been conducted to depict not only the value and impact of online learning but also the dynamics of online learning. However, while it is not within the scope of this chapter to have an in-depth conversation about online learning, a few key dynamics will be highlighted.

First, online learning creates opportunities for flexibility and accessibility for students and teachers alike, in terms of both location and time, and can create further opportunities for better learning, resources, and collaborative teaching. According to Wallen and Hyun, online learning gives students and faculty more flexibility than the traditional classroom. They further argue that online learning gives students the opportunity to attend lectures from wherever they are and promotes accountability and time management, especially in higher education. A further benefit of online learning is the opportunity it provides to students to take full control and accountability for their learning.[7]

The flexibility of online learning provides spaces that will reduce the stress and pressure that are normally found in the traditional classroom. Flexible learning allows the student to work out when and how they will learn by adapting their course to their own competencies. Siegenthaler

---

6. Arenson, "More Colleges Plunging," para. 2.
7. Wallen and Hyun, *How to Design*, 1125–60.

articulates that flexibility is considered a significant model in individualizing the learning and teaching process, enfolding all activities from entry to classes to the end of the learning process beyond the flexibility of place and time.[8]

Second, online learning provides pedagogical synergy. Most of the online management systems used in online learning create a dynamic interaction process between the instructor and the students and among the students themselves. Waghid et al. add that "the synergy that exists on the online platform is one of the most vital and unique opportunities that online learning can provide."[9] Pedagogical synergy in online learning provides robust engagement for self-development among teachers and students.

Third, online learning creates prospects for collaboration and collaborative learning. Through online learning, students are able to partake in high-quality learning situations with different people from different parts of the world. Collaboration can also be enhanced between teachers of different institutions in the teaching-learning process, where ideas are shared and thus a wide range of pedagogical dynamics created that are both local and global. Students can participate in classes from anywhere in the world, giving the lecturer also an opportunity to engage with more guest lecturers, hence providing variety.

Fourth, online learning enhances creative teaching. The features of the independent and self-directed sphere of online learning make new and imaginative methodologies for teaching and learning even more significant.[10] In the online environment, the teacher and student collaborate to create a dynamic learning experience. Online learning challenges teachers to transform their pedagogical approaches to make learning not only creative but also a joyful experience. Facilitating an engaging online class will require the teacher to develop strategies that will enhance student participation and build a sense of learning community.

As mentioned above, the dynamics of online learning are so numerous that it is not in the scope of this chapter to discuss all of them. The few that have been discussed here provide a bird's eye view of some of the dynamics that accompany online learning.

---

8. Siegenthaler, "Relationship," 101–3.
9. Waghid et al., "Assessing," 415.
10. Hajdúk et al., "Psychotic Experiences."

CHALLENGES OF TEACHING AND LEARNING ONLINE: TEACHING AND LEARNING IN CRISIS

Despite the numerous positive dynamics of online teaching, there are several factors that deprive online learning of joy and fun, especially during a period of crisis. In order to restore joy and tenacity in online learning, especially during a crisis, we need to consider some of those factors and find out how to forge a way through for joy and tenacity using online teaching and learning, even in the midst of crisis. Theological educators often struggle with how they should address a crisis or tragedy, especially if it doesn't seem to have an obvious connection to their course content.

Several studies have been conducted on the impact of online learning, especially during the COVID-19 pandemic. Again, the aim of this chapter is not to offer a comprehensive discussion regarding the impact of online learning. However, brief reference will be made to that in order to lay the foundation for the focus of this chapter. This reference will be heavily dependent on the existing studies conducted mainly between 2020 and 2021.

First, studies have shown that online learning can affect the mental health of students, parents, and teachers. According to Dhawan, the side effect of online learning, especially during the COVID pandemic, is "that three-fourths of university students suffered from different depressive symptoms, half of which had moderate to extreme levels of depression."[11] The lack of interaction with other peers and the hours spent in front of computers without playtime with friends further contributed to the deterioration of mental health among students. Additionally, another study conducted by Major found that many students suffered from fear and anxiety, especially during online exams. Furthermore, in many countries there was an increase in the number of hospital admissions for students with existing mental problems as a result of online learning.[12]

Similarly, teachers have increased workloads and were normally pressured by their institutions to deliver quality online learning with minimal training or orientation. As a result, many teachers succumbed to depression, and some had to quit their jobs. Baker et al. add that "many teachers suffered from mental health issues during the COVID pandemic as a result of online learning, more than health workers who are on the front line of dealing with the pandemic."[13] Many teachers suffered anxiety and depres-

---

11. Dhawan, "Online Learning," 20.
12. Major, "Innovations in Teaching."
13. Baker et al., "Experience of COVID-19," 493.

sion as a result of work overload and limited social interaction with both students and other teachers.

Additionally, many parents also suffered from mental health issues as a result of online learning. Parents became teachers and were helping with schoolwork without any training. Parents became proxy educators and were getting more involved with their children's schoolwork to ensure their children learned well and maintain good grades. This additional responsibility of combining their personal work and the involvement in their children's teaching and learning process caused many parents to suffer anxiety and even depression. Parents were not prepared to handle the additional responsibility presented by either the school or the government.

Second, online learning can cause fatigue. Lu and Qi define online learning fatigue as "the overwhelming sense of exhaustion, anxiety, stress, or burnout that students feel due to constant presence online." Online classes bombard students with overload information and prolonged hours on the screen, which can be mentally draining. As a result, it is more challenging for students to learn new information, and even though they just sit in front of the computer, they feel physically sick. Online learning fatigue is real, and it may lead to anxiety and stress for both students and teachers. The term "Zoom fatigue" was coined during the pandemic to refer to exhaustion after long Zoom classes or video conference calls.[14]

Third, online learning can create a lack of interaction and social isolation for both students and teachers. Adam in his study found that since the COVID pandemic, there has been a lack of interaction on the part of both students and teachers that has created a huge gap of social isolation. The academic environment is not just a place where learning takes place through teaching and learning from books, but the extra and hidden curriculum activities provide spaces for friendship and fun. Furthermore, social skills are developed and learned with social interaction, which forms the basis of living in a community.[15] Many theories of social development argue that the lack of social interaction can lead to feelings of loneliness, lack of motivation, and isolation. Anderson sums up by adding that "communication and social skills are best learned with social interaction."[16]

Fourth, online learning comes with many technical issues and challenges. Even though we live in a digital era, digital literacy is totally a new concept to many teachers and students, especially in theological education. Learning online requires multiple resources like computers, the internet,

---

14. Lu and Qi, "Fatigue Detection Technology," 273.
15. Adam, "Social Isolation and Loneliness."
16. Anderson, *Theory and Practice*, 14.

and some basic knowledge of how the online world operates. A study conducted among 30 theological institutions in Africa reveals that 90 percent of the teachers lack digital literacy, 80 percent of the students do not have access to personal computers and 75 percent of both teachers and students do not have regular access to the internet.[17]

The technical issues surrounding online learning created a bigger crisis in some contexts than the COVID pandemic itself. Many theological institutions were forced to shut down, and many struggled to maintain their students even with the provision of online spaces. Many lecturers are still struggling to learn the ropes of the intricacies of online learning. The reality is that in order to proficiently learn through an online system, it will require an understanding of the workings of multiple software, which presents a huge learning curve.

Fifth, online learning redefines teaching and learning. "The notion of an educator as the knowledge-holder who imparts wisdom to their pupils is no longer fit for the purpose of 21st-century education."[18] The reality of teaching and learning online must be redefined because students can now gain access to comprehension and can learn professional skills with a click of a button. The assumption that the teacher holds the key to learning and knowledge is no longer the case in online learning. This may imply the changing role of educators shifting to *enabling* the teaching-learning process, rather than being the sole custodians of knowledge and learning.

With the above-discussed challenges of online learning, teaching and learning can be very difficult, especially during a crisis. The next section will discuss the main focus of this chapter on how we can restore joy and tenacity in teaching and learning during a crisis, especially in terms of theological education.

RECLAIMING JOY AND TENACITY THROUGH ONLINE LEARNING: PEDAGOGICAL IMPLICATIONS (TEACHING AND LEARNING)

Developing strong attitudes toward learning, especially during crisis, can help students and teachers to reduce some of the difficulties discussed above. It becomes more expedient for theological educators because they deal with adult learners. Positive attitudes are required in order to develop joy and tenacity during a crisis. Studies have shown that students' attitudes

---

17. Oliver, "Digital Game-Based Learning," 1–8.
18. Souers with Hall, *Fostering Resilient Learners*, 12.

and disposition to learn during the crisis are dependent to a great degree on the support they receive from their teachers and other family members. Hence, theological educators must align themselves with these findings and find a way to promote joy and tenacity in teaching and learning.

Theological education systems must aim to strengthen engagement between schools, teachers, and learners in order to improve the goals, objectives, and formational needs of students. At the same time, "teachers need support to incorporate technology effectively into their teaching practices and methods and help students overcome some of the difficulties that are associated with an online form of the learning environment."[19] Supporting teachers' professional development on the use of digital resources for pedagogical practice and promoting teaching practices adapted to the context of theological education is key to ensuring joy and tenacity in online learning. In order to accomplish that, the following considerations have to be taken seriously.

First, theological education must focus on intrinsic elements of learning. Intrinsic motivation is a type of motivation that pushes individuals to be motivated by their goals and activity, rather than by external consequences of one's involvement in a task. Intrinsic motivation is considered to be innate, while external motivation is cultivated through internalization. Simply, intrinsic motivation happens when someone does something because they enjoy it or find it very interesting. Then if theological educators are to restore joy and tenacity in teaching and learning during a crisis, then we must find a way to motivate our students intrinsically. Theological educators must take into account that with crisis comes a lot of distractions and a lack of focus.

Both students and teachers begin to question the value of learning and the cause of the difficult circumstances. Moreover, with the challenges of online learning mentioned above, theological educators will need to create an online learning community that will be motivated by intrinsic learning. Online learning must focus on creating a community of inquirers because there is the joy of self-discovery. Intrinsic elements of learning create joy naturally because there is joy in self-discovery. Poor motivation has been identified as a key factor that contributes to many students dropping out of online learning.[20] In contrast, Schunk et al. add that "motivated students are more likely to undertake daring activities, be actively engaged, enjoy and adopt a deep approach to learning, and demonstrate enhanced performance,

---

19. Rotar, "Missing Element," 12.
20. Rotar, "Missing Element," 13.

tenacity, and creativity."[21] Theological educators will need to find a way to indulge their students in the joy of discovery, with the joy of discovery comes tenacity, because students are intrinsically motivated to learn.

Developing a strong attitude of joy and tenacity toward learning can help students remain focused and motivated. A positive attitude will help students embrace learning, with the intrinsic motivation that will not only bring out the best in them, but that will also allow the teacher to create joy and tenacity in the classroom and beyond.

Second, theological educators must communicate that they care during crisis. A caring teacher-student relationship in crisis leads to a transformational relationship, that places the teacher in a position to be trusted by the students and to be confident even to share things they are struggling with during crisis. It is important that theological educators express that they care about their student's personal life, not just the academic process and their success. The resulting anxieties, depression, and other challenges brought into the classroom can affect the teaching-learning process. As theological educators, the tendency is for us to focus more on covering our teaching contents and syllabus at the expense of showing our students that we care about them. Some crises are very visible, but others are not, the attitude of showing we care can facilitate helping students to open up and be free to share their struggles. Kithule makes the following suggestions of some sample language to use and adapt by educators to show a caring attitude: 1) acknowledge the real impact on students; 2) normalize struggles by admitting stress impacts you, too; 3) suggest ways to get help; and 4) reinforce that you care about their success.[22]

Admittedly, sometimes students may want to direct their emotional responses to issues in a nonsensitive way. As a teacher, you can acknowledge their concerns and gently nudge them back to applying class concepts to the issues at hand. Students will be motivated to stay focused despite their situation once they know the teacher cares for them and their circumstances. As teachers, we will need to create a warm and inviting space that will make learning joyful and adventurous.

Third, in order to reclaim joy and tenacity in teaching and learning during crisis, theological educators should allow some flexibility on timelines and deadlines. While you cannot schedule in advance for an unexpected crisis, as theological educators we must be aware of scheduling issues that might arise as a crisis unfolds. If you have the ability to shift your class schedule and move deadlines, students may be able to better attend to your

---

21. Schunk et al., *Motivation in Education*, 56.
22. Kithule, "Helping Students."

assignments. Trying to compete with a crisis for students' emotional and cognitive capacity won't work well for anyone. According to Maslen and Lupten, having flexibility in the teaching-learning process during crisis is not a sign of weakness but rather of accommodation. The teacher identifies with the students in their moment of crisis and struggle. Hence students will learn joyfully amid their difficult circumstances.[23]

Curtain argues that the success of online teaching and learning largely depends on the ability of the teacher to help students make a necessary adjustment during crisis.[24] Theological educators are not just teachers, but agents of hope. As theological educators, we will need to share with the students the necessary adjustments we have made in order to accommodate them and their crisis and to clearly create a manageable path that will help them to adopt. We will also need to make sure that the various tasks and assessments are relevant, appropriate, and worthy of the student's attention.

Fourth, to encourage joy and tenacity in online learning and teaching during crisis, theological educators should support students with needed resources. Providing support in terms of resources is one of the critical elements of online learning. Rotar emphasizes that the help given to students is important for the success of teaching and learning and guaranteeing positive and joyful interaction, motivation, and realization in the teaching and learning process online.[25] With adequate support, online learning provides ample opportunities for students to become more creative and embrace the complexities of the online world. The online world is full of opportunities that can provide joy and tenacity in teaching and learning during crises. According to Anderson, "The online world itself affords new tools for communication, knowledge and skill acquisition, and peer and group support that was not available to earlier generations of distance students."[26]

According to Kruger, theological students will require technical support in online learning and especially during crisis. He argues that theological educators will need to foster technical proficiency in their students. For many students, especially in Africa, this may be their first foray into online learning. Some of the students in rural areas may be seeing a computer for the first time during online learning. Online learning without technical support may be a huge challenge to many, and the reality is that, because of a crisis, that is the only mode of learning made available to them. Kruger further asserts that studies have shown that familiarity with the online

---

23. Maslen and Lupten, "Qualitative Study."
24. Curtain, "Scaffolding Critical Reflection."
25. Rotar, "Missing Element," 13.
26. Anderson, *Theory and Practice*, 23.

learning platform can be a good predictor of students' attitudes and success. For many who may not have the technical proficiency, learning could be a huge challenge and they may be deprived of joy.[27]

Another support that students will need is in the area of how to get online resources. It is one thing to have the technical skill to navigate online learning, it is another thing entirely to learn how to get online resources that are required for online learning. Students may have access to a range of technologies and resources, but not all of them will be beneficial or adequate for teaching learning engagement.

Fifth, theological educators must embrace self-care. It is important that in the midst of teaching and learning during crisis, as teachers we learn to take care of ourselves. Practicing self-care for theological educators is never an option, but it becomes even more critical during crisis. Educators are expected to extend care to students as an integral part of their calling. In as much as this is the right thing to do, we also need to ask a pertinent question as to who is taking care of the teachers. "The ultimate goal of care is to perpetuate others' capacity to care well. When we demonstrate healthy self-care by extending grace to ourselves, we empower others to do the same."[28] Oftentimes during crisis the focus and attention of the institution is to push faculty to deliver and the expense of their mental health. Educators must also recognize their immune stressors and design a way to take care of themselves. Freytag aptly notes that "to care for others well, teachers must care for themselves in healthy and responsive ways," recognizing the fact that crisis does not only affect students but affects teachers as well.[29]

Theological educators must pay attention to intentionally taking care of their physical, emotional, and mental health. This intentionality needs to include mind, body, and emotions. Arguably, self-care is prioritizing one's holistic health. For joy and tenacity to be achieved in teaching and learning during crisis, it is essential for true vitality to ensure that theological educators draw from the whole person. The adage that "you can't give what you don't have" really comes into play when it comes to teaching and learning during crisis.

Similarly, theological institutions must take workload into consideration during crisis in order to allow self-care for faculty members. Experiencing a lot of stress and change in the teaching-learning process due to crisis can diminish teachers' capacity to handle a large workload. Theological institutions must be considerate in reducing workloads or re-strategizing

---

27. Kruger, "Spiritual Formation," 87–89.
28. Souers with Hall, *Fostering Resilient Learners*, 13.
29. Freytag, "Embodying and Modeling," 20.

in order to allow practical self-care by teachers. A study conducted by Zamora-Antuñano et al. found out that many teachers considered resigning from their jobs during COVID due to the increase in workloads. The study further revealed that most teachers felt physically, emotionally, and mentally exhausted. Additionally, some felt unvalued and unheard and were forced to choose between their mental health and their income.[30] If teachers are at risk of poor emotional well-being, the achievement of joy and tenacity will be equal to an impossibility.

In practicing self-care, theological educators must learn to build a support system that will help them create a joyful environment in the classroom. Building a network of support systems, especially during a crisis, must be considered by theological educators to be an essential, ethical responsibility.

IMPLICATIONS FOR THEOLOGICAL EDUCATION/ EDUCATORS (FOR TEACHERS AND SCHOOLS)

Teaching and learning during a crisis can be a huge challenge. More so, the crisis of COVID-19 that for theological institutions necessitated the migration of learning online has proven that in order to maintain joy and tenacity in the teaching and learning process, more than technical know-how and the availability of connectivity and content is necessary. Teaching and learning during a crisis—and especially online—requires significant dedication from teachers and students. There has to be the motivation that will create joy and tenacity and will help students not only cope with the crisis but also with new pedagogical engagements in theological education. Thus, for safeguarding teaching and learning during a crisis, for online theological institutions as much as for other educational establishments, teachers must be provided with technological and pedagogical support to help them remain resilient as we all to adapt to the new normal.[31] The reality is that there will always be crises, and online learning is here to stay. Hence, the mandate to promote joy and resilience in teaching and learning is not optional. In order to ensure the sustainability of the process the following implications must be taken seriously by all theological institutions.

Theological institutions must invest in the development of teachers' online pedagogical skills. The technological skills cultivate an ability to teach efficiently using information and communication technologies, rather than just training them on how to use technology. Furthermore, theological educators must be equipped, trained, and empowered on "how to combine

30. Zamora-Antuñano et al., "Emergency Remote Education."
31. Kruger, "Spiritual Formation."

multiple modes of delivery (i.e., online, offline, and blended) to effectively facilitate learning."[32] These skills are essential in knowledge delivery and in the enhancement of the motivation of both students and learners.

Theological educators must take advantage of the opportunities online learning has created: the opportunities for collaboration, and the interconnectedness of teaching and learning around the world. Online learning is creating an opportunity for theological educators to educate glocal citizens, citizens who can focus locally but with a global perspective. The COVID-19 pandemic proved how globally interconnected we are. It broke down physical boundaries and showed there is no such thing as isolated social action. Theological educators should be able to capitalize on this interconnectedness and navigate teaching and learning in a globally collaborative way. Hence, resilience and adaptability will be crucial factors in online learning, especially for engaging the next generation.

Theological educators must summon the courage to unlock technology in order to deliver education that will be joyful; promote resilience and tenacity; and above all create a learning community that will not only change the future of theological education, but will shape the *nature* of theological education.

CONCLUSION

Reclaiming a sense of joy and tenacity in teaching learning during crisis is a responsibility that theological educators must take seriously. This chapter has argued that teaching and learning during crisis can be a challenge. However, buried in the challenge is a huge possibility and potential that theological educators can use to restore joy and tenacity in teaching and learning during crisis. One of the greatest opportunities in the world of online learning has proven to be a place where a learning community could be created, and joy and tenacity equally created. Joy and tenacity hold a key to creating a thriving online community that can make teaching and learning enjoyable despite crisis. The reality in the world we live in is that we will always have crises of different sorts, however, our role and desire as theological educators is to embrace the pedagogy of hope by creating an atmosphere of joy and tenacity in order to deliver theological education that will bring about the desired outcome and transformation.

---

32. Anderson, *Theory and Practice*, 23.

BIBLIOGRAPHY

Adam, Herman. "Social Isolation and Loneliness in Online Learning: Can Use of Online Social Media Sites and Video Chats Assist in Mitigating Social Isolation and Loneliness?" *Gerontology* 65 (2021) 121–24.

Al-Rabiaah, Abdulkarim, et al. "Middle East Respiratory Syndrome-Corona Virus (MERS-CoV) Associated Stress among Medical Students at a University Teaching Hospital in Saudi Arabia." *Journal of Infection and Public Health* 13 (2020) 687–91.

Anderson, Terry, ed. *The Theory and Practice of Online Learning*. Alberta: Athabasca University Press, 2008.

Arenson, Karen W. "More Colleges Plunging into Uncharted Waters of Online Courses." *New York Times*, Nov. 2, 1998. https://archive.nytimes.com/www.nytimes.com/library/tech/98/11/biztech/articles/02online-education.html.

Baker, Courtney, et al. "The Experience of COVID-19 and Its Impact on Teachers' Mental Health, Coping, and Teaching." *School Psychology Review* 50 (2021) 491–504.

Bakker, Arnold B., and Evangelia Demerouti. "The Job Demands-Resources Model: State of the Art." *Journal of Managerial Psychology* 22 (2007) 309–28.

Curtain, Leonard. "Scaffolding Critical Reflection in Online Learning: Teachers Helping Students Think." *Journal of Teacher Education* 14 (2020) 321–33.

Dhawan, Shivangi. "Online Learning: A Panacea in the Time of COVID-19 Crisis." *Journal of Educational Technology Systems* 49 (2020) 5–22.

Dubey, Akash Dutt, and Shreya Tripathi. "Analysing the Sentiments towards Work-from-Home Experience during COVID-19 Pandemic." *Journal of Innovation Management* 8 (2020) 13–19.

Freytag, Cathy E. "Embodying and Modeling Healthy Self-Care in Teacher Education." *International Christian Community of Teacher Educators Journal* 11 (2016) art. 3.

Hajdúk, Michal, et al. "Psychotic Experiences in Student Population during the COVID-19 Pandemic." *Schizophrenia Research* 222 (2020) 520–45.

Hofer, S. I., et al. "Online Teaching and Learning in Higher Education: Lessons Learned in Crisis Situations." *Computers in Human Behavior* 121 (2021) 106789.

Kithule, Martin. "Helping Students through Education Crisis." *Kappan* 20 (1978) 296–300.

Kruger, Trust. "Spiritual Formation in Online Theological Education." *Christian Education Journal* 5 (2010) 85–102.

Kumashiro, Kevin K. "Teaching and Learning through Desire, Crisis, and Difference: Perverted Reflections on Anti-Oppressive Education." *Radical Teacher* 58 (2000) 6–11.

Lu, Jun Jie, and Chao Qi. "Fatigue Detection Technology for Online Learning." In *2021 International Conference on Networking and Network Applications (NaNA)*, 272–77. Lijang City: IEEE, 2021. 10.1109/NaNA53684.2021.00054.

Major, Christopher. "Innovations in Teaching and Learning during a Time of Crisis." *Innovative Higher Education* 45 (2020) 265–66.

Maslen, Sarah, and Deborah Lupton. "'You Can Explore It More Online': A Qualitative Study on Australian Women's Use of Online Health and Medical Information." *BMC Health Services Research* 18 (2018) 1–10.

Nicola, Maria, et al. "The Socio-Economic Implications of the Coronavirus Pandemic (COVID-19): A Review." *International Journal of Surgery* 78 (2020) 185–93.

Oliver, Erna. "Digital Game-Based Learning and Technology-Enhanced Learning for Theological Education." *Verbum et Ecclesia* 39 (2018) 1–8.

Rotar, Olga. "A Missing Element of Online Higher Education Students' Attrition, Retention and Success: An Analysis through a Systematic Literature Review." Lancaster University, 2020. https://www.research.lancs.ac.uk/portal/en/publications/a-missing-element-of-online-higher-education-students-attrition-retention-and-success(9555562c-2eac-4269-9ffa-9295997614b4).html.

Schunk, Dale H., et al. *Motivation in Education: Theory, Research, and Applications*. 3rd ed. Upper Saddle River, NJ: Pearson, 2008.

Siegenthaler, Eva. "The Relationship between Flexible and Self-Regulated Learning in Open and Distance Universities." *IRRODL* 13 (2012) 101–23.

Souers, Kristin, with Pete Hall. *Fostering Resilient Learners: Strategies for Creating a Trauma-Sensitive Classroom*. Akron: ASCD, 2016.

Sutcher, Leib, et al. *A Coming Crisis in Teaching? Teacher Supply, Demand, and Shortages in the U.S.* ERIC, 2016. https://files.eric.ed.gov/fulltext/ED606665.pdf.

Waghid, Zayd, et al. "Assessing Cognitive, Social and Teaching Presences during Emergency Remote Teaching at a South African University." *International Journal of Information and Learning Technology* (2021) 413–32.

Wallen, Norman, and Helen H. Hyun. *How to Design and Evaluate Research in Education*. 7th ed. New York: McGraw-Hill, 2012.

Zamora-Antuñano, Marco Antonio, et al. "Analysis of Emergency Remote Education in COVID-19 Crisis Focused on the Perception of the Teachers." *Sustainability* 13 (2021) 3820.

Chapter 15

The Transformative Power of Cultural Immersion Practices in a Master of Theology Module?

Reflections on Opportunities and Challenges with Regards to Engaging Students on Poverty and Inequality in South Africa Today

Nadine Bowers Du Toit and Ralph Afghan

INTRODUCTION

Mezirow highlights the fact that transformative learning paradigms empower and affirm learners towards personal transformation.[1] For the past seven years we (a lecturer in Theology and Development/Diaconia at Stellenbosch University and a clergyperson who is deeply passionate about the missional role of congregations) have been co-lecturing in a block master's module. This module is part of a broader master of theology qualification in "missional leadership" targeted largely at clergy, and our module seeks to help students in understanding their own positioning and role as agents of change as church and community leaders within the complex South African context of poverty and inequality. This module has been developed over the years into a unique learning environment that "front-loads" immersive cross-cultural/cross-socioeconomic experiences and exercises at the

---

1. Mezirow, "Perspective Transformation," 100.

beginning of the module before formal lectures take place and allows for reflexive and dialogical learning. According to Tomlinson-Clarke and Clarke, such immersion experiences "exposes learners to culturally dissimilar situations that may be unfamiliar. Immersion in a new and different culture (or socio-economic context) can serve as a disorientating cultural dilemma from which beliefs and values about the self and culturally dissimilar others are challenged."[2] We have found this approach to be initially disorientating, but also instrumental in facilitating deep critical reflection and discourse within the course and ultimately towards critical self-reflection—even transformation—of the individual participants/learners. In this chapter we will seek to reflect on our teaching praxis as it has developed over the years in light of scholarly thought on transformative learning theories that advance both personal transformation and, ultimately, social justice, such as the model of cultural immersion.

THE CONTEXT OF THE MODULE

This module is situated within the MTh ministry practice, which has a "specific focus on missional leadership in the African context."[3] This structured master's degree, which consists of six modules taught by a range of academic lecturing staff and qualified practitioners, was introduced in 2011 and is presented over two years. It mainly targets clergy and usually sees an average of ten to twelve students per annum join the program from a range of denominational backgrounds (Anglicans, Reformed, Methodist, Congregational, Pentecostal) and is diverse also in terms of race, class, and gender. As noted, the majority of the students are clergy; however, in terms of ministry experience they have ranged from probationer ministers to clergy with thirty years of ministry experience. In terms of ministry contexts they minster in contexts as diverse as rural towns where their congregants are farmers, wealthy urban megachurches and township contexts where congregants are impoverished. In recent years, we have seen the increase in bi-vocational ministers entering the program. There are various reasons that bi-vocational ministry has taken shape in denominations, as some contexts cannot afford a full-time minister for economic reasons or others have a twofold ministry. Secondary to this, some of the students are within their second professional vocation, after retiring from their current work and sensing the call of God upon their lives to ministry. Robust conversations about race and the need for socioeconomic alignment or adjustments are often taken personally by

---

2. Tomlinson-Clarke and Clarke, "International Cultural Immersion," 25.

3. Nell, "MTh Ministry Practice Information," 1.

The Transformative Power of Cultural Immersion Practices 223

those who lived through the apartheid era and were privileged due to race during this era. In recent years, its teaching staff have also become more diverse in terms of confessional status and gender profile.

The program's pedagogy is described in the following way:

> The program offers students a unique learning experience. The program focuses on developing students' skills as missional leaders through a reading program on missional theory; deep ecumenical interaction; contextual exposure; and exercises in innovative missional practices. The learning experience will include:
>
> - the reading of academic books and articles.
> - reflection in an ecumenical learning community.
> - exposure to diverse contexts and ministries.
> - gaining expertise through exercising new skills; and
> - articulating and integrating theory through the writing of module assignments for each module and a research assignment at the completion of the program.
>
> The learning experience is rooted in an ecumenical discerning community of fellow students and lecturers.[4]

The program is based on a hermeneutical-rhetorical framework and is made up of six modules.

Our module was first revised in 2016 after two cohorts of students expressed a need to have more engagement around the topic of the local church in the context of community, whereafter we created this new module, centered and front-loaded around immersive learning experiences. At the time of our module revision, it is important to note that we were the only teaching team who were people of color, and this remained the case for a number of years within the program. More recently this has changed. The module's outcomes were targeted at developing missional skills "needed by church leaders to cross boundaries and also integrate missional theological skills in their congregations ministries"; guiding students to "recognize missional opportunities for themselves and their communities"; encouraging missional habits (spiritual discernment practices); and, of course, exploring missional transformation theories, which encourage church leaders "to not only reflect on how they should proclaim and embody the gospel for their contexts, but also what the real content of the gospel is in terms of hope for those contexts."[5] Their ethnographic experiences in their particular context

---

4. Nell, "MTh Ministry Practice Information," 1.
5. Bowers Du Toit, "MTh Ministry Practice Module," 1.

would, in this module, point out the identity of their church and the gaps in their understanding with regards to what it means to be church in the African context.

In 2019, the program was revised to better address the needs of church stakeholders. This module, which was previously the fifth module of six and offered in the second year of the course, was then moved to become the second module that students take. This would later be changed back, due to the positive effect this module had had when it was previously located in the second year as the fifth module of six. By module 5, the students would know each other and thus be ready for robust engagement and interrogation of current and relevant issues. The module was previously named Kingdom Communities and in the current revised curriculum is called Churches in a (South) African Context. This course, unlike the others in the MTh, has always been taught off site at the Methodist church where one of us—namely, Ralph Afghan—is the minister, and at a local NGO, The Warehouse. From the first day we sought to immerse students in the context of the church where we hold the classes and engaged them in immersive experiences, exploring various tools, which, it is hoped, would encourage them to reflect more deeply on their own ministerial contexts of church and community. These experiences and tools are explored in more depth later in this chapter. This approach is influenced by theorists such as Kolb and Kolb and Barber who champion the facilitation of a "process of integration by linking existing student knowledge and information to a larger foundational schema in order to make meaning out of experiences. This transfer of learning encompasses experiential learning elements not found in traditional academic settings."[6]

As facilitators we bring an average of twenty years each in terms of ministry and academic experience respectively and have both been formed and informed by a critical consciousness. Both of us are situated in cross-cultural and multilingual contexts, where mostly we have been in the minority in terms of race and language. We are passionate and committed to helping clergy to think and act compassionately, justly, hopefully, and innovatively in addressing the very challenging issues of poverty, inequality, and racism within our own South African context. This has deeply influenced how we approach teaching this module each year.

---

6. Lewis et al., "Creative Teaching and Reflection," 31.

TOWARDS DEFINING HOPEFUL TRANSFORMATIVE LEARNING IN A SOUTH AFRICAN CONTEXT

South Africa has a complex and divided history that has resulted in deep racial, ethnic, and socioeconomic divisions. When placing diverse individuals—all of whom are master's students and largely church leaders already positioned in further diverse contexts—to engage theologically with issues of racial and socioeconomic inequality more especially, it is holy ground. South African educationist Jonathan Jansen writes about "knowledge in the blood," which he defines as the knowledge that is "embedded in the emotional, psychic, spiritual, social, economic, political and psychological loves of a community."[7] Tomlinson-Clarke and Clarke note that this knowledge is transmitted, and "influences how individuals see the world, and themselves and how they understand others. Engaging in difficult dialogues and interactions with diverse others deepens understanding of the critical issues underlying social justice, suggestive suggesting ways to interrupt the habitual flow of knowledge and to develop what Jansen refers to as empathetic knowledge that is not compromised by defensive knowledge."[8]

This "knowledge in the blood" in South Africa is of course deeply influenced by our colonial and apartheid past—a past that was deliberately built not only on the separation of races and a racial hierarchy and resulted in socioeconomic inequality but that, for many, still continues to dictate racially and culturally exclusive social interactions today—not least within the social milieu of South African churches. The spatial reality of churches during apartheid created "make-shift" and congested impoverished communities in black areas, compared to white suburban areas where locations can be utilized fully and are privileged both economically and socially.[9] It is, therefore, no easy feat to move students towards engaging in difficult dialogues and interactions with diverse others—more especially with regards to issues of social justice in a context wherein injustice was also shaped by theological underpinnings. Nevertheless, as noted by Dames in his article "A Dangerous Pedagogy of Discomfort," this is needed in theological education in South Africa today.[10] So, while we don't believe that we would easily find a clergy person who would still subscribe to the crude and racist beliefs of apartheid theology and ideology, its continued influence on the way that we minister and gather as faith communities is evident.

---

7. Jansen, *Knowledge in the Blood*, 171.
8. Tomlinson-Clarke and Clarke, "Complex Hope," 148.
9. Resane, "White Fragility, White Supremacy."
10. Dames, "Dangerous Pedagogy of Discomfort," 10.

The need for difficult dialogues and interactions in our quest to interrupt this "knowledge in the blood" and assist student clergy in moving towards critical reflection on their own and others positioning and place (also as theologians) is, therefore, a challenging one as it often brings to the surface emotions and microaggressions. In this respect, bi-vocational ministry can be both a blessing and a curse. The blessing of the bi-vocational minister is that they understand that they have agency and often exercise their presence and voice to create dialogue in critical life-changing moments for their community in relation to justice and discipling. However, if one is not fully embedded in the "soil" of ministry then this is also a barrier. These ministers often struggle with being fully present and engaging critically and theologically with issues of social justice.

As theologians, we are fascinated that hope and hopefulness are also identified by secular scholars as essential characteristics for effective educational leadership. Perhaps we should affirm that our hope as theological educators has been firmly rooted in the kingdom vision of shalom, which includes justice, equality, freedom, peace, restoration, and healing in all its forms.[11] After all, if we reflect on it, this is how we specifically interpret the very vague inherited moniker for this course—initially named Kingdom Communities. Indeed, our hope is to not only to move students, as Jansen says, from defensive knowledge towards empathetic knowledge,[12] but also how we empower and affirm learners towards personal transformation as church and community leaders. Public theologian and former rector of the University of Stellenbosch Russell Botman drew extensively on the work of Paulo Freire in believing that the use of critical pedagogy could play a role in stimulating critical thinking and critical consciousness in people in such a way that "they may free themselves from oppression, poverty, injustice and difficult task of living peacefully."[13] This is not a false or utopic hope, but one rooted, as Freire argues in an "existential, concrete imperative"—critical hope—which seeks to put hope into action and which demands of progressive educators that they not only engage students with regards to a political analysis that "leads to an understanding of the historical, economic and social processes producing conditions that lead to despair" but also seeks to unveil hope in a seeking for transformative action.[14]

---

11. Bragg, "From Development to Transformation," 28–47.
12. Tomlinson-Clarke and Clarke, "Complex Hope," 148.
13. Botman, "Case for Relevant University," 14.
14. Botman, "Case for Relevant University," 16.

FRONT-LOADING IMMERSIVE LEARNING AS PEDAGOGICAL TOOL

One of the key ways in which we sought to unlock transformative dialogue shaped by empathetic rather than defensive knowledge, was to front-load immersive learning. Immersion is defined as "exercises which provide occasions for trainees to personally experience immersion in a culture different from their own."[15] In our case, owing to the fact that the group is usually all South Africans and culturally diverse, we position the course in a geographical context (not necessarily a culture) that is generally unfamiliar to all of them and then provide occasions for not only cross-cultural but cross-class (and also cross-denominational) interactions, seeing that the course is about cultivating church leaders who are able to work and engage with the complex issues of poverty, inequality, and race in self-reflexive and transformative ways. Tomlinson-Clarke and Clarke discuss a cycle of immersive learning, which we adapt here.[16]

The cycle usually starts with a *disorientating dilemma*, which provides learners with the opportunity to engage in culturally (or in our case culturally or socioeconomically) different individuals interacting in their community and to see how their values are expressed in relationship. The first two days of the course, therefore, start with two such experiences and on the fourth day there is another experience. This means that there are a few cycles of these disorientating dilemmas.

Day 1: Transect walk (a kind of observation walk) of an economically divided community—they need to observe issues of race, class, and social movement—marginalized people, the economic state of the area, etc. We even encourage them to engage with people they meet along the walk. This exercise is new to them in that we found that not many clergy have even done this exercise in their own community (some having been ministering in their communities for more than ten years) and because this walk is not their community, they are more observant of what is going on. They usually come back from that exercise disturbed by what they hear and see, as they suddenly see issues of racial and social inequality much more clearly in a context that is not their own and are forced to relocate themselves in their own community.

Day 2: Attend a cross-cultural church service, which is hosted by Zimbabwean refugees in their language of Shona—a language that usually no one in the class speaks. They attend the service as guests, and this is followed

---

15. Ridley et al., "Multicultural Training," 263.
16. Tomlinson-Clarke and Clarke, "International Cultural Immersion," 25–26.

by a meal with the congregants. This exercise is disruptive to church leaders, because in church they are usually the host and power holder. Here they are the guests who cannot speak the language of the liturgy. Their hosts are also socioeconomically poorer than they, and in a country where xenophobia is rife, year on year this experience was pivotal and transformational.

In the revised module, which began in 2020, the church service changed location and context and was hosted not by your traditional theological trained pastor, but by a person who has a passion for homeless people, and who seeks to provide hope and dignity to them. We gather at six a.m. at Thomas House, which is a safe house and place of hope and restoration for street homeless people, and here a social worker is provided to help with the social restitution of the homeless back into society and family. After debriefing, the students prepare breakfast and tea for the homeless community and participate in an open-air street chapel service. For many, it is their first encounter ministering in such a way.

Days 3 and 4 are facilitated training on community discernment processes with a nongovernmental organization that assists church leaders in understanding and addressing issues in their communities. This is a tool that they are trained in and it provides them with some time to process the other experiences. During this training they also begin to understand how their immersions also mirror what is being taught by this tool.

Day 5: On the morning of this day, Nadine Bowers Du Toit teaches in the morning on the theological foundations for the church engaging in issues of poverty and inequality, where they are also encouraged to reflect on the ways in which their own theologies hinder or help in their churches engagement with society. On that afternoon we practice "open chapel" (in line with the Wesleyan notion of "the world is my parish"), which consists of the class being divided into groups and positioning themselves in a socio-economically poor, yet busy, urban economic hub and offering prayer from a couch or chair to passersby. This exercise often takes these clergy far beyond their comfort zones, and it is an exercise that they often find both simultaneously tremendously challenging and inspirational in their ministry journeys when they reflect back on the experience. We recall one very conservative clergyman even refusing to participate, but we will reflect on this further in the chapter.

The next stages in the cycle are critical reflection and critical discourse. Opportunities for critical reflection and discourse are provided throughout the course. Each morning we have both a debrief of the previous day's immersion or learning experience and what we call "dwelling the word." This is a practice popularized in missional church circles and which is described as "a practice of a repeated communal listening to a passage of Scripture

The Transformative Power of Cultural Immersion Practices 229

over long periods of time in order to enable a Christian community to undertake its decisions and actions in line with the biblical meta-narrative."[17] The biblical text—it is the same one every day—is read through various lenses: power, leadership, our context of south Africa's land issue, etc. This debriefing and time of "dwelling in the word" often provides fruitful times of critical discourse and reflection on their experiences in a diverse group context, which "helps learners/students to consider differing worldviews and to engage in critical discourse about situations that may differ from one's own."[18] This biblical narrative exercise where they read the text together and in context catches them off guard and is not the norm of what they had been doing in the previous modules. From day one, the emerging text and context are real, and they are confronted with themes they often ignore or are afraid to address in their current context. The point of the immersion experiences or disorientating dilemmas we created is, as Tomlinson-Clarke and Clarke note, to provide a context whereby cultural (and we would add, socioeconomic and racial) "assumptions are challenged, prejudice and racism are reduced and multicultural competencies are increased."[19] The dialogue is at times heated, and often the disorientation students feel when confronted with new experiences and the challenging of their own assumptions of dominance or privilege is to lash out at us as the facilitators. In one of the earliest times of offering this module, one of the students, a white women, reached her limit in terms of confronting the hard issues of the ways in which poverty, inequality, and race intersect in South Africa and addressed us very defensively. This usually happens on the days that are taught days and where they are encouraged to engage in reflection and discussion. As facilitators we simply attempt to "hold the space" and often pose probing or critical questions and facilitate the dialogical engagement within the class as well as of course seeking to integrate prescribed content. As facilitators we have come to recognize these outbursts (and we have had more than one over the years, especially from white students) as the point of transformation and not to personalize them. In fact, scholars note that these experiences in socioeconomically diverse environments "encourages learners to engage in critical self-reflection to challenge cultural assumptions, cultural biases and perceptions often triggered by emotionally charged situations."[20] They also note that what is needed is that "encouragement and support must also be an essential part of critical discourse in order for learners to dig

17. Nel, "Influence of Dwelling," 1.
18. Nel, "Influence of Dwelling," 1.
19. Tomlinson-Clarke and Clarke, "International Cultural Immersion," 26.
20. Tomlinson-Clarke and Clarke, "International Cultural Immersion," 34.

deeper into their emotional reactions."[21] The latter often requires skill and discernment from us as course facilitators, and we have learned not to be defensive or "shut down" these reactions—even if they are triggering to us as people of color or personal in terms of the outburst. We will often share that this is normal for this part of the process as these students are often embarrassed once they understand their response. Other scholars note that in their own experiences of facilitating such courses, students often find that their emotions are "abundant and overwhelming" or contain mixed feelings of "joy and anger."[22] Tomlinson-Clarke and Clarke note that "it is perhaps through these emotional triggers that personal transformation and the desire or awakening towards social justice advocacy is codified."[23] Coble et al. note that "building a sustaining and common representational space requires group members to engage in dialogue, hold tension and operate within a context of risk and uncertainty" but that "the benefits outweigh the risks because enriching the common representational space also enriches the personal representational space of each participant."[24]

The next aspect is critical self-reflection. Lewis et al. cite Ash and Clayton, who note that "critical reflections can be transformative in promoting personal development and professional growth as students connect ideas, engage in self-assessment, and consider alternative viewpoints to surpass superficial learning methods."[25] One of the pillars of this course's pedagogy is that students journal their experiences on each day and hand in their reflection electronically at the end of each day. We are clear that the aim of the journal is not just to produce and hand in a summary of their experiences, but to really reflect deeply and self critically on what they felt and thought about as they experienced these encounters. They are also encouraged to reflect in light of their prescribed course readings and each morning after these experiences there is a debrief. It is here where we often sense where shifting in their own theological understanding of church and kingdom perspectives of ministry has taking place. In others, the ignorance of denial and their prejudices becomes clear. We then provide feedback engaging them to think deeper or differently or identify blind spots in their reflections through probing questions and open reflection and discourse during and private feedback to their journal reflections. This is because "our meaning

---

21. Tomlinson-Clarke and Clarke, "International Cultural Immersion," 34.
22. Tomlinson-Clarke and Clarke, "International Cultural Immersion," 26.
23. Tomlinson-Clarke and Clarke, "International Cultural Immersion," 26.
24. Coble et al., "Opening Up," 26.
25. Lewis et al., "Creative Teaching and Reflection," 30.

perspective must be challenged in developing more culturally appropriate assumptions and alternatives."[26]

We allow six weeks for students to hand in their final paper, which we term an "integrated reflexive assessment." In this paper we now ask them to integrate their learnings from the immersive experiences, tools, lectures, and prescribed readings and consider how their learning could shape their engagement as clergy with the socioeconomic issues in their own communities. Often this time allows them to process and digest the immersion experiences, dialogue and content and to critically self-reflect from a different perspective and in conversation with theological texts. It is usually in these assignments—six weeks after they have left the course—that they really understand how the course has been a catalyst for personal change. *This is the final stage of the process—personal transformation (social justice leadership and advocacy).* Brookfield notes that this will occur only where those reflecting must try to identify the assumptions they hold and learn to examine their own "emotional responses to certain situations as learned."[27] The very woman who was previously mentioned as having been offended by the discourse on race later reflected in her integrated assessment how she had (through further reflection upon her course readings and having had time to process her feelings and response) come to a better understanding of her positionality and committed herself to social change. We remain in close contact with her. We also especially remember one clergyperson who was challenged on the course about the way his congregation treated a staff member of another race as well as the way they ran community projects, and who told us that the course changed the way he interacted with black colleagues and the way his church ran their community projects—which they had transformed from one-way paternalistic charity into more dignifying and participatory projects. Lest it be thought that personal transformation relates to only one race group, we have also witnessed over the years how clergy of color find their voice and space in this context and have also been challenged with regards to their own community engagement. One clergyperson of color was especially challenged by the closed ecclesiology of his congregation and as a result of the course has changed his understanding of the church's role in community.

---

26. Tomlinson-Clarke and Clarke, "International Cultural Immersion," 26.
27. Brookfield, "Transformative Learning," 127.

CONCLUSION

Suffice it to say, this course is not for the fainthearted—and that refers to both students and lecturer-facilitators—as it often unearths deep-seated beliefs and requires self-reflexivity. In many ways, the immersive learning process is not predictable as it is process related and, therefore, often messy. As a past student recently commented to current students of the module, they need to "trust the process." According to Smit, Russel Botman, public theologian and the first rector of color at the University of Stellenbosch, liked to say that all transformation takes place "on shifting ground." According to him, "We partake in making history as limping people, dependent on grace, on gifts, on surprises, on blessing, on the sunrise. We partake in making history, deeply conscious of the limitations, shortcomings and provisional nature of our achievements—grateful for 'early gains'!, yet self-critical and therefore open and receptive."[28] Perhaps this is a good descriptor of where we find ourselves as facilitators of this course—we remain deeply conscious and grateful for the gains of personal transformation many of the students have undergone, yet self-critical and receptive to adjusting our pedagogy as the context shifts.

BIBLIOGRAPHY

Botman, Russell. H. "The Case for the Relevant University." *SAJHE* 25 (2011) 14–24.

Bowers Du Toit, Nadine. "MTh Ministry Practice Module 5 Outline." Photocopy, Department of Practical Theology and Missiology, University of Stellenbosch, Stellenbosch, 2018.

Bragg, Wayne. "From Development to Transformation." In *The Church in Response to Human Need*, edited by Vinay Samuel and Christopher Sugden, 20–51. Oxford: Regnum, 1987.

Brookfield, Stephen. "Transformative Learning as Ideology Critique in Learning and Transformation." In *Learning as Transformation: Critical Perspectives on Theory in Progress*, edited by John Mezirow and Associates, 125–46. San Francisco: Jossey-Bass, 2000.

Coble, Theresa G., et al. "Opening Up to Hard History: Activating Anti-Racism in an Immersive Ed.D. Cohort Experience at Heritage Sites in Montgomery, Alabama." *Impacting Education* 5 (2020) 26–32.

Dames, Gordon. E. "A Dangerous Pedagogy of Discomfort: Redressing Racism in Theology Education." *HvTSt* 75 (2019) 1–11.

Jansen, Jonathan. *Knowledge in the Blood: Confronting Race and the Apartheid Past*. Palo Alto, CA: Stanford University Press, 2009.

---

28. Smit, *Making History*, 629.

Lewis, Melinda, et al. "Creative Teaching and Reflection in Non-Traditional Settings: Regional, National, and International Experiences." *Social Development Issues* 39 (2017) 29–40.

Mezirow, John. "Perspective Transformation." *Adult Education* 28 (1978) 100–110.

Nel, Marius. "The Influence of Dwelling in the Word within the Southern African Partnership of Missional Churches." *Verbum et Ecclesia* 34 (2013) 1–7.

Nell, Ian. "MTh Ministry Practice Information Booklet." Photocopy, Department of Practical Theology and Missiology, University of Stellenbosch, Stellenbosch, 2023.

Resane, Kelebogile. "White Fragility, White Supremacy and White Normativity Make Theological Dialogue on Race Difficult." *In die Skriflig/In Luce Verbi* 55 (2021) 1–10.

Ridley, Charles R., et al. "Multicultural Training: Reexamination, Operationalisation and Integration." *Counselling Psychologist* 22 (1994) 227–89.

Smit, Dirkie. "Making History for the Coming Generation: On the Theological Logic of Russel Botman's Commitment to Transformation." *Stellenbosch Theological Journal* 1 (2015) 607–32.

Tomlinson-Clarke, Saundra M., and Darren Clarke. "Complex Hope: Developing Leadership for Social Justice." In *Social Justice and Transformative Learning: Culture and Identity in the United States and South Africa*, edited by Saundra M. Tomlinson-Clarke and Darren Clarke, 143–56. Routledge Research in Educational Equality and Diversity. New York: Routledge, 2019.

———. "International Cultural Immersion: Exploring Culture and Society within the Context of the United States and Post-Apartheid South Africa." In *Social Justice and Transformative Learning: Culture and Identity in the United States and South Africa*, edited by Saundra M. Tomlinson-Clarke and Darren Clarke, 24–39. Routledge Research in Educational Equality and Diversity. New York: Routledge, 2019.

Chapter 16

(Im)possibilities of Malawian Postgraduates Studying at Stellenbosch University during the COVID-19 Crisis

Chrispine Nthezemu Kamanga

INTRODUCTION AND BACKGROUND

The "paradoxical community" that ensues is caught in a historical temporality of partial and double identifications that exist side-by-side in Ethical and Political life—at once "same and other"; at once indigenous and foreign; at once citizen and alien; at *once jus sanguinis and jus soli.*[1]

By shedding the unhomely element in her life, that is the disturbing aspects of the neighborhood, the house, and the home, she is left with very little more than her veiled body. Self-covering, in this context, goes beyond what conventions ask for: it is a self-imprisoning act, a self-censoring performance.[2]

The dawn of the COVID-19 pandemic brought different dynamics to the life and operations of different people in different spaces. The education sector was and continues to be greatly impacted by COVID-19. While doing a postgraduate degree in a foreign country has its challenges, the COVID-19 pandemic added its own dynamics for Malawian postgraduate students at Stellenbosch University. This chapter brings to the fore the experiences of a selected group of Malawian postgraduate students at Stellenbosch University

---

1. Bhabha, *Our Neighbours, Ourselves*, 2.
2. Ghazoul, "Iraqi Short Fiction," 8.

during the COVID-19 crisis. The population of this study consisted of Malawian postgraduate students at Stellenbosch University who were either in Malawi or at Stellenbosch at the time of the lockdown(s) implemented by the South African government to curtail the spread of coronavirus. The study explores the nature of postgraduate research in challenging environments. What would such environments mean to postgraduate students in the Global South in general and Malawi in particular? The study is set in both Malawi and South Africa (Stellenbosch) where selected Malawian postgraduate students were at the time of the COVID-19 pandemic outbreak and the subsequent implementation of measures meant to contain the virus, including lockdown.

Most postgraduate Malawian students whom I interviewed were sponsored by their employing organization. A good number of these postgraduate students were married and were therefore responsible for their families while at the same time pursuing their studies. The COVID-19 pandemic revolutionized many sectors, including academic studies, and most academic institutions transformed their traditional physical classroom setting to hybrid online classes.[3] The national lockdowns in the wake of COVID-19 forced these postgraduate students to turn to the internet for academic meet-ups on Zoom and other online platforms.[4] The online learning was a perfect option for these postgraduate students, allowing them to be close to their families and their workplaces while studying.[5] At the dawn of the pandemic and the introduction of lockdowns to contain the spread of coronavirus, many Malawian students were stuck in either Malawi or Stellenbosch. However, the challenge with this online mode of study for the postgraduate students in Malawi was that the internet was sometimes slow, unreliable, and expensive and that the students had to respond to the recurring needs of their families and their workplaces while pursuing their studies. This was at the same time as the pandemic seemed to suggest that the education sector was shifting to a digital space and providing a new normality.[6] At the time the measures to contain COVID-19, like lockdown, were being implemented by the South African government, some of the Malawian students were in Malawi. This meant that they could not travel back to Stellenbosch immediately. Others were in Stellenbosch and consequently could not travel back to Malawi as they wished. These unavoidable circumstances caused

---

3. Carius, "Network Education," 3; Blizak et al., "Students' Perceptions"; Selwyn and Jandrić, "Postdigital Living."
4. Murphy, "COVID-19 and Emergency eLearning," 496.
5. Adnan and Anwar, "Online Learning"; Dhawan, "Online Learning," 14–15.
6. Tesar, "Towards a Post-Covid-19," 558.

by the pandemic created panic and affected their economic status and the duration of studies. Those students who were still in Malawi had to carry on with their studies while responding to the demands of their families and employers, while those in Stellenbosch had to continue their studies in a quiet and lonely environment where they could not move around at will. Depending on where these students were trapped, they faced challenges related to the continuation of their postgraduate studies. Despite the challenges that they faced; opportunities to proceed with their studies were also created.

This chapter engages exploratory, descriptive, and qualitative study design to reflect on the experiences of selected Malawian postgraduates at Stellenbosch University and suggests workable modes of studies in the COVID-19 era. The study participants were recruited from willing members of a WhatsApp group of the Malawi students at Stellenbosch University (MSSU), which comprises students who were studying at Stellenbosch. The group had twenty-seven participants (seventeen male, ten female). The researcher created a Google form, which was an effective data collection tool for quick and accurate data processing. The questionnaire contained an introduction to the study, aims of the study, guarantee of confidentiality for the participants, and six open questions. Participants were sent the questionnaire through their WhatsApp numbers. The questionnaire was sampled among three students who were later excluded from participation. Out of the twenty-four remaining participants, nineteen responded to the questionnaire, representing a 79-percent response rate. The questions were as follows:

1. What are the challenges you have encountered because of undertaking a postgraduate degree during COVID-19 pandemic?
2. In your view, what are the opportunities that the pandemic has brought to the postgraduate studies?
3. In your view, what are the complications or disadvantages the pandemic has brought to the postgraduate studies?
4. How do you describe the usage of the internet during the study process in the COVID-19 era?
5. What do you suggest would be the best way of undertaking postgraduate studies in this time of crisis?
6. Please add any other comment you may find relevant to the topic.

THEORETICAL FRAMEWORK

This study deploys Homi Bhaha's idea of home as utilized by Rostami and Parvaneh in their recent work.[7] Bhabha theorizes home to be a place of stable identity where one has been and is understood.[8] In nation and cultures that are experiencing oppression, home is linked to a positive version of the past as argued by Toni Morrison and Nadine Gordimer on their reflection on racism and apartheid in South Africa.[9] To them, home means a life before oppression. In other words, home is tied to freedom. Bhabha develops the notion of "unhomely" by referring to some work of postcolonial literature that problematizes the idea of the real and stable home. Bhabha lays emphasis on the instability of home and of the past. The word *unhomely* is the translation of *unheimlich*, which is the opposite of *heimlich*. Bhabha argues that the place between the *heimlich* (homely) and *unheimlich* (unhomely) is a postcolonial place, a space in which one can see how a person's identity is a mixture of what is unfamiliar or foreign and what is familiar.[10]

The idea of homely and unhomely echoes the work of Sigmund Freud.[11] To Freud, as the subconscious creeps and moves into the conscious, it creates an uncanny moment. It is the same when the world creeps into the home and shakes an identity that was thought to be stable and secure. This shock of recognition is commonly considered to be negative. Alienation is a very painful experience that one thinks to be familiar, but it is not. Bhabha suggests that the alienation that a person experiences in the "unhomely" moment may also present an opportunity to reevaluate one's identity. Bhabha talks about his own origins and does not claim a stable and fixed identity. He suggests that Parsis have transformational experiences and hybrid identity. We should know that homelessness is real as well as metaphorical.

> I have lived that moment of scattering of the people that in other times and other places, in the nations of others, becomes a time of gathering. Gathering of exiles and émigrés and refugees; gathering on the edge of foreign cultures; gathering at the frontiers; gatherings in the ghettoes or cafes city centres; gathering in the half-life, half-light of foreign tongues or in the uncanny fluency of another's language.[12]

7. Rostami and Parvaneh, "Notion of Unhomeliness," 157.
8. Ghazoul, "Iraqi Short Fiction," 2.
9. Morrison, *Beloved*, 198–99; Gordimer, *My Son's Story*, 249.
10. Rostami and Parvaneh, "Notion of Unhomeliness," 157.
11. Cixous, "Fiction and Its Phantoms."
12. Bhabha, *Nation and Narration*, 291.

Bhabha suggests the uncanny concept as the unhomely too. He evokes the uncanniness of migrant experience through a series of familiar ideas such as half-life (the partial presence of colonial identity) that repeat the life lived in the country of origin. However, the repetition is not identical. It introduces transformation and difference. He also says, further, that this repetition is a way of reviving that past life and keeping it alive in the present. All the uncertainties, hesitations, and ambivalences that colonial authority and its figures are imbued with are characterized in terms of the uncanny. In other words, the split in political subject can be described as uncanny. Sigmund Freud and Julia Kristeva use the idea of the uncanny.[13] This influenced Bhabha and his sense of the hybrid, postcolonial perspective.

According to Bhabha, culture has dual identity. On the one hand, it is homely or realistic, asserting its stability and coherence; on the other hand, it is unhomely because it is always changing; it is always made meaningful by others. Culture, to Bhabha, is never coherent and self-sufficient. Though its narratives seem confident and stable, they are always drawn into displaced relationship. They are in relationship with other cultures, texts, or disciplines. He says migrants can be a good example of this dual nature of culture; they are always situated in relation to both an original culture and a new place and location. Bhabha argues that the uncanny possibly has more power when it is applied to the homeliness of the colonizer, when it is used to explore the foreignness that is central to original and self-sufficient source of colonization. Bhabha points out that the relationship between self and other is always an uncanny one. He says uncanniness is not only a question of place, but also of time since our sense of national identity is open and static. We don't "own" our nation, as it is something that is our own and at the same time it is not ours, because its identity is always changing or coming from the future. He adds, like culture, Western knowledge is homely and unhomely or canny and uncanny. Bhabha believes in Western and non-Western identities. Because the concept of "uncanny" undermines the stability of all concepts in general, it seems to be a slippery concept. Bhabha is supposed to be an expert in transforming concepts into his theoretical strategies. The slippery aspect means it tends to elude definite theorization. By using canny and uncanny, Bhabha focuses the colonial relationship—as the simple division of self and other.[14]

This chapter uses the ideas of home and unhomely borrowed from Bhabha to indicate that the Malawian postgraduate students undertaking

---

13. Kristeva, *Strangers to Ourselves*, 13.

14. See Bhabha, *Nation and Narration*; and Rostami and Parvaneh, "Notion of Unhomeliness."

their studies in South Africa during the COVID-19 pandemic were placed in between spaces. While they were home, they needed to be relevant elsewhere (at school, at work, and to their families), yet with COVID-19, such freedom was not guaranteed. The pandemic seems to have continuously placed the students at home and not at home.

DATA COLLECTION APPROACHES AND TRUSTWORTHINESS

To increase the credibility of collected data and to determine the appropriateness and usefulness of the central question ("What are the challenges you have encountered because of undertaking a postgraduate degree during COVID-19 pandemic?"), the questionnaire was piloted with three participants. These three participants formed part of the population but were not included in the main study.[15] After piloting, the questionnaire was deemed appropriate to collect the data that would answer the research question and was used to gather the data.

To enhance the trustworthiness of the study, *credibility* was achieved through purposive sampling and through analysis triangulating by both researchers analyzing the data and reaching consensus on the identified themes.[16] The study further achieved *dependability* and *confirmability* of data through well-kept documentation and transparency in the methodology, data analysis, and conclusions. By getting responses from nineteen out of twenty-four participants, the research enhanced and achieved *transferability*, while *authenticity* of the study was achieved through the written responses from the participants, including direct quotations from study participants in the description of findings.[17]

DATA ANALYSIS AND RESULTS

Data was analyzed through thematic qualitative content analysis and measures to ensure trustworthiness was in place. The study identified three themes with categories, namely, institutional challenges (i.e., lack of access to academic facilities, provision of data bundles, power outages, high cost of internet, delayed feedback from supervisors and ethics board); personal

---

15. Fouché et al., *Research at Grass Roots*, 53.
16. Holloway and Galvin, *Qualitative Research*, 40.
17. Holloway and Galvin, *Qualitative Research*, 41; Polit and Beck, *Essentials of Nursing Research*, 33; Connelly, "Demographic Data."

challenges (mental health, finances, employment, and family); and opportunities (financial savings on accommodation and flights, the future of academia and meetings, availability to family and employment). Here, below, I discuss further the outcome of data analysis:

INSTITUTIONAL CHALLENGES ENCOUNTERED WHILE UNDERTAKING A POSTGRADUATE DEGREE DURING THE COVID-19 PANDEMIC

The study established several challenges that were encountered while undertaking a postgraduate degree during the COVID-19 pandemic. A critical synthesis of responses reveal that respondents encountered the following challenges while studying a post graduate degree during the pandemic period: limited access to physical and social interaction such as the library; library resources and friends; network problems; intermittent blackouts; difficulties in time management; restriction of movements and hiking of transport prices; delaying studies and disturbing the family time. All these challenges could be stated to respond to institutional challenges. One participant stated:

> Online classes have been my greatest challenge because I have always been good at my studies in my previous stages, however, studying online has proven to be a challenge. Social interactions have also been a challenge. Without a real time class where you meet and interact with classmates, I have only myself to talk to. I am glad I came with other members of our scholarship who are doing a different program altogether, but I still feel alone.[18]

Further, another participant, while agreeing with the previous participants, adds another challenge that they encountered regarding their supervision and intermittent internet services in saying that "I would say that the first challenge was the stoppage of face-to-face interaction with my supervisor. The second problem was unreliable internet services that hindered me from submitting my assignments on time."[19] Directly impacted by limited face-to-face meeting between people in responding to ways of controlling the spread of the COVID-19, another participant lamented that "I had limited access to library resources and the library itself during lockdown."[20] The fact that the internet was erratic and the library inaccessible meant

18. Participant 4.
19. Participant 9.
20. Participant 1.

that the student had little if nothing to do in their research journey. It is worth noting that Stellenbosch University provided internet bundles to all registered students who were within the borders of South Africa. This opportunity was not granted to international students even though they were registered at the time of lockdown.[21]

Studies that needed ethical approval from both South Africa and Malawi experienced significant delay due to uncertainty about the meeting of the boards. This led to more time for studies, and in some cases, it led to economic hurdles. One student stated:

> The research required that ethics approval should be obtained in both South Africa and Malawi. In both countries, the process was slowed down due to the COVID-19 pandemic. There were drastic changes in the application and approval process as well as the requirements in the application forms. The ethics committees strongly recommended an immediate reduction of all research activities until such a time as the infection rate went down to below 5% in the research implementation country. All these led to delays in the approval process and subsequent research activities.[22]

In what looked like a combination of different challenges coming from the institution, family duties, and internet, a participant stated:

> Power cuts in Malawi, handling "homeschooling" aka online learning for my kids (South Africa and Malawi) and expensive and slow internet which rendered online meetings difficult, and almost made my final submission impossible (I had to submit without final edits as I couldn't download final comments from supervisors).[23]

This annoyance was also shared by another participant who stated that "internet has been the very biggest challenge of all since, when I need to study or write exams even during assignments, there has been network disruption, especially with our local providers. In addition to this the buying of bundles is very expensive."[24] Further, another participant explained that "whenever I was in Malawi, it was hard to stay online and save backup

---

21. De Villiers, "Information Update," lines 34–36.
22. Participant 10.
23. Participant 3.
24. Participant 16.

copies of documents, use Mendeley and Teams. Because internet charges were too high and too slow, and options were limited."[25]

One participant who was working as a lecturer at the time of data collection lamented on the poverty levels of most students in Malawi who may not even benefit from online learning. Such students, the participant shared, have no money to acquire a smartphone. In his own words, he said:

> I think generally, the global south has been heavily affected by coronavirus as far as education is concerned. In one forum, I had shared that, as a lecturer, you can find some students who literally do not have a smart phone and a laptop, and they depend on face-to-face teaching and use school facilities when it comes to IT. This is the biggest challenge. Poverty is so high amongst school students in Africa and particularly Malawi. Worse, is the provision of IT services by mobile companies. The internet speed and bandwidth are very poor so that online studies in some cases is almost impossible.[26]

PERSONAL EXPERIENCES IN THE EVENT OF CLOSENESS TO THE EMPLOYERS/FAMILY DURING THE COVID-19 PANDEMIC PERIOD

Respondents were asked to give their experiences in the event of closeness to their employers/family during the COVID-19 pandemic period. The results of the study revealed a mixed reaction in terms of the experiences that the students had, as they were close to their employers and families. On the positive side, the study established that some family encouragement was imperative on the success of the studies, and this made most respondents to work extra harder. On the other hand, it was revealed that closeness to employers and family members was an impediment to the success of studies. In this case, it was revealed that respondents were given some responsibilities at work, yet they were on study leave. On account of that, they encountered difficulties in time management, especially when it came to balancing work, family, and community expectations. One participant was able to give both sides of the coin regarding their positive and negative experiences related to the COVID-19 crisis and being closer to their family and to their workplace. They stated:

---

25. Participant 18.
26. Participant 11.

> My experience has been both positive and negative. They (family) gave me courage and at the same time, there was a need to attend to their daily needs. This has negatively affected on the duration of the study. You need to be a father, a brother, an uncle, an employee, and a student at the same time.[27]

Due to the demands of academic work, family affairs, and employer expectations, a participant stated that they had a mental load that directly affected their time management and their output. They stated: "Time management has been a challenge because of the demands both at work and my family even the demands of the community where I live. Mental load in short."[28] The negative experience was also shared by two more participants who stated that "my employers expected me to show up at work and do some light jobs including meetings. My extended family expected me to attend the usual family gatherings like funerals, weddings, and others."[29] This chimed with the other participants, who shared that "the disturbances of work and family renders a student inefficient and they cannot concentrate on their studies."[30]

The mixed experience was also reported by another participant who indicated that the travel restrictions that were imposed due to COVID-19 made them stagnate. They stated:

> As a matter of fact, it was a mixed experience. I was on study leave meaning I was not supposed to work. I had the energy to concentrate on studies but would not do so due to the lock down and travel restrictions imposed as precautionary measures for the COVID-19 pandemic.[31]

Two participants were joyful at the very fact that they were closer to their families, necessitated by the lockdown in South Africa. By the time the lockdown was announced, these two students, like others, were in Malawi with their families. Unlike most of the participants, who were negative about the experience, these two stated that "staying closer to family helped me to appreciate the role they play in postgraduate studies"[32] and that "I felt a lot of support being around family."[33] Unlike the joys that were shared,

---

27. Participant 6.
28. Participant 5.
29. Participant 2.
30. Participant 10.
31. Participant 16.
32. Participant 11.
33. Participant 18.

another participant's experience in being closer to the family was the exact opposite. He stated:

> Towards the end of my studies when I was finalizing my research I was back in Malawi and stayed in with my parents. Being the oldest in the family at times I would sacrifice my research times for family matters. For example, I had to be there when my dad was sick and taken to the hospital in the middle of the night. Sometimes family members will not give you the space to work on your academic assignments if they see you around.[34]

However, a participant who was in Stellenbosch at the time of the lockdown shared that they were depressed for a good part of the time due to lack of interaction with other people. But later on, when the lockdowns relaxed, the participant was able to attend some gatherings just to meet people and remove stress. They said:

> During my studies I have not been close to my family nor my employers. However, there were a couple of events which brought a lot of people together and interacted. At these times, I would remove some of my depression and would also meet people who are vital to my project.[35]

Economically, COVID-19 restrictions spearheaded by the South African government impacted heavily on most participants in the study. Among them, one participant shared that he travelled with their children to South Africa on a short visit. While there, the lockdowns were announced. This meant that the participant had to stay with their three children in South Africa on a very limited budget and space. This is what was shared:

> I just wanted to state that I lived with my three kids in SA until after they allowed international travel during lockdown. It was hard, so I brought the kids home. I worked from home until they settled in school before returning to Stellenbosch for four months. I was on an external scholarship i.e., the Stellenbosch University one, not from my home university.

---

34. Participant 14.
35. Participant 1.

THE OPPORTUNITIES BROUGHT BY THE COVID-19 PANDEMIC TO THE POSTGRADUATE STUDIES

The other question required participants to express their views regarding the opportunities brought by the COVID-19 pandemic to the postgraduate studies regardless of its negative repercussions. Results obtained revealed that the COVID-19 pandemic brought some opportunities to the postgraduate studies. It was revealed that the pandemic brought opportunities for online studies. Besides that, it was also revealed that a great deal of time was saved in online studies as compared with physical studies, as testified by a participant who said:

> Now, the world can agree with me that more time was wasted through in-person meetings. Aaaah, you know what! while this came at a greater cost of obstruction from studies in early 2020 when it was still new to study online, the recent times show that it is time-efficient.[36]

Additionally, there was exploration of some new businesses, especially for companies responsible for the provision of digital learning platforms. Apart from that, there was discovery of more social media platforms. Moreover, the study also found that there was enhancement of students' digital competencies during this period. The COVID-19 crisis enabled many people to realize that there are other online platforms to be used for communication, for example, Zoom, Microsoft Teams, Webex Meetings, RingCentral MVP, GlobalMeet Collaboration, 3CX, Fuze, Google Workspace, GoTo Meeting, BlueJeans Meetings, etc. A participant in this study mentioned that the pandemic "made me discover the world of social media, which I believe is the future of everything, especially finance and investment."[37] The data analysis also established that there was the possibility of attending to personal engagements such as work, family, and friends while studying, and having the flexibility to telecommute. The study further established that the pandemic promoted learner-centered pedagogy. It was interesting to hear that some students economically benefited from the lockdowns initiated by the COVID-19 crisis. A participant joyously said:

> Let me say this with confidence, the pandemic has opened a new way of studying which is online. Studying online has dramatically decreased the costs of studying since no travel and accommodation costs are incurred. You no longer need to travel all

---

36. Participant 13.
37. Participant 15.

> the way to Stellenbosch to undertake your exam. You can do it at home.[38]

Apart from the internet being a tool in aiding studies during the pandemic, it was interesting to learn that the same internet made some people closer to their families than they were before, and it provided a new way of living. One participant shared:

> The internet has been my very livelihood. Being away from my family and not being able to attend classes face to face meant that one must use the internet for communication as well as for learning. Streaming YouTube videos for some extra lessons as well as attending webinars. It's all been the internet during the COVID pandemic.[39]

While the opportunities are celebrated, some participants indicated that they had challenges with laboratory-based research. They stated:

> The COVID-19 pandemic led to changes in postgraduate studies delivery at Stellenbosch. Some activities were digitized and went online. These activities include, student registration, supervisory meetings, ethics application processes. It was also encouraged that some student research activities, for example, social surveys should be electronic. All these changes made it possible for studies to continue despite the COVID-19 pandemic challenges. However, laboratory-based research activities were seriously affected.[40]

DISCUSSION

This study identified challenges and opportunities that Malawian postgraduate students met while undertaking postgraduates' studies both at "home" and away from "home." Such challenges included institutional challenges, personal challenges, and opportunities that other studies have highlighted, even before the COVID-19 outbreak.[41] Regarding institutional challenges, the participants in the study indicated lack of access to academic facilities, provision of data bundles, and delayed feedback from supervisors and ethics board as some of the challenges. Unlike the challenges that were faced

---

38. Participant 19.
39. Participant 15.
40. Participant 13.
41. Essa, "Reflecting"; Clerehan et al., "Saudi Arabian Nurses' Experiences," 217.

(Im)possibilities of Malawian Postgraduates

by Malawian students in relation to Stellenbosch University, the response to a similar scenario in Trinidad and Tobago also proved to be problematic because of their population, which is multicultural, multiethnic, and stratified by race, class, and culture.[42] Similarly, another university in Indonesia experienced related challenges, though their major obstacle was the introduction of the online learning platform by the university.[43]

Further, economic challenges are common and relate to the direct cost of education whether in pre-COVID or post-COVID times: fees and educational debt, cost of living away from home, and the inability to earn an income if the student is not employed.[44] It seems to be common that most African countries do not have funding for postgraduate research.[45] If a student has limited financial resources, it means that such students will have problems purchasing data bundles, paying for accommodation, and buying the basic necessities of life.[46] One participant had mentioned that at the time of the lockdown, he had already taken his children and a wife for a short stay in Stellenbosch. After the lockdown was announced, it meant more money to feed and accommodate the family, a view shared by other scholars on the economic crisis of migrating graduate students.[47]

Postgraduate students in this study, especially those who were in Malawi at the time of lockdown, reported that having no travel and no accommodation in Stellenbosch helped them save some money, yet they still managed to progress with their studies.[48] This view on the economic saving is also shared by Clerehan et al., who state that accommodation is a critical issue for all students.[49]

Still, for those students who were closer to their workplaces and their families, they experienced a high workload, which affected the progress of their studies. This experience is in line with the challenges experienced by postgraduate students in other studies reporting that most postgraduate scholars were employed adults who also had other responsibilities.[50] Such circumstances bring worry about meeting expectations, taking time off

---

42. Kalloo et al., "Responding to the COVID-19 Pandemic," 453.
43. Khuluqo et al., "Postgraduate Students' Perspective," 620.
44. Perna, "Understanding Decision to Enroll."
45. Mutula, "Challenges of Postgraduate Research," 186–87.
46. Roets and Maritz, "Challenges, Opportunities and Achievements," 75.
47. Cairns, "Exploring Student Mobility," 345. See also Cao et al., "Psychological Impact."
48. Fatonia et al., "University Students Online."
49. Clerehan et al., "Saudi Arabian Nurses' Experiences," 218.
50. Essa, "Reflecting," 255.

from study to attend to work, or about dealing with family matters, a view shared by Maasdorp and Holtzhausen.[51]

On one hand, the participants on the Malawian side in this study alluded to having experienced an imbalance in relation to their studies, employment, and family responsibilities. On the other hand, they indicated that their families also acted as a support system in their academic journey. Essa states that balancing of academic, work, and family responsibilities is a challenge for postgraduate students who may be employed and have families of their own.[52] Benshoff et al. also indicate that fulfilling numerous roles, responsibilities, and expectations is a common feature of postgraduate studies.[53]

In agreement with the challenges faced by the participants in this study in relation to work and family engagements, Essa states that the limited time for student engagement and support becomes a cause of isolation and mental health-related challenges in many postgraduate students.[54]

The postgraduate students' experiences of supervisors delaying in giving responses is also corroborated by Essa and Clereham et al., who report that many postgraduate students felt that the lecturers were distant, inaccessible, unapproachable, and abrupt.[55] On the same point, Wadesango and Machingambi argue that the importance of support cannot be underestimated.[56] They emphasize that the supervisor-supervisee relationship is central to progress and completion.

Interestingly, the study has revealed opportunities brought by studying in the pandemic situation. Most participants indicated that the future of academia and work meetings lies in a hybrid internet setup. In this way, one can be available to the family and for work commitments while undertaking higher academic qualification. These opportunities are shared in detail by other scholars such as Gamage et al. but also by Carr et al. in discussing how the COVID-19 pandemic is reversing the tide.[57] Further, Van der Walt has explored the value of an e-learning bundle in the acquisition of a clinical

---

51. Maasdorp and Holtzhausen, "Bridging the Gap," 38.

52. Essa, "Reflecting," 255.

53. Benshoff, "Graduate Students on Campus," 83–84.

54. Essa, "Reflecting," 255. See also Cao et al., "Psychological Impact."

55. Essa, "Reflecting," 255; Clerehan et al., "Saudi Arabian Nurses' Experiences," 218.

56. Wadesango and Machingambi, "Post Graduate Students' Experiences," 31.

57. Gamage et al., "Online Delivery," 1; Carr et al., "Academic Careers."

skill in the era of the pandemic in South Africa, where participants in the study liked and recommended the idea of e-learning.[58]

LIMITATION OF THE STUDY

The fact that this study targeted only Malawian postgraduate students who were on the MSSU WhatsApp group provides a valid limitation of the research. Further, the electronic response to the questionnaire limited in-depth exploration of the matter at hand through probing by the researcher. As such, this study cannot be replicated elsewhere. In view of these limitations, the suggestion is that in the future a study of this type should involve participants from more than one country and more than one university who should engage in comprehensive interviews and even in focus group discussions.

RECOMMENDATION

In view of the challenges and opportunities reflected in this chapter, the study recommends that prerecorded and streamed lectures, frequent virtual meetings, and student response systems should be implemented to improve learning outcomes. Similarly, the university should consider financial support during the period of online study to reduce some of the financial burden for students buying internet bundles. In other words, the university should put in place measures for all students (including foreign students) to ensure that they all have access to computers and the internet. This venture should be supported by study sponsors that include government ministries, companies belonging to the government, and charitable organizations to create a conducive environment for students who are sent to foreign universities.

Lastly, the study supports the view that using the internet to study remains a better option, despite the high costs attached to it and power outages occurring in some parts of the world. From the study, it is clear that education in Malawi and the entire Global South has been greatly affected by coronavirus. Those students who do not have a smart phone and a laptop to make study efficient come mostly from the Global South. These students depend solely on face-to-face teaching and rely on school facilities when it comes to IT. This is the biggest challenge. Poverty is not the only problem here. The provision of IT services by mobile companies in Malawi is not as

---

58. Van der Walt, "Value of e-Learning Bundle," 18.

efficient as in other countries. Internet speed and bandwidth are very poor, so much so that online studies in some cases are almost impossible.

Lastly, since laboratory-based research activities were negatively affected during the time, efforts should be made to enhance the capacity of laboratories in Malawi. There should also be collaborative work between laboratories in Malawi and their counterparts in South Africa to improve postgraduate training in the sciences.

CONCLUSION

This study reflected on the challenges experienced by Malawian postgraduate students at Stellenbosch University during the COVID-19 pandemic. Institutional challenges, personal challenges, and economic implications were identified as main themes of the study. These challenges are not confined to Malawi, as they are similar to challenges reported in other international studies. Conversely, apart from the challenges, the study revealed that due to their stay in their home country, Malawi, some students were able to save on travel and accommodation expenses. It is in this regard that the study recommends that the education sector maximize the opportunities provided while the university and sponsoring organizations engage in establishing and maintaining a supportive culture for students, providing a conducive environment for better learning outcomes at times of crisis such as the COVID-19 pandemic.

This study received approval from the Department/Faculty of Ethics Screening Committee (DESC/FESC): Faculty of Theology, Stellenbosch University, and was classified as a low-risk project with ID 26825.

BIBLIOGRAPHY

Adnan, Muhammad, and Kainat Anwar. "Online Learning amid the COVID-19 Pandemic: Students' Perspectives." *Online Submission* 2 (2020) 45–51.
Benshoff, James M., et al. "Graduate Students on Campus: Needs and Implications for College Counselors." *Journal of College Counseling* 18 (2015) 82–94.
Bhabha, Homi K., ed. *Nation and Narration*. Berlin: Routledge, 2013.
———. *Our Neighbours, Ourselves: Contemporary Reflections on Survival*. Hegel Lectures. Berlin: De Gruyter, 2011.
Blizak, Djanette, et al. "Students' Perceptions Regarding the Abrupt Transition to Online Learning during the COVID-19 Pandemic: Case of Faculty of Chemistry and Hydrocarbons at the University of Boumerdes—Algeria." *Journal of Chemical Education* 97 (2020) 2466–71.

Cairns, David. "Exploring Student Mobility and Graduate Migration: Undergraduate Mobility Propensities in Two Economic Crisis Contexts." *Social & Cultural Geography* 18 (2017) 336–53.

Cao, Wenjun, et al. "The Psychological Impact of the COVID-19 Epidemic on College Students in China." *Psychiatry Research* 287 (2020) 112934.

Carius, Ana Carolina. "Network Education and Blended Learning: Cyber University Concept and Higher Education Post COVID-19 Pandemic." *Research, Society and Development* 9 (2020) e8209109340.

Carr, Rotonya M., et al. "Academic Careers and the COVID-19 Pandemic: Reversing the Tide." *Science Translational Medicine* 13 (2021) eabe7189.

Cixous, Hélène. "Fiction and Its Phantoms: A Reading of Freud's *Das Unheimliche* (The 'Uncanny')." *New Literary History* 7 (1976) 525–48, 619–45.

Clerehan, R., et al. "Saudi Arabian Nurses' Experiences of Studying Masters Degrees in Australia." *International Nursing Review* 59 (2012) 215–21.

Connelly, Lynne M. "Demographic Data in Research Studies." *MEDSURG Nursing Journal* 22 (2013) 269–71.

De Villiers, Wim. "Information Update: Online Learning and Residence Cancellations." Stellenbosch University, Apr. 20, 2020. https://t.co/UZPMzjS9th.

De Vos, A. S., et al. *Research at Grass Roots: A Primer for the Social Science and Human Professions.* 4th ed. Pretoria: Van Schaik, 2011.

Dhawan, Shivangi. "Online Learning: A Panacea in the Time of COVID-19 Crisis." *Journal of Educational Technology Systems* 49 (2020) 5–22.

Essa, Ilhaam. "Reflecting on Some of the Challenges Facing Postgraduate Nursing Education in South Africa." *Nurse Education Today* 31 (2011) 253–58.

Fatonia, N. A., et al. "University Students Online Learning System during Covid-19 Pandemic: Advantages, Constraints and Solutions." *Systematic Reviews in Pharmacy* 11 (2020) 570–76.

Fouché, C. B., et al. *Research at Grass Roots: For the Social Sciences and Human Service Professions.* 5th ed. Pretoria: Van Schaik, 2021.

Gamage, Kelum A. A., et al. "Online Delivery and Assessment during COVID-19: Safeguarding Academic Integrity." *Education Sciences* 10 (2020) art. 301.

Ghazoul, Ferial. "Iraqi Short Fiction: The Unhomely at Home and Abroad." *Journal of Arabic Literature* 35 (2004) 1–24.

Gordimer, Nadine. *My Son's Story*. Chichester, UK: A&C Black, 2003.

Holloway, Immy, and Kathleen Galvin. *Qualitative Research in Nursing and Healthcare.* 4th ed. Chichester, UK: Wiley & Sons, 2016.

Kalloo, Rowena Constance, et al. "Responding to the COVID-19 Pandemic in Trinidad and Tobago: Challenges and Opportunities for Teacher Education." *Journal of Education for Teaching* 46 (2020) 452–62.

Khuluqo, Ihsana El, et al. "Postgraduate Students' Perspective on Supporting Learning from Home to Solve the COVID-19 Pandemic." *International Journal of Evaluation and Research in Education* 10 (2021) 615–23.

Kristeva, Julia. *Strangers to Ourselves.* Translated by Leon S. Roudiez. New York: Columbia University Press, 1991.

Maasdorp, C., and S. M. Holtzhausen. "Bridging the Gap towards Postgraduate Studies at the Central University of Technology, Free State." *Interim: Interdisciplinary Journal* 10 (2011) 38–51.

Morrison, Toni. *Beloved.* New York: Vintage, 2004.

Murphy, Michael P. A. "COVID-19 and Emergency eLearning: Consequences of the Securitization of Higher Education for Post-Pandemic Pedagogy." *Contemporary Security Policy* 41 (2020) 492–505.

Mutula, Stephen M. "Challenges of Postgraduate Research: Case of Developing Countries." *South African Journal of Libraries and Information Science* 77 (2011) 184–90.

Perna, Laura W. "Understanding the Decision to Enroll in Graduate School: Sex and Racial/Ethnic Group Differences." *Journal of Higher Education* 75 (2004) 487–527.

Polit, Denise F., and Cheryl Tatano Beck. *Essentials of Nursing Research: Appraising Evidence for Nursing Practice*. Philadelphia: Lippincott Williams & Wilkins, 2010.

Roets, Lizeth, and J. E. Maritz. "Challenges, Opportunities and Achievements of Nurses' Research Supervision across Language Borders." *African Journal for Physical Health Education, Recreation and Dance* 19 (2013) 68–79.

Rostami, Ali Akbar Moghaddasi, and Farid Parvaneh. "The Notion of Unhomeliness in the Pickup: Homi Bhabha Revisited." *Advances in Language and Literary Studies* 7 (2016) 157–60.

Selwyn, Neil, and Petar Jandrić. "Postdigital Living in the Age of Covid-19: Unsettling What We See as Possible." *Postdigital Science and Education* 2 (2020) 989–1005.

Tesar, Marek. "Towards a Post-Covid-19 'New Normality?' Physical and Social Distancing, the Move to Online and Higher Education." *Policy Futures in Education* 18 (2020) 556–59.

Van der Walt, Lizanne. "The Value of an e-Learning Bundle in the Acquisition of a Clinical Skill: Exploring the Perceptions of Third-Year Medical Students at Stellenbosch University, South Africa." Master's thesis, Stellenbosch University, 2022.

Wadesango, Newman, and Severino Machingambi. "Post Graduate Students' Experiences with Research Supervisors." *Journal of Sociology and Social Anthropology* 2 (2011) 31–37.

Chapter 17

Learning and Teaching from the Margins

An Autoethnographic Reflection upon Theological Formation That Is Committed to the Cause of Justice

Dion A. Forster

INTRODUCTION

What are the leading considerations that should shape our approach to the formation of theological students in relation to some of the crises we face in contemporary South Africa? Who are we forming, in what contexts does formation take place, and to what end are we forming theological graduates in South Africa? This chapter presents some tentative answers to these questions. The answers emerged from a critical autoethnographic study of my development as a theological educator who has taught, and studied, theology during various moments of crisis in South Africa's history.

Mercy Amba Oduyoye, the "mother" of African theology and the founder of the Circle of Concerned African Woman Theologians, says that "theology remains a story that is told, a song that is sung and a prayer that is uttered in response to experience and expectation."[1] My own story is intertwined with the stories and lives of the students I have journeyed with in the last twenty-five years. Together we have sought to understand, and witness to, the "story" of our faith in times of crisis. Our learning was shaped in

---

1. Oduyoye, *Introducing African Women's Theology*, 22.

"response" to the inescapable injustices of apartheid and the "expectation" of a better life for all South Africans.

This chapter will show how my own theological biography and educational journey emerged within the context of the struggle for justice and healing among South Africans and within South Africa. It will explain how my pedagogical philosophy has been shaped by generations of activist scholars who have sought to reflect theologically the crises of our history, to gain knowledge, values, and skills that can contribute towards a more just, inclusive, and equitable world.

ON CRITICAL AUTOETHNOGRAPHY, DECOLONIZATION, AND THE SCHOLARSHIP OF EDUCATIONAL LEADERSHIP

Teaching in times of crisis must take seriously the context in which teaching and learning takes place. Crises are inherently contextual in nature. They way in which a community responds to danger, threat, or injustice takes on a unique character based on unique interplay between crisis inducing factors and the people who are facing the threat. As such, while generalized or universal responses to moments of crisis may hold some general value, the most effective responses will need to be particular to the context itself. One approach to this call for reflective particularity among scholars in the so-called majority world is a commitment to decolonization. Among other things, this means decentering foreign knowledge systems, recentering contextual experience, and advocating approaches to formation that are suited to the challenges and opportunities of the context.[2]

Like higher education itself, the archive of scholarship on learning and teaching needs both methodological and thematic decolonization.[3] As a systematic theologian, I remind my students that considering *what* an individual or community believes is only a part of interrogating and understanding their truth claims. In addition to understanding *what* is believed, we also need to know *why* a person or group believes that their claim is true, and *how* they come to hold (or construct) this "truth." The decolonial imperative is thus not only about particularizing knowledge, but also about accounting for the different ways in which particularity has meaning and value.[4] Hence, we ask not only what counts as truth, but also what counts

---

2. D. Forster, "African Realities."
3. Mbembe, "Decolonizing the University"; Mbembe, "Decolonizing Knowledge."
4. Andreotti et al., "Mapping Interpretations," 22.

as contextually relevant truth, where and how such truth is discovered, and how it can be reliably, credibly, and ethically accessed and represented. This presupposes both epistemological and methodological creativity. Decolonizing theological higher education requires both thematic and methodological shifts if it wishes to address the ongoing crises of our context and reflect a commitment towards justice.[5]

With this in mind, I have opted to use a critical autoethnographic methodological approach in this chapter since it is contextually oriented towards knowledge generation and dissemination. Autoethnography is a subcategory of ethnographic research. It is finding increasing purchase among researchers in the majority world.[6] In ethnographic research the researcher(s) aim to understand a culture, or aspects of a culture, from the perspective of participating research subjects.[7] Autoethnography is a research approach that uses "writing, story, and method that connect the autobiographical and personal to the cultural, social, and political. In autoethnography, the life of the researcher becomes a conscious part of what is studied."[8]

This approach could offer a valuable contribution to both the discipline of systematic theology and the context of theological education in South Africa since there are, to date, no critical self-reflections on pedagogy and teaching philosophy by systematic theologians, ethicists, or public theologians teaching at South African universities. Moreover, much of the scholarship on the learning and teaching of theology in higher education comes from persons, locations, institutions, employing approaches that exemplify the dominance of Western worldviews, epistemologies, primary questions, and methodologies. This does not mean that such contributions hold no value, but rather that they should be decentered in the Southern African conversation in favor of contextually relevant contributions.[9]

In what follows I will present a critical autoethnography that draws upon a "personal narrative" of my own educational formation and journey in learning in teaching. The "personal narrative" is an academically credible approach to autoethnography, in which the researcher takes on their "dual academic and personal identities" to "understand a self or some aspect

---

5. Chan-Tiberghien, "Towards 'Global Educational Justice'"; Costandius et al., "#FeesMustFall"; Waghid, "Decolonising African University Again"; Fataar, "Placing Students at Centre."

6. Belbase et al., "Autoethnography"; Mackinlay, *Critical Writing*; Hagoel and Kalekin-Fishman, *From the Margins*.

7. Given, *Qualitative Research Methods*, 1:288.

8. Given, *Qualitative Research Methods*, 1:48.

9. Vellem, "Un-Thinking the West."

of a particular life lived in a cultural context."[10] It is presented as a critical approach since it will explore, and point out, failings and inadequacies as part of the narrative process. The narrative that is presented will be in the first person, since I aim to explain, reflect upon, and present experiences, encounters, and ideas from my own journey as a learner and teacher. To demarcate the narrative, I shall employ three limits. First, I shall focus on my engagement with the disciplines that I am trained in, and currently teach (namely, systematic theology, theological ethics, and public theology). Second, I will reflect on my own learning and growth; both formal learning related to the award of qualifications in the discipline (which includes formal disciplinary and pedagogical training) and informal learning related to the social, cultural, and political environment in which I was formed. Third, the narrative will have a clear telos or intent. Namely, it will point towards how I have come to understand theological formation as contributing towards justice in a manner that is socially engaged, embodies disciplinary excellence, and has contextual relevance for learners and our network of stakeholders.

THE CONCEPTS AND CONTEXTS THAT SHAPE MY TEACHING AND EDUCATIONAL LEADERSHIP EXPERIENCES

As you will see in the sections that follow, my teaching and learning philosophy is closely linked to concepts such as justice, human dignity, planetary flourishing, and the common good. This can be related to both my personal life and my professional life. While I am an educator in a public university, I am also a person who holds deep personal moral commitments, and I have a history of being committed to justice and transformation. Of course, all of us are formed by our contexts, histories, and biographies.

In this regard Miguel De La Torre, the Latin American ethicist and educator, writes,

> The task of educators, specifically those who call themselves ethicists, is to cultivate students' ability to find their own voices by creating an environment in which individual and collective consciousness-raising can occur.[11]

This notion shapes my understanding of why education matters, and how and where it takes place. So much of my work has been shaped by the

---

10. Given, *Qualitative Research Methods*, 1:50–51.
11. De La Torre, *Doing Christian Ethics*, xi.

understanding that teaching and learning finds their proper setting against the backdrop of an ethical horizon.[12] At times, this ethical horizon is recognized and explicated. At other times, it may be recognized and not explicated. At other times still, it may go unrecognized and remain a hidden force in social formation (sometimes for good at other times for evil). People are formed and learn in order to grow and develop in appropriate knowledge, skills, and values so that they can achieve what they believe is good or desirable. For the theological educator, and particularly for the theological ethicist, theological formation takes place in relation to the fostering of the common good of both individuals and society at large. Hence, the task of the theological educator is to sensitively facilitate spaces and opportunities in which constructive formation takes place through an interplay between disciplinary specificity, institutional expectation (e.g., graduate attributes), the social context of learning, and the needs and expectations of the learner and their stakeholders.

Like De La Torre, I am trained as a systematic theologian and ethicist. Over the last twenty-five years I have journeyed with learners as we faced the challenges of social identity complexity (racism and race identity in particular), economic inequality, and historical and contemporary privilege (particularly the pervasiveness of white privilege), while seeking to gain knowledge and skills and engage values that can better our lives and contribute to society at large. Moreover, as an educator at Stellenbosch University in South Africa, I am deeply aware that, as De La Torre rightly notes, "our education system is far from being neutral or objective."[13] As we have discovered at Stellenbosch University, and continue to discover, the "classroom is appropriately named, for it is indeed a room of class—a room where students learn the class they belong to [or do not belong to] and the power and privilege that come with that class."[14]

The experiences, learning, convictions, and ideas that will be shared in what follows have been shaped by my interaction with students, peers, the university as institution, our local context, and the national and international debates, on ethics and human dignity. In short, they are responses to both crisis and opportunity. I am reflecting upon my experiences of journeying with students in a second-year ethics module that focusses on Human Dignity, and a third-year ethics module that focusses on Public Theology (Faith

---

12. D. Forster, "Living More Decently." Three percent of South Africans indicate that they are religious (in fact, 85.6 percent of the population claim to be Christian).

13. De La Torre, *Doing Christian Ethics*, xi.

14. De La Torre, *Doing Christian Ethics*, xi. For a very helpful engagement with the complexities of white privilege and theological education, please see Wepener and Nell, "White Males Teaching Theology," 1.

and Public Life), as well as first-year and fourth-year systematic theology modules. I currently also serve as the chair of the Department of Systematic Theology and Ecclesiology. As a result, I have had formal training in Scholarship of Teaching and Learning (SOTL) and in Scholarship of Educational Leadership (SOEL). How I teach and assess my courses and support my colleagues in teaching their courses are inextricably linked to the social context of learning. The #OpenStellenbosch, #RhodesMustFall, and #FeesMustFall movements that emerged in 2015–2016 played a very important role in forming my thinking. Together with this, I have had to consider disciplinary specificity (and the conceptualization of the curriculum amid calls of decolonization and Africanization of approaches to learning and learning content)[15] and institutional requirements (such as the university's language policy and quality assurance criterion), as well as the university's social location, and the complexity of social, political, and economic factors among an extremely diverse student population in these modules.

EDUCATIONAL PHILOSOPHY, DISCIPLINARY SPECIFICITY, AND THEIR IMPACT ON TEACHING AND LEARNING

This section presents some commitments that have emerged within my educational philosophy over the last decades. I have come to critically evaluate how important my own experiences and life have been in shaping my educational and leadership commitments. I currently serve as a professor of systematic theology and ethics with a focus on public theology and ethics at Stellenbosch University. My primary responsibilities are to facilitate learning at undergraduate and postgraduate levels (from first-year undergraduate students all the way up to PhD, and also postdoctoral supervision), to develop credible and sustained research outputs that further disciplinary knowledge in the South African context and shape the international theological discourse, to facilitate socially engaged research that benefits society at large, and to serve as the chair of our department and the director of the Beyers Naudé Centre for Public Theology (a research institute in the faculty). As the chair of the Department for Systematic Theology and Ecclesiology, I bear responsibility for managing the quality control and curriculum design in our department, as well as supporting our students and colleagues in their teaching and learning needs.

My first experience as a teacher was as an ordained minister of the Methodist Church of Southern Africa in the transition from South Africa's

---

15. D. Forster, "African Public Theology?"; D. Forster, "Public Theology in Africa."

unjust apartheid system to democracy.[16] In the mid 1990s, I served as a member of the academic staff and management of a private higher education provider (John Wesley College, the seminary of the Methodist Church of Southern Africa). The seminary was mandated to train clergy and laity for South Africa's largest, predominantly black, so-called mainline Christian denomination—the Methodist Church of Southern Africa.[17] From the late 2000s, I served as a contracted university lecturer at both distance learning institutions (such as the University of South Africa [UNISA]) and residential institutions (such as the University of Pretoria and Stellenbosch University). I took up my current post at Stellenbosch University in 2014.

This diverse set of experiences shaped my commitment to forming people theologically to respond to the crises and opportunities of the South African context. I would like to highlight a few points that I feel are important emphases and discoveries in my educational teaching and leadership philosophy:

Communities of learning—among the most noteworthy series of events, indeed crises, during this period was the emergence of the #OpenStellenbosch, #RhodesMustFall, and #FeesMustFall movements.[18] These movements invited reflection on what I was doing, what values I held, and how

---

16. The time spent as a minister was extremely valuable in forming both my views of teaching and learning, as well as in gaining understanding of the social, economic, and political complexity in which teaching and learning takes place in South Africa. I served in various township churches before the end of political apartheid (notably, Soweto, Khutsong, and Khokhosi). This experience introduced me to challenges of resource-scarce environments, the historical inequalities of "Bantu education," and basic issues of survival and justice in South African society. For more on the historical injustice and legacy of apartheid era education, please see M. Forster, "Deliberative Democratic Theory," 21–80.

17. I first served as a lecturer and course coordinator/subject matter expert for the Joint Board for Theology, and later as the chairman of the Joint Board for Theology in Southern Africa. This body regulated and ensured quality assurance for Southern African theological education institutions during a period when the apartheid government would not recognize or accredit such educational institutions for predominantly Black churches. I later went on to serve as a course designer, assessor, and moderator for the Theological Education by Extension College. Finally, I served as the dean of John Wesley College, the seminary of the Methodist Church of Southern Africa. During this time, I had responsibility for the management and administration of the academic programs. I learned a great deal about course design and the necessary balance between learning outcomes that address contextual needs held in tension with international and national academic trends and standards.

18. Costandius et al., "#FeesMustFall"; Habib, *Rebels and Rage*; Baloyi and Isaacs, "#FeesMustFall."

I would enact these values in my classes and leadership in the department and faculty. Several of the key leaders in these movements in Stellenbosch were (and some still are) members of my classes. Since my subject field engages issues of ethical concern, and my own specialization is in economic and political (social) ethics, I was deeply challenged by the complexity of the demands and requirements of the students. For me, there were aspects of the movements that were valuable and challenged unquestioned or entrenched social and educational systems. These include modes of instruction, discourses and scholars that inform the curricular content, the priority of South African contextual issues, the languages of instruction, epistemologies of knowledge (especially Western epistemologies), and of course the social identities of the persons facilitating learning (such as myself).[19] Yet, at the same time, there were some aspects of these movements that I felt uneasy about. These included shallow political populism that informed the politics of identity, a seeming disregard of historiographical rigor and positionality, an uncritical disregard of persons and contributions based on race, gender, social class (e.g., disregarding contributions by women and so-called "colored" people), party political interference, and allegations of sexual and physical violence.[20]

Yet, as a consequence of the importance of these movements, I worked very hard to become aware of the power dynamics at work in the classes I participated in (particularly as a white, male professor), and so deliberately sought to build a collaborative community of learning in my classes. We also shared in tasks of seeking to read texts on decolonization theory and postcolonial approaches to learning.[21]

The classroom, and the university setting, is an important space to facilitate noncompetitive, collaborative learning, in which students from different contexts and backgrounds bring their strengths, experiences, and insights to bear on helping one another (and their lecturers) to learn and grow. The result is that my classes frequently require group work and peer support. Such activities are carefully planned and facilitated to allow different types of contributions to find expression (e.g., lived experience, indigenous knowledge systems, formal reading or research, visual presentation, reflective learning). I encourage students to develop patience with one another (and me), and to deepen their relationships of trust and support. This is not always easy, and with some of the cultural and social pressures

---

19. Grassow and Le Bruyns, "Embodying Human Rights."

20. Habib, *Rebels and Rage*.

21. Costandius et al., "#FeesMustFall"; Grassow and Le Bruyns, "Embodying Human Rights"; Mbembe, "Decolonizing the University"; Naudé, "Decolonising Knowledge"; D. Forster, "Translation and Politics"; D. Forster, "Can Contextual Theology."

that we face in South Africa, it can lead to conflict or withdrawal, which requires different strategies for engagement and learning. However, when collaboration and shared responsibility is achieved, it leads to far deeper and more meaningful learning.

Authentic education, blended learning, and embedded/embodied knowledge—the time that I spent as a minister serving in township settings required a great deal of education and the facilitation of learning, as well as personal growth (particularly during the apartheid era when the church served an important role in the conscientization of citizens and the raising of resistance to apartheid).[22] This period first introduced me to the lived experience and context in which most of South Africa's citizens form their identity, values, and frame their learning.

This had two effects on my teaching philosophy. First, I came to understand that education has a crucial role to play in the constructive development of individual and social systems. Notions such as race, gender, and economic class are contested identifiers in South African society. Public institutions, such as universities, and the educators in those systems, have a moral responsibility to facilitate learning, conduct research, and contribute to knowledge production that can better serve the common good. Second, this period of my life helped me to understand some of the challenges and barriers that the majority of our population face in their educational journey. Many of the students in my classes, and particularly the students who participated in the classes I taught, came from economically disadvantaged contexts. As a minister in Soweto, Khutsong, and Khokhosi, I came to understand the challenges of spatial (geographic) apartheid, which placed communities long distances from basic amenities, places of work, and necessary resources. Moreover, the legacy of the "Bantu education" system has left many communities without adequately educated parents or grandparents who could support current students with their studies.[23] Finally, the economic reality frequently meant that people did not have sufficient means to provide for their basic needs (food, shelter, health), let alone acquire books or equipment for self-study.[24] Another consequence of the apartheid system is that students not only face economic and social inequality—they also face educational inequality.[25] The demographic makeup of my current classes reflects a number of students from economically and educationally

---

22. The term *conscientization* was coined by the Brazilian educator Paulo Freire in relation to radical social change—please see Lloyd, "Freire, Conscientization."
23. M. Forster, "Deliberative Democratic Theory."
24. Fataar, "Towards a Humanising Pedagogy."
25. M. Forster, "Deliberative Democratic Theory," 21–80.

disadvantaged contexts. The Faculty of Theology is the most racially diverse faculty at the University of Stellenbosch. We serve a predominantly black and so-called "colored" student population, many of whom are "second-career" or "mature" students. This means that our students grapple with many of the historical legacies of poverty and inequality.[26]

Since not all of the students in our context have had access to the same educational experiences, a textured and varied approach to learning is encouraged and valued in our courses. For example, some students have lived experiences of the topics under discussion, such as suffering from economic inequality, being prejudiced by patriarchal social systems, or having their identity denied and misrecognized. These students help other students in their peer group to access different knowledge systems (e.g., indigenous knowledge systems through oral histories, postcolonial and African epistemologies of knowledge, diversities of public opinion, theological meaning-making in contexts of suffering and injustice, etc.). Other students may have access to computers and libraries in their schools or homes—these students help their peers to learn how to source, utilize, and present such materials. Hence, a communal, blended learning, approach is favored that allows for learning, assessment, and collaboration in various settings (including the classroom, online resources, such as chat groups and forums, and shared tasks), and where feasible, "out of class" group work is encouraged.[27] As a result, attempts to develop and foster varied approaches to knowledge acquisition are valued.[28] These include taught classes that can facilitate technical and discipline-specific learning, self-study for heuristic learning, group projects to foster collaborative learning, and community engagement activities that connect knowledge to a broader social context. Such approaches not only introduce students to different forms of knowledge and help them to learn how to gather and present what they have learned, they also place their learning within a broader educational framework; i.e., their learning is not confined to the university classroom or library; rather, it builds bridges of knowledge into society at large, and from the varied publics of society at large back into the university setting.[29]

---

26. Nattrass and Seekings, "Two Nations?"; Seekings and Nattrass, *Class, Race, and Inequality*.

27. Shea and Bidjerano, "Learning Presence"; cf. Rovai and Jordan, "Blended Learning."

28. Nell and Bosman, "Integrating Graduate Attributes"; Bozalek et al., "Transforming Teaching"; Hay, "Nuts and Bolts"; Jacobs and Strydom, "From 'Matie' to Citizen."

29. For more on the "three publics" of theology (church, academy, and society at large), please see Tracy, "Religion in Public Realm."

Shared responsibility for learning between facilitator and learner, university and community—over the years I have become acutely aware that we make the mistake of giving preference to certain forms of knowledge while disregarding or undervaluing other forms of knowledge in university settings.

An important phase in my development as a teacher was once I had completed my first PhD and was appointed as a lecturer and administrator at the seminary of the Methodist Church of Southern Africa (John Wesley College, Pretoria) from 2002 to 2008. During this period, I came to realize that my own academic training had been somewhat jaundiced. It privileged a certain kind of academic knowledge over other knowledge systems. While it had a high level of discipline-specific academic content, it was not very contextual or connected to my own social engagement. My academic formation had encouraged exclusive, competitive achievement, rather than collaborative learning. The content of my knowledge was almost exclusively linked to published research, which was not always contextual to Africa or African indigenous knowledge systems. As a member of a predominantly Black Southern African community, I soon came to realize the importance of collaborative learning strategies where knowledge is sourced from different settings and has value for different purposes.[30] Moreover, I became conscious of the way in which published academic content was privileged, and how this perpetuated learning inequality in South Africa. Different forms of knowledge held value in different contexts. My experience, at present, is that the richness of diversity, lived experience, and cultural specificity, adds to the rich tapestry of ideas and forms of knowledge in the student and content interactions. As a result, I have been working in African empirical ethics for the last decade or more. My last book, *The (Im)possibility of Forgiveness?*, sought to listen to, and amplify, the voices of "ordinary Bible readers" in shaping the teaching and research of biblical ethics in South Africa.[31] I have also built in a lot more group engagement and personal reflection work into my classes, to draw upon the experience, wisdom, and situational knowledge of learners in classroom (and other learning) settings.

Of course I agree that one needs credible, rigorous, technical, formal research to develop and drive knowledge.[32] At the same time one also needs indigenous social knowledge, social values, virtue, and lived experience to deliver a particular "quality" of learning that is about more than just

---

30. See D. Forster, "Southern African Response."

31. D. Forster, "Public Theological Approach"; D. Forster, *(Im)possibility of Forgiveness*.

32. Kivunja and Kuyini, "Understanding and Applying," 26.

knowledge—it also engages values and develops contextually necessary skills.[33] These two forms of knowledge are not opposed to each other, they are coherent and mutually enriching. Moreover, since most of contemporary academic research emanates from Western knowledge contexts it was increasingly important to critically reconsider the value of such knowledge for contexts in the Global South.[34] During this period of my pedagogical and educational formation I also had the privilege of receiving further formal training as an assessor, curriculum designer, course writer, and academic administrator. I served on the Standards Generating Body (SGB) for unit standards in religion and theology, and the National Standards Body for qualifications in religion and theology (NSB7) in South Africa.

This was an invaluable experience since it allowed me, along with others, to ask critical questions about the "exit outcomes" and design criterion for qualifications in theology in South Africa.[35] What should a student know and be able to do, and what values should be engaged, through a course of study? How could such learning serve the common good in South Africa (particularly when education is such a scarce and rare commodity for most South Africans)? What is knowledge, how is it appropriated, and to what ends? And of course, how would South African theological qualifications articulate to, and relate to, other contexts around the world?

In the theological disciplines, and particularly in ethics, it is necessary to engage varied forms of knowledge. First, it stands to reason that learners will require some introduction to formal disciplinary knowledge systems of their field of study (history, theory, moral complexity, critical engagement). However, this knowledge does not constitute all that there is to know about a given subject. In theological study in South Africa, many of our students are second-career students who come to the learning process with a wealth of biographical and social knowledge and wisdom. Moreover, since the discipline of ethics has a tacit (and frequently expressed) intention of gaining knowledge and insight for the sake of good, an approach that shares responsibility for learning between the subject-matter "experts," practitioners of knowledge systems in communities, and the learners themselves is most helpful. In my own scholarship I have often spoken of these three interlinked "knowledges" as addressing the *head, heart, and hands* (i.e., knowledge as content, values, and skills). While the lecturer may have expertise in some fields (such as disciplinary content), members of the learning group

---

33. Fataar, "Towards a Humanising Pedagogy," 10.

34. Mbembe, "Decolonizing the University."

35. Kriel, "Proposed Norms and Standards," 20–38; Farisani, "New Policy Developments"; McCoy, "Restoring Mission"; Wethmar, "Theological Education."

may be able to facilitate learning in other areas (such as values or skills). As a result, our courses contain service-learning components, individual and peer assessment, and assessments that require both formal (academic) and nontraditional sources of knowledge acquisition and sharing.[36]

Maintaining a dialectic tension between contexts of knowledge—the next phase of my growth as a teacher and educational administrator was when I was appointed as a contract lecturer and researcher at various South African universities. During this period, I began to travel to other countries to participate in research projects, present at academic conferences, and teach at various international academic institutions. This period helped me to value the specific role of universities as institutions of learning and research in society in general. Between receiving my PhD in 2006 and being appointed to Stellenbosch University in January 2014 I taught at the University of Pretoria (New Testament and Greek) and UNISA (systematic theology and ethics). These settings introduced me to different learning populations.

The University of Pretoria had a similar student body than that I have since encountered at Stellenbosch, i.e., a number of middle-class students, or emerging middle-class students. They had some support from their families, communities, or the state, to undertake their studies. The University of Pretoria and Stellenbosch also offer formal learning support for their students as part of the university's staffing and student offering (these include library support, tutors, academic development, writing laboratories, research assistance, etc.). At UNISA I encountered students who had to work while studying at a distance. This posed significant educational challenges, but, interestingly, offered an unexpected level of social depth and reflective richness that I had not encountered among the students at the University of Pretoria. UNISA students also tended to be slightly older, much more socially engaged, and were more deeply committed to gaining knowledge that could be of use in their vocation (rather than just getting a "degree"). Moreover, the mode of teaching (distance learning) meant that I had to consider the precision and clarity of my academic communication (written instructions, feedback on assessments, course materials, etc.).

---

36. My understanding of the importance of community-engaged learning and shared responsibility for learning has been informed by the service learning training I was privileged to undertake at Stellenbosch University, and the subsequent reading and reflection on this topic. For some insights into how this approach benefits learning, please see Astin et al., "How Service Learning Affects Students." In order to understand the importance of linking formal and nontraditional forms of learning (between the university and the broader community), please see Eyler, "Reflection." My own approach to service learning has been influenced by the ideas in Hay, "Nuts and Bolts."

During this period, I continued to study and develop my own academic competency. I worked towards completing a second PhD (2017) and gaining a postgraduate qualification in management and economic sciences at the University of Stellenbosch Business School (2009). I also undertook various short courses (such as isiXhosa language courses, blended learning courses, engaged teaching and learning courses, etc.) Being a student among students gave me a sense of shared responsibility for learning, but also helped me to consider the needs and pressures that students face, since I was facing these myself! It taught me to be very prudent about designing my modules to take account of "notional work hours," to ensure that there were clear outcomes to work towards, to set helpful assessments that would allow students to gauge their learning towards clearly described outcomes, and to ensure that teaching and learning was manageable and relevant to whatever they were preparing for (not only for credits on their degree, but as preparation for "life").

Lastly, I had the privilege of developing as a researcher with growing "subject matter expertise" in my own discipline. This allowed me to travel to international conferences, visit universities in other countries, spend time on my own research, and collaborate on various research projects. This exposure helped me to develop a more sober understanding of the challenges, and ideological influences, that come to bear on South African higher education. As a result, I have come to understand both the importance of contextual education, but also that it must be held in tension with international standards and trends in the various academic disciplines and discourses. In particular, those students who progress beyond undergraduate study must be prepared to be able to make both a contextual and a broader (transnational or international) academic contribution. We do them a disservice if we do not prepare them with the knowledge, values, and skills that they will need to engage their academic peers in other international contexts. Hence, my teaching and learning philosophy has gained a deeper commitment to discovering and fostering the African contextual contribution,[37] but also in preparing my own research and helping my students to prepare their research, to make a valid and worthwhile contribution to the global scholarly discourse.[38]

I have become increasingly aware of the importance of maintaining a dialectic tension between the value and importance of inter-contextual learning. It is my conviction that we have a moral responsibility to facilitate learning that is of value in both the "local" context, yet is credible in

---

37. D. Forster, "Public Theology in Africa"; D. Forster, "African Public Theology?"
38. D. Forster, "African Realities."

international (academic) settings. As a teacher at a church seminary in the late 1990s, my primary role was to facilitate theological formation for ministry in the specific South African context. This required particular attention to contextual knowledge, skills, and values that could help to shape the students to make a pragmatic contribution towards justice in their contexts. However, in later years as I taught at South African and other international universities, I realized that I had had a responsibility to form students for further study and research that may need to engage with knowledge from other contexts around the world. In this sense, the task of theological formation required critical reflexivity. Students need to be formed to reflect upon both the promise and the peril of their own values, histories, and commitments in relation to the perspectives of others. Moreover, they had to be equipped to be able to bring their contextual contributions into conversation with other contextual contributions in order to further knowledge, shapes disciplines, and critique themselves and others. Hence, the first inter-contextual dimension I have in mind is that of the quality assurance criteria of the university as an institution that shapes people for both vocational readiness and academic research. In relation to the ideological calls for transformation and renewal that emerge from our immediate South African social context, I recognize that the African theological voice, and African theological epistemologies, have not found sufficient recognition at Stellenbosch or in the broader theological academy.[39] So, the development of these perspectives, and their critical engagement, should be undertaken in ways that valorize and explicate the local context while holding on to the value of the history and tradition of the development of disciplinary specificity and standards.[40] As such, it has been my approach to develop my understanding of decolonizing and African methodologies and epistemologies, to work alongside colleagues and students, and to try to hold some

---

39. Nel, "Visual Redress"; Bowers Du Toit et al., "Born Free?"; Weber, "Practical Theology"; Weber, "Decolonising Youth Ministry Models?"

40. As part of my own growth, in conjunction with students and peers, I have been researching the complexity of Africanization and decolonization theory. It is my contention that, at present, the African voice must gain priority in our context so as to engage, and decenter, unquestioned and entrenched Western epistemological approaches to knowledge. However, the intention is not to replace one "center" (Western knowledge systems) with another (African knowledge systems), as if one system could be superior to another. Rather, it is an attempt to redress the silencing of one perspective by the other, and to seek to equalize the power dynamics of knowledge in the medium– and long term. For some helpful reading in this regard, please see Mbembe, "Decolonizing Knowledge"; Naudé, "Decolonising Knowledge"; Chan-Tiberghien, "Towards 'Global Educational Justice'"; Chinn, "Decolonizing Methodologies"; Zeleza, "Africa's Struggles for Decolonization"; Smith, *Decolonizing Methodologies*; Nell, "We Know"; Andreotti et al., "Mapping Interpretations of Decolonization."

inter-contextual complexity in tension in both the design and implementation of the courses I am responsible for.

Naturally there are other general elements in my educational philosophy, such as academic rigor, lifelong learning, respect for learners, commitment to values, etc., that I shall not be able discuss in detail in this narrative. The points mentioned above seemed most pertinent to reflect upon in light of my personal narrative.

REFLECTING ON SHORTCOMINGS AND AREAS FOR PERSONAL, PEDAGOGICAL, AND INSTITUTIONAL GROWTH

It has been a valuable exercise to reflect upon, and write up, some of the aspects of my educational philosophy and the implementation of my understanding of educational "leadership" (as an educator and administrator). The process has helped me to see what I value as an educator and educational administrator, and what has informed those values. Moreover, it has also helped me to identify gaps that exist between my values and my implementation of those values in practice.

I recognize that there are some aspects of my values and skills that have shortcomings. I still need to develop and implement the following aspects more intentionally:

The ongoing value of collaborative learning—while I value collaborative learning a great deal, the reality is that at times it is easier to "fall back" into teaching conceptual knowledge (course content). I also need to encourage my colleagues in the department to include collaborative learning in our collective work. Simply "teaching" disciplinary "content" requires less effort because of having some experience in my field, and since I have access to materials and resources related to my discipline. Moreover, it requires work (planning, preparing people, and resources), resources (relationships with people, venues, nontraditional materials), and trust (trust *in* people and systems, and trust *from* people and systems) to teach and learn in a collaborative manner. I am conscious of my own constraints in terms of time, energy, and resources and need to plan more carefully and rely a little more on others for assistance and input in this regard.

Contextualizing knowledge generation and acquisition—I have already noted that I value the inter-contextual tensions that allow for creative and nuanced knowledge to emerge in communities of learning. That being said, I do frequently find myself being pressed into generating knowledge for my own academic research in "standard" (Western) ways. I am also aware that I still have many "blind spots" and often find my ideas, and manner, challenged by students. Since the pressure is high to publish scholarly articles and monographs, and publishers have particular requirements and expectations (often shaped by their commitments, contexts, and needs), I do find that I compromise on this principle at times and simply "fall into" using Western sources, and Western methods and knowledge systems, and develop and distribute my research and learning in largely Western academic settings. I realize that what is needed is more balance—the tension needs to be maintained between meeting external expectations, and forging a credible, yet avant-garde, approach to African theological scholarship.

Mentoring and development—a further area of shortcoming that I recognize in my own approach is that I have not capitalized on the privilege of service in my department to share discoveries, ideas, and approaches with colleagues and senior students. I currently serve as the chair of department and have a strong sense that I should be utilizing this unique opportunity to encourage colleagues to not only excel in research, but also to take teaching and learning as crucial elements of their professional academic development and contribution to the University and society. I have supported colleagues to undertake the Professional Educational Development for Academics course and engage in SOTL, but I realize the importance of collaborating in SOEL and SOTL research with them. All of these formal programs are offered to the full-time teaching staff of the University of Stellenbosch. I benefitted a great deal from undertaking these courses, learning in a community of teachers and assessors, being introduced to new literature and theory, and being invited to reflect critically on my pedagogical philosophy and practice. I will encourage colleagues to undertake some of these courses, since they are extremely beneficial for fostering reflective and intentional growth in teaching and learning that takes the context seriously and equips one to face both the crises and opportunities of teaching, learning, and assessment within our context.

I still have a great deal to learn and have a responsibility to do so and to share what I am learning. This project between Stellenbosch and NLA has been a rare, and important, opportunity to reflect on what I am learning, and what still needs to be engaged.

CONCLUSION

As I reflect upon my journey thus far, I can see that my understanding of, and approach to, teaching and learning, and educational leadership, has shifted over the years. In large measure that has been a "story that is told, a song that is sung and a prayer that is uttered in response to experience and expectation."[41]

I realize that more changes and challenges, even crises, will come in the years ahead. At this stage, however, I can conclude that the South African higher educational context requires engaged citizens whose educational responsibility is shaped against the backdrop of our moral concern and the tension between international and national needs. I feel a sense of responsibility to use the privilege and opportunity that I have to facilitate spaces and opportunities for mutual engagement with students, communities, and expertise, that allows for transformation and the development of rigorous, credible, contextual, knowledge that serves the common good. As the Stellenbosch University slogan says, *Sonke Siya Phambili! Forward together! Saam Vorentoe!*

BIBLIOGRAPHY

Andreotti, Vanessa de Oliveira, et al. "Mapping Interpretations of Decolonization in the Context of Higher Education." *Decolonization: Indigeneity, Education & Society* 4 (2015) 21–40.

Astin, Alexander W., et al. "How Service Learning Affects Students." *Higher Education* (2000) 144. http://digitalcommons.unomaha.edu/slcehighered/144/.

Baloyi, Basani, and Gilaad Isaacs. "#FeesMustFall: What Are the Student Protests About?" *CNN*, Oct. 28, 2015. http://www.cnn.com/2015/10/27/africa/fees-must-fall-student-protest-south-africa-explainer/index.html.

Belbase, Shashidhar, et al. "Autoethnography: A Method of Research and Teaching for Transformative Education." *Journal of Education and Research* 1 (2008) 86–95.

Bowers Du Toit, Nadine, et al. "Born Free? South African Young Adults, Inequality, and Reconciliation in Stellenbosch." *International Bulletin of Mission Research* 46 (2022) 200–210. https://doi.org/10.1177/23969393211010747.

Bozalek, Vivienne, et al. "Transforming Teaching with Emerging Technologies: Implications for Higher Education Institutions." Self-published, 2013. http://dx.doi.org/10.20853/27-2-252.

Chan-Tiberghien, Jennifer. "Towards a 'Global Educational Justice' Research Paradigm: Cognitive Justice, Decolonizing Methodologies and Critical Pedagogy." *Globalisation, Societies and Education* 2 (2004) 191–213.

Chinn, Pauline WU. "Decolonizing Methodologies and Indigenous Knowledge: The Role of Culture, Place and Personal Experience in Professional Development." *Journal of Research in Science Teaching* 44 (2007) 1247–68.

Costandius, Elmarie, et al. "#FeesMustFall and Decolonising the Curriculum: Stellenbosch University Students' and Lecturers' Reactions." *SAJHE* 32 (2018) 65–85.

De La Torre, Miguel A. *Doing Christian Ethics from the Margins*. Maryknoll, NY: Orbis, 2014.

---

41. Oduyoye, *Introducing African Women's Theology*, 22.

Eyler, Janet. "Reflection: Linking Service and Learning—Linking Students and Communities." *Journal of Social Issues* 58 (2002) 517–34.

Farisani, Elelwani. "Impact of New Policy Developments in Higher Education on Theological Education." *Studia Historiae Ecclesiasticae* 36 (2010) 1–10.

Fataar, Aslam. "Placing Students at the Centre of the Decolonizing Education Imperative: Engaging the (Mis)Recognition Struggles of Students at the Postapartheid University." *Educational Studies* 54 (2018) 595–608. https://doi.org/10.1080/00131946.2018.1518231.

———. "Towards a Humanising Pedagogy through an Engagement with the Social-Subjective in Educational Theorising in South Africa." *Educational Research for Social Change* 5 (2016) 10–21. https://doi.org/10.17159/2221-4070/2016/v5i1a1.

Forster, Dion A. "African Public Theology? A Conceptual Engagement to Keep the Conversation Alive." *In die Skriflig/In Luce Verbi* 56 (2022) a2849. https://doi.org/10.4102/ids.v56i1.2849.

———. "African Realities and Resilient Religion? An Invitation to Africanize the Conversation." In *Resilient Religion, Resilience and Heartbreaking Adversity*, edited by C. A. M. Hermans and Kobus Schoeman, 83–100. International Practical Theology 24. Münster: LIT, 2022. https://www.lit-verlag.de/isbn/978-3-643-91500-9.

———. "Can Contextual Theology Bridge the Divide? South Africa's Politics of Forgiveness as an Example of a Contextual Public Theology." In *Contextual Theology: Skills and Practices of Liberating Faith*, edited by Sigurd Bergmann and Mika Vähäkangas, 15–33. Routledge New Critical Thinking in Religion, Theology and Biblical Studies. New York: Taylor & Francis, 2021. https://doi.org/10.4324/9780429348006.

———. *The (Im)possibility of Forgiveness: An Empirical Intercultural Bible Reading of Matthew 18:15–35*. Eugene, OR: Wipf and Stock, 2019.

———. "Living More Decently in an Indecent World? The Virtues and Vices of a Public Theologian." Lecture at Stellenbosch University, S. Afr., Aug. 16, 2022. https://doi.org/10.13140/RG.2.2.15535.82089.

———. "A Public Theological Approach to the (Im) Possibility of Forgiveness in Matthew 18:15–35: Reading the Text through the Lens of Integral Theory." *In die Skriflig/In Luce Verbi* 51 (2017) a2108. https://doi.org/10.4102/ids.v51i3.2108.

———. "Public Theology in Africa." In *T&T Clark Handbook of Public Theology*, edited by Christoph Hübenthal and Christiane Alpers, 469–88. T&T Clark Handbooks. New York: Bloomsbury Academic, 2022.

———. "A Southern African Response to 'Pastoral Theology as Attention.'" *Contact* 153 (2007) 33–35. http://dx.doi.org/10.1080/13520806.2007.11759075.

Forster, Dion Angus. "Translation and the Politics of Forgiveness in South Africa? What Black Christians Believe, and White Christians Do Not Seem to Understand." *Stellenbosch Theological Journal* 14 (2018) 77–94. http://dx.doi.org/10.17570/stj.2018.v4n2.a04.

Forster, Megan. "Deliberative Democratic Theory in Relation to Private General and Further Education and Training." PhD diss., Stellenbosch University, 2022.

Given, Lisa M., ed. *The SAGE Encyclopedia of Qualitative Research Methods*. 2 vols. Los Angeles: SAGE, 2008.

Grassow, Lisa, and Clint Le Bruyns. "Embodying Human Rights in #FeesMustFall? Contributions from an Indecent Theology." *HvTSt* 73 (2017) 1–9. https://doi.org/10.4102/hts.v73i3.4799.

Habib, Adam. *Rebels and Rage: Reflecting on #FeesMustFall*. Johannesburg: Ball, 2019.

Hagoel, Lea, and Devorah Kalekin-Fishman. *From the Margins to New Ground: An Autoethnography of Passage between Disciplines*. Rotterdam: Sense, 2016.

Hay, H. R. "The Nuts and Bolts of a Service-Learning Programme: Research in Higher Education." *SAJHE* 17 (2003) 184–91.

Jacobs, Cecilia, and Sonja Strydom. "From 'Matie' to Citizen: Graduate Attributes as Signature Learning at Stellenbosch University." *Independent Journal of Teaching and Learning* 9 (2014) 63–74.

Kivunja, Charles, and Ahmed Bawa Kuyini. "Understanding and Applying Research Paradigms in Educational Contexts." *IJHE* 6 (2017) 26–41. https://doi.org/10.5430/ijhe.v6n5p26.

Kriel, Aletha Catharina. "Proposed Norms and Standards for Pastoral Counsellors/Therapists." MTh thesis, University of South Africa, 2001.

Lange, Hans-Christoph Thapelo. "An Experiential-Realist Approach to Theology? An Interview with Prof Klaus Nürnberger." *Stellenbosch Theological Journal* 7 (2021) 2–24.

Lloyd, Arthur S. "Freire, Conscientization, and Adult Education." *Adult Education* 23 (Sept. 1972) 3–20. https://doi.org/10.1177/074171367202300101.

Mackinlay, Elizabeth. *Critical Writing for Embodied Approaches: Autoethnography, Feminism and Decoloniality*. Cham, Switz.: Springer, 2019.

Mbembe, Achille. "Decolonizing Knowledge and the Question of the Archive." WISER, 2015. http://wiser.wits.ac.za/system/files/Achille%20Mbembe%20-%20Decolonizing%20Knowledge%20and%20the%20Question%20of%20the%20Archive.pdf.

Mbembe, Achille Joseph. "Decolonizing the University: New Directions." *Arts and Humanities in Higher Education* 15 (Feb. 2016) 29–45. https://doi.org/10.1177/1474022215618513.

McCoy, Michael. "Restoring Mission to the Heart of Theological Education A South African Perspective." Paper presented at meeting of Inter-Anglican Standing Commission on Mission and Evangelism, Larnaca, Cyprus, Feb. 2005.

Nattrass, Nicoli, and Jeremy Seekings. "'Two Nations'? Race and Economic Inequality in South Africa Today." *Daedalus* 130 (2001) 45–70.

Naudé, Piet. "Decolonising Knowledge: In What Sense Is an 'African' Ethic Possible?" Scholar, Apr. 2017. http://scholar.sun.ac.za/handle/10019.1/101556.

Nel, Reggie. "Visual Redress: Decolonising the Faculty of Theology at Stellenbosch University?" In *Evoking Transformation: Visual Redress at Stellenbosch University*, edited by Aslam Fataar and Elmarie Costandius, 220–38. Stellenbosch, S. Afr.: African Sun Media, 2021.

Nell, I. A., and J. P. Bosman. "Integrating Graduate Attributes into a Master of Divinity Programme at a South African University." *SAJHE* 31 (2017) 175–90. http://dx.doi.org/10.20853/31-1-868.

Nell, Ian. "We Know to Whom We Belong? The Drama of Ministerial Practice in a Post-Colonial Africa Context." Lecture presented at the Faculty of Theology, Stellenbosch, S. Afr., Apr. 6, 2017.

Oduyoye, Mercy. *Introducing African Women's Theology*. London: A&C Black, 2001.

Rovai, Alfred P., and Hope Jordan. "Blended Learning and Sense of Community: A Comparative Analysis with Traditional and Fully Online Graduate Courses." *IRRODL* 5 (2004). http://www.irrodl.org/index.php/irrodl/article/view/192.

Seekings, Jeremy, and Nicoli Nattrass. *Class, Race, and Inequality in South Africa.* New Haven, CT: Yale University Press, 2008.

Shea, Peter, and Temi Bidjerano. "Learning Presence: Towards a Theory of Self-Efficacy, Self-Regulation, and the Development of a Communities of Inquiry in Online and Blended Learning Environments." *Computers & Education* 55 (2010) 1721–31.

Smith, Linda Tuhiwai. *Decolonizing Methodologies: Research and Indigenous Peoples.* 2nd ed. New York: Zed, 2012.

Tracy, David. "Religion in the Public Realm: Three Forms of Publicness." In *At the Limits of the Secular: Reflections on Faith and Public Life*, edited by William A. Barbieri, 29–51. Grand Rapids: Eerdmans, 2014.

Vellem, Vuyani S. "Un-Thinking the West: The Spirit of Doing Black Theology of Liberation in Decolonial Times." *HvTSt* 73 (2017) a4737. https://doi.org/10.4102/hts.v73i3.4737.

Waghid, Y. "Decolonising the African University Again." *SAJHE* 35 (2021) 1–4. https://doi.org/10.20853/35-6-4875.

Weber, Shantelle. "Decolonising Youth Ministry Models? Challenges and Opportunities in Africa." *HvTSt* 73 (2017) 1–10. https://doi.org/10.4102/hts.v73i4.4796.

———. "Practical Theology Rooted in and from Africa." In *The Wiley Blackwell Companion to Theology and Qualitative Research*, edited by Pete Ward and Knut Tveitereid, 58–66. Wiley Blackwell Companions to Religion. Wiley & Sons, 2022. https://doi.org/10.1002/9781119756927.ch7.

Wepener, Cas, and Ian Nell. "White Males Teaching Theology at (South) African Universities? Reflections on Epistemological and Ontological Hospitality." *Academia Letters*, art. 3304 (Aug. 25, 2021). https://doi.org/10.20935/AL3304.

Wethmar, Conrad J. "Theological Education in an Ecumenical Context: Principles and Procedures of the Pretoria Model." In *Theology between Church, University and Society*, edited by N. F. M. Schreurs et al., 61–74. Studies in Theology and Religion 6. Leiden, Neth.: Brill, 2003.

Zeleza, Paul Tiyambe. "Africa's Struggles for Decolonization: From Achebe to Mandela." *Research in African Literatures* 45 (2014) 121–39.

Chapter 18

Epilogue: Learning Theology in Crisis by Reading the Times

A Question of Leadership

BÅRD NORHEIM AND SHANTELLE WEBER

READING THE TIMES AS A POETIC AND PROPHETIC ENTERPRISE

Every year on Christmas Eve the South African Anglican archbishop of Cape Town, Thabo Makgoba, gives a sermon at midnight Mass at St George's Cathedral in Cape Town. On Christmas Eve in 2014, the archbishop preached on courage.[1] Makgoba described the year that had passed as a *crisis*, "a difficult year for South Africa." He mourned that we "seem to have been living in a country whose leaders, despite the emancipation of democracy, do not look after the needs of their people."[2]

The experience of crisis is manifold around the world and not confined to postapartheid South Africa. Some of the acute crises always seem to catch our attention—like the outbreak of a war or natural disaster, say, a flood or an earthquake. At the same time, an ongoing crisis, such as the crisis of poverty and social injustice, is equally worthy of attention.

---

1. The sermon was also a point of reflection for a short case study discussion on co-teaching in ch. 13 on training courage in theological education, in pt. 3 of this book.

2. Makgoba, "Welcome Season of Light," para. 6. For a broader analysis of Makgoba's sermons, see Wepener and Steyn, "Struggle for Hope Continues."

Epilogue: Learning Theology in Crisis by Reading the Times

So, where do we start—and where do we end? This book does not in any way take on the ambition to cover any experience with crisis. The focus of this book is somewhat selective as we have focused on three crises in particular: First, the climate crisis, which affects the whole world at large. Second, we have explored the crisis of youth involvement and youth citizenship, which affects both the current and future political state of the world. Finally, we have looked at the crisis of the church's changed position in society, which affects how theology and theological education are configured. We have proposed a new paradigm for theological teaching and learning in the light of crisis—*glocal theological education*.

In the first part of the book, we started by naming the reality of different crises to discuss *where* we may learn from crisis. In the second part of the book, we explored *how* we can learn from crisis both digitally, globally, and locally. In the third part, we discussed *what* we may learn from crisis: Are there any virtues and skills that are worthy of attention as we seek to strengthen theological discernment among students of theology?

In this final chapter of the book, the epilogue, we want to examine the experience of crisis and its relevance for theological education and the developing of theological discernment through the lens of leadership. Globalization has broken down national and territorial boundaries and compressed time and space. It has brought convenience to social life and connection among people.[3] An important task for any theologian, therefore, involves reading the times. Evaluating the time we live in implies offering a response to people's most acute question to any leader: What's going on? Or more precisely: What time is it? Is this a time for rejoicing or lamenting? Should we keep peace or go to war? What should we make of the world around us and how should we respond to it? Should we protest or salute?[4] The imaginative and poetic craftsmanship of trying to read the times is a contested and difficult enterprise, perhaps because reading the times involves looking both backwards and forwards. A well-known example of what it means to read the times by looking backwards is announced every year in January, when members of the Bulletin of the Atomic Scientists publish the so-called Doomsday Clock.[5] The clock operates as a metaphor: It looks back at the year that has passed and describes the current threats to humanity and portrays the hypothetical global catastrophe as midnight. In declaring the number of minutes or seconds to midnight it describes the current stance of the world: How close is humanity to a worldwide disaster, that "would

---

3. Pui-Lan et al., *Teaching Global Theologies*, 12.
4. Norheim and Haga, *Four Speeches*, 29.
5. Spinaze, "Doomsday Clock."

inflict irrevocable harm to humanity"? Currently, the clock is set at ninety seconds to midnight, the closest the clock has ever been set to midnight.[6]

When it comes to predicting the future before it happens, Nassim Nicholas Taleb has become famous for his theory of the Black Swan, on how to look to the future by assessing the impact of the highly improbable. Taleb was received as a prophetic voice, particularly as he was able to prophesize the arrival of the financial crisis in 2008 and onwards.[7] In this book, we have tried to offer signposts for theological education in times of crisis, learning from a glocal learning community of theological leaders who become more capable of reading the times together, by both looking backwards and forwards.

As Jeffrey Bilbro has pointed out, reading the times is fundamentally a practice of the community. It is also crucial to remember that, from the perspective of a Christian worldview, we read the news to love our neighbor. Bilbro also warns against the danger of "attending to trivia."[8] Within the realm of contextual theologies, the emergence of local theologies and an increasing sensitivity to history and culture has created an important shift in perspective of Christian self-awareness and theology, both among churches in the north and south. This then means that while theology is contextual, our contexts are increasingly interconnected and we cannot do theology limited to our local contexts.[9] So, how do we engage interdisciplinary theologians teaching into their varying contextual realities to read the times locally and glocally? How do we develop and enhance the poetic and situational discernment that grows out of intimate knowledge of Scripture and tradition and dedicated attention to the critical questions that any contemporary crisis evokes? Put bluntly, how do we train theologians as both poets and prophets?[10]

READING THE TIMES AS AN ACT OF LEADERSHIP

To further explore what it means to read the times as theologians, we need to consider in more detail what leadership is. Why is that? Well, reading the times is an act of pursuing influence, and leadership is intrinsically linked

---

6. Norheim and Haga, *Three Fears*, 41–42.
7. Taleb, *Black Swan*.
8. Bilbro, *Reading the Times*, 20.
9. Pui-Lan et al., *Teaching Global Theologies*, 14–15.
10. On what it takes for the theologian or pastor to develop the role of both poet and prophet, see Roxburgh, *Missionary Congregation*, where the threefold leadership of a theologian is described as that of the *poet*, the *prophet*, and the *apostle*.

Epilogue: Learning Theology in Crisis by Reading the Times

to the pursuit of exhibiting influence. However, the conceptualization of the phenomenon called "leadership" has changed over time, and contemporary definitions of leadership often emphasize leadership as a potential that exists in everyone, rather than a calling reserved only for people with special character traits. Current conceptions of leadership also argue for the prominence of vision and purpose over position and power. Aligned with this, the leader is often pictured as the key player in a team, rather than a solo player.[11]

But what characterizes the practice of leadership? Well, one thing is rather obvious: A leader invites followers. Put bluntly, a leader with no followers is not a leader. This applies to the gift of reading the times as well. Reading the times is a poetic and prophetic calling that invites an audience, underscoring that leadership is a fundamentally relational enterprise. The prophet engages in envisioning another future. The prophet does not ask if the vision can be implemented, for questions of implementation are of no consequence until the vision can be imagined. The imagination must come before the implementation. Our current culture seems to be competent at implementing almost anything, but at the same time seems to imagine almost nothing.[12] However, leadership cannot be defined by relational dynamics alone. The purpose of any leadership, even that of trying to discern and read the time, is not just to create something relational, but to point out and work towards a future goal by the means of leading and influencing others.[13]

If leadership is about influence, the practice of leadership—and subsequently trying to read the times—is not a neutral thing. How we evaluate the practice of leadership, depends on how we evaluate the aim and quality of the intended influence that the process of reading the times is supposed to produce. Is the purpose of reading the times to manipulate followers or to respond to particularly critical questions and dilemmas that an ongoing crisis may evoke? This contested element of reading the times reminds us that any prophesy needs to be tested—and tested by a community. This is also why reading the times, discerning theologically, is a gift belonging to a communal and glocal learning community.[14] Students on university campuses are bombarded with so many worldviews, lifestyles, and even perceptions of faith. Holistic mission equips them not only to be the salt and light they are called to be, but also to live among others knowing who they are and

---

11. See, for instance, Kellerman, *End of Leadership*.

12. Brueggeman, *Prophetic Imagination*.

13. Yukl, *Leadership in Organizations*, 26; Kotter, *Leading Change*, 9; Northouse, *Leadership*, 6–7; Grint, *Leadership*, 85.

14. See also Norheim, "Leadership as Christian Practice."

what they believe. Faith communities view themselves as living in relationship with God and, by extension, in relation to their past and future the present generation) derive our ethics of responsibility for the communities. Christ who took responsibility for us and transcends time is the one who is always coming and keeps acting on our behalf. Therefore, we do not take responsibility for future generations because of how they can reciprocate, but because Christ took responsibility for us; even so, future generations (like present generations) are not exempt from acting responsibly themselves.[15]

If reading the times is an attempted act of influence, the question of authority comes to the fore, and even the question of what constitutes and legitimizes the authority to offer a poetic and prophetic reading of times in a particular crisis. In *The End of Leadership*, Barbara Kellerman discusses how different conceptualizations of leadership relate to authority. She argues that leadership as a phenomenon should be recognized as an equilateral triangle, with three equal parts—the leader, the followers, and the context. For Kellerman, the "context" points to the cultural and social environment that both leaders and followers must engage and interact with to assess the situation—or read the times. The critical point in order to avoid harmful leader-centrism, according to Kellerman, is that followers need to subscribe voluntarily to the message of the leader, even in times of crisis.[16] Although people may have a basic need for authority, as Freud found, in times of crisis and insecurity a leader who attempts to read the times and name reality does so by inviting the followers to commit voluntarily to the reading and vision that the leader presents. The alternative would be granting the leader some sort of absolute authority. Sometimes, and particularly in times of uncertainty, this sort of leadership could appear attractive, Kellerman finds, drawing on Thomas Hobbes: The leader—like a king in the old days—would be granted absolute power by followers by offering what they want and need in return—protection and security. This bond was in many ways the introduction of the social contract.[17] Education should therefore play a role in changing the world for the better by stimulating critical thinking and empowering people so that they may free themselves from oppression, poverty, injustice, and the difficult task of living peacefully with former oppressors after political liberation. In this sense there needs to be a shift from an individualistic to a communal sense of educational agency that takes place for this to become a reality.[18]

15. Weber, "Necessity of Intergenerational Dialogue."
16. Kellerman, *End of Leadership*, 200.
17. Kellerman, *End of Leadership*, 6–7, 10.
18. Msila and Gumbo, *Africanisation of Education*.

Epilogue: Learning Theology in Crisis by Reading the Times 279

Training theological leaders to read the times, however, must be rooted in a conviction that the potentially authoritative act of leadership that reading the times involves demands the critical and voluntary response of followers. Such an understanding of reading the times as an act of leadership also implies bidding farewell with the conception that the leader is a genius with a special *charisma*, who is set apart from the rest of the community. However, as Max Weber sometimes argues, it is also possible to interpret the charisma of the leader as something dynamic, dialogical, and dialectical—a gift attributed to the leader *by* the community.[19] Theological education without the spiritual formation of its students is not holistic. This lack of continuity between what theology students are learning in the classroom and what they need to know once they enter the ministerial context is thus a source of concern. Students arrive at institutions of theological education already formed in different ways by faith communities and numerous other communities in which they grew up and participated. The practicing theologian is one who seeks to bridge action and reflection, or practice and the reflection on practice. Theologians as leaders in varying contexts need to become reflective practitioners and scholarly leaders to enhance their theological training.

READING THE TIMES AS AN ACT OF CHRISTIAN LEADERSHIP?

Is there then a particularly Christian way to read the times? The more fundamental question here, however, is whether there is such a thing as Christian leadership at all. David I. Smith has explored whether there is anything particularly Christian about teaching by asking if there "is such a thing as teaching Christianly." Succinctly put, Smith investigates whether there is a way in which "faith forms" the practice of teaching and the whole concept of teaching.[20] Similarly, one may ask if the act of leadership involved in the attempt to read the times, to discern and exercise sound judgement, may be taken to be a Christian endeavor.

It seems obvious that reading the times is hardly an exclusively Christian enterprise. Like all leaders, theological leaders read the times in times of crisis to name reality and envision a path toward the future. Perhaps, though, it may be possible to speak of a Christian end or purpose involved in reading the times? The goal of this activity may be interpreted as being in Christian in some sense, given that reading the times has the needs of the

19. Haslam et al., *New Psychology of Leadership*, 2–5.
20. Smith, *On Christian Teaching*, preface.

neighbour in mind—and perhaps more radically—even the needs of the enemy.[21]

More fundamentally, any theory on leadership, as it proposes a vision of a preferred future, implicitly makes theological claims, and more explicitly challenges theological imagination. More precisely, it challenges theological interpretations of change and transition and modes for leading human beings into change and in times of change, which is an essential element in reading the times. In what sort of theological anthropology do we need to anchor the leadership practice of trying to read the times? In Christian theology the *historicity* and *plasticity* of human beings are fundamental modes of change. They are inscribed in the sacramental and Christological narrative of the reality of change promised through the hope of resurrection.[22]

Reading the times therefore needs to be rooted in Christian eschatology, where one must remember that the theological telos of change finds its ultimate response in the hope of resurrection. Since this is the case, the telos of change is fundamentally a hope for a new creation. German theologian Jürgen Moltmann finds that "the kingdom of God can mean no less than resurrection and new creation and hope in the kingdom can be satisfied with no less than this."[23] The hope Moltmann here proposes is fundamentally imbedded in a *communal* telos, highlighting that the biblical hope of resurrection from the dead is a collective term. Reading the times under the hope of a future resurrection implies that the theological telos of reading the times also invites a call to name reality in solidarity with all of creation, cf. Rom 8:22.[24] Hope, on one hand, is an absurdity too embarrassing to speak about, for it flies in the face of all those claims we have been told are facts. Hope is the refusal to accept the reading of reality that is the majority opinion; and one does that only at great political and existential risk. On the other hand, hope is subversive, for it limits the grandiose pretension of the present, daring to announce that the present to which we have all made commitments is now called into question.[25]

---

21. See Norheim, "Leadership as Christian Practice," on what sort of telos may qualify leadership as a Christian practice.

22. Norheim, "Grain of Wheat."

23. Moltmann, *Theology of Hope*, 223.

24. Pannenberg, *What Is Man*, 138. The irony here is that death as the ultimate anthropological category for change appears utterly individual. Simultaneously, finitude is something all human beings have in common; see Moltmann, *Theology of Hope*, 223.

25. Brueggemann, *Prophetic Imagination*.

HOW TO TRAIN SOUND THEOLOGICAL DISCERNMENT—IMPROVISATION AND PLAY

Developing the art of reading the times as a key practice in theological training presupposes that the church and theology find their place at the *glocal* marketplace. However, this comes with a certain cost. Meeting people at the marketplace implies living with the possibility of being rejected. People may turn the church and her message down. Everyone who attempts to read the times may not just be overlooked or rejected but may even fail. So, the church, then, and her theologians need to rehearse living with the fear of being rejected. Perhaps a more self-critical assessment by the church and her leaders would make her ethos on the marketplace more credible, particularly when a leader of the church attempts to read the times?

Any poet and prophet who is not sensitive to the possibility of *misreading* the times is embarking on a dangerous path. The problem, however, is that the fear of failing may result in the fear of making choices. It takes a certain amount of courage to dare to take a decision that might prove to be wrong. However, the problem when decisions are postponed is the potential lack of trust among the leader's followers, which may involve running the risk of losing the dedication and passion of your coworkers.[26]

In times of crisis the church enters a liminal stage, where she needs to rediscover her story or message—the logos—anew. This happens by carefully examining both the situation and the tradition. Reading the times as a Christian practice may hence be interpreted as a sort of improvisation art. Samuel Wells has argued that the church needs to rediscover and rehearse the art of improvising faithfully. However, Wells dismantles the idea that improvisation is about being original. To think of oneself as original, even in reading the times, is in a certain sense a sin, as the reader puts oneself at the center of a one-act play. Rather, in a Christian view of the world, the leader may attempt to read the times—improvise rooted in the Christian tradition and the practice of the church, the community of saints. This improvisation implies living with the possibility of failure and misinterpretation. Wells argue that, unlike heroes, saints expect to fail, as they acknowledge the influence of the fall. And even as important, unlike the hero, who stands alone against the world, saints, even in the biblical narrative, are never alone.[27] Therefore, the practice of improvisation that reading the times involves must account for the possibility of failure. It must also fundamentally understand itself as a communal practice of church: "The church is God's new

---

26. Brunstad, *Beslutningsvegring*.
27. Wells, *Improvisation*, 128, 67, 44.

language, and it speaks not of a country fit for heroes to live in but of a commonwealth of saints."[28] In the everyday practice of many pastors and other church leaders, conversations represent a laboratory for such improvisation art, whether it is meeting people at the local market place or online or for a planned conversation with families mourning one of their loved ones. For the pastor, the call to discernment is equally important in any conversation. Training this conversational discernment is often helped by playful exercise of improvisation along with self-reflection, often helped by mentoring.

In the TLC project—Teaching and Learning Theology in Crisis—we have also seen many examples of this improvisation art. We have seen it as students are exposed to new contexts of learning and must try out new modes of speaking and practicing together with other students through the online co-teaching. Another essential part of the project that this book bears witness to are the student internships. Here, students cannot simply disappear into traditional modes of study, but through exposure to new ways of living, playing, and worshipping they must learn to improvise—and potentially fail and learn from failure. All in order to develop and strengthen theological discernment that enables you to exercise leadership in the face of crisis.

This implies that one's theology and sense of mission is challenged during times of crisis. The COVID-19 pandemic has impacted people across the globe politically, economically, socially, and spiritually. Religious institutions, including churches, have also been impacted and pushed to think about how we understand and experience church. Institutional church buildings were closed, restricting churches from gathering for their usual ministerial activities. The very notion of church has been challenged from varying perspectives.[29]

How do you train to live with the challenge of being rejected, then? Ironically, by learning to play. The importance of play in times of crisis has been discussed in more depth in an earlier chapter of this book on the crisis of the church and its consequences for theological educations, and in the chapter on training to develop courage. Here it is just worth reminding the reader, that play teaches those who participate the necessity of making choices, with the constant risk of making the "wrong" choice—of failing. Play literally forces you to learn from your mistakes. If you play hide-and-seek, it is essential to learn from your mistakes in the previous round. In many ways, playing is like the *inventio* stage of a creative, rhetorical process where you radically pursue any idea available.

28. Wells, *Improvisation*, 44.
29. Weber, "Children."

Epilogue: Learning Theology in Crisis by Reading the Times 283

Learning to play may help the church to follow in the footsteps of St. Paul on Areopagos, speaking boldly about the relevance of the Christian faith among other competing worldviews on the marketplace. Developing a mode of playfulness allows the person who attempts to read the times a space for vulnerability. Training to read the times in theological education is therefore a reminder that humans can interpret and handle the experience of both brokenness and discontinuity, being both *able to* relate to their surroundings in an interpretive manner and being to a certain extent *dependent on* these surroundings. This *historicity* and *situatedness* of human beings are what makes us capable of reading the times by looking at ourselves from the outside in a certain sense. To exercise reading the times invokes the importance of the church and her leaders *historicizing* themselves.[30] Acknowledging the *historicity* of human beings is of great value for anyone who wants to exercise the poetic and prophetic gift of reading the times. For one thing, it opens a larger time span in which to interpret a crisis. The focus on historicity even emphasizes the radical situatedness of a crisis, the importance of different contexts. Ultimately, to historicize oneself when confronted with the Christian narrative implies reading the times in the light of U-shaped *comedy structure* of the Christian story.[31]

Fundamentally, embracing the importance of play in theological training therefore brings theology back to its heart—worship: Worship is much like a game. It is a sort of play that comes with "its own rules, customs, and etiquette." Worship even "suspends normal patterns of thought and behavior." And, like play in general, it "takes place in its own controlled space and time," and most importantly, "it is undertaken for its own sake, for no other purpose."[32] The latter point resembles Alasdair MacIntyre's definition of social practices:

> Any coherent and complex form of socially established cooperative human activity, through which goods internal to that form of activity are realized in the course of trying to achieve those standards of excellence which are appropriated to, and partially

---

30. Pannenberg, *What Is Man*, 138. Pannenberg elaborates more broadly on the historicity (*Geschichtlichkeit*) of human beings in Pannenberg, *Anthropologie*, 472–501. Jürgen Moltmann also emphasizes the importance of *historicity* for a Christian anthropology but finds that the future should hold a prerogative: "The whole present situation must be understood in all its historic possibilities and tasks in the light of the future of the truth" (Moltmann, *Theology of Hope*, 288).

31. Frye, *Great Code*, 169. Frye argues that the "entire Bible, viewed as 'divine comedy,' is contained with a U-shaped story . . . one in which man, as explained, loses the tree and water of life at the beginning of Genesis and gets them back at the end of Revelation."

32. Wells, *Improvisation*, 85.

definitive of, that form of activity, with the result that human powers to achieve excellence, and human conceptions of the ends and goods involved, are systematically extended.[33]

This perspective on theological education and its capacity to foster leaders who can read the times faithfully fixes the importance of developing a theologian's character. For someone who wants to explore both poetic and prophetic roles on the glocal marketplaces virtues like self-awareness,[34] authenticity, and maturity become all the more important.[35]

Drawing on Augustine and the Greek fathers such as Gregor of Nyssa, American theologian Kathryn Tanner argues that the reflexive capacities of self-formation imply that humans can try to reshape themselves in a self-critical fashion, including even desires they cannot help having by nature.[36] However, changing your own self-reflection, approach, tactics, and awareness takes time and requires work. For someone who wants to train reading the times, it is important to remember that "you are a system as complex as the one you are trying to move forward,"[37] and therefore "your whole self constitutes a resource for exercising leadership."[38]

Finally, developing the theological discernment necessary to read the times does not stop at simply noting what time it is. Naming reality in poetic and prophetic ways may even involve engaging in more subversive practices, like vigilance awareness, resilience, and even resistance and protests.[39]

READING THE TIMES AS AN ART OF ADAPTIVE LEADERSHIP: THE VULNERABILITY OF LEADERS

To name reality in a crisis is certainly an adaptive challenge, as it involves addressing necessary changes in "people's priorities, beliefs, habits and loyalties."[40] Perhaps the ability to read the times may be conceptualized as a sort of adaptive leadership, a "practice of mobilizing people to tackle tough

---

33. MacIntyre, *After Virtue*, 187.
34. Heifetz et al., *Practice of Adaptive Leadership*, 45–46.
35. Roxburgh and Romanuk, *Missional Leader*, 141.
36. Tanner, *Christ the Key*, 41, 47. "Becoming a human image of God through the impress of the divine image is just an extreme case of having one's character made over by relations with what one is not—God, what is most unlike creatures generally" (Tanner, *Christ the Key*, 41).
37. Heifetz et al., *Practice of Adaptive Leadership*, 181.
38. Heifetz et al., *Practice of Adaptive Leadership*, 38.
39. See, for instance, Jones and Hammersley, "Social Protest as Formation."
40. Heifetz et al., *Practice of Adaptive Leadership*, 19.

challenges and thrive."[41] Anyhow, when you address a conflict or a crisis it could be compared to the dissonance that creates tension in music, "causing the listener to naturally want some kind of resolution."[42]

In the practice of adaptive leadership, shifting between the perspective of the dance floor and the balcony as you try to diagnose the current crisis or challenge both culturally and structurally is emphasized.[43] Trying to diagnose a crisis and read the times, you may start at high levels of abstraction, then frame the work at the lowest level of abstraction, or the opposite way around. The point is to shift your perspective to exercise and enhance your analytical bandwidth,[44] your repertoire. Any leader who wants to speak convincingly in a crisis needs to know and constantly expand their rhetorical wardrobe. A rhetorical wardrobe is the rhetorical "garments" a leader may use with credibility and integrity to read the times. It implies the use of words, gestures, metaphors, stories, symbols, examples, deductive arguments that fit both you and the current crisis.[45] Reading the times means applying your bandwidth and your wardrobe in naming the reality of the crisis.

At the same time, every speaker may work to expand their rhetorical wardrobe—crafting new metaphors, reflecting on gestures, and the use of examples. In any case, it is key that the rhetorical "clothes" you put on are perceived to be your own, even if you have borrowed them.

CONCLUSION: THEOLOGICAL TRAINING IN CRISIS— EDUCATING GLOCAL THEOLOGICAL LEADERS WHO READ THE TIMES

It is of course important to point out that theological training involves more than the mere training of pastors, but rather training all of God's people for ministry and theological discernment. The fact that Jesus weeps and that he is moved in spirit and troubled contrasts remarkably with the dominant culture. That is not the way of power, and it is scarcely the way among those who intend to maintain firm social control. But (in John 11:33–35), Jesus is engaged not in social control but in dismantling the power of death, and he

---

41. Heifetz et al., *Practice of Adaptive Leadership*, 14.
42. Heifetz et al., *Practice of Adaptive Leadership*, 151.
43. Heifetz et al., *Practice of Adaptive Leadership*, 58–78.
44. Heifetz et al., *Practice of Adaptive Leadership*, 205.
45. Norheim and Haga, *Four Speeches*, 111–13.

does so by submitting himself to the pain and grief present in the situation, the very pain and grief that the dominant society must deny.[46]

Theological training that is reflective of the context and times our students live in therefore requires that we be dependent on God's Spirit for wisdom, creativity, humor, and flexibility in how we train and prepare students. In this sense, it requires the self-awareness that the teachers are no longer viewed as the solemn expert in the classroom. Faced with a crisis, even teachers of theology are forced to learn by trying to interpret and name reality. In trying to exercise leadership by reading the times in this manner, theological teachers may become facilitators in students' education. Learning in glocal communities of practice therefore requires that we know the local yet engage with the global, with the aim of fostering sound judgment and mature leadership among theological students.

BIBLIOGRAPHY

Bilbro, Jeffrey. *Reading the Times: A Literary and Theological Inquiry into the News*. Downers Grove, IL: IVP Academic, 2021.
Brueggemann, Walter. *The Prophetic Imagination*. 2nd ed. Minneapolis: Fortress, 2001.
Brunstad, Paul Otto. *Beslutningsvegring—et ledelsesproblem*. Oslo: Gyldendal Akademisk, 2017.
Frye, Northrop. *The Great Code: The Bible and Literature*. San Diego: Harcourt Brace Jovanovich, 1983.
Grint, Keith. *Leadership: A Very Short Introduction*. Very Short Introductions. Oxford: Oxford University Press, 2010.
Haslam, S. Alexander, et al. *The New Psychology of Leadership: Identity, Influence, and Power*. New York: Psychology, 2011.
Heifetz, Ronald, et al. *The Practice of Adaptive Leadership: Tools and Tactics for Changing Your Organization and the World*. Boston: Harvard Business Review, 2009.
Jones, Ian, and Peter Hammersley. "Social Protest as Formation for Prophetic Ministry: An Experiment in Transformative Theological Education." *Journal of Adult Theological Education* 6 (2009) 176–93.
Kellerman, Barbara. *The End of Leadership*. New York: HarperBusiness, 2012.
Kotter, J. P. *Leading Change*. Boston: Harvard Business Review, 1996.
MacIntyre, Alasdair. *After Virtue: A Study in Moral Theory*. Notre Dame, IN: University of Notre Dame Press, 1984.
Makgoba, Thabo. Archbishop Thabo Makgoba, Dec. 25, 2014. "Welcome the Season of Light by Becoming a Society of Long Spoons." https://archbishop.anglicanchurchsa.org/2014/12/welcome-season-of-light-by-becoming.html.
Moltmann, Jürgen. *Theology of Hope*. Translated by J. W. Leitch. New York: Harper & Row, 1967.
Msila, Vuyisile, and Mishack Gumbo. *Africanisation of Education and the Search for Relevance and Context*. Stellenbosch, S. Afr.: African Sun Media, 2016.

---

46. Brueggeman, *Prophetic Imagination*.

Norheim, Bård. "Leadership as a Christian Practice." *Scandinavian Journal for Leadership & Theology* 10 (2023) 533–44.

Norheim, Bård, and Joar Haga. *The Four Speeches Every Leader Has to Know*. London: Palgrave Macmillan, 2020.

———. *The Three Fears Every Leader Has to Know: Words to Use in a Crisis*. London: Palgrave Macmillan, 2022.

Norheim, Bård Eirik Hallesby. "A Grain of Wheat: Towards a Theological Anthropology for Leading Change in Ministry." *Journal of Religious Leadership* 13 (2014) 59–77.

Norheim, Bård Eirik Hallesby, and Joar Haga. "The Impotent Leader and the Legacy of the Church: The Farewell Sermon as a Bishop's Last(ing) Act of Leadership." *Scandinavian Journal for Leadership & Theology* 8 (2021) 1–20.

Northouse, Peter G. *Leadership: Theory and Practice*. 9th ed. Los Angeles: Sage, 2022.

Pannenberg, Wolfhart. *Anthropologie in theologischer Perspektive*. Göttingen: Vandenhoeck & Ruprecht, 1983.

———. *What Is Man? Contemporary Anthropology in Theological Perspective*. Translated by D. A. Priebe. Philadelphia: Fortress, 1970.

Pui-Lan, Kwok, et al., eds. *Teaching Global Theologies: Power & Praxis*. Waco: Baylor University Press, 2015.

Roxburgh, Alan J. *The Missionary Congregation, Leadership, and Liminality*. Harrisburg, PA: Trinity International, 1997.

Roxburgh, Alan J., and Fred Romanuk. *The Missional Leader: Equipping your Church to Reach a Changing World*. San Francisco: Jossey Bass, 2006.

Smith, David I. *On Christian Teaching: Practicing Faith in the Classroom*. Grand Rapids: Eerdmans, 2018.

Spinaze, Gary. "Press Release: Doomsday Clock Set at 90 Seconds to Midnight." Bulletin of the Atomic Scientists, Jan. 24, 2023. https://thebulletin.org/2023/01/press-release-doomsday-clock-set-at-90-seconds-to-midnight/.

Taleb, Nassim Nicholas. *The Black Swan: The Highly Improbable*. New York: Random House, 2010.

Tanner, Kathryn. *Christ the Key*. Cambridge: Cambridge University Press, 2010.

Weber, Shantelle. "Children in South African Churches: The Place and Role of Children in South African Churches during the Covid-19 Pandemic." In *Covid-19 in Congregations and Communities: An Exploration of the Influence of the Coronavirus Pandemic on Congregational and Community Life*, edited by Ian Nell, 75–94. Johannesburg: Naledi, 2021.

———. "The Necessity of Intergenerational Dialogue on Social Justice within the South African Church." In *Powers, Inequalities and Vulnerabilities: Impact of Globalisation on Children, Youth and Families and on the Mission of the Church*, edited by Johannes L. Knoetze and Valentin Kozhuharov, 267–92. Reformed Theology in Africa 4. Cape Town: AOSIS, 2020. https://doi.org/10.4102/aosis.2020.BK229.13.

Wells, Samuel. *Improvisation: The Drama of Christian Ethics*. Grand Rapids: Brazos, 2004.

Wepener, Cas, and Marileen Steyn. "The Struggle for Hope Continues: The Christmas Sermons of Archbishop Thabo Makgoba, 2009–2019." Thabo Makgoba, n.d. https://www.thabomakgoba.online/acmp/images/TheStruggleforHopeWepenerSteyn.pdf.

Yukl, Gary. *Leadership in Organizations*. New York: Pearson, 2010.

Index

21st/Twenty-first century skills, 130

Academic flexibility, 30
Academic formation, 263
Academic literacy, 156–61, 165–68
Academic support, 158–59
Action research, 113, 145–49, 190
Adaptive leadership, 284–85
Agency, 30, 226, 278
Anthropocentrism, 49
Anthropology, biblical/theological, 86, 280
Apartheid, 223, 225, 237, 254, 259, 261
Arminianism, 85
Aristotle, 2, 81, 189–190, 197–198
Assessment, 102, 109–10, 119–20, 137, 152, 164, 173–74, 178, 230–31, 262, 265, 269
Attention, 94, 96–7, 103, 108–10, 119, 122–24, 274–76
Augustine, 80, 192, 284
Authority, 20, 27, 55, 85, 150–52, 160, 199, 238, 278
Autoethnography, 176–77, 183, 254–55
Autonomous learning, 104, 108

Bandwidth, 190, 285
Bantu education, 259, 261
Berlin Wall, 194–95
Bi-vocational ministry, 222, 226
Biblical studies, 5, 53–5, 73
Bildung, 51
Blended learning, 98, 129, 135, 261–62, 266
Boesak, Allan, 4, 9

Bonhoeffer, Dietrich, 198–203
Botman, Russel, xi, 8, 226, 232
Bronfenbrenner, Urie, 178

Chikane, Frank, 4
Childlessness, 61, 63–4, 74
Christology, 9, 48–9, 55
Christ's presence, 8–9, 24, 27–8
Citizenship, youth citizenship, xiii, 5–6, 32, 34, 37, 275
Classroom observation, 173
Climate change, 7, 31, 40, 44–5, 47–52, 84
Climate crisis, xi, xiii, 5–7, 10, 46–55, 57, 189, 275
Co-teaching, xiii, 6–8, 40, 274, 282
Cognitive engagement, 94
Collaborative inquiry, xii
Collaborative learning, 118, 131, 134, 138, 168, 209, 260, 262–63, 268
COIL (collaborative online international learning), 111–20, 124–25
Colleague observation, 173–75, 177, 179
Common good, 256–57, 261, 264, 270
Communities of practice, 117, 153, 286
Confession, confession of sins, 49–50, 201–3
Conradie, Ernst M., 45–48, 50
Consumerism, 50, 97
Contemplatio, 3–4
Counterculture, 73
Courage, 88, 189–203, 218, 243, 274, 281–82
Covid-19, 7, 10–11, 93–110, 111, 114, 128, 131–32, 134–35, 157,

163, 165, 171, 182, 206, 210–12, 217–18, 234–36, 239–48, 250, 282
Creation, xiii, 9, 24–25, 48, 50, 55, 68, 79, 83, 206, 210–12, 217–18, 234–36, 280
Creativity, 26, 128–38, 214, 255, 286
Crisis, 1–5
Critical discourse, 228–29
Critical reflection, 36, 72, 167, 222, 226, 228–29
Critical thinking, xi, 11, 32, 37, 68, 119, 122–123, 129–30, 162, 226, 278
Cultural flexibility, 19
Curriculum, 7, 27, 31, 33, 37, 39, 41, 57–58, 72, 115, 117–18, 143–44, 146–47, 149, 152, 156, 158, 164, 201, 211, 224, 258, 264
Cyber-slacking, 96–97, 103–4, 108–9

Decolonization, 31, 35, 142, 168, 254, 258, 260, 267
Death, 8, 31, 79, 84, 189, 191–92, 200, 280, 285
Diakonia/diaconia, 36, 61, 64, 68–69, 71–74, 221
Dialogic turn, 112–13
Dialogue, 32, 62, 69, 84, 112, 173, 179–180, 226–27, 229–31
Digital learning, 129–38, 245
Disability, 68, 70, 74
Discernment, xii, xiii, 2–6, 10, 12, 39–40, 275–76, 281–85
Discerning community, 4, 223
Discipleship, 24, 39, 198, 201
Disorientating dilemma, 222, 227, 229
Dispositio, 26
Disruption, 93, 172, 241
Domination, 17, 50, 196
Doomsday Clock, 275

Ecclesial agoraphobia, 20–21, 25, 27
Ecological hermeneutics, 45, 52–55
Ecology, 47–49, 51–52, 55, 176
Eco-theology, 49, 52–53, 55
Ecumenical, 9, 33, 35, 40, 47, 67–69, 223

Educational leadership, 142, 226, 254–58, 269
Educational philosophy, 258, 268
Elocutio, 26
Embodied knowledge, 261
Environmental ethics, 45
Epistemology, 152
Equity, 143, 158, 160
Escapism, 2, 97
Eschatology, xii, 280
Ethical leadership, 153
Ethos, 101, 193, 281
Evil, xii, 48, 79–88

Face-to-face teaching, 8, 94, 97–98, 101–2, 107, 112, 120, 132, 126, 240, 242, 246, 249
Fatigue, 211
Fear, 20–21, 25, 27, 67, 72, 189–92, 197–98, 210, 281
Fertility, 62, 65–67, 71–72
Fight-Flight-Freeze, 20
Finkenwalde, 198, 201–3
Flipped classroom, 55
Formation, 4, 31–33, 51, 56, 68, 74, 101, 115, 201, 253–256, 263–64, 267, 279, 284
Freedom, 23, 55, 57–58, 83, 85, 117, 193–95, 226, 237
Freud, Sigmund, 237–38, 278

Games, 23, 201
Gender, 62–63, 70, 72, 151, 222–23, 260–61, 31–33, 38
Global awareness, 119, 122–23, 125
Globalization, 21, 275
Glocal, glocal theology, glocal learning, xi, xiii–xiv, 7–11, 21, 25, 40–41, 129, 172, 175, 177–78, 183, 190, 218, 275–77, 284–86
Grace, 83, 198, 216, 232
Greed, 50

Hamartiocene, 47
Hammarskjöld, Dag, 23
Historicity, 280, 283
HIV/AIDS, 63–64, 67

Holistic mission, 277
    Holocaust, 86
Homo Ludens, 23
Huizinga, Johan, 23
Humor, 194, 202–3, 286
Hybrid learning, 97–98, 106–8, 120, 235, 248

Identity, 9, 32–33, 64, 68, 103, 116–17, 152, 160, 237–38, 257, 260–62
Idolatry, 50
Imagination, xii, 2, 25, 202, 277, 280
Immersive learning, 223, 227, 232
Improvisation, xii, 22, 26, 134–35, 281–83
Inequality, 31, 221, 224–25, 227–29, 257, 261–63
Infertility, 61–74
Influence, 3–4, 18–21, 26–27, 37, 70, 122, 145, 149, 175–82, 198, 225, 266, 276–78
Innovation, 3–4, 26, 51, 57, 128, 131, 137, 171, 173, 175–77, 202
Inter-contextual learning, xi–xii, 266
Interdisciplinary learning, 119, 125
Interaction, xii, 62, 73, 109, 114–15, 119, 132–37, 175–80, 209–11, 215, 223, 240, 244, 257
Interpretation, xii, 4, 38, 45, 130, 173–74, 178
Intrinsic motivation, 25, 120, 202, 213–14
Inventio, 26, 282
IVF, 65–66

Jenkins, Philip, 17–19
Jenson, Robert W., 4
Joy, 23, 206–218, 230, 243, 245
Judgment, xiii, 1–5, 8, 50, 55, 57, 174, 178, 196–98, 202–3, 286
Judicium, xiii, 2, 198–99, 203
Justice, 4, 37, 39, 68, 80, 82, 158–61, 168, 189, 199, 222, 225–26, 230–31, 254–56, 259, 267
Justification, 81–84

Kerygmatic model, 69
Kimani, Martin, 195–96, 203

Kristeva, Julia, 238
Kyoto Protocol, 46

Lament, 78, 80, 81, 85–86
Leadership, xii, 3, 10–11, 117–22, 142–43, 147–53, 176, 190–91, 197, 221–22, 226, 229, 231, 254–60, 268–69, 274–86
Leader-centrism, 278
Leadership characteristics, 149–52, 226
Learning community, 25, 107–8, 201–3, 209, 213, 218, 223, 276–77
Learning environment, 114, 118, 133, 135–37, 164, 166, 168, 197, 201–2, 213, 221
Learning goals, 25
Learning process, xi, 6, 93–95, 104–5, 109, 116, 118, 135–37, 145, 166, 168, 173, 206, 208–17, 232, 264
Liberation theology, 9
Literacy, academic and digital literacy, 109, 120, 123, 129, 135–37, 156–58, 211–12
Lifelong learning, 268
Lockdown, 93, 95–100, 108, 235, 240–47
Logos, 193, 281
Luther, Martin, 3, 8, 55

Makgoba, Thabo, 190, 274
Martyrdom, 192, 200
Meaning-making, 121, 160, 262
Meditatio, 3
Memoria, 26
Memory, 87, 95, 147
Mental health, 106, 108, 168, 210–11, 216–17, 240, 248
Migrant, 238
Migrating, 8–9, 247
Ministerial formation, 32–33, 74
Moltmann, Jürgen, 23–24, 80, 280, 283

Naming reality, 9–10, 122, 196, 203, 284
Naudé, Beyers, 4, 9, 258

Oduyoye, Mercy Amba, 253
Online learning, 105, 114, 129, 131–132, 136, 165, 206–18, 235, 241–42, 247
Oratio, 3–4

Pandemic, xi–xii, 6–7, 30, 64, 98, 100, 106, 111–14, 123, 128–38, 157–63, 166, 171–72, 182, 206–12, 218, 234–50, 282
Participatory citizenship, 5
Pastoral counseling, 5, 61, 67–74
Pathos, 193
Pedagogy, 111, 116, 120–25, 129, 137, 144, 168, 172–73, 181–83, 218, 223, 225–26, 230, 232, 245, 255
Performative discernment, xi
Persuasion, 122, 193
Play, xii, 18, 21–28, 202–3, 281–83
Play-based learning, 25
Poet, 276, 281
Political, 9, 30, 37–38, 44–49, 54, 144, 146, 176–77, 183, 196, 198, 200, 225–26, 234, 238, 255–60, 275, 278, 280
Postcolonial, 237–38, 260, 262
Poverty, 37, 119, 221, 224, 226–29, 242, 249, 262, 274, 278
Practical Theology, xii, 5, 34, 38, 56, 68, 71, 98, 107, 112–13, 117, 119, 125, 165
Prevention, 46
Pride, 50, 201
Proclamation, 84
Professional skills, 180, 212
Program leader, 142–55
Prophet, 18, 276–77, 281
Prophetic diakonia, 71
Protest, 37, 40, 275
Public sphere, 18–21, 27, 200
Public theology, 71, 256–58, 266

Rationality, 84–87, 180, 196
Reagan, Ronald, 194–96, 203
Relationship building, 164
Reflective practitioner, 179–80
Reflexivity, 143, 232, 267

Relevance, 3, 10, 18, 21, 36, 38, 41, 52–53, 56, 256, 275, 283
Repetition, 25, 180, 238
Reproductive technology, 62–66
Resilience, 217–18, 284
Resistance, xii, 36, 116, 198, 261, 284
Responsible Imagination, xii
Rhetoric, 26, 117, 119, 121, 193, 203
Rhetorical wardrobe, 285
Root, Andrew, 17, 25, 201

Sin, 44–58, 69, 84, 281
Secularization, 19
Self-care, 216–17
Self-discovery, 213
Self-evaluation, 125, 174, 178–80
Self-formation, 284
Self-reflection, 172, 180, 183, 198, 202–3, 222, 229–30, 255, 282, 284
Semantic theory construction, 172, 174, 178, 183
Shalom, 226
Sloth, 50–52
Social justice, 4, 39, 158–61, 168, 222, 225–26, 230–31
Social practices, 112
Solidarity, 39, 46, 80, 87, 199, 280
Sound judgment, xiii, 1–5, 8, 62, 196–98, 202–3, 279, 286
Spiritual growth, 104–5
Stakeholders, 5, 144–45, 151, 224, 256–58,
Stark, Rodney, 17
Stewardship, 48, 55, 68
Student collaboration, 130–37
Student creativity, 128–38
Student performance, 158, 163–65
Suffering, 23, 48, 50, 65, 78, 80, 87, 121, 192, 199–201, 262
Surrogate motherhood, 72–73
Sustainability, 52, 217
Systematic Theology, 5, 55–56, 73, 165, 255–58, 265

Tanner, Kathryn, 9, 284
Taylor, Charles, 19–20, 82
Teacher-student relationship, 176–214

Technology-mediated learning
  (TML), 93–110
Telos, 39, 189, 256, 280
Tenacity, 206–18
Tentatio, 3–5
Theological discernment, 6, 10, 12,
  152, 275, 281–85
Theological learning, 8, 25, 62, 67, 69
Theological resistance, xii
Therapeutic model, 69
Transformation, 9, 17, 25, 39, 52,
  68, 144–45, 147, 168, 201, 218,
  221–23, 229–232, 238, 256, 267,
  270
Transcendence, xii, 78, 81
Tutu, Desmond, 4

Unhomely, 234, 237–38
United Nations, 62

Virtue, 5, 189–93, 196–98, 203, 263
Vulnerability, 179, 202, 283–84

Welcome, 26
Women for Christ, 64–65

Youth citizenship, xiii, 6, 275
Youth involvement, 5, 7, 10, 275
Youth participation, 40

Zoom fatigue, 211

www.ingramcontent.com/pod-product-compliance
Lightning Source LLC
Chambersburg PA
CBHW071234230426
43668CB00011B/1432